PROJEKTFELD AUSSTELLUNG
PROJECT SCOPE: EXHIBITION DESIGN

Aurelia Bertron, Ulrich Schwarz, Claudia Frey

PROJEKTFELD AUSSTELLUNG
PROJECT SCOPE: EXHIBITION DESIGN

Eine Typologie für Ausstellungsgestalter, Architekten und Museologen
A Typology for Architects, Designers and Museum Professionals

VORWORT PREFACE

Das Projektfeld Ausstellung und Museum wird zunehmend als interessanter und wachsender Arbeitsbereich für Architekten, Designer und Museologen erkannt. Das vorliegende Buch wendet sich an alle, die Ausstellungen konzipieren, gestalten, planen und produzieren. Mit seinen erklärenden und praktischen Hinweisen dient es aber auch Studierenden der Fachbereiche Architektur, Innenarchitektur, Ausstellungsdesign, Szenografie und Visuelle Kommunikation als Einführung in das Thema Ausstellung und Museumsgestaltung. Alle Autoren leisten mit ihren Texten einen Beitrag zur Entwicklung des Themengebiets. Sie stellen ihre durchaus neuen und ungewöhnlichen Positionen dar und regen damit den Diskurs an. Jede Ausstellungsart stellt spezifische Bedingungen an Autorschaft und Ausstellungsgestaltung. Diese werden durch Parameter wie inhaltlicher Fokus, Art der Exponate, Anlass, Ziel und Zweck der Ausstellung bestimmt. Es spielt auch eine Rolle, wie lange eine Ausstellung gezeigt werden soll, ob es sich um eine temporäre, eine Wechselausstellung oder eine Dauerausstellung handelt. Und nicht zuletzt bestimmen finanzielle und zeitliche Rahmenbedingungen die Dramaturgie der Präsentation.

Wie diese Parameter die praktische Gestaltung beeinflussen, belegen die im Folgenden vorgestellten exemplarischen Ausstellungen zu den großen Themenbereichen Natur, Archäologie, Geschichte, Kunst und Wissenschaft.

So unterschiedlich diese Themenbereiche sind, so unterschiedlich können auch die Gestaltungslösungen sein. Die analytische Betrachtung der gezeigten Beispiele lässt einerseits gleiche, die Bereiche übergreifende Elemente erkennen, andererseits aber auch ganz spezifische Anforderungen, die nur für einen klar definierten Bereich gelten. Untersucht man die Erscheinungsformen mit der Methode des morphologischen Kastens, so wird eine Typologie erkennbar, die es erlaubt, Ausstellungen

The project area focusing on exhibitions and museums is being increasingly recognized by architects, designers, and museologists as an interesting and expanding field of work. This book is directed at all those involved in the conception, design, planning, and production of exhibitions. However, the explanations and practical tips it provides also make it suitable as an introduction to the theme of exhibition and museum design for students of architecture, interior architecture, exhibition design, scenography, and visual communication. All the authors represented in this book have contributed to the development of this topic. In presenting their new and unusual positions they are helping to enliven the discourse in this field. Every type of exhibition places specific demands on its authors and designers. These demands are determined by parameters such as thematic focus, types of exhibits and the occasion, as well as the goal and purpose of the exhibition. Another factor is the projected duration of the exhibition – whether it is intended as a temporary or permanent installation. The dramaturgy of the presentation is also affected not least by the financial considerations and the time frame available for its design and production.

Just how these parameters influence the practical process of design is illustrated by the exhibitions presented here as examples relating to the broad thematic areas of nature, archeology, history, art, and science. These are very different topics and the range of options open to exhibition designers is correspondingly wide. An analytic consideration of the examples presented here reveals, on the one hand, shared elements that can be applied to all the themes being dealt with, and, on the other, very specific requirements that only apply to a clearly defined area. Investigating the different forms exhibitions can take using the morphological box method reveals a typology that allows

hinsichtlich der eingesetzten Mittel und deren Wirkungen zu vergleichen. Die Typologie arbeitet das Spezifische der verschiedenen Museen und Ausstellungen heraus. Die Beschreibung und Betrachtung möglichst vieler Parameter, die den Duktus, die Anmutungsqualität ausmachen, bietet Ausstellungsgestaltern ein umfassendes Entwurfsrepertoire.

Es gibt aber auch verbindende Elemente. Alle Ausstellungstypen werden von folgenden gleichen Bausteinen gebildet.

Inhalt und Objekt
Informationen müssen dargestellt werden. Dies erfolgt mehr oder weniger mit Hilfe von Objekten und den zu ihnen gehörenden Aussagen und Erklärungen.

Präsentation und Vermittlung
Die Form der Darstellung entscheidet darüber, wie die Inhalte und Objekte vom Publikum aufgenommen und verstanden werden.

Gestalterische und technische Qualität
Die Aufgabe des Gestaltungskonzeptes ist die Festlegung von ästhetischen Kriterien und technischen Vorgaben für die Ausführung. Die Vorgaben erfolgen durch präzise Beschreibungen mit erläuternden Skizzen, Darstellungen, Zeichnungen, Modellen und Prototypen.

Das Spezifische der vorgestellten Typen von Ausstellungen verdeutlichen exemplarische Fallstudien mit Textbeiträgen zur Theorie und Praxis des Ausstellungsgestaltens. Skizzen, Grundrisse, Visualisierungen und zahlreiche Fotografien verdeutlichen eine Vorgehensweise, die in ihrer Struktur gleich ist, jedoch für jedes Thema eine andere Lösung findet. Alle Elemente der Betrachtung folgen einem analytischen Raster steigender Komplexität. Grundsätzlich sind – so die Haltung von BERTRON SCHWARZ FREY – immer die Inhalte der jeweiligen Ausstellung die Basis für den Gestaltungsprozess. Die Frage nach dem, was gesagt und gezeigt werden soll, steht grundsätzlich vor der Frage, wie es gezeigt wird.

us to compare exhibitions in terms of the materials and approaches they utilize, and their effects. This typology addresses the specific character of the different museums and exhibitions under consideration. The description and consideration of a range of parameters instrumental in generating a specific appeal offers exhibition designers a comprehensive conceptual repertoire.

On the other hand, there are also elements shared by all types of exhibitions, and these can be categorized in terms of the following building blocks.

Content and object
Information must be presented. The communication of such information relies more or less on objects, and the statements and explanations accompanying them.

Presentation and communication
The form the presentation takes is decisive in determining how the content and objects involved are perceived and understood by the public.

Design and technical qualities
The task of the design concept is to define the aesthetic criteria and technical specifications relevant to the execution of a project. These specifications take the form of precise descriptions accompanied by explanatory sketches, depictions, drawings, models, and prototypes.

The specific features of the types of exhibition presented are illustrated by exemplary case studies accompanied by texts addressing the theory and practice of exhibition design. Sketches, ground plans, visualizations, and numerous photographs help to shed light on a process that is characterized by the same basic structure yet generates a different solution for each different theme. All elements considered here accord with an analytical model of increasing complexity. In principle – in terms of the approach adopted by the BERTRON SCHWARZ FREY design office – the content of the respective exhibition always forms the foundation of the design process. The question of what is

Die dokumentierten Projekte vermitteln die jeweilige Stimmung, die emotionale Qualität der Ausstellung über große, doppelseitige Fotografien. Grundrisse, Skizzen, Darstellungen und Detailfotos erklären dagegen die Gestaltung und die technischen Lösungen. Eine „Statusleiste" am Fuß jeder Seite ordnet die gezeigten Themen und Beispiele und gibt Quellenverweise. Vorgestellt werden aktuell gestaltete Ausstellungen, zum Beispiel für das Museum für Naturkunde und das Jüdische Museum in Berlin, das Pommersche Landesmuseum in Greifswald und das Landesmuseum Württemberg in Stuttgart.

to be said and shown always precedes the question of how it is to be shown.
The presentation of projects is accompanied by large, double-page photographs that communicate the atmosphere and emotional quality generated by the respective exhibitions. Ground plans, sketches, depictions and detail photos, on the other hand, shed light on the specifics of the design itself, and the technical solutions involved. A status bar at the foot of each page links the themes and examples shown with categories, and provides references.
We have also included exhibitions here that are currently being designed, for example, the Museum of Natural History and the Jewish Museum in Berlin, the Pomeranian State Museum in Greifswald, and the Württemberg State Museum in Stuttgart.

Projektfeld Ausstellung Project Scope: Exhibition Design

„Museen gehören zu den erfolgreichsten und dynamischsten Medien der Informationsgesellschaft. ... – erfolgreicher als Bibliotheken, Theater und Universitäten".[1] Ausstellungen bilden die Schnittstelle zwischen Museum und Benutzer. So ist die Ausstellung nicht nur Medium, sondern auch Interface für die Informationen, die in Depots, Sammlungen und Forschungsarbeiten gespeichert sind.

Das moderne Museum entfernt sich in zum Teil bedenklicher Weise vom klassischen Museumsbild, wie es im 19. und 20. Jahrhundert entstand, als Direktoren und Kuratoren ihre Aufgabe hauptsächlich als Sammeln und Bewahren von Kulturgegenständen verstehen konnten und Besucher die Forschungstätigkeiten eher störten. Es bewegt sich hin zu einem Publikumsforum, das mit seinen Angeboten immer breitere Schichten der Bevölkerung erreicht und damit Bildungsaufgaben, aber auch Wünsche nach Unterhaltung und Erholung erfüllt. Der Besuch einer Ausstellung zählt zu den geschätzten Freizeitaktivitäten und ist häufig der Anlass zu Reisen. Die Anzahl der professionellen Büros für Ausstellungsgestaltung hat sich, verglichen mit den achtziger Jahren, in denen es nur einige wenige gab, vervielfacht. Das Interesse des Publikums an Museums- und Ausstellungsbesuchen ganz allgemein ist enorm gestiegen. Ausstellungen sind längst zu einem wichtigen Wirtschaftsfaktor und zu einem sehr interessanten Projektfeld für Gestalter geworden. Ein Indikator dafür ist die Zunahme hervorragender Beispiele, die aus diesem Bereich publiziert werden.[2]

Der Begriff „Ausstellung" ist sehr weit gefasst. Eine lexikalische Suche ergibt lediglich eine unscharfe Definition, wonach eine Ausstellung eine „Veranstaltung"[3] oder Einrichtung ist, bei der es um Gegenstände geht, die gewerblicher, künstlerischer oder wissenschaftlicher Natur sind. Unter Gegenständen können sowohl Dinge als auch Sachverhalte verstanden werden. Um das

"Museums are among the most successful and dynamic media of the information society ... more successful than libraries, theaters, and universities."[1] Exhibitions form the point of contact between the museum and its user. In this sense the exhibition is not only a medium but also an interface for the information that is stored in repositories, collections, and research projects. The modern museum is departing – in sometimes questionable ways – from the classical notion of the museum that emerged in the nineteenth and twentieth century, when directors and curators understood their task as one of the collection and preservation of cultural artifacts and saw visitors as a more or less as a necessary disturbance to research. The museum is now becoming a forum for the public that is reaching ever greater parts of the population and in the process fulfilling educational tasks as well as responding to demands for entertainment and recreation. A visit to an exhibition is now regarded as a valuable recreational activity and often forms the focus of a trip outside one's own locality. Whereas in the 1980s only a few professional offices devoted to exhibition design existed, this number has now multiplied significantly. The general interest of the public interested in visiting museums and exhibitions has grown enormously. Exhibitions have now become important in economic terms and a highly interesting project field for designers. One indicator of this development is the increase in the number of high-quality publications generated by this field.[2]

The term "exhibition" is an extremely broad one. A lexical search merely yields the rather vague definition of an exhibition as an "event"[3] or presentation dealing with objects of a commercial, artistic, or scientific nature. Objects in this context can be understood as things or information. In order to take a more in-depth look at this field, we need first to delimit it. Trade fairs

[1] Gottfried Korff: „Sechs Emder Thesen zur Rolle des Museums in der Informationsgesellschaft", in: *Museumskunde*, Bd. 73, 2, 2008, S. 19.
[1] Gottfried Korff, "Sechs Emder Thesen zur Rolle des Museums in der Informationsgesellschaft," in *Museumskunde*, vol. 73, no. 2 (2008): p. 19.

[2] Uwe J. Reinhardt, Philipp Teufel: *New Exhibition Design 02*, Ludwigsburg 2010. Die Publikation verzeichnet mit 120 herausragenden Projektbeispielen gegenüber der vorhergehenden Ausgabe eine Zunahme um fast 100 Prozent.
[3] Vgl. wikipedia.de und wissen.de.

2 Uwe J. Reinhardt and Philipp Teufel, *New Exhibition Design 02* (Ludwigsburg 2010). This publication documents 120 outstanding projects, a figure which represents an increase of almost one hundred percent compared to the previous edition.
3 See wikipedia.de and wissen.de.

Feld eingehender zu betrachten, müssen Abgrenzungen vorgenommen werden. Auch auf Messen werden Gegenstände einem Publikum zugänglich gemacht und bieten einen kulturellen Nutzen. Was Ausstellungen auf Messen von denen in Museen unterscheidet, ist der gewerbliche Charakter. Für die Planung und Produktion von Ausstellungen ist diese Unterscheidung essenziell, da sich aus ihr vollkommen unterschiedliche Anforderungen an die Ausstellungsgestalter ergeben. Messebau bedeutet, unter großem Druck und innerhalb einer sehr kurzen Bearbeitungsfrist hochwertige Ausstellungsbauten zu fertigen, die dann über einen meist sehr begrenzten Zeitraum von sehr vielen Besuchern benutzt werden. Das Museum dagegen plant mit wesentlich längeren Bearbeitungszeiten. Selbst Wechselausstellungen benötigen meist mehr als eine einjährige Vorlaufzeit. Dafür können Dauerausstellungen in den meisten Fällen noch zehn weitere Jahre, Messen aber meist nur zehn Tage lang besucht werden.

Die Art der Tätigkeiten und die zur Erstellung einer Ausstellung notwendigen Arbeitsphasen gleichen sich weitgehend – selbst die Budgets und die Besucherzahlen liegen in vergleichbarer Größenordnung. Unterschiede ergeben sich in den zu erfüllenden technischen Anforderungen. Das Museum stellt besondere Bedingungen an den Ausstellungsbau, um die Exponate zu schützen. Es geht dabei meist um das Abwenden schädigender Klimaeinflüsse, wie Temperatur, Luftfeuchte, Staub und Chemikalien.[4] Dies schränkt die Auswahl der zu verwendenden Materialien drastisch ein. Auch die Bearbeitungsmethoden unterscheiden sich. Wo Messebauer eine Pulverbeschichtung als Standard ansehen, erfordert die Ausstellung in denkmalgeschütztem Umfeld eine Lackierung von Hand und mit dem Pinsel – im Ansehen des Messeprofis eine minderwertige Arbeit, nach Überzeugung der Denkmalschützer unter Umständen die einzig akzeptable. Aus diesen Gründen konzentrieren sich die folgenden Betrachtungen fast ausschließlich auf Ausstellungen in Museen oder im

also present objects to a public and have a cultural use. What distinguishes exhibitions at trade fairs from those in museums is the former's commercial character. This distinction is essential when it comes to the planning and production of exhibitions since exhibition designers face very different demands in these two different instances. Mounting a trade fair involves the tightly scheduled construction of high-quality exhibition facilities that are then used by visitors for what is mostly a very limited time. By contrast, the time taken to design and mount a museum exhibition is far longer. Even temporary exhibitions usually require more than one year of preparation. On the other hand, in most cases permanent exhibitions can be visited over a period of years, whereas trade fairs are usually only open for a few days.

The activities involved and the work phases required to produce an exhibition in these two areas are broadly similar – even the budgets and visitor numbers are comparable. The differences lie in the technical requirements that have to be met in each case. Museums present particular demands regarding the protection of exhibits, for the most part with regard to potentially damaging environmental factors such as temperature, air moisture, dust, and chemicals.[4] This drastically limits the choice of materials that can be used. The way in which exhibition facilities are finished also differs. Whereas trade-fair builders regard a powder coating as standard, an exhibition in a heritage-protected location must be hand-painted with a brush – a method regarded as inferior by trade-fair professionals but as the only acceptable one in certain circumstances by preservationists. For these reasons, the following comments focus almost exclusively on exhibitions in museums or museum environments, although obviously many of the statements made here can also be applied to other fields of spatial design. In order to describe this project field it is necessary to classify and order the diverse range of tasks and materials it involves and thereby to generate

---

Projektfeld Ausstellung
Project Scope: Exhibition Design

[4] Vgl. dazu Alexandra Schlieweck, Tunga Salthammer: *Schadstoffe in Museen, Bibliotheken und Archiven*, Fraunhofer Institut 2006.

[4] See Alexandra Schlieweck and Tunga Salthammer: *Schadstoffe in Museen, Bibliotheken und Archiven* (Fraunhofer Institut 2006).

musealen Umfeld, wobei selbstverständlich viele Aussagen auch für andere Bereiche des raumbezogenen Entwerfens gelten. Zur Beschreibung des Projektfeldes ist es erforderlich, das vielfältige Material zu ordnen, um eine Grundlage für eine Typenerkenntnis zu erhalten. Das Feld definiert sich durch verschiedene Parameter, von denen einige als Konstante, andere als Variable gelten. Eine wesentliche Konstante ist, dass allen beschriebenen Beispielen eine gestalterische Haltung zugrunde liegt, die alle Ausstellungstypen übergreift.

Die Ausstellungsprojekte entstanden zwar in unterschiedlichsten Arbeitszusammenhängen, haben jedoch als gemeinsames Merkmal, dass zumindest ein Mitglied von BERTRON SCHWARZ FREY am Entwurfsprozess maßgeblich beteiligt war. Diese Beschränkung des Betrachtungsrahmens erlaubt einen geschärften Blick auf die Variablen, die Typologien definieren.

Publikationen zur Theorie der Ausstellungsgestaltung entstehen aus unterschiedlichsten fachlichen Richtungen und verfolgen dem jeweiligen Blickwinkel entsprechende Ansätze. Zwangsläufig führen unterschiedliche Blickwinkel zu unterschiedlichen Einschätzungen, Vorgehensweisen und Lösungen.[5] Denn an der Entstehung von Ausstellungen sind unterschiedliche Disziplinen beteiligt. Rollen und Aufgaben, die diese übernehmen, überschreiten oft die eigentliche Bestimmung ihrer Disziplin. Selbst wenn man es sich manchmal anders wünscht – Ausstellungsgestaltung entsteht im Regelfall nicht autokratisch, sondern in einem Dialog, der viele Fachrichtungen einschließt: Autoren und Wissenschaftler auf der einen Seite und auf der Seite der Umsetzung Ausstellungsgestalter, Architekten, Innenarchitekten, Szenografen, Künstler, Fachleute aus den Bereichen der Visuellen Kommunikation, Illustration, Informations- und Produktgestaltung, Mediengestaltung, Animations- und Videofilm, gelegentlich auch Landschaftsarchitekten und Wissenschaftsjournalisten.

an exhibition typology. As a field, exhibition design is defined by different parameters, some of which can be seen as constants and others as variables. One fundamental constant in the present context is the fact that all the examples described are based on a design approach that applies to all types of exhibition.

Although the exhibition projects discussed here were created in extremely diverse working contexts, they are linked by the fact that at least one member of BERTRON SCHWARZ FREY was significantly involved in the design process in each case. Limiting the framework of discussion in this way has the advantage of allowing us to focus more precisely on the variables central to the definition of a typology.

Publications on the theory of exhibition design come from a wide range of areas of expertise and are based on approaches consistent with the respective perspectives involved. Different perspectives in turn lead to different assessments, procedural methods, and solutions.[5] To some extent this is inevitable because the process of producing exhibitions is one that draws on different disciplines. Moreover, the roles and tasks that these disciplines are required to adress in this context often exceed their normal parameters of enquiry and expertise. Even though we would sometimes prefer it to be otherwise, as a rule, exhibition design is not an autocratic process, but one that unfolds through a dialog involving many specializations: on the one hand there are the authors and scholars and, on the other, exhibition designers, architects, interior architects, scenographers, artists, specialists from the fields of visual communication, illustration, information and product design, media design, animation and video production, and occasionally also landscape architects, and science journalists.

[5] Vgl. dazu Brigitte Kaiser: *Inszenierung und Erlebnis in kulturhistorischen Ausstellungen*, Bielefeld 2006, S. 14.

[5] See Brigitte Kaiser, *Inszenierung und Erlebnis in kulturhistorischen Ausstellungen* (Bielefeld, 2006): p. 14.

Typologie und Morphologie

Brauchbare Ansätze wissenschaftlicher Autoren helfen bei der Suche nach einer geeigneten Typologie, mit deren Hilfe das Medium Ausstellung aus gestalterischer Sicht untersucht werden kann. Joachim Baur versucht sich dem Thema mit einer „kleinen Taxonomie des Museums"[6] auf phänomenologische, etymologische, historiografische und definitorische Weise zu nähern. Für Gestalter ist es vor allem die phänomenologische Betrachtung, die das Arbeitsfeld am besten beschreibt. Baur unterscheidet nach der Größe von Depot- und Ausstellungsflächen, aber auch nach der Anzahl der Mitarbeiter, nach dem „Alter" des Museums – handelt es sich um eine Neugründung oder ein Traditionshaus? –, nach wissenschaftlichen Disziplinen, nach Trägerschaft, nach dem Bezugsrahmen – lokal oder international – oder nach anderen Besonderheiten – Benennung, Arbeitsweise mit oder ohne Sammlung, Forschung, Vermittlung.

Auf den ersten Blick scheint aus Sicht der Ausstellungsgestalter die Unterscheidung nach Alter bei der Untersuchung des Feldes wenig hilfreich. Doch bei analytisch genauerer Betrachtung macht gerade die zeitgeschichtliche Entwicklung und Einordnung Sinn, denn alle vergangenen Museums- und damit auch Ausstellungsformen sind in ihren wesentlichen Ausprägungen als Spuren bis heute an vielen Stellen immer noch präsent.[7]

Die These von Wulf Herzogenrath lautet, dass sich für jede Form der Vergangenheit eine zeitgenössische Interpretation findet. Die Museumsentwicklung reicht, ausgehend von Wunderkammern und Kuriositätenkabinetten über das „Gelehrtenmuseum" des Bürgertums im späten 19. Jahrhundert, das Volksmuseum mit Erziehungsauftrag, das ganzheitliche, inszenatorische Museum, das spezialisierte Sparten-, Medien- und Künstler-Museum, das Sammlermuseum bis hin zum „Architektur-Museum", dem ökonomischen Museum und dem Erlebnismuseum, wo Entertainment als Tourismusmagnet eingesetzt wird. David Dernie et al. unterscheiden dagegen nach szenografisch-

Typology and Morphology

Scholarly authors have formulated a number of approaches that can be useful in the search for a typology appropriate to the examination of the medium of the exhibition from a design perspective. Joachim Baur, for instance, has created a "small taxonomy of the museum"[6] that combines phenomenological, etymological, historiographical, and definitional elements. For designers it is above all the phenomenological point of view that best describes their field of work. Baur draws distinctions based on the size of repository and exhibition areas as well as the number of staff involved, the "age" of the museum (determining if it is a new building or an established institution?), scholarly disciplines, frame of reference (local or international), funding bodies and other particularities – title, work method (with or without collection, research, educational program).

At first glance, the distinction according to age hardly seems helpful to an investigation of this field from the point of view of the exhibition designer. However, when looked at more closely in analytical terms, the concept of historical development and classification makes sense on the grounds that all past forms of museum and thus exhibition retain a presence today in terms of their fundamental character as traces at many sites.[7]

Wulf Herzogenrath argues that a contemporary interpretation can be found for every form of the past. The development of the museum form extends from the cabinets of curiosities produced in Renaissance Europe to the "scholars' museum" of the late nineteenth century bourgeoisie, the folk museum with its educational function, the integrated, "stage-directed" museum, the specialized museum, the media museum, the artist museum and the collector's museum to the "architecture museum," the economic museum and the experiential museum, where entertainment is used to created a magnet for tourists. By contrast, David Dernie et al. use scenographic-semantic criteria to differentiate museums

[6] Joachim Baur: „Was ist ein Museum?", in: *Museumsanalyse – Methoden und Konturen eines neuen Forschungsfeldes*, Bielefeld 2010.
[6] Joachim Baur, "Was ist ein Museum?" in *Museumsanalyse – Methoden und Konturen eines neuen Forschungsfeldes* (Bielefeld, 2010).

[7] Wulf Herzogenrath: „Die Museen aus der Vergangenheit fit für die Zukunft", in: *Museumskunde*, Bd. 71, 2, 2006, S. 16 ff.
[7] Wulf Herzogenrath, "Die Museen aus der Vergangenheit fit für die Zukunft," in *Museumskunde*, vol. 71, no. 2 (2006): p. 16 ff.

semantischen Kriterien in narrativen Raum, performativen Raum und simulierten Raum.[8] Eine ungewöhnliche Sicht auf die zeitgenössische Entwicklung der Museen ermöglicht Victoria Newhouse.[9] Sie betrachtet ausschließlich Kunstausstellungen, diese jedoch in verschiedenen Ausprägungen. Außerdem sieht sie die Architektur als wesentlichen Bestandteil der Gestaltung von Museumserlebnissen. Museumskultur versteht sie als sich stets neu erfindenden Prozess. Dies erläutert Newhouse sehr gut im ersten Kapitel ihres Buches, das von Kunstsammlungen handelt, die ursprünglich aus den italienischen „studiolo" des frühen 16. Jahrhunderts oder den „Wunderkammern" herausgelöst wurden. Diese Sammlungen hatten im Gegensatz zu religiösen Sammlungen, die devotionalen und didaktischen Zwecken unterworfen waren, in erster Linie die Aufgabe, das Publikum zu unterhalten. Ihr Beitrag zur Bildung von Museumskategorien vermittelt sich über eine große Anzahl von unterschiedlichsten Beispielen: vom mono-grafischen Museum über das Museum als Ort der Unterhaltung oder das Museum als „heilige Halle" bis zu dem Museum als „Environmental Art".[10]

Im Seminar „Museografie und Ausstellungsgestaltung" im Studiengang Visuelle Kommunikation der Universität der Künste in Berlin werden aktuelle Ausstellungen der Stadt anhand eines vorgegebenen Rasters, das sich in Form eines morphologischen Kastens abbildet, analysiert. Dieser morphologische Kasten ist ein Instrument des programmatischen Entwerfens[11] und geht in seinen Grundzügen davon aus, dass Ideen aus der möglichst vollständigen Kenntnis aller Möglichkeiten entstehen können. Entwerfen wird in diesem Zusammenhang als Auswahlprozess begriffen, in dem ein erster Arbeitsschritt versucht, alle Bereiche aufzulisten, die für die Betrachtung des Gegenstandes relevant sind. Auf dieser Basis werden alle möglichen Ausprägungen, die Variablen, formuliert. Aus der so gewonnenen Übersicht lassen sich nun sehr vielfältige – wenn auch nicht zwangsläufig sinnvolle – Lösungen generieren.

in terms of narrative space, performative space, and simulated space.[8] An unusual view of the contemporary development of museums is provided by Victoria Newhouse.[9] She focuses exclusively on art exhibitions although in different variants. In addition, she sees architecture as a fundamental element in shaping experiences of museums. She understands museum culture as a process that is constantly reinventing itself. This phenomenon Newhouse illustrated very clearly in the first chapter of her book, which deals with art collections originating from the Italian "studiolo" of the early sixteenth century and from "chambers of curiosities." In contrast to religious collections, which were used for devotional and didactic purposes, the role of these collections was above all to entertain the public. Their contribution to the formation of museum categories can be seen in a large number of diverse examples: from the monographic museum to the museum as a site of entertainment, from the museum as "sacred space" to the museum as "environmental art."[10]

The seminar "Museography and Exhibition Design" that forms part of the Visual Communications course at the Berlin University of the Arts involves the analysis of exhibitions currently on show in the city with reference to a standardized grid that forms a kind of "morphological box." This morphological box provides an instrument for programmatic design[11] and is based on the idea that the full range of possibilities can unfold when the knowledge of a field is as complete as possible. In this context design is understood as a process of selection in which the first step entails listing all the areas relevant to the consideration of an object, and thereby formulating all the possible variables involved. The overview achieved in this way provides a foundation for the generation of highly diverse – albeit not necessarily sensible – solutions. On the one hand, this method is eminently suited to the analysis of exhibitions while on the other it provides us with a syntax relating to their design.

[8] David Dernie, Martina Fiess, Elke Walter: *Ausstellungsgestaltung: Konzepte und Techniken*, Ludwigsburg 2006.
[8] David Dernie, Martina Fiess and Elke Walter, *Ausstellungsgestaltung: Konzepte und Techniken* (Ludwigsburg, 2006).

[9] Victoria Newhouse: *Towards A New Museum*, New York 2006.
[9] Victoria Newhouse, *Towards A New Museum* (New York, 2006).

[10] Ebd.: Der englische Begriff „environment" (dt: „Umgebung") bezieht sich auch auf Innenräume.
[10] Ibid.: The term "environment" here relates to interior spaces.

Parameter	Variable A	Variable B	Variable C
Parameter	Variable A	Variable B	Variable C
Kategorie/Inhalte	Naturkundliche Ausstellung	Naturwissenschaftliche Ausstellung	Kunstausstellung
Category/Content	Natural history exhibition	Natural sciences exhibition	Art exhibition
Träger	Staatliche Museen	Landesmuseen	Stadtmuseen
Supporting institution	State museums	National museums	Municipal museum
Art	Archiv	Studiensammlung	Schausammlung
Type	Archive	Collection	Exhibition collection
Ort	Innenraum	Außenraum	
Location	Interior	Exterior	
Bedeutung	Lokal	Regional	National
Importance	Local	Regional	National
Aufwand/Budget	0	XS	S
Expenditure/Budget			
Präsentation	Authentisch	Museal	Didaktisch
Presentation	Authentic	Museal	Didactic
Thematische Struktur	Chronologisch	Thematisch	Synchronoptisch
Thematic structure	Chronological	Thematic	Synchronoptic
Objekte	Original	Replik	Faksimile
Object	Original	Replica	Copy
Vermittlung/Stil	Interpretativ	Hermeneutisch	Belehrend
Communication/Style	Interpretive	Hermeneutic	Instructive
Vermittlung	Visuell [a]	Auditiv	Audiovisuell
Communication	Visuals [a]	Auditory	Audio visual
Vermittlung/Mittel	Text/Sprache	Bild	Bewegtbild
Communication/Means	Text/Language	Picture	Moving image
Zugang/Rezeption	Explorativ	Narrativ	Spielerisch
Access/Reception	Explorative	Narrative	Playful
[a] Mittel	Typografie	Grafik/Illustration	Tabellen
[a] Means	Typography	Graphics/Illustrations	Tables
[b] Modelle	Funktionsmodelle	Geomorphologische Modelle	Architektur-Modelle
[b] Models	Functional models	Geomorphological models	Architectural Models

| Projektfeld Ausstellung | [1] Karl Gerstner: *Programme entwerfen*, Teufen 1963. | |
| Project Scope: Exhibition Design | [1] Karl Gerstner, *Designing Programmes* (Baden, 2007). | |

Variable D	Variable E	Variable F	Variable G
Variable D	Variable E	Variable F	Variable G

Baudenkmäler Schlösser Freilichtmuseen Monuments Palaces Open-air museums	Archäologische Ausstellung Archeological exhibitions	Historische Ausstellung Historical exhibitions	Erinnerungs- und Gedenkstätten Memorials

Firmenmuseen Company museum	Privatmuseen Private museum	Sonstige Träger Other supporting institution	

Dauerausstellung Permanent Exhibition	Wechselausstellung Temporary exhibition	Wanderausstellung Traveling exhibition	Event Event

International			
International			

M	L	XL	

Szenisch Scenic	Partizipativ Participatory		

Synergetisch Synergetic	Exemplarisch Exemplary	Pointiert Emphasis	

Bauwerk Building	Inventar Inventory	Ausstattung Equipment	

Interaktiv Interactive	Kontemplativ Contemplative	Unterhaltend Entertaining	Kommunikativ Communicative

Interaktiv Interactive			

Objekt/3d[b] Object/3D [b]	Grafik[a] Graphics[a]		

Faktisch Factual			

Diagramme Diagrams	Karten Charts	Bewegtbild Moving image	Fotografie Photography

Szenische Modelle Scenic models	Simulationen Simulations	Dioramen Dioramas	

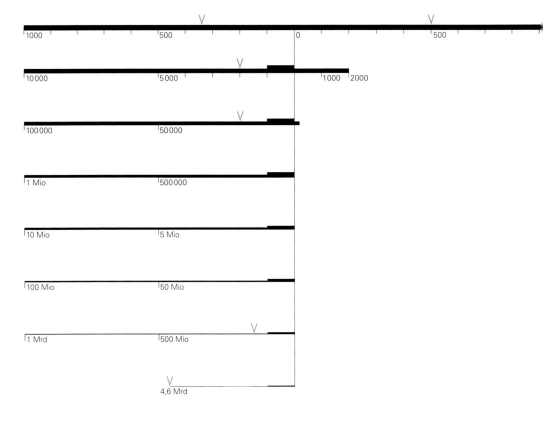

Werden die Ausstellungsprojekte auf einer Zeitachse verortet, entsteht ein geordnetes Archiv,
und 4,6 Mdr. Jahre sind als Autobiografie lesbar:

Vor 4,6 Mrd. Jahren   Entstehung des Weltalls / Museum für Naturkunde
Vor 150 Mio. Jahren   Dinosaurier im Tendaguru des Jura / Museum für Naturkunde
Vor 20 000 Jahren   Entstehung der Maare in der Vulkaneifel
Vor 4 000 Jahren   Entdeckung des Königreiches Qatna / Württembergisches Landesmuseum
Vor 2 360 Jahren   Idee der Verknüpfung von Philosophie und Natur / Botanischer Garten
Vor 1500 Jahren   Die Slawen / Pommersches Landesmuseum
Vor 600 Jahren   Regensburg / UNESCO-Welterbe-Besucherzentrum
Vor 200 Jahren   Deutsche und Juden zugleich / Jüdisches Museum
Vor 66 Jahren   WAS BLEIBT / KZ-Gedenkstätte Flossenbürg

The exhibition project will be organized according to a timeline, in which the archive,
and 4.6 billion years are read as an autobiography:

4.6 billion years before   The creation of the universe / Natural History Museum
150 million years ago   Dinosaurs roamed in the Jurassic Tendaguru / Museum of Natural History
20,000 years before   The emergence of Crater Lakes in the Volcanic Eifel
4,000 years before   The Discovery of the Kingdom Qatna / Württemberg State Museum
2360 years ago   The idea of linking philosophy and nature / Botanic Garden
1500 years before   The Slavs / Pomeranian State Museum
600 years ago   Regensburg / UNESCO World Heritage Visitors Center
200 years ago   German and Jew simultaneously / Jewish Museum
66 years ago   WHAT REMAINS / Flossenbürg Concentration Camp

Projektfeld Ausstellung
Project Scope: Exhibition Design

Diese Methode eignet sich einerseits hervorragend zur Analyse von Ausstellungen andererseits aber auch als Syntax für das Gestalten von Ausstellungen.

Die Erkenntnisse der ursprünglich für die Sprach- und Literaturwissenschaften entwickelten Methode der Semiotik sind auch auf bildliche und räumliche Phänomene übertragbar. Der Vorteil einer bildlichen Sprache ist ihre universelle Verständlichkeit. In der Sprachforschung versteht man unter Morphologie der Sprache die Lehre von der Struktur und Funktion der Morpheme und deren Bezug zur Syntax. Das gilt auch für eine visuelle Sprache, für die Visuelle Kommunikation. In einer „visuellen Grammatik" untersucht die Morphologie die Veränderung der Erscheinungsform, die „Gestaltveränderung" (Flexion) der kleinsten Parameter (Morpheme), die Gestaltung tragen.

Unterscheidung und Kategorie
Der Aufgabe, das Feld der Ausstellungen und Museen in Kategorien zu beschreiben, kann man sich auf unterschiedliche Weise nähern. Kriterien für eine Ordnung können sowohl chronologischer als auch thematischer Art sein. Die chronologische Betrachtung ist besonders dann aufschlussreich, wenn sie über ein „Schon die Römer haben..." hinauswächst. 4,6 Milliarden Jahre sind ein Zeitraum, den sich viele weder vorstellen noch in Relation zum eigenen Erleben setzen können. Die abgebildete Grafik veranschaulicht diese Zeit von der Entstehung der Erde bis heute.

Eine einfache thematische Ordnung gliedert das Feld in folgende Kategorien:
– Natur
– Kunst
– Technik
– Wissenschaft

The findings of semiotics – an analytic method originally developed in the context of linguistics and the study of literature – can also be applied to pictorial and spatial phenomena. The advantage of a pictorial language is its universal comprehensibility. In linguistics the morphology of language relates to the doctrine of the structure and function of morphemes and their relationship to syntax. This also applies to visual language, and to visual communication. In the context of a "visual grammar," morphology involves the investigation of the changes in the manifestation, the modification (inflection), of the smallest parameters (morphemes) underlying the design.

Differentiations and categories
The task of describing the field of exhibitions and museums can be approached from different angles. The criteria of classification can be chronological or thematic. The chronological approach is particularly instructive when it moves beyond the "already in Roman times" approach – 4.6 billion years is a time frame that is very difficult to imagine or relate to our own experience. The diagram shown here provides a visual representation of this time period stretching from the origin of the Earth until the present.

The following categories form the basis for a simple thematic form of classification:
– Nature
– Art
– Technology
– Science

Es gibt aber auch gewachsene Gruppie-
rungen, die sich aus gemeinsamen oder
trennenden Merkmalen und Interessen
ergeben. Sowohl ICOM[12] als auch der
Deutsche Museumsbund haben ihre Arbeit
in Komitees organisiert, deren Titel und
Schwerpunkte die Arbeitsfelder bezeichnen
und eingrenzen.
Eine weitere, vielleicht die interessanteste
Unterscheidungsmöglichkeit ergibt sich aus
Titeln und Themen der Ausstellungsstätten,
denn die Namen der Museen sagen bereits
etwas über den Inhalt, den sie vermitteln.
– Naturkundemuseum
– Naturwissenschaftliches Museum
– Technikmuseum
– Archäologisches Museum
– Geschichtsmuseum
– Erinnerungs- und Gedenkstätte
– Völkerkundemuseum
– Volkskundemuseum (Heimatmuseum)
– Kulturhistorisches Museum
– Kunstmuseum
– Freilichtmuseum
– Baudenkmal, Schloss

In der Kunst, aber auch in der Biologie würde
man von Gattungen sprechen. Die Kunst
unterscheidet dabei nach Ausdrucksmitteln:
bildende und darstellende Kunst, Literatur
und Musik.
Die Art kennzeichnet die speziellen Merkmale. Bei Ausstellungen ist ein entschei-
dendes Merkmal der Zeitrahmen, in dem
die Ausstellung gezeigt wird. Dauerausstellungen sind, der Name sagt es bereits, auf
Dauer angelegt. Das Museumswesen geht
im Allgemeinen davon aus, dass Dauerausstellungen über einen längeren Zeitraum
aktuell bleiben. Demzufolge ist die wichtigste
Anforderung an die Ausstellungsgestaltung,
Formen zu finden, die nicht zu schnell „ver-
greisen", und Materialien zu verwenden,
die einen jahrelangen Gebrauch überstehen.
Diese Materialanforderungen gelten jedoch
meist auch für Wechselausstellungen, die in
ihrer Form zwar den Zeitgeist widerspiegeln
können, aber in einem begrenzten, kurzen
Zeitraum ebenso viele Besucher anziehen,
wie manche Dauerausstellungen über viele
Jahre.

However, there are also more complex
groupings based on shared or distinct
features and interests. Both ICOM[12] and the
German Museums Association have organized their operations into committees with
titles and emphases that denote and delimit
the fields of work involved.
A further and perhaps the most interesting
method of differentiation is based on the
titles and themes of exhibition locations,
since the names of museums already tell
us something about the content of their
holdings.
– Museum of natural history
– Natural science museum
– Technology museum
– Archeological museum
– Historical museum
– Memorial center
– Ethnological museum
– Museum of folk culture
  (local history museum)
– Museum of cultural history
– Art museum
– Open-air museum
– Historic monument, castle

Such categories correspond to what are
referred to in art as genres. In art a distinction is made between forms of expression,
between fine and performing arts, literature
and music.
The type indicates the specific features. In
the case of exhibitions a decisive feature
is the time frame in which the exhibition is
shown. Permanent exhibitions, as the name
suggests, are presented over the longer
term. In general, museum organizations assume that such exhibitions will retain their
currency over a long period of time. The
most important requirement placed on exhibition design in this context is therefore to
find forms that do not date too quickly, and
to use materials that can withstand years of
use. However, in most cases this requirement in terms of materials also applies to
temporary exhibitions, which, although they
may take a form that is suited to a particular
zeitgeist, are still exposed to a number of
visitors equal to that attending many permanent exhibitions over many years.

Projektfeld Ausstellung
Project Scope: Exhibition Design

[12] Internationaler Museumsrat ICOM

[12] International Council of Museums
ICOM

Wanderausstellungen stellen darüber hinaus die Anforderung, dass die Ausstellung leicht auf- und abgebaut sowie transportierbar sein muss. Die Elemente müssen einerseits variabel gestaltet werden, andererseits sind Wanderausstellungen, denen man es ansieht, dass sie für den Transport und nicht für das Publikum gestaltet wurden, wenig attraktiv. Bei der Planung sind die verschiedenen räumlichen Situationen, in denen die Ausstellung stattfinden kann, besonders zu beachten. Unterschiedliche Ausstellungslokale unterliegen oft verschiedenen Bedingungen. Architektur und Veranstaltungstechnik sind nicht standardisiert. Besonders die Lichtsituation und Beleuchtungsmöglichkeiten variieren. Deshalb ist eine Wanderausstellung, die sich mit ihren Ausstellungselementen praktisch autark in die jeweilige Umgebung transferieren lässt, ideal.

Die räumlichen Gegebenheiten beeinflussen aber nicht nur bei Wanderausstellungen die Gestaltungsentscheidungen. Unabhängig vom Thema und der inhaltlichen Aufarbeitung wirkt die architektonische Umgebung auf den Gesamteindruck, den eine Ausstellung beim Publikum hinterlässt. Die weiß gestrichene Ausstellungshalle bedingt zweifellos einen anderen gestalterischen Umgang wie ein im 17. Jahrhundert erbautes Schloss. Die räumliche Organisation einer Ausstellung steht in Wechselwirkung zur Architektur. Eine wesentliche Gestaltungsentscheidung betrifft dementsprechend den grundsätzlichen Umgang mit ihr: Harmonisiert die Ausstellungsgestaltung mit der formalen Sprache der Architektur, oder bildet sie einen Kontrast? Ein gutes Beispiel für das Erstere ist die Gestaltung der neuen Säle im Museum für Naturkunde Berlin[13]. Die Ausstellung fügt sich harmonisch in die Architektur ein, ohne sich anzubiedern. Die Formen der Ausstellung heben sich mit ihrer Materialwahl und Farbe erkennbar von der architektonischen Hülle ab, respektieren jedoch diese als eigenständige ästhetische Erscheinung. Als Gegenbeispiele lassen sich die Ausstellungen im Landesmuseum Württemberg[14] anführen, die eigene, dominante, raumbildende Ausstellungselemente in den historischen Raum bringen und diesen

Traveling exhibitions involve the additional requirement that the exhibition must be easy to erect, dismantle, and transport. On the one hand the elements used have to be variable, but on the other travelling exhibitions that have obviously been designed for transport rather than for the public tend to be less attractive. When planning such exhibitions, particular attention needs to be paid to the different spatial contexts within which the exhibition may be mounted. Different exhibition locations are often subject to different conditions. Architecture and technological facilities are not subject to any standard, and variations are encountered particularly when it comes to natural light and artificial lighting possibilities. For this reason, the ideal traveling exhibition is one equipped with self-sufficient elements that can be transferred to practically any environment.

However, design decisions are not only influenced by spatial conditions in the case of traveling exhibitions. Irrespective of the theme and content presentation, the architectural environment of an exhibition shapes the overall effect that an exhibition exerts on its public. A white-painted exhibition space undoubtedly requires a design approach different from that of a castle constructed in the seventeenth century. The spatial organization of an exhibition and the architecture of the exhibition location have an interdependent relationship, and how one approaches this architecture is a fundamental design decision. Should the exhibition design harmonize or contrast with the formal vernacular of the surrounding architecture? A good example of the former approach can be found in the new spaces in the Berlin Museum of Natural History. The exhibition integrates harmonically with the architecture without pandering to it. The materials and colors selected for the exhibition clearly set it apart from its architectural envelope while also respecting it as an independent aesthetic phenomenon. A contrasting example is provided by the exhibitions in the Württemburg State Museum,[14] which add independent, dominant, space-defining elements to the historic space

[13] Siehe Seite 30:
Museum für Naturkunde Berlin.
[13] See page 30:
The Berlin Museum of Natural History.

[14] Siehe Seiten 156 und 242:
Schätze des Alten Syrien – Die Entdeckung des Königreichs Qatna und *Das Königreich Württemberg. 1806–1918 Monarchie und Moderne.*

[14] See pages 156 and 242:
The Treasures of Ancient Syria – Discovery of the Kingdom of Qatna and *The Kingdom of Württemberg 1806–1918: Monarchy and Modernity.*

vollständig überformen. Die Grundbedingung ist jedoch immer die Einbeziehung des Denkmalschutzes und der behutsame Umgang mit der historischen Bausubstanz. Ausstellungen im Außenbereich stellen besondere Anforderungen an die Wetterbeständigkeit der Materialien und insbesondere an den Druck der Informationsflächen. Man muss mit starken Temperaturschwankungen, intensivem Sonnenlicht, Wind, Regen, Schnee und Eis rechnen. Die Farben dürfen nicht ausbleichen, und die Materialien müssen besonders robust sein, da nicht nur Umwelteinflüsse zu vorzeitiger Abnutzung führen, sondern auch die Gefahr mutwilliger Beschädigungen besteht. Nicht immer sind es jedoch die besonders starken Ausführungen, die Beschädigungen verhindern – auch die umgekehrte Strategie kann erfolgreich sein. So kann etwa mit der Verwendung des Materials Glas eine relativ hohe Hemmschwelle gegen Beschädigungen gesetzt werden. Eine andere Strategie verfolgt den Einsatz von Materialien, die nachgeben oder mit einer Sollbruchstelle ausgestattet sind. Originale Objekte können unter diesen Bedingungen nur in sehr seltenen Fällen gezeigt werden.

and completely reshape it. Nevertheless, the exhibition still adheres strictly to the precepts of heritage preservation and great care has been taken to protect the historic building fabric.

Open-air exhibitions present particular demands in terms of ensuring the weather-resistance of materials and in particular the durability of print on information panels. The designer must reckon with temperature fluctuations, intensive sunlight, wind, rain, snow, and ice. Colors need to be fade-proof, and the materials must be particularly robust not only to protect against the effects of weather but also possible vandalism. However, it is not always the sturdiest form of construction that can prevent such damage – in some cases the opposite strategy can also be successful. The use of glass, for example, can provide a relatively high inhibition threshold against such damage. Another strategy involves the use of materials that give under pressure or are equipped with a predetermined breaking point. Such conditions, however, seldom permit the exhibition of original objects.

Alamannenmuseum Weingarten
Alemanni Museum Weingarten
Museum für Naturkunde Berlin
The Berlin Museum of Natural History

Das Königreich Württemberg
Kingdom of Württemberg
Schätze des Alten Syrien
Treasures of Ancient Syria
Otto Bock Science Center Medizintechnik
The Otto Bock Science Center

Die Charité zwischen Ost und West
The Charité between East and West
Bauernhaus im Freilichtmuseum Beuren
The Farmhouse in the Beuren Open-Air Museum

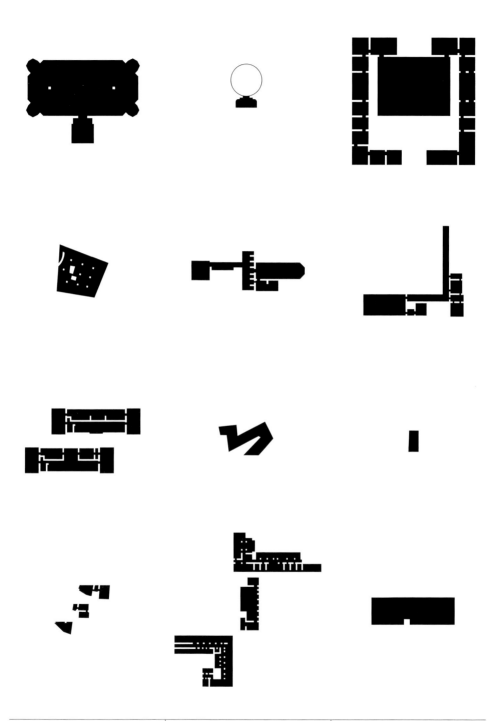

Gemäß ihrer Aufgabe legen Museen Sammlungen an, die meist nicht vollständig in Ausstellungen gezeigt werden können. Zur Aufbewahrung der Sammlungsgegenstände dient das Depot. Archive und Depots werden gelegentlich auch für Publikum zugänglich gemacht. Depotausstellungen zeigen als Schausammlung die Objekte in geordneter Form, ohne weitere didaktische Aufbereitung. Diese Präsentation kann auf das Publikum durch ihre Fülle eine besondere Faszination ausüben. Ein sehr gutes Beispiel, ein Archiv für das Publikum interessant zu machen, wurde im Literaturarchiv Marbach gefunden. Dort zeigt eine ständige Ausstellung Archivalien. Da die Schriftstücke besondere konservatorische Bedingungen an die Beleuchtung stellen, werden diese in einem bestimmten Turnus gewechselt. Die Konservatoren gehen davon aus, dass nicht nur die Lichtmenge, sondern auch die Dauer der Ausstellung die Originale schädigt.

Die Frage, wer Träger einer Ausstellung ist, hat für Ausstellungsgestalter, aber auch für die Besucher und letztlich auch für Wissenschaftler, Auftraggeber und Veranstalter entscheidende Bedeutung. Die Träger selbst unterliegen verschiedenen Prinzipien und Vorschriften:
– Privatpersonen
– Firmen
– Vereine
– Institutionen
– Stiftungen
– Städte
– Bundesländer
– Staatliche Museen

Der Verwaltungsaufwand ist für eine Privatperson oder eine Firma, die sich schnell und unkompliziert für eine bestimmte Qualität entscheiden können, in der Regel geringer als für eine staatliche Stelle, die ein genaues und langwieriges Vergabeverfahren befolgen muss, das durch die VOB[15] und VOL[16] gesetzlich geregelt ist. Es unterscheiden sich:
– Öffentliche Ausschreibung
– Beschränkte Ausschreibung
– Beschränkte Ausschreibung nach
   öffentlichem Teilnahmewettbewerb

The function of museums means that they assemble collections only part of which can usually be shown in exhibitions. The objects making up collections are stored in repositories. Archives and repositories are occasionally also opened to the public. Such repository exhibitions present the objects in an ordered form without any further didactic elements. The sheer plenitude of such presentations can exert a particular fascination for the public. A very good example of how an archive can be made interesting for the public can be seen in the literary archive in Marbach, which contains a permanent exhibition of archival materials. Since the historical documents are particularly sensitive to light, they are rotated at certain intervals to restrict the amount of light and the duration of exposure.

The question of who funds an exhibition is a decisive one not only for exhibition designers but also for visitors and ultimately also for scholars, commissioning bodies, and organizers. Exhibition sponsors fall into a number of different categories that are subject to different principles and prescriptions:
– Private individuals
– Firms
– Associations
– Institutions
– Foundations
– Cities
– Federal states
– National museums

For a private individual or a firm that is able to decide quickly and easily for a certain quality, the job of administering the project is usually less arduous that for a state authority, which is required to conduction a precise and lengthy tendering process that is legally regulated – in Germany, for example, by the VOB[15] and the VOL.[16] Distinctions are made between:
– Public calls for tender
– Restricted calls for tender
– Restricted calls for tender following a
   public competition
– International calls for tenders
– Open procedures

---

[15] Vergabe- und Vertragsordnung für Bauleistungen.
[15] Construction Contract Procedures.

[16] Vergabe- und Vertragsordnung für Leistungen.
[16] Servce Contract Procedures.

– Internationales Ausschreibungsverfahren
– Offenes Verfahren
– Nicht offenes Verfahren
– Freihändige Vergabe
– Verhandlungsverfahren

Oft fällt die Entscheidung zugunsten des niedrigsten Preises, obwohl auch die engen Vorschriften ein Instrumentarium bieten, den Bieter zu beauftragen, der am besten für die Aufgabe geeignet ist, und nicht den, der am billigsten ist. Dazu sind jedoch aufwendige Maßnahmen notwendig. Durch einen Teilnahmewettbewerb kann der Kreis der Bieter eingeengt werden. Danach jedoch muss der Günstigste beauftragt werden.
Das Ziel, die höchste Qualität mit dem wirtschaftlichsten Angebot zu verknüpfen, wird am besten durch einen differenzierten Bewertungsschlüssel erreicht, bei dem die Höhe des Preis-Angebots nur zu einem gewissen Prozentsatz den Ausschlag gibt. So können von den Bietern Nachweise für die Qualifikation durch Referenzen, die wirtschaftliche und technische Leistungsfähigkeit sowie auch Erfahrung auf dem speziellen Gebiet der Aufgabenstellung verlangt werden. Referenzprojekte werden persönlich in Augenschein genommen, dokumentiert und nach festgelegten Kriterien bewertet. Diese Kriterien müssen rational begründet sein. Wenn die Reisen zu lang und aufwendig sind, kann die Bewertung auch bei den jeweiligen Auftraggebern erfragt werden. Bewertet wird nach einem vorher festgelegten und in der Ausschreibung bekannt gegebenen Punktesystem.

Beispiel: 100 Punkte verteilen sich auf fünf Referenzprojekte der Bieter. Die Referenzprojekte wiederum werden nach weiteren Kriterien beurteilt: Verarbeitungsgenauigkeit der Materialien Glas, Holz, Metall, Homogenität der Oberflächen, Präzision der Stöße, Sauberkeit der Verklebung, Dichtheit der Verschlussmechanismen. Es können auch Erfahrungen mit der Herstellung hochwertiger Oberflächenbearbeitungen wie spezielles Lackieren, Polieren, Glasperlstrahlen, Brünieren, Bürsten usw. zur Bedingung

– Restricted procedures
– Direct agreements
– Negotiated procedures

Decisions are often taken based on the lowest price even though the strict regulations actually offer an instrument for choosing the bidder best suited to the task rather than the one offering the lowest price. However, applying such regulations is an elaborate process. A competition can be held to restrict the number of bidders but once this has been done the cheapest offer must be selected.
The best means of linking the best quality with the lowest possible price involves the use of a differentiated valuation scale in which price is only one factor determining the outcome. For example, bidders can be asked to provide proof of their qualifications in the form of references, documentation of their economic and technical capacities, and records of their experience in the specific area in question. Reference projects can be examined in their original condition, documented and assessed according to fixed criteria. The criteria must be substantiated in rational terms. If the projects are located too far away, the assessment can also be based on information provided by the respective client. Valuation should be based on a fixed points-based system that is explained in the call for tenders.

For example, one hundred points are distributed over five reference projects presented by the bidder. The reference projects are in turn assessed according to further criteria: precision with which materials such as glass, wood, and metal are used, as well as homogeneity of surfaces, precision of joints, neatness of bonded joints, and tightness of closing mechanisms. Other criteria could include experience with high-quality surface processing techniques such as varnishing, polishing, glass-bead blasting, burnishing,

gemacht werden. Jedes Projekt erfordert eine andere Gewichtung der Kriterien. Bei hochempfindlichen Objekten mit besonderen konservatorischen Bedingungen steht die Präzision, mit der eine Vitrine verarbeitet wird, an erster Stelle und bestimmt die Bewertung zu einem festgelegten Anteil.

brushing etc. Each project requires specific weighting of the criteria involved. In the case of highly sensitive objects subject to particular conservational conditions, the precision with which a display case is worked is of primary importance and will form a fixed factor in the assessment.

Präzision
– Staubdichte
– Anpressdruck der Vitrinentüren
– Stabilität
– Sauberkeit der Verklebungen

Precision
– Dust-proofing
– Pressure resistance of display case doors
– Stability
– Neatness of bonded joints

Verarbeitung
– Verglasung
– Oberflächen
– Sichtbare oder verdeckte Verschlüsse
– Verklebungen

Processing
– Glazing
– Surfaces
– Visible or concealed fastenings
– Bonded joints

Bedienbarkeit
– Öffnungsmechanismus
– Bestückung
– Zugänglichkeit
– Justierbarkeit
– Wartung
– Revision der Beleuchtung
– Revision der Feuchtekontrolle

Usability
– Opening mechanism
– Assembly
– Accessibility
– Adjustability
– Maintenance
– Adjustability of lighting
– Adjustability of humidity regulation

Sicherheit
– Technik
– Verriegelung

Security
– Technology
– Locking systems

Anmutungsqualität
– Erscheinungsbild
– Qualität
– Optischer Eindruck

Appeal
– Appearance
– Quality
– Optical effect

Die Zuverlässigkeit des Bieters sowie seine wirtschaftliche und technische Leistungsfähigkeit zeigt der Umsatz der letzten drei Geschäftsjahre, wichtig ist auch die Qualifikation der Mitarbeiter in den Bereichen der technischen Bearbeitung, Werkstattfertigung und Montage. Diese Angaben können durch Informationen über die technische Ausrüstung wie CAD-Arbeitsplätze, Werkstattausrüstung und Maschinen ergänzt werden.

The reliability of the bidder and their respective economic and technical capacities are indicated by turnover from the last three financial years. Another important factor is the qualifications held by staff members in the areas of technical processing, production in the workshop, and assembly. These details can be supplemented by information regarding technical equipment such as CAD work stations, workshop equipment, and machinery.

Projektfeld Ausstellung
Project Scope: Exhibition Design

[17] Ein „Repronat" stellt eine nicht ganz ernst gemeinte, aber kennzeichnende Begriffsschöpfung von Bodo-Michael Baumunk dar. In: *Museumsblatt. Mitteilungen aus dem Museumswesen Baden Württembergs*, Heft 36, 2004.

[17] Addressing the subject of reproductions in this context Bodo-Michael Baumunk coins the not completely serious term "Repronat" – a play on the German term "Exponat" (exhibit), in *Museumsblatt. Mitteilungen aus dem Museumswesen Baden Württembergs*, vol. 36 (2004).

Deponat und Exponat

In Ausstellungen geht es um zwei wesentliche Punkte: Objekte zeigen und Geschichten erzählen. Objekte werden zum Exponat, wenn sie ihren Weg aus dem Depot in die Ausstellung finden. Sind Originale nicht verfügbar, kommen Reproduktionen oder Repliken zum Einsatz. Die Ausstellung von „Repronaten"[17] als Surrogate oder Ersatzmaterialien wird kontrovers diskutiert. Die Frage, ob es sich für den Besucher lohnt, wegen einer ausgestellten Fotokopie Hunderte von Kilometern zurückzulegen, ist an dieser Stelle jedoch verständlich und berechtigt. Das typische, museale Objekt ist ein „aus der realen Umwelt, aus dem üblichen System synchroner und diachroner Zusammenhänge herausgelöster, herausgebrochener Träger sozialer, naturhistorischer und ästhetischer Informationen. ... Das museale Objekt ist ein authentisches Objekt."[18] Das Objekt ist per Definition der Gegenstand der Betrachtung und steht dem Subjekt, dem Publikum, gegenüber. Das Objekt[19] ist der Gegenstand, auf den sich das Subjekt erkennend oder handelnd richtet.

Für die Gestaltung von Ausstellungen wird gegenwärtig häufig der Begriff „Szenografie" bemüht. Gemeint ist damit das Inszenieren von Räumen. Die Gestaltung von szenischen Bildern bezieht ihr formales Verständnis aus dem Bühnenbild des Theaters. Es geht darum, ein großes Bild zu schaffen, das als superiertes Zeichen für die Erzählung einer Geschichte steht. Das einzelne Objekt ist dabei nicht so wichtig. Demgegenüber könnte die Gestaltung von Ausstellungen mit Objekten, das Zeigen, die „Beschreibung" der Sammlung mit dem in Frankreich öfter benutzten Begriff Museografie belegt werden. Das museografische Bild entsteht durch die Anordnung und Kombination der Exponate. Diese vermitteln ein authentisches Bild. „Das Museum hat eigentlich nicht mit Visualisierung zu tun, sondern das Museum stellt aus, arrangiert anschaubare Objekte im Raum. Visuell sind seine Bauelemente eo ipso und nicht nur seine didaktische Strategie. Das Museum bebildert nicht; es ist Bild."[20]

Deposits and Exhibits

Exhibitions have two fundamental goals: to display objects and to tell stories. Objects become exhibits when they make their way from the repository into the exhibition. If originals are not available, reproductions or replicas are used. The exhibition of reproductions[17] as surrogates or substitute material is a subject of some controversy. Of course, the question of whether it is the worth the effort of traveling hundreds of kilometers to see a photocopy is an understandable and justified one. The typical museum object is a "bearer of social, natural historical and aesthetic information that has been decoupled, dragged out of the real environment, from the usual system of synchronic and diachronic interconnections … the museum object is an authentic object."[18] The object is by definition the object of consideration and confronts the subject, the public. The object[19] is that to which the subject orients himself in terms of recognition or action.

Currently a term often associated with the design of exhibitions is that of "scenography." This refers to the way space is staged. In formal terms, the design of scenic images is based on stage design in the theater. The aim is to create a large image that functions as an integrated symbol for the narration of a story. The individual object is not very important in this context. On the other hand, the design of exhibitions presenting objects, the process of showing, of "describing" the collection, can perhaps best be summed up by the concept of museography. The museographic image emerges through the ordering and combination of exhibits. These communicate an authentic image. "The museum actually has nothing to do with visualization; the museum presents, arranges viewable objects in the space. Its structural elements are eo ipso by the fact alone visual and not only its didactic strategy. The museum does not picture, it is picture."[20]

---

[18] Vgl. Reinhardt, Teufel (Anm. 2) S. 28.
[18] See Reinhard and Teufel (note 2) p. 28.

[19] „Obiectum", lat. das „Entgegengestellte" oder „Entgegengeworfene".
[19] "Obiectum", lat. the "opposed."

[20] Gottfried Korff: *Museumsdinge deponieren – exponieren*, Köln 2002, S. 144.
[20] Gottfried Korff, *Museumsdinge deponieren – exponieren* (Cologne, 2002): p. 144.

Vermittlung und Publikum

Die Frage, an wen sich die Ausstellung wenden solle, wird allzu oft mit „an alle" oder „an Acht- bis Achtzigjährige" beantwortet. Tatsächlich kann der fertigen Ausstellung meist eine besser definierbare Zielgruppe zugeordnet werden. Die Qualität einer Ausstellung ließe sich wesentlich steigern, wenn der Fokus von Anfang an auf einem spezifisch ausgewählten Publikum oder einem entschiedenen Duktus läge. Experimente entstehen, wenn der Blickwinkel verändert wird. Eine gute Möglichkeit dazu bietet die Betrachtung der Besuchergruppen mit den Augen der Psychologie.

Ausstellungsgestalter sind sich vermutlich nicht bewusst, dass es in der Hauptsache zyklothyme[21] Ausstellungen sind, die sie entwerfen. Sie wenden sich mehr oder weniger unbewusst an Menschen pyknischen[22] Körperbaus mit dem dazugehörigen Temperament von leichtem Wechsel zwischen Heiterkeit und Traurigkeit bei entsprechend hoher Psychomobilität. Der Gegensatz dazu wäre eine Ausstellung, die sich an den kühlen, empfindsamen und sprunghaft Denkenden und Fühlenden wendet – an den konstitutionellen Leptosomen. Diese Frage ist interessant: Wie sehen Ausstellungen aus, die für bestimmte Temperamente und Konstitutionen gebaut sind – Pykniker, Athletiker, Leptosome, Sanguiniker, Choleriker, Melancholiker, Phlegmatiker, Extravertierte, Introvertierte? Doch das sind nicht die einzigen Fragen, die sich Gestalter bei der Planung von Ausstellungen stellen sollten. Die wohl wichtigste Frage von allen ist die nach der Qualität. Folgende Kriterien bieten dazu einen Ansatz:

– Dauerhaftigkeit
– Zweckmäßigkeit
– Anmutung, Ästhetik, Schönheit
– Originalität, Attraktivität
– Angemessenheit der Mittel
– Logik der Zuordnungen

Communication and the Public

The question as to whom the exhibition should be directed at is all too often answered with "at everybody" or "at everyone between eight and eighty." In fact a finished exhibition can be connected with a more well-defined target group. The quality of an exhibition can be greatly increased when it is focused from the outset on a specifically selected public or a characteristic style. In this context it possible to experiment with changes in perspective. One possibility is here involves looking at visitor groups from the point of view of psychology.

Exhibition designers are probably not aware that for the most part they are designing cyclothymic[21] exhibitions. Their work tends to be unconsciously directed at people of a pyknic[22] physique, a temperament the shifts between cheerfulness and sadness, and a high level of psycho-mobility. The opposite would be an exhibition directed at people who tend to exhibit a cooler temperament, and are sensitive and somewhat erratic mentally and emotionally – constitutional ectomorphs. This is an interesting question: What do exhibitions look like that are designed for particular temperaments and constitutions – endomorphs, athletic types, ectomorphs, sanguine types, choleric types, melancholic types, phlegmatic types, extroverts and introverts? But these are not the only questions that designers need to ask themselves when planning exhibitions. Probably the most important question has to do with quality. The following criteria can be used as the basis for an approach in this regard:

– Durability
– Fitness for purpose
– Appeal, aesthetic, beauty
– Originality, attractiveness
– Appropriateness of approach and materials
– Logic of classifications

Projektfeld Ausstellung
Project Scope: Exhibition Design

[21] Zyklothym meint „gesellig", „aufgeschlossen", „abwechslungsreiche Stimmung".
[21] Cyclothymic refers here to notions of "gregarious," "outgoing" and "changeable mood."

[22] Pyknisch meint „untersetzt", „zu Fettansatz neigend".
[22] Pyknic is defined as "pudgy", „tending to fat".

Weitere Fragen, die das raumbezogene Entwerfen unterstützen können:

Was ist der Anlass der Ausstellung?

Was sind die Kernaussagen?

Welches sind die Schlüsselobjekte, die wichtigsten Exponate?

Welche Rolle spielen die Objekte?

Werden diese angemessen präsentiert?

Wie ist die Wechselwirkung der Einzelteile zum Gesamten?

Wie werden Bedeutungen kommuniziert?

Welche atmosphärische Stimmung entsteht?

Wie verläuft die Dramaturgie des Ausstellungsrundganges?

Wie werden Themen und Inhalte umgesetzt?

Welche Erkenntnisse können gewonnen werden?

Lohnt sich ein zweiter Besuch?

Die Antworten fallen für jede Ausstellung anders aus. Die folgenden Beispiele sollen verdeutlichen, dass jede Aufgabenstellung ihre eigene angemessene Lösung verdient und dass das Museum ein Ort der Erkenntnis, der Aktualität, Authentizität, Kommunikation und Interaktion ist, aber eben auch ein Ort der Kontemplation und des Staunens.

Other questions that can be useful in the context of spatially based design include:

What is the reason for the exhibition?

What are the core statements?

What are the key objects, the most important exhibits?

What role do the objects play?

Are these appropriately presented?

What is the relationship between the individual parts and the whole?

How are meanings communicated?

What kind of mood or atmosphere is generated?

How does the dramaturgy of the exhibition tour function?

How are themes and content implemented?

What kind of knowledge can be gained?

Does the exhibition merit a second visit?

The answers to these questions will be different for every exhibition. The following examples are designed to show that every task in this field deserves its own appropriate solution and that the museum is a place of knowledge, topicality, authenticity, communication, and interaction but also a place of contemplation and wonder.

NATURKUNDLICHE AUSSTELLUNGEN
NATURAL HISTORY EXHIBITIONS

Naturkundemuseen beschäftigen sich vorwiegend mit den beschreibenden Wissenschaften. Die Beispiele im folgenden Kapitel behandeln Präsentationen aus der Paläontologie, Geologie, Geografie, Zoologie, Biologie und Botanik. Themen aus der Physik, Chemie oder Mathematik finden sich dagegen häufiger in Technikmuseen und Science Centern.[1]

Bedeutende Institutionen sind in Deutschland die Senckenberg-Museen in Frankfurt, Görlitz und Dresden sowie das Museum für Naturkunde in Berlin. Beim weltweiten Vergleich der Ausstellungen solcher Institutionen ist vor allem das American Museum of Natural History in New York mit seinen fantastischen Dioramen und der betont sachlich gestalteten Saurierausstellung hervorzuheben; aber auch das Natural History Museum in London, dessen Saurierausstellung sehr populär ist und vom Film *Jurassic Parc* beeinflusst erscheint, muss erwähnt werden. Einen Meilenstein der Museumsgestaltung setzte ferner das Pariser Muséum national d'Histoire naturelle mit seiner opulenten Szenografie des „Zuges der Tiere" in der Grande Galerie de l'Evolution, die in hartem Kontrast zu der weitgehend unveränderten Präsentation in den benachbarten Galeries de Paléontologie et d'Anatomie comparée steht und auf faszinierende Weise den Geist des Ausstellens im ausgehenden 19. Jahrhundert widerspiegelt.

Gemeinsames Merkmal dieser Institutionen ist ihre intensive Forschungstätigkeit, die sich auch positiv auf die inhaltliche Qualität der Ausstellungspräsentationen niederschlägt. Dies unterscheidet sie von Science Centern und deren durchaus attraktiven und vor allem publikumswirksamen Ausstellungen wie zum Beispiel das inatura in Dornbirn, Vorarlberg.

Natural science museums are predominantly concerned with the descriptive sciences. The examples in the following chapter deal with presentations in the fields of paleontology, geology, geography, zoology, biology, and botany. Themes relating to the fields of physics, chemistry and mathematics are more commonly presented in museums of technology and science centers.[1]

Leading natural science museums in Germany include the Senckenberg museums in Frankfurt, Görlitz, and Dresden and the Museum of Natural History in Berlin. In the international context, the American Museum of Natural History in New York, with its amazing dioramas and emphatically fact-based dinosaur exhibition, is worthy of particular mention, as is the Natural History Museum in London, which features a very popular dinosaur exhibition that seems to have been influenced by the film *Jurassic Park*. The Muséum national d'Histoire in Paris has created a new milestone in museum design with its "procession of animals" in the Grande Galerie de l'Evolution, which contrasts starkly with the largely unchanged presentation in the nearby Galeries de Paléontologie et d'Anatomie comparée and provides a fascinating reflection of the exhibition ethos prevailing in the late nineteenth century.

All these institutions place a strong emphasis on research, something that is positively reflected in the quality of the content of their exhibition presentations. This distinguishes them from science centers such as the inatura in Dornbirn, Austria, which offer highly attractive exhibitions designed above all to have an impact on the public.

[1] Vgl. Kapitel „Science Center", Seite 340.

[1] See the chapter "Science Center," page 340.

Die großen Häuser verfolgen unterschiedliche Präsentations- und Vermittlungsstrategien. Während die einen – dem Zeitgeist entsprechend – einen massiven Medienauftritt wählen, um das Publikum anzuziehen, zeigen andere opulente, kontextualisierende Szenografien oder verzichten eben gerade darauf, um auf die auratische[2] Wirkung der Objekte zu bauen.

Die gezeigten Objekte stellen hinsichtlich ihrer Präsentation andere Anforderungen als Kultur- oder Kunstgegenstände in geschichtlichen Ausstellungen. Zum einen dienen sie mehr als bei allen anderen Ausstellungsarten der Wissensvermittlung und benötigen deshalb eine wohl durchdachte Erklärungsebene, die sich durch Kürze und Prägnanz auszeichnen muss; zum anderen fordern die Objekte selbst besondere konservatorische Bedingungen an die Ausstellungsgestaltung. Tier- und Pflanzenpräparate sind lichtempfindlich und müssen zudem vor Schädlingsbefall geschützt werden, was oft zu weiteren Problemen führt. Geologische Exponate dagegen sind gegen Schwankungen der Temperatur und Luftfeuchte zu schützen.

Ein Vergleich der großen Naturkundeausstellungen lässt den Schluss zu, dass die wirklich nachhaltig beeindruckenden Ausstellungen das Exponat mit seinen Erklärungsschichten und nicht die Inszenierungen in den Mittelpunkt der Gestaltungsüberlegungen stellen.[3]

The large institutions employ different strategies of presentation and communication. While some choose to follow the prevailing zeitgeist and use large-scale media-based presentations to attract the public, others present opulent, contextualizing scenographies or dispense with all such presentational tools to allow maximum scope for the auratic effect of their exhibits.[2] The requirements involved in the presentation of natural scientific exhibits are different to those associated with the exhibition of cultural or art objects. On the one hand, more than any other type of exhibition, natural science exhibitions are concerned with conveying knowledge and therefore require a well-thought-out explanatory system that offers information in a brief and engaging way. On the other hand, the exhibits themselves place particular conservational conditions on the exhibition design. Animal and plant specimens are sensitive to light and require protection from pest infestation, which can also lead to further problems. Geological exhibits, on the other hand, need to be protected from variations in temperature and humidity.

A comparison of the great natural science exhibitions suggests that exhibitions leaving a genuinely lasting impression are those that focus on the exhibit and its associated levels of explanation rather than on the overall staging of the presentation.[3]

[2] Walter Benjamin: *Das Kunstwerk im Zeitalter seiner technischen Reproduzierbarkeit*, Frankfurt am Main 1963.
[2] Walter Benjamin, *The work of art in the age of mechanical reproduction (London, 2008)*.

[3] Zum Beispiel das Museum für Naturkunde Berlin, American Museum of Natural History und Galeries de Paléontologie et d'Anatomie comparée.

[3] E.g. The Berlin Museum of Natural History, American Museum of Natural History, and Galeries de Paléontologie et d'Anatomie comparée.

Museum für Naturkunde Berlin The Berlin Museum of Natural History

Die großen naturhistorischen Museen in aller Welt sind „Registraturen" für die belebte und unbelebte Natur sowie Zentren zur Erforschung ihrer Vielfalt und Entwicklungsgeschichte. Das Berliner Museum für Naturkunde ist weltweit eines der wenigen, deren Sammlungen über 30 Millionen Objekte zählen. Wertvollste Objekte der wissenschaftlichen Sammlungen sind Zehntausende von Typusexemplaren, jenen Tieren der Vergangenheit und Gegenwart, die der Namensgebung der jeweiligen Arten zugrunde liegen und die für die Forschung besonders wichtig sind. In den Ausstellungen werden einmalige Schätze präsentiert. Mit seinen Sammlungen und Ausstellungen zählt das Museum für Naturkunde zu den bedeutendsten derartigen Institutionen der Welt.

Konzeption der neuen Ausstellungen

Ausstellungen sollen informieren – dabei aber auch unterhalten. Sie sollen ein zeitgemäßes Erscheinungsbild besitzen, ohne der Versuchung zu erliegen, schnell sich ändernden Trends nachzulaufen. Mit der Konzeption der vier neuen Ausstellungssäle bestand die Möglichkeit, der neuen „alten" Philosophie des Museums für Naturkunde gerecht zu werden: als Kommunikationszentrum zwischen Wissenschaft und Öffentlichkeit aufzutreten. Deshalb wurden bei der Konzeption und Umsetzung zwei wichtige Vorgaben beachtet. Einerseits sollten die Ausstellungsinhalte von Wissenschaftlern des Hauses erarbeitet werden, andererseits bei der Objektauswahl – wo immer möglich – zuerst Originale aus den Sammlungen des Museums berücksichtigt werden. Wo Fossilnachbildungen zum Einsatz kommen mussten, sind diese als solche kenntlich gemacht. Damit unterstreichen wir nicht nur die Authentizität der Ausstellung, sondern auch die Authentizität der Wissenschaft.

Insgesamt wurde vier Jahre an dem Projekt gearbeitet. An der größten Umgestaltung der Dauerausstellung seit Jahrzehnten waren über 40 Wissenschaftler des

The major museums of natural history around the world serve as registries for animate and inanimate nature – and as centers for examining natural diversity and evolutionary history. The Berlin Museum of Natural History is one of the few museums worldwide that have more than 30 million objects in their collections. The most valuable items in its scientific collections are the tens of thousands of "type specimens" – animals from the past and present that have lent their names to their respective species, and are particularly important for research purposes. The museum's exhibitions present unique treasures. With its collections and shows, the Berlin Museum of Natural History ranks among the most important of its kind in the world.

Designing the New Exhibitions

Exhibitions are supposed to not only teach, but also to entertain. They must have a modern design yet not succumb to the temptation of following quickly changing fads. When the four new exhibition rooms were designed, the museum had the chance to live up to its new "old" philosophy: to act as a communication center mediating between science and the public. For this reason, it observed two important guidelines when developing and implementing the exhibition concept. On the one hand, the museum's own researchers created the content of the exhibitions; on the other, whenever possible, original objects from the museum collections were favored when objects were selected. If fossil reproductions had to be used, these were marked as such. This approach has allowed us to emphasize not only the authenticity of the exhibition, but also the authenticity of science.

All told, four years of work went into the project. More than forty of the museum's researchers were involved in the most important redesign of the permanent exhibition in decades – developing concepts, selecting objects and implementing the ideas. The institution's taxidermists,

Naturkundliche Ausstellungen
Natural History Exhibitions

Museum für Naturkunde Berlin
The Berlin Museum of Natural History

Leibniz-Institut für Evolutions- und
Biodiversitätsforschung
an der Humboldt-Universität zu Berlin
Invalidenstraße 43
10115 Berlin

Amtierender Generaldirektor
Acting General Director:
Dr. Ferdinand Damaschun

Museums an Konzeption, Objektauswahl und Umsetzung beteiligt – Präparatoren, Pädagogen, Grafiker und Techniker des Hauses arbeiteten gemeinsam mit externen Partnern.

Die Forschung steht im Museum für Naturkunde unter dem Generalthema „Evolution der Vielfalt – Entwicklung der Erde und des Lebens". Im Fokus befindet sich die Erforschung jener Vorgänge, die zum einen zur Entwicklung der Erde und zum anderen zur Entstehung der biologischen Vielfalt und Fülle an Lebensformen und Organismen geführt haben, die bis heute unseren Planeten kennzeichnen. Entsprechend diesem Generalthema wurden vier Aspekte der Evolution aufgegriffen und in den Sälen der neuen Ausstellungen umgesetzt.

Auf einen vorgegebenen Rundgang wurde bewusst verzichtet. Der Besucher soll sich auf seine eigene und ganz persönliche „Forschungsreise" begeben. Digitale und audiovisuelle Medien werden in der Ausstellung zurückhaltend eingesetzt. Wir nutzen vor allem ihre Möglichkeit, Objekte zu erläutern und diese in einen didaktischen Zusammenhang zu stellen. Unser „heimlicher Medienstar" sind die „dynamischen Legenden" – hinterleuchtete Textflächen mit integrierten Monitoren. Ganz nach dem Vorbild der Links im Internet werden mit Hilfe sensitiver Textbereiche Objekt, Text und Bewegtbilder punktgenau verknüpft. Auf diese Weise werden spannende Inhalte zeitgemäß vermittelt. Tragendes Element der neuen Ausstellung bleiben jedoch die originalen Objekte.

Diese Idee ist im zentralen Saal „Die Welt im Oberen Jura" konsequent umgesetzt. Hier zeigen wir die wissenschaftlichen Ergebnisse der weltweit spektakulärsten und erfolgreichsten paläontologischen Grabungen am Berg Tendaguru im heutigen Tansania. Die Grabung dauerte von 1909 bis 1913 und förderte große Mengen unterschiedlicher Fossilien zutage, die es den Wissenschaftlern im Hause ermöglichen, den Lebensraum am Tendaguru vor 150 Millionen Jahren zu rekonstruieren. Die eindrucksvollen Dinosaurierskelette repräsentieren das Leben auf dem Land. Daneben

educators, graphic artists, and technicians worked together with external partners.

At the Berlin Museum of Natural History, research is carried out under the general heading of "The Evolution of Diversity – The Development of the Earth and the Origins of Life." The processes are examined that led to the development of the Earth and the emergence of the biological diversity, and profusion of organisms/life forms that continues to characterize the planet today. In keeping with this general theme, four aspects of evolution were selected and presented in the new exhibition spaces.

We consciously decided against a prescribed tour of the exhibitions. The idea was to have visitors embark on their own personal expedition. Digital and audiovisual media are used sparingly throughout. We primarily exploit their potential to explain objects and place them in an educational context. Our secret media stars are what we call "dynamic captions": backlit text areas with integrated monitors. Modeled on Internet links, these media tools precisely link objects, texts, and animated images using touch-sensitive text areas. This concept has enabled us to convey exciting content in a modern way. However, the original objects are the central element in the new exhibition.

These ideas were systematically implemented in the central space, entitled "The World in the Late Jurassic." It presents the scientific results of the world's most spectacular and successful paleontological excavation, carried out between 1909 and 1913 at Mount Tendaguru in present-day Tanzania. The excavations unearthed vast quantities of fossils from a variety of animals, which museum researchers used to reconstruct the environment at Mount Tendaguru 150 million years ago. Spectacular dinosaur skeletons give visitors an idea of the life that existed on land, while the fossilized remains of many other important animal groups from the same period show the animals that colonized the seas, and lived in the air. Visitors are given a window to the distant past.

When developing the exhibition concept, we decided to remove text elements, media

Autoren / Kuratoren Authors/Curators: Wissenschaftliches Team aus über 40 Wissenschaftlern Scientific research team made up of over 40 scientists

Projektleitung Project Management: Dr. Ferdinand Damaschun Wissenschaftlicher Projektleiter Scientific Project Manager: Uwe Moldrzyk

Verantwortliche für einzelne Bereiche Departmental Directors: Dr. David M. Unwin, PD Dr. Oliver Hampe, Dr. Kristian Remes, PD Dr. Thomas Kenkmann, Prof. Dr. Wolfgang Kießling, Dr. Ansgar Greshake, Dr. Matthias Glaubrecht, Dr. Michael Ohl

sind Fossilien von vielen anderen wichtigen Tiergruppen zu sehen, die zur gleichen Zeit die Meere und die Lüfte besiedelten. Dem Besucher öffnet sich so ein Zeitfenster in eine ferne Vergangenheit.

Bei der Konzeption der Ausstellung haben wir uns dafür entschieden, Textelemente, Medien und Lebendrekonstruktionen der Tiere und Pflanzen der Jurazeit aus der Blickachse des Besuchers zu nehmen, wenn dieser den Saal betritt. Als Erstes sollen die Exponate wirken. Weckt eine bestimmte Objektgruppe das Interesse, tritt der Besucher näher, und nun werden auch die zugehörigen Informationssysteme wahrgenommen. Sie nehmen Bezug auf die Objekte der Ausstellung und bieten dabei wissenschaftlich interessante Details an. Es wird aber nicht nur scheinbar abgeschlossenes Wissen vermittelt, sondern es werden auch wissenschaftliche Prozesse oder alternative Hypothesen dargestellt. „Juraskope" bieten die Möglichkeit, eine mediale Reise in den Oberen Jura zu unternehmen und „unsere" Saurier in ihrem Lebensraum zu beobachten.

Ingesamt ist eine Ausstellung entstanden, die in wunderbar restaurierten Räumen die drei Kernaufgaben des Museums vereint: Sammlung, Forschung und öffentliche Bildung. Wer die Ausstellung mit wachem

and reconstructions of Jurassic-period plants and animals from the visitors' visual axis when they enter the hall. The exhibits are supposed to catch their eye first. If the visitors' interest is aroused by a specific group of objects, they can move closer to these objects, and will then see the accompanying information systems. These refer to the exhibited objects and offer interesting scientific details. Yet the exhibits present not only complete knowledge but also research processes, and alternative hypotheses. The "Jurascopes" enable visitors to take a media journey to the Late Jurassic period and observe our dinosaurs in their habitat.

All told, we have created an exhibition that unites three of the museum's central goals in beautifully restored spaces: to collect, research, and educate the public. Anyone who views the exhibition with an inquisitive mind is bound to realize that the only way to solve the major problems of our time such as global climate change, and the consequences of dwindling biodiversity, is by applying the integrative knowledge of researchers from different professional disciplines, including paleontology, zoology, geology, and the mineralogy.

Editing: Ferdinand Damaschun

Naturkundliche Ausstellungen
Natural History Exhibitions

Museum für Naturkunde Berlin
The Berlin Museum of Natural History

Dauerausstellung
Permanent Exhibition
Träger zur Zeit der Projektlaufzeit
Supporting Institution for the Duration of the Project:
Humboldt-Universität zu Berlin

Brachiosaurus brancai
Das zwischen 1909 und 1913 im heutigen Tansania ausgegrabene und nahezu vollständige, 150 Millionen Jahre alte Saurierskelett wird im Original gezeigt. Es ist mit ca. 13 Metern das höchste in einem Museum aufgestellte Saurierskelett.

Geist betrachtet, wird erkennen, dass auch die anstehenden großen Fragen unserer Zeit wie globaler Klimawandel und die Folgen schwindender Biodiversität nur mit dem integrativen Wissen von Forschern aus den unterschiedlichen Fachdisziplinen – zu denen auch die Paläontologie, die Zoologie, die Geologie und die Mineralogie gehören – gelöst werden können.
Redaktion: Ferdinand Damaschun

Zum Entwurf der vier neuen Säle

Der Leitgedanke der Ausstellungsgestaltung ist „Respekt" im Sinne von Achtung, Rücksicht und Anerkennung. Die Idee der Gestaltung besteht darin, eine neue, zeitgenössische Schicht über die Ausstellungsräume zu legen, sodass wertvolle, historische Teile nicht überlagert werden. Vielmehr werden die bereits vorhandenen qualitätvollen Elemente in eine neue Gesamtkonzeption integriert. Dies bedeutet auch, den historischen Raum zu akzeptieren, sich dem Baudenkmal unterzuordnen. Die Architektur bietet den Rahmen für die ausgestellten Objekte.
Die originalen Objekte stehen im Mittelpunkt der Überlegungen. Im Dienst der Wissensvermittlung stellt das Objekt selbst, nicht das Beiwerk der opulenten Inszenierung die Attraktion dar. Objekte

On the Design of the Four New Halls

The main idea behind the exhibition design is "respect" in the sense of regard, consideration, and appreciation. The design task involves adding a contemporary "layer" to the exhibition spaces in a way that does not obscure valuable, historical elements but rather integrates them into a new overall concept. This also means accepting the historical space as it is, respecting its status as a historic monument, and allowing the architecture to provide a framework for the exhibits.
The focus is on the original objects on display. It is the object itself and not its opulent staging that conveys information, and is therefore the real attraction. Objects "speak" – but not in language understandable to the public. In this context, scholars assume the role of translators and exhibition designers have the task of conveying the translated knowledge and making it easily accessible.
Particular respect is owed to the visitors; they want to be taken seriously. The aim is to facilitate a playful engagement with natural history wherever possible. However, this playful aspect is never deployed as an end in itself but is used to scale the presentation of information in a way that facilitates the acquisition of more detailed knowledge.

Brachiosaurus brancai
Excavated in 1909–1913 in present-day Tanzania, an almost complete, 150 million year old dinosaur skeleton is shown in the original. It is about 13 meters, the highest assembled dinosaur skeleton in a museum.

Archaeopteryx lithographica
Der Urvogel Archaeopteryx ist das wohl berühmteste Fossil der Welt. Er steht nach heutiger Kenntnis am Anfang der Evolution der Vögel und zeigt deren Verwandtschaft zu den Dinosauriern.

Archaeopteryx lithographica
The archaeopteryx is the most famous fossil in the world. According to current knowledge the fossil is on the cusp of the early evolution of birds and shows their relation to the dinosaurs.

„sprechen" – jedoch nicht in einer Sprache, die dem Publikum verständlich ist. Wissenschaftlern kommt die Rolle der Übersetzer zu, Ausstellungsgestaltern die Aufgabe, das übersetzte Wissen zu vermitteln und leicht zugänglich zu machen.

Besonderen Respekt verdienen die Besucher. Sie wollen ernst genommen werden. Das Ziel ist, wo immer möglich einen spielerischen Zugang zur Naturkunde zu schaffen. Dabei wird das Spiel jedoch nie als Selbstzweck eingesetzt, sondern bietet durch eine klare Informationsstaffelung die Möglichkeit der vertiefenden Wissensaneignung. Auch für den Besucher mit Vorkenntnissen muss die Ausstellung bereichernd sein. Es ist zu bedenken, dass viele Kinder und Jugendliche längst ein leidenschaftliches Interesse zum Beispiel an Sauriern entwickelt haben und über erstaunliche Fachkenntnisse verfügen. Ein Faszinosum entsteht besonders, wenn es gelingt, Unsichtbares sichtbar zu machen. Die neuen Medien mit ihren umfangreichen didaktischen Möglichkeiten finden ihren sinnvollen Einsatz genau da, wo sie naturwissenschaftliche Sachverhalte interessant und lebendig vermitteln.

It is important that the exhibition also offers an enriching experience for visitors with prior knowledge of a particular subject. For example, many children and young people have a passionate interest in dinosaurs and often bring an astounding level of knowledge of the subject to the exhibition. A particular fascination is generated when an exhibition manages to make the invisible visible. The new media offer a range of didactic possibilities for conveying scientific knowledge in an interesting and vivid way.

Naturkundliche Ausstellungen
Natural History Exhibitions

Museum für Naturkunde Berlin
The Berlin Museum of Natural History

Foto Photo:
Carola Radke, Museum für Naturkunde
Museum of Natural History
Foto auf Seite 33 Photo on page 33:
Christoph Hellhake, München

Ausstellungsfläche
Exhibition Area:
2 100 m²
Ausstellungseröffnung: 13. Juli 2007
Opened on July 13, 2007

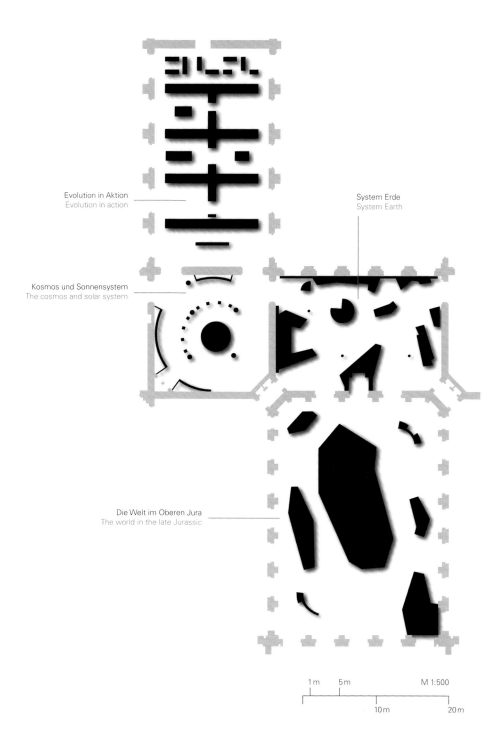

Evolution in Aktion
Evolution in action

System Erde
System Earth

Kosmos und Sonnensystem
The cosmos and solar system

Die Welt im Oberen Jura
The world in the late Jurassic

1 m   5 m   M 1:500

10 m   20 m

Entwurf

Der Arbeitsprozess zum Entwurf der Ausstellung entwickelt sich über Skizzen zur Fixierung und Kommunikation von Ideen, über einfache Modelle zur Veranschaulichung der raumbildenden Wirkung und zur Planung der Objektaufstellung, über ungewöhnliche Vorgehensweisen mit Analogien zur Verdeutlichung von Entwurfsüberlegungen bis hin zu konkreten maßstabsgerechten Zeichnungen.

Design

The working process for the exhibition design develops through the use of sketches for determining and communication of ideas; either using simple models to illustrate the space-creating effect and for the planning of the object list, through unusual practices with analogies to illustrate design considerations to concrete scale drawings.

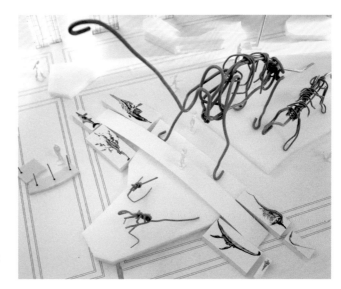

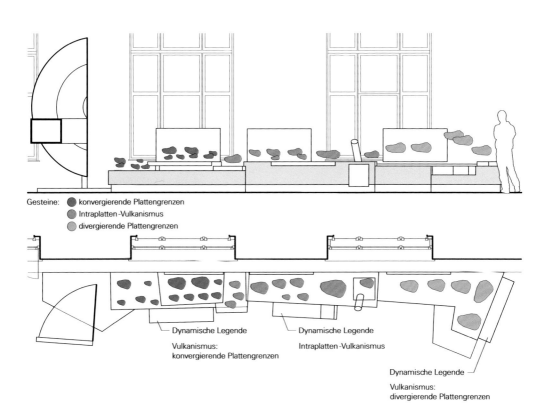

Gesteine: ● konvergierende Plattengrenzen
● Intraplatten-Vulkanismus
● divergierende Plattengrenzen

Dynamische Legende

Dynamische Legende

Vulkanismus:
konvergierende Plattengrenzen

Intraplatten-Vulkanismus

Dynamische Legende

Vulkanismus:
divergierende Plattengrenzen

Naturkundliche Ausstellungen
Natural History Exhibitions

Museum für Naturkunde Berlin
The Berlin Museum of Natural History

Architektur Architecture:
Diener & Diener Architekten

Generalplaner und Neue Medien
General Planner and New Media:
ART+COM AG

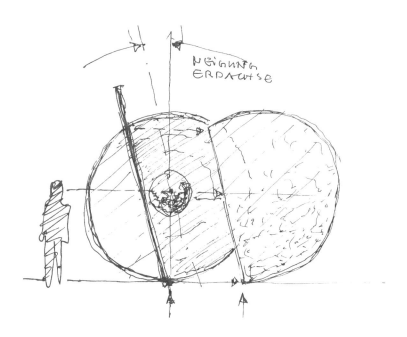

NEIGUNG
ERDACHSE

Ausstellungsgestaltung
Exhibition Design:
BERTRON SCHWARZ FREY

Projektleitung und Planung
Project Management and Planing:
SchielProjekt GmbH
Daniel Konstantin Schiel
Dorit Rudolph

Entwurfsleitung Head of Exhibition Design
Prof. Ulrich Schwarz
Entwurfsleitung Neue Medien
Head of New Media Design:
Prof. Joachim Sauter
Entwurfsleitung Grafik Design
Head of Graphic Design:
Aurelia Bertron

Farben und Materialien

Das Konzept basiert auf den von den Restauratoren im Befund festgestellten historischen Farbwerten. Da die starken Farben des Gebäudes denen der ausgestellten Objekte ähneln, braucht es für die Ausstellungselemente eine neutrale Farbstellung. So wirkt zum Beispiel das Anthrazit des gesinterten Stahls der Podeste als visuelle Sperrschicht zwischen Exponat und Architektur.

Colors and Materials

The concept is based on the color values identified and discovered by the conservators. Since the strong colors of the building are similar to that of the exhibit objects it was necessary to select a neutral color scheme. For example, the anthracite of the sintered steel pedestals acts as a visual barrier between the exhibits and the architecture.

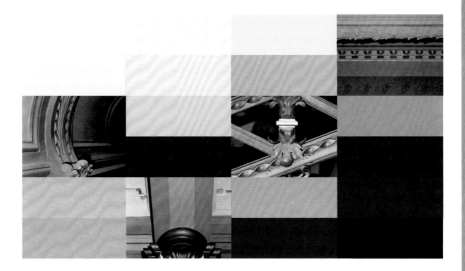

Naturkundliche Ausstellungen
Natural History Exhibitions

Museum für Naturkunde Berlin
The Berlin Museum of Natural History

Grafik Design/Layout
Graphic Design/Layout:
Monika Richter, Gert Albrecht,
Franziska Morlok, Emily Smith
Illustration Illustration:
Prof. Günther Biste, schreiberVIS

Konzept und Einleuchten
Concept and Lighting:
Delux AG Rolf Derrer, Tobias Mühlemann
Ausführungsplanung
Planning and Execution:
Studio Dinnebier

Bildnachweis Images:
Alexandra Restaurierungen
Büro für Bauforschung, Restaurierung
und Architektur, Berlin

Aufgabe neuer Medien

Bei sinnvollem Einsatz bieten die interaktiven Medien gegenüber allen klassischen Medien (wie Texttafeln, Video und Audio) die Möglichkeit eines echten Dialogs mit den Ausstellungsinhalten und Objekten. Durch die Interaktion erfahren die Besucher selbstbestimmt die zu vermittelnden Inhalte. Sie können sich, je nach Interesse, nur oberflächlich oder auch intensiv in ein Thema vertiefen. Gut konzipierte und realisierte Medien sprechen Besucher mit unterschiedlichem Wahrnehmungsverhalten an:
– explorativ
– narrativ
– spielerisch
– faktisch

Eine überzeugende Gestaltung stellt Medien nie als Pseudo-Objekte oder Inszenierungen vor die Originalexponate, sondern versteht die mediale Aufarbeitung des Themas als integralen Bestandteil der Ausstellung. Aufgabe der Medien ist dabei, das Unsichtbare sichtbar zu machen, zu kommentieren, den Besucher zu informieren, aber auch zu unterhalten.
Damit eng verknüpft ist die gestalterische Absicht, technische Geräte wie zum Beispiel Computermonitore oder Tastaturen an keiner Stelle sichtbar werden zu lassen. Die Technologie verschwindet hinter Exponaten, Installationen und Inszenierungen. Neue Medien werden die klassischen Vermittlungstechniken nicht ersetzen, sind aber nachweislich eine sinnvolle und wichtige Komponente in modernen Ausstellungen. In der Ausarbeitung war auf Bedien- und Wartungsfreundlichkeit sowie Haltbarkeit besonderer Wert zu legen.
Joachim Sauter

The Role of New Media:

Interactive media provides a meaningful use of traditional media (such as text panels, audio and video) the possibility of a genuine experience with the exhibition content and its objects. Through the interaction, the visitors were able to select the instructional content themselves. Depending on the respective interests the visitor is able to decide if they prefer to intensely delve into, or rather briefly learn about the subject. Well designed and implemented media speak to visitors with differing perception:
– explorative
– narrative
– playful
– factual

A well thought out design should never present media as pseudo-objects or stagings of the original exhibits, but rather underscores medial processing of the topic as an integral part of the exhibition. The task of the media is to make the invisible visible, to comment, to inform the visitors, but also to entertain. The design incorporates the idea that all technical devices such as computer monitors or keyboards are removed from sight. The technology disappears behind exhibits, installations, and scenes. New media will not replace traditional informational techniques, but have however, proved a useful and an important component in modern exhibitions. During the preparation it was particularly important to place special consideration on the operation and maintenance, as well as the durability of the media.
Joachim Sauter

Naturkundliche Ausstellungen
Natural History Exhibitions

Museum für Naturkunde Berlin
The Berlin Museum of Natural History

Wie groß wird der Krater?

Größe und Gestalt von Meteoritenkratern hängen von Geschwindigkeit und Größe des kosmischen Körpers ab. Je schwerer und schneller der Körper, desto größer der Krater. Bei normalen Geschwindigkeiten von etwa 20 km/s ist der Kraterdurchmesser ungefähr 10 bis 20 Mal so groß wie das Projektil. Auch der Winkel, mit dem das kosmische Geschoss auf die Erde trifft, beeinflusst die Kraterform. Einschläge von 100 Meter großen Asteroiden geschehen statistisch alle 3000 Jahre. Zehn Kilometer große Asteroiden dagegen treffen die Erde nur alle 100 bis 200 Millionen Jahre.

How large will the crater be?
The size and shape of meteorite craters depends on the speed and size of the cosmic body. The heavier and faster the body, the larger the crater. At normal speeds of around 20 km/s the crater diameter is about 10 to 20 times as large as the projectile. The angle at which the cosmic projectile hits Earth also affects the crater form. Statistically speaking, asteroids around 100 metres in diameter hit Earth every 3000 years. Ten-kilometre-large asteroids hit the earth every 100 to 200 million years.

Impakt-Kalkulator
Medieninstallation zur Berechnung der Größe des Kraters, den ein Meteorit bei unterschiedlichem Gewicht und Aufschlagwinkel verursachen würde.

Impact Calculator
Media installation in which visitors are able to calculate of the size of the crater, which a meteorite with various weights and angles would cause.

Foto unten Photo below:
Antje Dittmann, Museum für Naturkunde

Dynamische Legenden

Erklärungspulte, auf denen Texte, Grafiken, schematische Darstellungen, Diagramme, Fotos und Screens integriert sind, finden als „dynamische Legenden" in allen Sälen Anwendung. Die Texte sind kurz und präzise. Obwohl zusätzliche Texte über die Bildschirme vermittelt werden könnten, verzichtet dieses speziell entwickelte Medienformat darauf und konzentriert sich ausschließlich auf Fotos, Bewegtbild und Animationen.

Dynamic Legends

Information tables, or "dynamic captions" on which texts, graphics, schematics, diagrams, photographs and screens are integrated, are available in all the rooms. The texts are short and precise. Although additional texts could be imparted through the screens, this specially developed media format forgoes such texts and rather focuses exclusively on photographs, moving images, and animations.

System Erde - d
System Earth - T

Di

System Erde - der dynamische Planet : Vulkanismus **Impakt** Tektonik Gebirgsbildung Atmosphäre
System Earth - The dynamic Planet : Volcanism Impact Tectonics Mountains Atmosphere

Die Projektile

Unser Planet ist einem ständigen kosmischen Bombardment ausgesetzt. 30 Tonnen kosmische Staubpartikel [x] treffen täglich auf die Erde und verglühen im Schutzschild der Erde, der Atmosphäre und Stratosphäre, als Sternschnuppen Kleinere Objekte bis Dekametergröße zerbrechen beim Eintreffen in die Stratosphäre, werden wirkungsvoll abgebremst und fallen als *Meteoriten* [xx][xx] zu Boden. Gelegentlich werden solche Meteoritenfälle [xx] beobachtet. Die Geschwindigkeit von ungebremsten Projektilen liegt zwischen 11 und 72 km/s.

Zu den kosmischen *Projektilen* zählen Asteroiden und Kometen. *Asteroiden* stammen aus dem Asteroidengürtel, der zwischen der Umlaufbahn von Mars und Jupiter liegt. Asteroiden sind die Mutterkörper der Meteoriten. Ihre Größe reicht von wenigen Kilometern bis zu fast 1000 km Durchmesser. Ihre Oberflächen sind selbst von Kratern übersäht.

Asteroide, die der Erde nahe kommen (Near Earth Asteroids) werden heute durch eine »Task Force« der NASA überwacht und ihre Umlaufbahnen und Vorbeiflugdistanzen zur Erde bestimmt. Das Kollisionsrisiko wird in einer Bedrohungsskala erfasst.

The Projectiles

This, of course, is not the real copy for this Text.
30 tons of cosmic dust particles [xx] will be written once you have approved the headline. Rest assured, the words will expand the concept. With clarity, Conviction. And even a little wit. *Meteorites* [xx][xx] in today's competitive marketing environment [xx], the body copy of your Text must lead the reader through a series of disarmingly simple thoughts.

All your *projectiles* supporting arguments must be communicated with simplicity and charm. *Asteroids* and in such a way that the reader will read on. And by the time your readers have reached this point in the finished copy, you will have convinced them that you not only respect their intelligence, but you also understand their needs as consumers.

Kometen
der soge
umgibt. I
ihrem Ur
Sonnens
zu verda
bezeichn
konnte d
eines Ko

Kollisio
Planeter
Erde, zu
nachgeo
Davor ga
größerer
dem die

Lebender Kolumnentitel

Titel einzeilig

Dynamische Legende Feld links	Dynamische Legende Feld links	Bildfeld Screen	Dynami
Text deutsch 6 Units	Text englisch 4 Units		Text de

Naturkundliche Ausstellungen
Natural History Exhibitions

Museum für Naturkunde Berlin
The Berlin Museum of Natural History

Erde unte

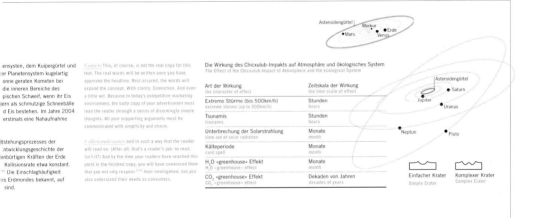

ensysten, dem Kuipergürtel und
er Planetensystem kugelartig
onne geraten Kometen bei
die inneren Bereiche des
pischen Schweif, wenn ihr Eis
ern als schmutzige Schneebälle
d Eis bestehen. Im Jahre 2004
erstmals eine Nahaufnahme

tstehungsprozesses der
ntwicklungsgeschichte der
enbürtigen Kräften der Erde
Kollisionsrate etwa konstant.
Die Einschlaghäufigkeit
s Erdmondes bekannt, auf
sind.

Comic: This, of course, is not the real copy for this
text. The real words will be written once you have
approved the headline. Rest assured, the words will
expand the concept. With clarity. Conviction. And even
a little wit. Because in today's competitive marketing
environment, the body copy of your advertisment must
lead the reader through a series of disarmingly simple
thoughts. All your supporting arguments must be
communicated with simplicity and charm.

Collisionsdesaster and in such a way that the reader
will read on. (After all, that's a reader's job: to read,
isn't it?) And by the time your readers have reached this
point in the finished copy, you will have convinced them
that you not only respect [link] their intelligence, but you
also understand their needs as consumers.

Die Wirkung des Chicxulub-Impakts auf Atmosphäre und ökologisches System
The Effect of the Chicxulub-Impact of Atmosphere and the ecological System

Art der Wirkung	Zeitskala der Wirkung
the character of effect	the time scale of effect
Extreme Stürme (bis 500km/h)	Stunden
extreme storms (up to 500km/h)	hours
Tsunamis	Stunden
tsunamis	hours
Unterbrechung der Solarstrahlung	Monate
time out of solar radiation	month
Kälteperiode	Monate
cold spell	month
H_2O »greenhouse« Effekt	Monate
H_2O »greenhouse« effect	month
CO_2 »greenhouse« Effekt	Dekaden von Jahren
CO_2 »greenhouse« effect	decades of years

Asteroidengürtel
Merkur
Mars · Erde
Venus

Asteroidengürtel
Jupiter · Saturn
Uranus
Neptun · Pluto

Einfacher Krater   Komplexer Krater
Simple Crater   Complex Crater

Dynamische Legende Feld rechts

Text englisch 4 Units

Dynamische Legende

Feld optional Tabelle/Datengrafik/Illustration/Karte

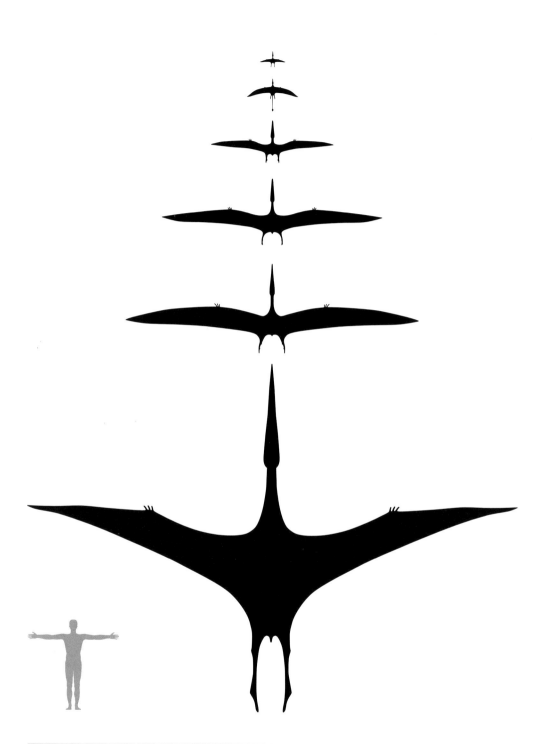

Naturkundliche Ausstellungen
Natural History Exhibitions

Museum für Naturkunde Berlin
The Berlin Museum of Natural History

Thema Evolution
Die grafische Darstellung vermittelt durch
den Mensch als Maßstab eine Vorstellung
der tatsächlichen Größe.

Evolution
By using the human form as a gauge the
graphic representation provides an idea
of the actual size.

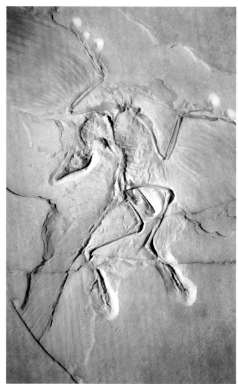

Von allen Archaeopteryx-Funden ist das Berliner Exemplar am besten erhalten und gilt als das bekannteste Fossil der Welt. Es ist 150 Millionen Jahre alt. Das Exponat präsentiert sich mit auratischer Wirkung in einem eigens dafür geschaffenen Raum unter Panzerglas. Die Beleuchtung umrundet das Objekt und lässt seine Schatten in verschiedenen Lichtsituationen erscheinen.

Of all the archaeopteryx discoveries the Berlin specimen is considered the best preserved and most famous fossil of the world – it is 150 million years old. The exhibit is presented with an auratic effect in a specially created room under bulletproof glass. The lighting surrounds the object and its shadow can appear different depending on the lighting situations.

Naturkundliche Ausstellungen
Natural History Exhibitions

Museum für Naturkunde Berlin
The Berlin Museum of Natural History

Foto rechts Photo right:
Antje Dittmann, Carola Radke,
Museum für Naturkunde

Juraskope

Interaktive Fernrohre „Juraskope"
genannt, ermöglichen die mediale
Verbindung zwischen den Original-
exponaten und Rekonstruktionen
der Dinosaurier. Der Effekt der
Medieninstallation ist besonders
wirksam.
Der Blick durch das Fernrohr zeigt
die reale Situation der Skelette
in ihrem heutigen Umfeld, dem
Museum. Die mediale Transformation zeigt dann, wie sich das
Skelett mit Muskeln bedeckt und
schließlich sich der Saurier in der
virtuell-realen Umgebung von vor
150 Millionen Jahren bewegt.

Jurascopes

Interactive telescopes called
"Jurascopes," allow for a media-
based connection between the
original exhibits and reconstructions of the dinosaurs. The
effect of the media installation
is particularly effective. The view
through the telescope is of the
skeletons as they appear in their
current environment, a museum.
The media transformation then
illustrates how the skeleton looks
when covered with muscles
and eventually how the dinosaur
moved into the virtual-real environment of 150 million years ago.

Naturkundliche Ausstellungen
Natural History Exhibitions

Museum für Naturkunde Berlin
The Berlin Museum of Natural History

Transformation vom Skelett zum Saurier
Kentrosaurus Transformation from
skeleton to Kentrosaurus

Bildnachweis Images:
ART+COM AG

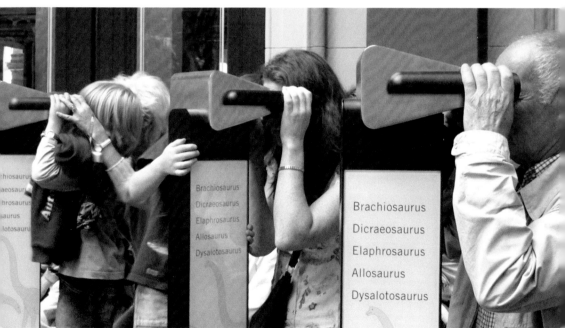

Brachiosaurus
Dicraeosaurus
Elaphrosaurus
Allosaurus
Dysalotosaurus

Juraskope ermöglichen einen Blick auf
das Leben vor 150 Millionen Jahren.

Jurascopes allow a view of life
150 million years ago.

Informationsgrafik
Zur Erklärung wissenschaftlicher
Sachverhalte dienen sachliche
Darstellungsmethoden, die
wesentliche Merkmale des
Gegenstands herausarbeiten,
aber nicht zwangsläufig ohne
Sympathiewert auskommen
müssen. Die Grundlage, die zur
Herstellung solcher Zeichnungen
befähigt, ist das akademische
Zeichnen, die grafisch generali-
sierend und reduzierend überar-
beitete Freihandzeichnung. Nicht
der individuelle Zeichenstrich, die
subjektive Illustration, sondern die
neutrale Sachdarstellung ist das
adäquate Mittel der Ausstellung.

Information Graphics
To explain scientific facts factual
presentation methods are utilized,
the essential features of the
subject are illustrated, but it does
not have to be reproduce in a
"dry" manner. The basis for the
production of such drawings, is an
academic drawing that is graphically generalizing and reduces
revised freehand drawing. It is
not the individual brushstrokes,
or the subjective illustration, but
rather the neutral presentation of
the facts that is considered to be
the adequate means of exhibition.

Landenge von Panama
ermöglicht Wanderung
von Tieren.
Isthmus of Panama
allows migration of
animals.

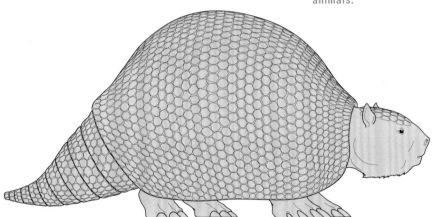

Glyptodon clavipes, **Owen** 1839

Naturkundliche Ausstellungen
Natural History Exhibitions

Museum für Naturkunde Berlin
The Berlin Museum of Natural History

Darstellung der plattentektonischen
Verbindung vor drei Millionen Jahren und
der Wanderung von Tiergruppen

Representation of the tectonic plate
connection and the migration of animal
groups three million years ago

Plattentektonik verbindet

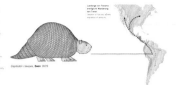

Glyptodon clavipes, **Owen** 1839

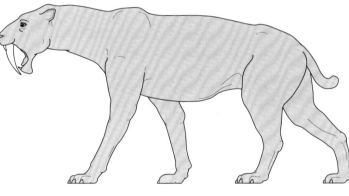

Smilodon populator, **Lund** 1842

Nächste Seite:
Das dreidimensionale Bild als Informationsträger und Sinnbild der Evolution; das Urpferdchen frisst von den Bäumen, der Nachfahre „Przewalski-Pferd" vom Boden.

Next page:
The three-dimensional image as an information carrier and a symbol of evolution; the prehistoric horse eats from the tree, the descendant of "Przewalski's horse" from the ground.

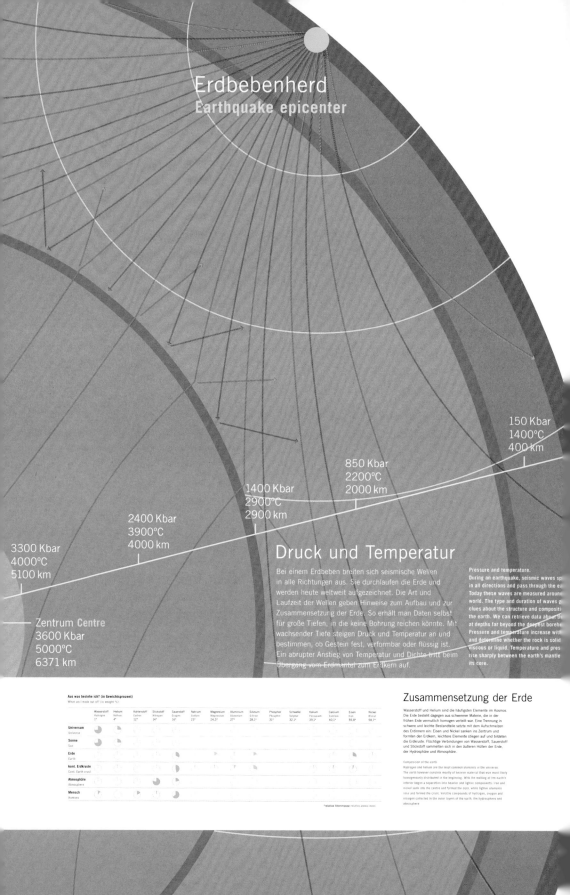

Erdbebenherd
Earthquake epicenter

150 Kbar
1400°C
400 km

850 Kbar
2200°C
2000 km

1400 Kbar
2900°C
2900 km

2400 Kbar
3900°C
4000 km

3300 Kbar
4000°C
5100 km

— Zentrum Centre
3600 Kbar
5000°C
6371 km

Druck und Temperatur

Bei einem Erdbeben breiten sich seismische Wellen
in alle Richtungen aus. Sie durchlaufen die Erde und
werden heute weltweit aufgezeichnet. Die Art und
Laufzeit der Wellen geben Hinweise zum Aufbau und zur
Zusammensetzung der Erde. So erhält man Daten selbst
für große Tiefen, in die keine Bohrung reichen könnte. Mit
wachsender Tiefe steigen Druck und Temperatur an und
bestimmen, ob Gestein fest, verformbar oder flüssig ist.
Ein abrupter Anstieg von Temperatur und Dichte tritt beim
Übergang vom Erdmantel zum Erdkern auf.

Pressure and temperature.
During an earthquake, seismic waves sp
in all directions and pass through the ea
Today these waves are measured around
world. The type and duration of waves g
clues about the structure and compositi
the earth. We can retrieve data about
at depths far beyond the deepest boreh
Pressure and temperature increase with
and determine whether the rock is solid
viscous or liquid. Temperature and pres
rise sharply between the earth's mantle
its core.

Zusammensetzung der Erde

Aus was bestehe ich? (in Gewichtsprozent)
What am I made out of? (in weight %)

	Wasserstoff Hydrogen 1*	Helium Helium 4*	Kohenstoff Carbon 12*	Stickstoff Nitrogen 14*	Sauerstoff Oxygen 16*	Natrium Sodium 23*	Magnesium Magnesium 24,3*	Aluminum Aluminum 27*	Silizium Silicon 28,1*	Phosphor Phosphor 31*	Schwefel Sulphur 32,1*	Kalium Potassium 39,1*	Calcium Calcium 40,1*	Eisen Iron 55,8*	Nickel Nickel 58,7*
Universum Universe															
Sonne Sun															
Erde Earth															
kont. Erdkruste Cont. Earth crust															
Atmosphäre Atmosphere															
Mensch Humans															

*relative Atommasse relative atomic mass

Wasserstoff und Helium sind die häufigsten Elemente im Kosmos.
Die Erde besteht dagegen aus schwererer Materie, die in der
frühen Erde vermutlich homogen verteilt war. Eine Trennung in
schwere und leichte Bestandteile setzte mit dem Aufschmelzen
des Erdinnern ein: Eisen und Nickel sanken ins Zentrum und
formten den Erdkern, leichtere Elemente stiegen auf und bildeten
die Erdkruste. Flüchtige Verbindungen von Wasserstoff, Sauerstoff
und Stickstoff sammelten sich in den äußeren Hüllen der Erde,
der Hydrosphäre und Atmosphäre.

Composition of the earth
Hydrogen and helium are the most common elements in the universe.
The earth however consists mostly of heavier material that was most likely
homogenously distributed in the beginning. With the melting of the earth's
interior began a separation into heavier and lighter components; iron and
nickel sank into the centre and formed the core, while lighter elements
rose and formed the crust. Volatile compounds of hydrogen, oxygen and
nitrogen collected in the outer layers of the earth, the hydrosphere and
atmosphere.

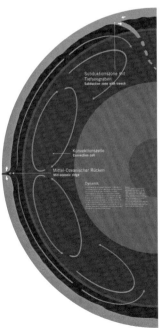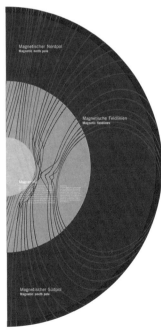

Ein multifunktionaler Globus im Durchmesser von drei Metern bildet den optischen Mittelpunkt des Saals. Der um den Globus herum gleitende Monitor zeigt Filmsequenzen von jeweils der Region, über der er gerade steht, und bezieht sich damit außerdem auf die um ihn herum gruppierten Themeninseln. In seiner zweiten Funktion vermittelt der Globus Einblicke in den schalenartigen Aufbau und die stoffliche Zusammensetzung der Erde.

The optical center of the room is a multifunctional globe with a diameter of three meters. The monitor which moves around the globe shows film clips of each region, on which the globe happens to be standing on, and which also refers to the grouped theme areas that surrounds it. In its second function the globe provides an insight into the shell-like structure and material composition of the earth.

Installation eines medial autoaktiv bespielten Globus im Ausstellungssegment „System Erde".

Media installation of an interactive recorded globe in the exhibition segment "System Earth".

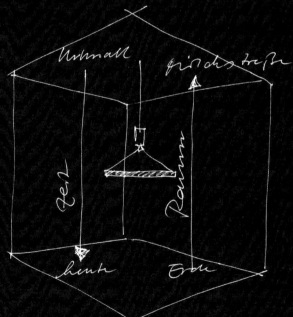

Naturkundliche Ausstellungen
Natural History Exhibitions

Museum für Naturkunde Berlin
The Berlin Museum of Natural History

Die Entstehung des Sonnensystems:
eine Reise durch die Zeit vom Urknall
bis heute und eine Reise durch den
Raum von der Erde bis ans Ende der
Milchstraße

The formation of the solar system: a
journey through time from the Big Bang
to the present day; and a journey through
space, from earth to the ends of Milky
Way

xien

atgalaxie, die Milchstraße, sehen wir als
helles Band am Sternenhimmel. Das ist so,
Milliarden Sterne in ihr nicht alle einzeln
r sind. Sie gehört zu den Spiralgalaxien, wie
hbarin·, die Andromeda-Galaxie. Beide werden
10 Milliarden Jahren zu einer Riesengalaxie
he Sterne der Milchstraße rotieren um ihr
Zentrum. Sie ·durchwandern· dabei die
Jnsere Sonne benötigt für einen Umlauf um
he Zentrum etwa 240 Millionen Jahre.

Besondere Bedingungen des Ausstellungsraumes

Treppenhäuser sind für Ausstellungen nur bedingt nutzbar. Es gelten strenge Vorschriften des Brandschutzes, und es besteht erhöhte Unfallgefahr durch mögliche Ablenkungen beim Begehen der Treppe.

Deshalb wird das Thema „Reise durch die Zeit" nicht an den Wänden, sondern im Auge des Treppenhauses durch eine runde Projektionsfläche dargestellt, die sich von der Decke herab auf die Zuschauer zubewegt.

Die Reise durch die Zeit endet im Naturkundemuseum über den Köpfen des Publikums, das anschließend von dort aus zu einem virtuellen Flug ins All startet.

Special conditions with regard to the exhibition space

Staircases render found within the exhibition space are only partly usable. There are strict fire safety rules, and there is an increased risk of accidents due to possible distractions when walking on the stairs. That is why the theme of "travel through time," is not illustrated on the walls but rather projected on the staircase by a circular projection, which extends from the ceiling and subsequently move through the audience. The journey through time ends at the Museum Natural History over the heads of the audience, which then launches to a virtual flight into space.

Unsere Heimatgalaxie, die Milchstraße, sehen wir als helles Band am Sternenhimmel. Ihre 100 Milliarden Sterne sind nicht alle einzeln wahrnehmbar.

We see our galaxy and the Milky Way as a bright band in the starry sky. Its 100 billion stars are not all individually visually perceptible.

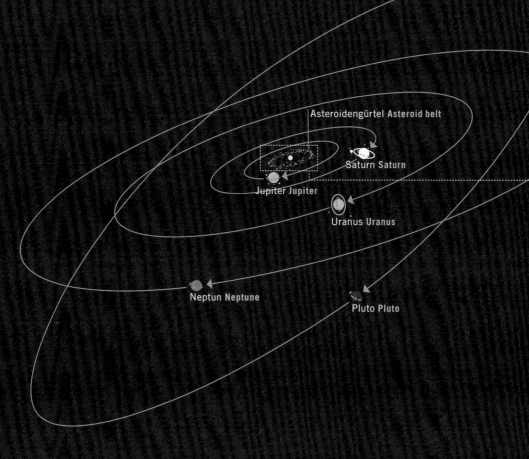

Asteroidengürtel **Asteroid belt**

Saturn **Saturn**

Jupiter **Jupiter**

Uranus **Uranus**

Neptun **Neptune**

Pluto **Pluto**

Wie Planeten wachsen

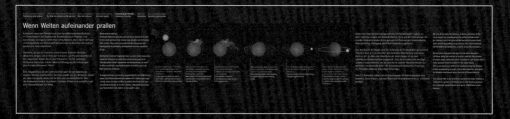

Wenn Welten aufeinander prallen

Naturkundliche Ausstellungen
Natural History Exhibitions

Museum für Naturkunde Berlin
The Berlin Museum of Natural History

Kollisionen zwischen Planeten gehören zu den entscheidenden Prozessen im Sonnensystem: Sie bewirken die Entstehung neuer Planeten und beeinflussen die Eigenschaften ihrer Umlaufbahnen. Auch die Entstehung und Entwicklung von Planetenatmosphären und die Evolution des Lebens werden von ihnen beeinflusst.

Collisions between planets are among the key processes in the solar system: they cause the formation of new planets and influence the properties of their orbits. Also, collisions also effect the formation and evolution of planetary atmospheres and the evolution of life.

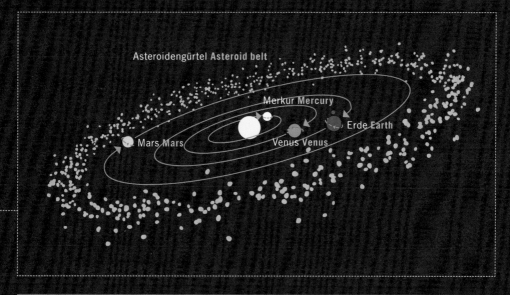

Asteroidengürtel **Asteroid belt**

Merkur Mercury

Mars Mars

Venus Venus

Erde Earth

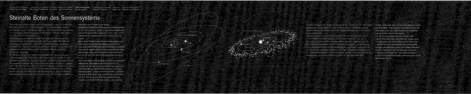

Steinalte Boten des Sonnensystems

Darstellungsmethode

Die Doppelseite zeigt drei
Informationsflächen, die das
Sonnensystem erklären. Der
Duktus der Zeichnungen bleibt in
der gesamten Ausstellung gleich.
Dabei ist es unerheblich, ob Tiere,
Pflanzen oder Planetenlaufbahnen
dargestellt werden (vgl. Seiten
54/55 und 66/67).
Es geht um die Vermittlung von
Inhalten im Überblick und im
Detail. Diese erfolgt sowohl mit
grafischen Mitteln in Form vergrö-
ßerter Ausschnitte, aber auch im
Gesamtzusammenhang.

Sprachentrennung

Das Layout organisiert in
geordneter Weise die Texte
in deutscher und englischer
Sprache.

Representative method

The double-page spread shows
three information areas that explain the solar system. The characteristic style of the drawings
remains the same throughout the
exhibition. It is irrelevant whether
it is animals, plants or the paths
of the planets careers (see pages
54/55 and 66/67).
In general it's about the placement of content and in the detail.
This is done both with graphic
means in the form of enlarged
sections, but also within the
overall context.

The language separation

The layout shows both the
German and English texts in an
organized manner.

Asteroide sind unregelmäßig geformte
Zwergplaneten und Gesteinskörper mit
einer Größe von bis zu 1000 Kilometern.
Eine Vielzahl dieser Körper befindet sich
auf Umlaufbahnen zwischen den Planeten Mars und Jupiter, im sogenannten
Asteroidengürtel, der sich an der Grenze
zwischen dem äußeren und dem inneren
Sonnensystem befindet.

Asteroids are irregularly shaped dwarf
planets and rock bodies with a size of up
to 1,000 kilometers. A number of these
bodies orbit between the planets Mars
and Jupiter, and in the so-called asteroid
belt, located in the area between the
outer and the inner solar system.

Die Entdeckung der biologischen Vielfalt

Zwischen 13 und 30 Millionen Tier- und Pflanzenarten
leben heute auf der Erde. Wissenschaftlich beschrieben
sind von dieser Biodiversität kaum mehr als zehn Prozent.
Das goldene Zeitalter der Biosystematik hat also gerade
erst begonnen. Denn allerorts werden neue Tierarten entdeckt, von kleinen unscheinbaren Insekten und Schnecken
bis hin zu Vögeln und Säugetieren. Dabei spielen heute
die Sammlungen der Naturkundemuseen eine ebenso große
Rolle wie früher Expeditionen in unerforschte Regionen.

The discovery of biological diversity.
Today between 13 to 30 million species of plants and animals inhabit the earth.
Hardly more than ten percent of them have been scientifically described.
Thus the golden age of taxonomy has only just begun. New species are being
discovered everywhere, from the smallest inconspicuous insects and snails
to birds and mammals. Today the collections of natural science museums are
just as important to these efforts as the expeditions to unexplored regions
were earlier.

Manteltiere
beschriebene Arten 2.566

Säugetiere
beschriebene Arten 5.416

Schwämme
beschriebene Arten 5.500
geschätzte Arten 18.000

Amphibien
beschriebene Arten 5.743
geschätzte Arten 7.500

Stachelhäuter
beschriebene Arten 7.000
geschätzte Arten 14.000

Reptilien
beschriebene Arten 8.300
geschätzte Arten 10.000

Nesseltiere
beschriebene Arten 9.000

Vögel
beschri
geschä

3.700.000

geschätzte Anzahl von Tierarten

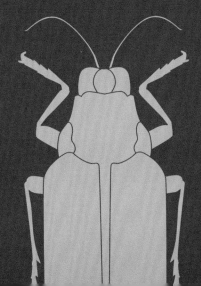

5.700.000

geschätzte Anzahl von Tierarten

1.324.442

beschriebene Anzahl von Tierarten

Ringelwürmer
beschriebene Arten 15.000
geschätzte Arten 30.000

Fische
beschriebene Arten 29.000
geschätzte Arten 35.000

Krebse
beschriebene Arten 40.000
geschätzte Arten 150.000

Weichtiere
beschriebene Arten 70.000
geschätzte Arten 120.000

Spinnentiere
beschriebene Arten 98.000
geschätzte Arten 600.000

Insekten
beschriebene Arten 950.000
geschätzte Arten 4.000.000

Übrige
beschriebene Arten 69.000
geschätzte Arten 690.000

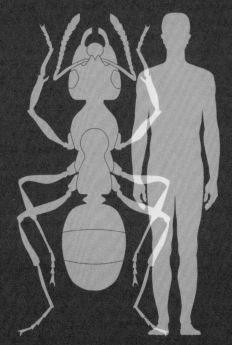

Ameisen – Die Masse zählt

Es sind etwa 10.000 Ameisen-Arten bekannt,
aber nur eine Menschen-Art. Es gibt auf der
Erde etwa 10.000.000.000.000.000 Ameisen
und 6.000.000.000 Menschen. Eine Ameise
wiegt durchschnittlich ein bis fünf Milligramm,
ein Mensch 55 Kilogramm. Alle Ameisen der
Erde wiegen zusammen etwa so viel wie alle
Menschen.

Nicht nur die Natur, auch die Naturbetrachtung hat ihre Evolution. Am Ende des Saales zum Thema Evolution repräsentieren Textzitate die Vielfalt des Denkens. So wird die Diversität der Biologie mit der Diversität der Geisteshaltungen konfrontiert. Was bedeutet uns die Natur? Was ist der Sinn des Lebens? Was ist Evolution? Was ist Leben? Was ist Wissenschaft? Was macht den Menschen zum Menschen? Was sagen Wissenschaftler über Gott? Die Installation spiegelt mit Hilfe der Zitate die vielfältigen Ansichten zu diesen Fragen wider und stellt damit gewissermaßen die geistige Vielfalt der biologischen Vielfalt gegenüber, die am Eingang gezeigt wird.

Not only nature, but the contemplation of nature has its evolution. At the end of the room on evolution text citations represent the diversity of such thought. Thus, the diversity of biology is confronted with the diversity of philosophies. What does nature mean? What is the meaning of life? What is evolution? What is life? What is science? What makes us human? What do scientists say about God? The installation reflects on the various thoughts through the use of quotes that considers these matters and in a way ensures the spiritual diversity of the biological diversity, and which is shown at the entrance.

Foto Photo:
Carola Radke, Museum für Naturkunde

THE ORIGIN OF SPECIES

BY MEANS OF NATURAL SELECTION,

By CHARLES DARWIN, M.A.,

Kosmos.

Entwurf

einer physischen Weltbeschreibung

Alexander von Humboldt.

...ALS ALLE TAGE VON MORGENS BIS ABENDS ETWAS TUM ZU H...

Vergegenständlichung durch große Bilder

Die Sammlungen des Museums für Naturkunde Berlin umfassen über 30 Millionen Objekte. Der Begriff der Biodiversität erklärt sich durch 1,8 Millionen wissenschaftlich beschriebene, registrierte und benannte Arten. In der Ausstellung vermittelt sich diese Vielfalt durch eine Großvitrine, die 2 000 Objekte zu einem großen Bild der Biodiversität zusammenfügt.

Das „große Bild" wird durch die mutige Entscheidung der Ausstellungsmacher gestützt, diese immense Anzahl von Objekten ohne direkte Beschriftung am Objekt zu präsentieren.

Wer sich für den genauen Namen der ausgestellten Präparate interessiert, kann ihn mit einer Lupe auf dem abgebildeten Dia finden.

Objectification through large-format pictures

The collection of the Museum of Natural History Berlin includes more than 30 million . The term biodiversity is explained by 1.8 million scientifically described, registered, and identified types. In the exhibition, this diversity is mediated by a large display case, which joins 2,000 objects together with a large picture of biodiversity.

The "big picture" is supported by the courageous decision of the curators to present this huge number of objects without a label directly on the object.

Those interested in learning the exact name of the exhibited objects can find it with a magnifying glass on the slide shown.

Links:
Historische Vitrinen mit nachgerüsteter Glasfaser-Beleuchtung.
Left:
Historical display case with retrofitted fiber-optic lighting.

Dia und Lupe als analoge Legende zur Vitrine „Biodiversität"
Slides and magnifying glass as an analogue legend for the biodiversity display case

Fotos Seiten 33, 50–53, 64 f., 72–77
Photos pages 33, 50–53, 64 f., 72–77:
Volker Kreidler

Das Große Tropenhaus im Berliner Botanischen Garten
The Main Tropical Greenhouse in the Berlin Botanic Garden

Den Anlass, die Ausstellung des Großen Tropenhauses neu zu konzipieren, gab die Restaurierung des denkmalgeschützten Wahrzeichens des Botanischen Gartens. Das bis 1907 erbaute Große Tropenhaus ist eines der imposantesten freitragenden Gewächshäuser der Welt. Die Konstruktion aus stählernen Dreigelenkbögen überspannt bei 26 Meter Höhe stützenfrei eine Grundfläche von 1750 Quadratmeter (60 x 29 Meter), die durch vier kleine Annexe jeweils in den Ecken des Gewächshauses ergänzt wird. Eine allseits umhüllende Fassade aus speziellem Isolierglas gewährleistet das für ein natürliches Pflanzenwachstum notwendige tropische Klima. Seit Anfang Mai 2009 kehrten die mehr als 4 000 ausgelagerten Pflanzen aus über 1 350 Arten in ihr Domizil zurück. Durch die Tropenhaussanierung werden 50 Prozent des bisherigen Energiebedarfs eingespart.

Der Botanische Garten in Berlin gilt als eine der weltweit führenden Einrichtungen seiner Art. Die Pflanzenvielfalt erforschen, dokumentieren, präsentieren, erklären und erhalten ist das Ziel der Zentraleinrichtung der Freien Universität Berlin. Schon Adolf Engler und Ignatz Urban hatten vor über 100 Jahren ein grundlegendes Konzept („Die Welt in einem Garten") entwickelt. Ihr pflanzengeografischer Ansatz, die Beschreibung der Pflanzenvielfalt nach ihrer geografisch-klimatischen Verbreitung, geht letztlich auf Alexander von Humboldt zurück, der diesen Erklärungsansatz während seiner berühmten Südamerikareise begründete. Die wissenschaftlich dokumentierte und genutzte Pflanzensammlung im Großen Tropenhaus stellt den tropischen Ausschnitt dieses Konzepts dar, das seine Ergänzung in den anderen Gewächshäusern und den Freilandanlagen auf dem 43 Hektar großen Areal findet. Für die Ausstellung war es daher wichtig, diesen tropischen Ausschnitt des Gesamtkonzeptes deutlich zu machen und in klarer Form Schnittpunkte mit den anderen Gartenausstellungen vorzudenken. Zentraler und hochkomplexer Gegenstand

The occasion for reconceptualizing the exhibition in the Main Tropical Greenhouse (*Grosses Tropenhaus*) was provided by the restoration of this historical landmark of Berlin's Botanical Garden. The Main Tropical Greenhouse, which was completed in 1907, is one of the most impressive freestanding glasshouses in the world. It is constructed from triple-hinged steel arches that reach a height of twenty-six meters, creating an uninterrupted interior space of 1,750 square meters (60 x 29 meter) that is supplemented by four small annexes positioned at its corners. The frame is covered by a specially insulated glass facade, which guarantees the maintenance of the tropical climate required for the natural growth of the plants inside. More than 4,000 plants comprising 1,350 species were relocated for the restoration, and have been returned to their domicile since May 2009. The restoration of the greenhouse has reduced its previous energy requirement by fifty percent.

The Botanical Garden in Berlin is regarded as one of the world's most important gardens. The garden is part of Freie Universität Berlin (Free University of Berlin), which is responsible for researching, documenting, presenting, explaining, and preserving its enormous variety of plants.

A fundamental concept informing the character of the garden ("the world in a garden") was already formulated one hundred years ago by two of the institution's founding figures, Adolf Engler and Ignatz Urban. Its plant-geographical approach, the description of plant varieties in terms of their geographical and climatic distribution, can ultimately be traced back to Alexander von Humboldt, who formulated this explanatory method during his famous journey through South America. The scientifically documented and utilized plant collection in the greenhouse represents the tropical segment of this concept, which has been applied throughout the other greenhouses, and outdoor garden areas across the entire forty-three hectare area. It was therefore important for the

Naturkundliche Ausstellungen
Natural History Exhibitions

Das Große Tropenhaus im Berliner Botanischen Garten The Main Tropical Greenhouse in the Berlin Botanic Garden

Botanischer Garten & Botanisches Museum Berlin-Dahlem, Freie Universität Berlin Botanic Garden and Botanical Museum, Freie Universität Berlin
Königin-Luise-Straße 6–8
14195 Berlin

Autoren/Kuratoren/Wissenschaftliches Team Authors/Curators/Research Team: Prof. Dr. Albert-Dieter Stevens, Direktor Director, Henrike Wilke, Gärtnermeisterin Gewächshäuser Greenhouse Horticulturalist, Christel Schrader, Gärtnerin im Tropenhaus Greenhouse Gardner, Harald Steinbrück,

der Ausstellung ist die Vielfalt von Bäumen, Sträuchern, Stauden, Epiphyten und Lianen aus allen Lebensräumen des tropischen Gürtels. Die Pflanzen werden in Beeten kultiviert, deren Pflanzensammlung dem historischen Ausstellungskonzept mit zwei Bereichen für die Tropen der Alten und der Neuen Welt folgen. Bei der Neuanlage wurde dieses Konzept mit einer Beetaufteilung jeweils für Mittelamerika (inkl. Karibik), Südamerika, Afrika, Asien und Ozeanien (inkl. Australien) verfeinert. Aus diesen Regionen werden exemplarisch Pflanzen(-arten) kultiviert, die ganz unterschiedlichen ökologischen Zonen und Vegetationstypen wie Savannen, Halbwüsten, feuchttropischen Tieflandwäldern oder tropischen Gebirgen entstammen.

Die Architektur des Großen Tropenhauses bedingt einen klimatischen Gradienten von trocken-warmen Kulturbedingungen der südwestlichen Seite bis zu schattig-feuchten der nordöstlichen. Ein Höhengradient wird durch die unterschiedliche Wuchsform der Arten, von Bäumen über Sträucher und Kräuter, vorgegeben. Ein spezielles Thema stellt die Entwicklungsgeschichte der Pflanzen dar. In vielen tropischen Regionen haben sich Relikte erhalten, deren Ahnen den Epochen der Urkontinente und Dinosaurier zugeordnet werden können. Der erdgeschichtliche Zusammenhang mit der heutigen pflanzengeografischen Verbreitung wird exemplarisch unter der Bezeichnung „Gondwana" dargestellt. Palmfarne, Schachtelhalme und weitere Arten werden auf einer naturnah gestalteten Felsengrotte mit kleinem Wasserfall oberhalb eines Wasserbeckens im hinteren nordöstlichen Teil gezeigt.

Weitere besonders interessante Pflanzengruppen, die spezielle Wuchsbedingungen erfordern, sind in den vier Annexen zu sehen. Dazu gehören die insektivoren Kannenpflanzen Südostasiens, *Welwitschia mirabilis*, eine urtümliche „Wunderpflanze" aus den Trockengebieten Südwestafrikas, die epiphytischen Trichterpflanzen (Bromelien) der Neotropis und schattenliebende, feuchtigkeitsbedürftige (circum-)tropische Moose.

exhibition to clearly identify this tropical segment as an underlying theme in the overall concept, and to consider points of intersection with the other garden exhibitions. The exhibition's central and highly complex subject is the variety of trees, bushes, shrubs, epiphytes, and lianas from all the habitats making up the tropical belt. The plants are cultivated in beds arranged in accordance with the concept originally developed for the Main Tropical Greenhouse, which made a distinction between plants from the old and new worlds. This concept was refined for the restored greenhouse with an added distinction between beds containing flora from Central America (including the Caribbean), South America, Africa, Asia, and Oceania (including Australia). The greenhouse contains examples of plant species from these regions that originate from a wide range of the different ecological zones, and vegetation types such as savanna, semi-arid areas, tropical lowland forests, and tropical mountain areas.

The architecture of the Tropical Greenhouse results in a climatic gradient that extends from dry and warm on the southwest side to shady and humid on the northwest side. An altitudinal gradient is produced by the different growth forms of the flora making up the collection, which ranges from trees to shrubs and herbage. The evolution of the plants is given particular consideration. In many tropical regions relics have survived whose ancestry can be traced back to the ages of the supercontinents and the dinosaurs. In the pavilion, this historical connection with the current geographical dissemination of plants is exemplified in the "Gondwana" section. Here, in the rear northeast section of the greenhouse, cycads, scouring rushes, and other species are presented in a rock grotto with a small waterfall above a pool.

Other particularly interesting plant groups that require special growing conditions can be found in the four annexes. These include the insectivore tropical pitcher plants (*Nepenthes*) of Southeast Asia, *Welwitschia mirabilis*, a traditional "miracle plant" from the arid regions of Southwest Africa, the

---

Reviergärtner im Tropenhaus Head Gardner Greenhouse, Kathrin Grotz, Museologin, Leiterin der Ausstellungen am Botanischen Garten und Botanischen Museum Museologin Museologist, Director of Exhibitions, Botanic Garden and Botanical Museum, Dr. Elke Zippel, Biologin Biologist,

Dr. Gerald Parolly, Biologe, Kustos am Botanischen Garten Biologist, Botanic Garden Curator, Birgit Nordt, Biologin Biologist, Dr. Beat Leuenberger, Kustos am Botanischen Garten (verstorben) Botanic Garden Curator (deceased)

Dauerausstellung Permanent Exhibition

Als Vertreter der neotropischen Pflanzenvielfalt sei der Ameisenbaum *(Cecropia
peltata)* – eine sogenannte Pionierart –
genannt, der in beispielhafter Weise die er-
staunlich komplexen Interaktionen zwischen
Tieren und Pflanzen verdeutlicht.
Als afrikanischer Vertreter ist mit *Adansonia
digitata*, der Affenbrotbaum, ein skurriler,
an offene Graslandschaften angepasster
Riesenbaum gewählt, der es schafft, trotz
lang andauernder Trockenphasen und
wiederkehrenden Feuern in der Savanne
auch für den Menschen vielseitig nutzbare
Früchte in großer Zahl zu produzieren. Er
steht gleichzeitig für viele andere dem
Menschen nützliche Arten, die schon früh,
in diesem Fall von arabischen Händlern
im 13. Jahrhundert, nach Indien gebracht
wurden und dort noch heute wachsen,
ohne Probleme zu bereiten.
Bambus steht für Asien, wird aber auch in
heimischen Breiten kultiviert und schließt
bei ca. 5000 Arten weltweit auch die größte
grasartige Pflanze, *Dendrocalamus giganteus*, ein, die bis zu 40 Meter hoch wachsen
kann. Bis zu 1,5 Milliarden Menschen leben
direkt oder indirekt von diesen vielseitig
verwendbaren biologischen Ressourcen. Sei
es als Nahrungsmittel oder für die Bauindus-
trie, als Energiequelle oder als Heilmittel –
Bambusarten haben viele noch ungenutzte

epiphytic bromeliads of the neotropical
regions, and (circum) tropical mosses,
which are particularly fond of shady, damp
conditions.
An interesting representative of the range
of neotropical plants is the Shield-leaved
Pumpwood *(Cecropia peltata)*, a so-called
pioneer species that exemplifies the
astoundingly complex interaction between
animals and plants.
A striking representative of African flora is
Adansonia digitata, the baobab, a bizarre,
giant tree adapted to open grassland which,
despite long dry spells and repeated fires
in the savanna, manages to produce large
amounts of fruit that has many versatile
uses, even for humans. The baobab is representative of an entire range of useful trees
that were brought early to India in this case
by Arab traders in the thirteenth century and
continue to grow there today without caus-
ing problems.
Bamboo is a symbol of Asia, however, it is
also cultivated in Europe and includes some
5000 species across the world including
the world's largest graminaceous plant,
Dendrocalamus giganteus, which can grow
to a height of forty meters. Up to 1.5 billion
people live directly or indirectly from this
versatile biological resource. Whether as
a food or building material, energy source

Naturkundliche Ausstellungen
Natural History Exhibitions

Das Große Tropenhaus im Berliner
Botanischen Garten The Great Pavilion in
the Berlin Botanic Garden

Träger Supporting Institutions:
Freie Universität Berlin, Land Berlin
Freie Universität Berlin, The State of
Berlin

Cecropia peltata (Ameisenbaum)
Cecropia peltata
(Shield-leaved Pumpwood)
Foto Photo:
Prof. Dr. Albert-Dieter Stevens

Potenziale, deren Nutzung von der Kenntnis ihrer Art abhängen. An diesen Beispielen mag deutlich werden, dass die Pflanzenvielfalt der tropischen Lebensräume wichtige geografische und klimatische Ursachen hat und dementsprechend ausgeprägt ist. Daneben muss die Vielfalt der Arten benannt werden, ihre Entstehungsgeschichte und Biologie müssen bekannt sein, um die komplexen Zusammenhänge in tropischen Lebensräumen und Ökosystemen erfassen zu können. Ohne dieses Verständnis kann weder ideell-ästhetisch noch materiell nachhaltiger Nutzen aus den tropischen Lebensgrundlagen gezogen werden.

Das Informationsangebot für die Besucher sollte die Ausstellungsobjekte, die Pflanzen, nicht verdrängen und deren eigene jahreszeitlich und altersabhängig wechselnde laubbildende, blühende oder fruchtende Erscheinung sollten im Mittelpunkt stehen. Gut lesbare aber unaufdringliche Namensetiketten zur Identifizierung der einzelnen Pflanzenarten sind ein unverzichtbares Element für eine wissenschaftlich ausgerichtete und forschende Einrichtung und machen deutlich, dass die Zusammenstellung der lebenden Objekte, die Pflanzensammlung, eine künstliche ist, die von einem wissenschaftlichen Verständnis der Vielfalt vorgegeben ist. Diese versucht, sich

or medicament bamboo species still have many unexploited potentials that researchers are yet to discover. These examples illustrate that the variety of plants growing naturally in tropical habitats have evolved as a result of important geographical and climatic influences.

In order to understand the complex relationships involved in these tropical habitats and ecosystems, this diverse range of species must be classified and named, and their evolutionary history and biology understood. Without this knowledge it will not be possible to use these tropical resources in a sustainable way, whether in aesthetic or material terms.

In an exhibition such found in the Tropical Greenhouse, it is important that information is not presented in an obtrusive way, and that the exhibits – the plants themselves and the individual and age-dependent phases in which they produce leaves, flower, and bear fruit – take center stage. Legible and unobtrusive labels for the identification of individual species are an indispensable element of every scientific and research-oriented institution, and make it clear that the combination of living objects, the plant collection, is an artificial one prescribed by a scientific understanding of the diversity involved that attempts to

Andansonia digitata (Affenbrotbaum)
Andansonia digitata (boabab)
Foto Photo:
Prof. Dr. Albert-Dieter Stevens

Dendrocalamus giganteus (Bambus)
Dendrocalamus giganteus (bamboo)
Foto Photo:
Dr. Yeon Ha

Eröffnung: 16. September 2009
Opened on September 16, 2009

an natürlichen Kategorien zu orientieren. Der Eintritt in die Pflanzenwelt der Tropen sollte über eine gesonderte Darstellung dieser wissenschaftlichen Vorstellungen oder Grundlagen erfolgen. Dazu bot sich der Vorraum zum Großen Tropenhaus an. An jeder geografischen Region im Tropenhaus wurden diese Grundlagen aufgegriffen, spezifiziert und exemplarisch an einzelnen Pflanzen detailliert dargestellt. Die Gestaltung und Materialität der Medien mussten den tropischen Kulturbedingungen wie hohe Luftfeuchtigkeit, künstlicher Regen und Nebel, Spritzwasser, Staub, hohe Sonneneinstrahlung usw. angepasst werden. Sie sollten trotz dezenter Darbietung leicht auffindbar und wiedererkennbar sein und außerdem eine spätere Ausdehnung des Konzeptes auf andere Bereiche des Gartens erlauben und ein Besucherleitsystem integrieren.

Albert-Dieter Stevens

orient itself according to natural categories. It seems appropriate that the entrance to the world of tropical flora should be marked by a separate presentation of its scientific fundamentals. In the case of the Main Tropical Greenhouse an opportunity in this regard was offered by the building's vestibule. The presentation mounted here illustrates these fundamentals in relation to each geographical region represented in the glasshouse, using specific and detailed examples of individual plants. It was important that the design and materials used here were adapted to tropical environmental factors such as humidity, artificial rain and mist, water spray, dust, and a high degree of solar radiation. While presentational elements needed to be restrained they also had to be easy to locate and recognize, and allow for subsequent application of the concept to other areas of the garden as well as integration into the signage system providing a guide for visitors.

Albert-Dieter Stevens

Naturkundliche Ausstellungen Natural History Exhibitions	Foto Photo: Ingo Haas	Ausstellungsfläche Exhibition Area: 1750 m²
Das Große Tropenhaus im Berliner Botanischen Garten The Great Pavilion in the Berlin Botanic Garden		

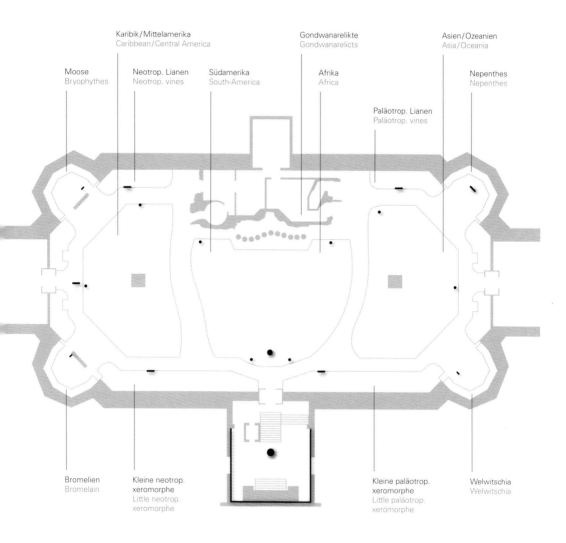

Moose
Bryophythes

Karibik/Mittelamerika
Caribbean/Central America

Neotrop. Lianen
Neotrop. vines

Südamerika
South-America

Gondwanarelikte
Gondwanarelicts

Afrika
Africa

Paläotrop. Lianen
Paläotrop. vines

Asien/Ozeanien
Asia/Oceania

Nepenthes
Nepenthes

Bromelien
Bromelain

Kleine neotrop.
xeromorphe
Little neotrop.
xeromorphe

Kleine paläotrop.
xeromorphe
Little paläotrop.
xeromorphe

Welwitschia
Welwitschia

1 m   5 m   M 1:500

          10 m   20 m

Naturkundliche Ausstellungen
Natural History Exhibitions

Das Große Tropenhaus im Berliner
Botanischen Garten The Great Pavilion in
the Berlin Botanic Garden

Die Planungsphase für das Informations-
system verläuft parallel zur Bauphase.

The planning phase for the information
system ran in parallel to the building
phase.

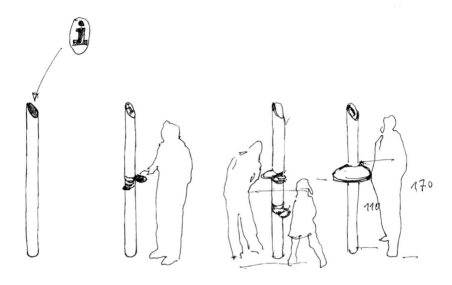

Das Gestaltungskonzept für die Besucherinformation bietet drei wesentliche Qualitäten:
– Information
– Orientierung
– Attraktion

Die Präsentation stellt die Einzigartigkeit der Sammlung in den Vordergrund, weswegen die Informationselemente nur dienenden Charakter haben. Der überwältigende Gesamteindruck soll erhalten bleiben. Der Fokus liegt eindeutig auf der Sammlung, ganz nach dem Leitsatz: „Das große Tropenhaus ist einzigartig".

Visitor information provides three essential qualities:
– Information
– Orientation
– Attraction

The presentation puts the uniqueness of the collection in the foreground, so that the information elements only have a "serving" character. The unique impression of the exhibition should remain in the mind of the visitor. In which the focus is clearly on the collection according to the motto: "The Main Tropical Greenhouse is unique."

Architektur Sanierung Building Renovation: HAAS Architekten

Leit- und Orientierungssystem, Informationsgrafik
Guidance and Orientation System, Informational Schematic:
BERTRON SCHWARZ FREY

Entwurf Design:
Aurelia Bertron, Prof. Ulrich Schwarz
Ausführungsplanung
Planning and Execution:
Prof. Claudia Frey, Sebastian Scheller
Grafik Graphic Design: Marie Lauenroth

Naturkundliche Ausstellungen
Natural History Exhibitions

Das Große Tropenhaus im Berliner
Botanischen Garten The Great Pavilion in
the Berlin Botanic Garden

Im Zentrum des Foyers vermittelt ein
Globus übergeordnete Zusammenhänge.
Das individualisierte vegetationsgeogra-
fische Kartenbild zeigt die ökologischen
Zonen.

Situated in the center of the foyer a globe
provides information on the individual-
ized vegetation-geographical map which
shows the ecological zones.

Die Besucherinformation strukturiert sich in drei Ebenen:
– Information/Präsentation
– Exponate
– Leit- und Orientierungssystem

Für das neue Informations- und Leitsystem dient die Geografie als räumliches und inhaltliches Gliederungsprinzip.
Die Pflanzen im Großen Tropenhaus präsentieren sich erstmals als Teil eines Gesamtkonzeptes. Das Vermittlungskonzept verdeutlicht, dass es „die" Tropen nicht gibt, sondern vielmehr unterschiedliche tropische Lebensräume, die sich klimatisch, geografisch und botanisch unterscheiden.
Ein Überblick über die Pflanzenwelt der Tropen wird im Foyer gegeben. Ein großer Globus und ein Panoramafries informieren hier über die weltweite Verteilung der tropischen Vegetations- und Ökozonen.

The visitor information is structured into three levels:
– Information/Presentation
– Exhibits
– Guidance and orientation system

Geography serves to guide the new information and guidance system as a spatial and content classification principle. For the first time the plants in the main tropical house are presented as part of an overall concept. The concept of mediation makes it clear that "they" are not tropical, but rather different tropical habitats, which differ in climate, geography and botany.
An overview of the plant world of the tropics is given in the foyer. A large globe and a panoramic frieze inform the visitor about the global distribution of tropical vegetation and ecozones.

Foto Photo:
Dirk Altenkirch

Analog zum Globus eine 360-Grad-Projektion der tropischen Vegetationszonen auf einem Wandfries mit kolorierten historischen Abbildungen

Globe with a 360-degree projection of the tropical vegetation zones on a wall frieze with color-coded historical pictures

Informationspylone
Formale Herleitung: Runde Stangen oder Säulen lassen den Blick auf die Pflanzen frei. Durch das farbliche Hervorheben der abgeschrägten Spitze sind die Pylonen schon aus der Entfernung sichtbar, ohne sich durch räumliche Ausbreitung in den Vordergrund zu drängen.

Information Pylones
Round poles or columns do not obstruct the view to the plants. By highlighting the beveled tip of the towers they are visible from a distance, allowing the plant exhibits to remain in the foreground.

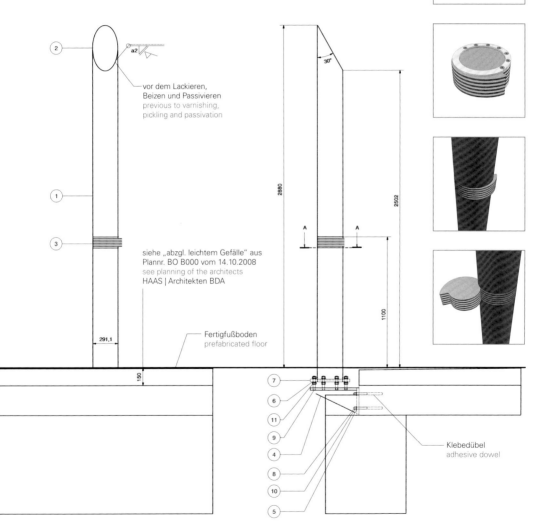

vor dem Lackieren, Beizen und Passivieren
previous to varnishing, pickling and passivation

siehe „abzgl. leichtem Gefälle" aus Plannr. BO B000 vom 14.10.2008
see planning of the architects
HAAS | Architekten BDA

Fertigfußboden
prefabricated floor

Klebedübel
adhesive dowel

Naturkundliche Ausstellungen
Natural History Exhibitions

Das Große Tropenhaus im Berliner Botanischen Garten The Great Pavilion in the Berlin Botanic Garden

Material: Stahlrohr, Lackierung DB 702, Anthrazit-Eisenglimmer, wie bereits am Bau verwendet
Material: steel pipe, paint DB 702, anthracite-iron mica, as previously used on the building

Konstruktionen Assembly:
Andreas Donner

Die geografische Einteilung der Beete kann an insgesamt acht Pylonen mit herausziehbaren Scheiben vertieft werden. Pylone dienen gleichzeitig zur themenbezogenen Navigation in den Häusern und als Basiselement des Leit- und Orientierungssystems auf dem Gelände. Das System folgt dem Grundsatz, immer an den gleichen definierten Stellen Informationen bereitzuhalten, an denen auch Orientierungsbedarf besteht. Vorteil: Das System der Orientierungsbeschilderung wird vom Besucher schnell verstanden, auf großformatige, auffällige Kennzeichnung kann verzichtet werden.

The geographical division of the beds can be deepened to a total of eight pylons with pull-out windows. Pylons are also used for the thematic navigation in the houses and on the grounds and serves as a basic element of control and guidance system. The system follows the idea to be able to obtain information always at the same areas, when an orientation is needed. Advantage: The system of signs used to guide visitors are easy to learn, and in that large-format, and eye-catching labels are done away with.

Unterkante Schrift deutsch 800 mm
lower edge of the german text 700 mm

horizontaler Mittelpunkt beider Zeilen: niedrigster Punkt von Schnittfläche

vertikaler Abstand zwischen beiden Grundlinien 80 mm

horizontaler Versatz zwischen beiden Zeilen 100 mm

Unterkante Schrift englisch 700 mm
lower edge of the english text 700 mm

horizontal center of the two lines: lowest point of the intersection

vertical distance between the two base lines 80 mm

horizontal drift between the two lines 100 mm

Unterkante Manschette 1310 mm
lower edge of the cuff 1310 mm

Auf umlaufenden Manschetten ist die Detailinformation zur Navigation innerhalb der Gewächshäuser platziert.

Detailed navigation information is placed on rotating cuffs and placed throughout the greenhouse.

Maßgenaue Positionierung der Beschriftungskomponenten
True-to-size positions of the labelling elements

Die Pylonen bieten nach Kontinenten gegliedert einen Überblick über die Verteilung trockener und feuchter Ökozonen in den Tropen. Auf herausziehbaren Scheiben werden interessante Phänomene exemplarisch an einzelnen Pflanzenarten erklärt.

Die Präsentation folgt konsequent der Themenmatrix:
Tafel 1:
Karte aller Vegetationszonen (FAO), entspricht dem im Globus verwendeten Kartenmaterial
Tafel 2:
Thementext
Tafel 3:
Darstellung von Vegetationsformationen
Tafel 4:
Adaptation am Beispiel einer Pflanze aus einer der beiden vorgestellten Formationen
Tafel 5:
Interaktionen am Beispiel einer Pflanze aus einer der beiden vorgestellten Formationen
Tafel 6:
Anthropogene Einflüsse in einer der beiden vorgestellten Formationen

The pylons are divided by continent and offer an overview of the distribution of dry and humid ecological zones in the tropics. On pull-out glass interesting phenomena are exemplarily explained regarding individual plant species.

The presentation follows the consistent theme format:
Table 1:
Map of vegetation zones (FAO), equivalent to the globe map material used
Table 2:
Topic text
Table 3:
Depiction of vegetation formations
Table 4:
The example of an plant adaptation from one of the two presented formations
Table 5:
Interactions utilizing the example of a plant from one of the two presented formations
Table 6:
Anthropogenic influences in one of the two presented formations

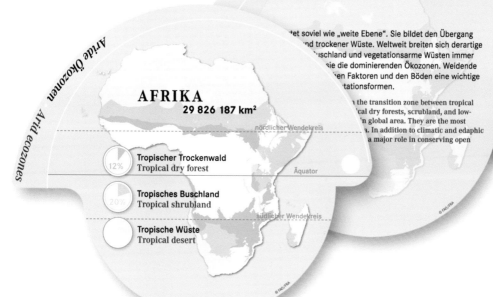

AFRIKA
29 826 187 km²

nördlicher Wendekreis

Äquator

südlicher Wendekreis

12%
Tropischer Trockenwald
Tropical dry forest

20%
Tropisches Buschland
Tropical shrubland

Tropische Wüste
Tropical desert

Aride Ökozonen Arid ecozones

Naturkundliche Ausstellungen
Natural History Exhibitions

Das Große Tropenhaus im Berliner Botanischen Garten The Main Tropical Greenhouse in the Berlin Botanic Garden

Bedruckung der Informationstablare in wetterbeständigem Spezialverfahren

Printing the information tables required a special weather resistant process

90

◀ *Adansonia digitata:*
Blüten- und Fruchtzweig
branch with flowers and fruits

"rucht fruit

Der bis zu 25 m hohe Baobab kann über 1.000
Jahre alt werden. Der Stammumfang erreicht bis zu
40 m, Blätter trägt er nur in der kurzen Regenzeit. Seine Blüten hängen an langen Stielen herab, messen
…is 12 cm und verbreiten einen unangenehmen Geruch.
…en Fledermäuse, Flughunde, Schwärmer und
…ls Bestäuber an. Die auffällig weißen Blüten
…s Salat gegessen oder als Aromastoff in
…det.

…e Früchte des Baobab. Sie und ihre Bestandteile
…ten als wichtige Nahrungsmittel gehandelt. Mit
…uchtfleisch wird als „Baobabmilch" verspeist.
…1 Vitamin-C-Gehalt und enthält Zucker und
…geröstet essbar und ihr Mehl verleiht
…icht mandelartigen Geschmack. Ge-
…als Kaffeeersatz verwendet.

…digita)

…erwachsenes ▲ *Adansonia digitata:*
Affenbrotbaum · Baobab

…itata) constitute an important source
…nonkeys. The entire fruit, seeds,
…led. Mixed with sugar and water,
…o milk". The pulp contains lots of
…e. Baobab seeds can be eaten
…heir flour is used for soups and
…a slight flavour of almonds to the dish.
…eds are also used as a substitute for

…ansonia digitata) ist gut an die trockenen
…ächst in Savannen vom Tiefland bis zu
…dicken, faserigen und kaum brennba-
…andhalten. Durch sein ausgedehntes
…r im dicken Stamm übersteht er
…ahrhundert brachten ihn arabische
…te anzutreffen ist.

…*itata:* ▶
…ower

…well adapted to the dry living
…annas from the lowland up to
…s thick, fibrous and almost
…thstand bush fires. It can also
…drought thanks to its vast root sys-
…em water reservoir. In the 13th
…rabian traders brought it to
…a where it still flourishes.

Akzentfarbe / accent colour cyan 100/0/0/0	
weiß / white	
schwarz / black	
0/0/0/80	Tropische Vegetationszonen Tropical Climate Zones
	Tropischer Regenwald / Tropical rainforest 70/0/100/20
100/80/0/0	Tropische humide Laub wer- fende Wälder / Tropical moist deciduous forest: 0/0/100/5
100/80/0/0 85%	Tropische Bergsysteme Tropical mountain systems 45/15/35/0
100/80/0/0 70%	Tropisches Buschland / Tropical shrubland 0/0/31/18
	Tropische Wüste Tropical desert 10/0/33/0
	Ozean / Ocean 15/0/0/9

Grundfarben des Planzenbestan-
des sind vorwiegend Erd- und
Grüntöne. Diese bilden den
Hintergrund für die Blüten, die
eine sehr nuancierte Farbigkeit
aufweisen.
Die Gestaltung räumt den Pflan-
zenexponaten den Vorrang ein.
Die Farben der Besucherinformation sollen sich harmonisch in das
Gesamtbild einfügen.

Basic colors for the pedestals are
predominantly earth tones and
greens. These form the background for the flowers, which
show a very subtle palette. The
design is intended to allow the
plants to remain in the foreground
of the exhibition. The colors used
for the visitor information were
selected to fit harmoniously into
the overall concept.

Die Farbauswahl setzt sich aus einer
erweiterten Blaupalette, Grautönen und
nur spartanisch eingesetzten, in ihrer
Menge äußerst begrenzten Akzentfarben
zusammen. Die Informationselemente
beziehen ihre Farbigkeit aus fotografi-
schen Abbildungen.

The color selection is made from an
expanded range of blue, shades of gray
and are only sparsely used, together
with a corresponding accent color. The
information elements derive their color
from photographic images.

…nas

…cher Plants

Ce…

Groß…

Main Tro…

Äquat…

© FAO/FRA

Alte Welt Afrika arid

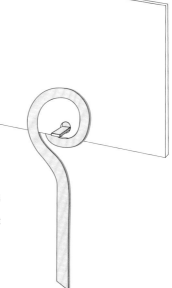

Die Etiketten sind leicht und kostengünstig zu produzieren. Die Halterung mit Sicherheitsdorn verhindert, dass sie abgezogen werden. Schriftgröße und -art sind so gewählt, dass gute Lesbarkeit gewährleistet ist. Die dunklen Etiketten fügen sich besser in das Pflanzenumfeld ein. Weiße Schrift hebt sich auf anthrazitfarbenem Untergrund sehr gut ab.

The labels are easy and inexpensive to produce. The support with integrated retainer prevents the labels from being removed. Font size and style are chosen to assure readability. The dark labels are better integrated into the plant environment; the white text stands out nicely on the anthracite surfaces.

Gebäudebeschriftung nach dem Prinzip der Direktbeschriftung

The building is labeled according to the principle of a direct labeling system.

Entwurfszeichnung
Design Drawing

Haus A|0

Großes Tropenh
Victoria Ha

Main Tropical Gre
Victoria Ho

KUNSTAUSSTELLUNGEN ART EXHIBITIONS

Kunst ist heute Inspirationsquelle für Ausstellungsgestalter – und Ausstellungsgestaltung spielt umgekehrt in der zeitgenössischen Kunst eine neue Rolle. Das war nicht immer so. In den Kunst- und Wunderkammern des 16. bis 18. Jahrhunderts waren Kunstwerke, technische Apparate und Naturobjekte in einer dichten Präsentation vereint. Von dort führte über die Welt- und Salonausstellungen des 18. und 19. Jahrhunderts der Weg zum White Cube und der damit verknüpften Vorstellung vom auratischen Kunstwerk und seinem Wirkungsraum.

Die bis heute dominante Museumsästhetik basiert auf einer Gestaltung, die Alfred H. Barr als Gründungsdirektor des New York Museum of Modern Art (MOMA), wohl auch beeinflusst vom Dessauer Bauhaus, 1929 als Erster realisierte: ein möglichst neutraler Raum, gleichmäßige Beleuchtung mit künstlichem Licht, helle, fast weiße Wandflächen, mit Abstand voneinander präsentierte Werke. Doch mit dieser Präsentation geht auch ein Ausschluss des Alltagslebens, der Natur und der Zeit einher – ein Umstand, der heute Gestalter und Ausstellungsmacher motiviert, den inzwischen klassischen White Cube zu dekonstruieren und neue Ausstellungsformen zu finden. Während sich also der pseudoneutrale „Container" des White Cube langsam auch unter den Anforderungen und der Mitwirkung der Künstler aufzulösen scheint, beschränkt sich die Gestaltung musealer Ausstellungen historischer Werke oft auf subtile Eingriffe in die Architektur, wie Beleuchtung, Wandfarbe oder die Integration eines Hängesystems. Dies ist nicht zuletzt konservatorischen Aspekten geschuldet. Wesentlich größer ist der Gestaltungsspielraum bei thematischen Ausstellungen zeitgenössischer Kunst oder Gruppenausstellungen. Hier kann mehr experimentiert und nach neuen Formen der Präsentation gesucht werden.

Today art is a potent source of inspiration for exhibition designers. Conversely, exhibition design is playing a new role in contemporary art. This was not always the case. In the cabinets of curiosities popular from the sixteenth to the eighteenth century, artworks, technical apparatus, and natural objects were combined in densely packed presentations. The world expositions and salon exhibitions of the eighteenth and nineteenth century were ultimately followed by the emergence of the White Cube and the associated notion of the auratic artwork and its scope of effect. The museum aesthetic that remains dominant today is based on a design first realized in 1929 by Alfred H. Barr, the founding director of the New York Museum of Modern Art (MOMA), who was probably influenced by the Dessau Bauhaus. This model comprises a space that is as neutral as possible, evenly illuminated with artificial lighting and with light-colored, almost white walls on which the works are presented separated by gaps. However, this form of presentation also entails an exclusion of everyday life, the natural environment and time – a situation that has motivated today's designers and exhibitionmakers to deconstruct the White Cube, and search for new exhibition forms.

While the pseudo-neutral "container" of the White Cube seems to be slowly disappearing, in part due to the demands and contributions of artists themselves, the design of museum exhibitions of historical works is still often restricted to subtle interventions in the architecture of the exhibition spaces, for example, in the form of lighting, wall colors, or the integration of suspended hanging systems. This low-key approach is due not least to conservational considerations. In the case of thematic exhibitions of contemporary art or group exhibitions the scope available to designers is far greater and allows for a great deal more experimentation in the search for new forms of presentation.

Kunstausstellungen
Art Exhibitions

Vor allem die neuen Medien verändern den Ausstellungsraum, sowohl in angewandter Form als Medien der Vermittlung als auch in der freien, künstlerischen Anwendung. Zeit-basierte, prozessuale Kunst verlangt neue Architekturen des Verweilens, der sozialen Interaktion und der Partizipation; Video- und andere Bewegtbildformate befreien sich zunehmend von ihren Black Boxes und bilden andere, permeablere Räume.

Insgesamt entwickelt sich der klassische, kontemplative Ausstellungsraum mehr und mehr zu einem dynamisierten Wissens- und Diskursraum, der tendenziell auch Online-Extensionen besitzt.

Parallel zu der Dynamisierung der Kunst-räume ist in den letzten Jahren auch Bewegung in das kreative Dreieck von Gestaltern, Kuratoren und Künstlern gekommen. Die vormals klareren Abgrenzungen zwischen denen, die aktiv an der Ausstellungsproduktion beteiligt sind, lösen sich auf. Künstler schlüpfen in die Rolle des Gestalters oder des Kurators – Gestalter erschaffen künstlerische Ausstellungsdisplays –, Kuratoren entwickeln Gestaltungskonzepte und ergreifen künstlerische Positionen. Die Herausforderung für alle Beteiligten ist, in diesem Dreieck, das bei jedem Ausstellungsprojekt neu ausbalanciert wird, ihre Rolle zu finden und die Suche nach adäquaten und innovativen Formen der Präsentation und Vermittlung gemeinsam fortzusetzen.

Susanne Jaschko

It is above all the new media that are altering the exhibition space, both in an applied form as media of communication and as artistic tools. Time-based, processual art demands new architectures of lingering, of social interaction and participation; video and other moving-picture formats are increasingly liberating themselves from their black boxes and forming other, more permeable spaces.

As a whole the classic, contemplative exhibition space is increasingly developing into a dynamic space of knowledge and discourse, one which is also being extended by online applications.

In recent years this dynamization of art spaces has been paralleled by new impulses in the creative triangle between designers, curators, and artists. The previously clear boundaries between these three groups active in the process of exhibition production are now dissolving. Artists are slipping into the role of the designer or the curator – designers are creating artistic exhibition displays – curators are developing design concepts and adopting artistic viewpoints. The challenge for all participants in this triangle, which is rebalanced with every new exhibition project, is to find their role and collaborate in the ongoing search for appropriate and innovative forms of presentation, and communication.

Susanne Jaschko

Gemäldegalerie im Quistorp-Gebäude Pommersches Landesmuseum Greifswald
Art Gallery in the Quistorp Building at the Pomeranian State Museum in Greifswald

In den Räumen des von Johann Gottfried Quistorp erbauten Schulgebäudes sollten die Bestände der Stiftung Pommern in Kiel mit den Gemälden des ehemaligen Städtischen Museums in Stettin, des Museums der Hansestadt Greifswald sowie ausgewählte Werke etwa aus dem Besitz der Universität Greifswald und aus Privatsammlungen zusammengeführt werden, um einen Überblick über die Sammlungstätigkeit und die künstlerische Produktivität der pommerschen Region zu geben.
Hinsichtlich der Strukturierung wurde die „klassische Variante" der chronologischen Präsentation von der Malerei des Barock bis ins 20. Jahrhundert gewählt. Durch die Dichte und Konzentration der Sammlung, etwa in der ersten Hälfte des 19. Jahrhunderts, wird dem Besucher die Betrachtung des „gleichzeitig Ungleichzeitigen" ermöglicht.
Caspar David Friedrich kommt als international bekanntestem Maler der Romantik eine Schlüsselstellung innerhalb der Galerie zu. Inzwischen ist es gelungen, ihn mit eigenen Werken und im Kontext seiner Freunde und Zeitgenossen in seiner Geburtsstadt zu präsentieren.
Vincent van Gogh würde man in Pommern nicht vermuten: Hier wartet die Sammlung mit „Weltkunst" auf, nach Stettin geholt durch den rührigen Museumsdirektor Walter

This project entails adapting the rooms in the school building built by Johann Gottfried Quistorp to house works held by the Pomeranian Foundation in Kiel, the paintings formerly held by the National Museum Stettin and the Greifswald Museum, and selected works from the Greifswald University collection and private collections in order to provide an overview of the history of art collection and artistic productivity in the Pomeranian region.
The "classic variant" arrangement approach was selected – a chronological presentation of painting from the Baroque to the twentieth century. The density and concentration of the collection, which places importance on the first half of the nineteenth century, allows the visitor to experience the "noncontemporaneous simultaneously."
As the most internationally renowned painter of the Romantic period, Caspar David Friedrich has been accorded a key position within the gallery, which provides a focus for this native of Greifswald's work in the context of that of his friends and contemporaries. One might not expect to find Vincent van Gogh in Pomerania, but this collection also includes works by the Dutch artist. These were originally acquired in 1910 by the energetic director of the museum in Stettin, Walter Riezler, at a time when van

---

Kunstausstellungen
Art Exhibitions

Gemäldegalerie im Pommerschen
Landesmuseum Greifswald
Art Gallery at the Pomeranian State
Museum in Greifswald

Pommersches Landesmuseum
Greifswald Pomeranian State Museum
in Greifswald
Rakower Straße 9
17489 Greifswald

C.D. Friedrich, *Ruine Eldena im Riesengebirge*, 1830/1834,
Öl auf Leinwand
C.D. Friedrich, *Eldena Ruin*, 1830/1834,
Oil on canvas

Riezler und das 1910, zu einer Zeit, als van Goghs Gemälde gerade erst ihren Einzug in die Museen hielten. Ähnlich verbinden sich auch beim Bildnis von Frans Hals pommersche Sammlungsgeschichte und hochkarätige Kunst.

Die Räume ordnen sich bewusst den zu präsentierenden Objekten unter. Alle technischen Objekte wie Lichtschalter, Heizung oder Klimaauslässe wurden „versteckt" angebracht: Die Wand gehört allein dem Bild. Passend zum klassizistischen Bau wurden dezente, nur in Nuancen spielende Wand- und Deckentöne gewählt. Auch die großen Bodenplatten (1x1 Meter) aus süddeutschem Kalkstein im Untergeschoss und der mit einer Schattenfuge frei schwebende Holzboden aus gekälkter Eiche tragen zur ruhigen Gesamtwirkung bei. Dieser schlichten Eleganz ordnen sich auch die Glasschilder für die Beschriftung unter, die mit etwas Abstand gesetzt sind.

Zusätzliche Informationsstände aus Edelstahl gibt es nur für ausgewählte Gemälde: Hier werden Besonderheiten aufgegriffen, und es wird auf Einzelheiten aufmerksam gemacht.

Zwei Glastafeln im Foyer geben Einblick in die Sammlungsgeschichte, ansonsten wurde auf Texte verzichtet, der Besucher kann aber auf ein mehrsprachiges akustisches

Gogh's paintings were first starting to find their way into established art galleries. A painting by Frans Hals also attests to the place of high-quality art in the history of collecting in Pomerania.

The exhibition spaces have been consciously designed to serve the presentation of the collection. All technical features such as light switches and heating and air-conditioning fixtures have been "hidden": the walls belong to the pictures alone. In keeping with the neo-classical character of the building, restrained, moderately nuanced colors have been used for the walls and ceilings. The large floor plates (1x1 meter) made of south German limestone on the basement level and the limed oak floor framed by a shadow gap also contribute to the overall atmosphere of calm.

The interior's simple elegance also extends to the glass plates bearing inscriptions, which are set slightly away from the walls. Additional information stands made of stainless steel are reserved for selected paintings and provide specific information about these works. Two glass panels in the foyer provide an insight into the history of the collection but otherwise the exhibition does not make use of texts. However, visitors have access to a multilingual acoustic guide system, which provides informally

Vincent van Gogh, *Allee bei Arles*, 1888, Öl auf Leinwand
Vincent van Gogh, *A Lane Near Arles*, 1888, Oil on canvas

Frans Hals, *Brustbild eines vornehmen Herrn*, Öl auf Leinwand
Frans Hals, *Portrait of a Gentleman*, Oil on canvas

Dauerausstellung Permanent Exhibition

Führungssystem zurückgreifen, das locker aufbereitete Informationen zu einzelnen Werken liefert. In den größeren Sälen gibt es Sitzmöglichkeiten in Form von ruhigen, geradlinigen Eichenbänken.

Durch die teilweise recht niedrigen Deckenhöhen und Unterzüge im Erdgeschoss ist das Lichtsystem dezent in die Decke eingelassen. Die Fenster des historischen Gebäudes, die teilweise den Schauwänden gegenüber liegen, wurden durch großzügige, bis knapp über den Boden reichende Verschattungselemente beruhigt, die mit den Wänden harmonieren. Um Hängeplatz zu gewinnen, wurde in den Kopfsälen das jeweils mittlere Fenster durch große, mit Seide bespannte Einstellelemente verstellt. Da sich die Eingangssituation im historischen Gebäude auf einer anderen Seite als die heutige befand, wurde nachträglich im Foyer eine Einstellwand eingezogen, die den Blick auf die historische Tür auch noch von den Seiten erlaubt. Hier hängt heute als erster Blickfang ein großformatiges Gemälde des niederländischen Malers Gerrit van Honthorst aus einer pommerschen Kirche. Ziel der Ausstellung war es, eine möglichst kontemplative Atmosphäre zu schaffen, die jenseits der Alltagswelt zu einer konzentrierten Versenkung in die Gemälde einlädt, ein Vorhaben, das auch durch die überschaubare Zahl der Räume und Werke unterstützt wurde.

Birte Frenssen

structured information on the individual works. The larger spaces are equipped with seating in the form of sedate, rectilinear oak benches.

Due to the low ceiling and joists in parts of the ground floor area, the lighting system has been discretely set into the ceiling. The windows of the historic building, which in some cases are positioned opposite the viewing walls, have been equipped with generous shading elements that extend down to just above the floor and harmonize with the walls. In order to gain more hanging space, the middle window in each of the main rooms has been blocked with large adjustable elements covered with silk. Since the present entrance to the building is located on a different side of the building than that of the original entrance, an adjustable wall has been added to the foyer so that the historic doors can be kept in view. The wall features a large painting by the Dutch artist Gerrit van Honthorst that once hung in a Pomeranian church.

When designing the exhibition, the goal was to create a contemplative atmosphere that would invite visitors to leave behind their everyday world and immerse themselves in the paintings, an atmosphere also promoted by the limited number of rooms and works.

Birte Frenssen

Kunstausstellungen Art Exhibitions	Träger Supporting Institution: Landesmuseen State Museums	Ausstellungsfläche Exhibition Area: 1 100 m²
Gemäldegalerie im Pommerschen Landesmuseum Greifswald Art Gallery at the Pomeranian State Museum in Greifswald		

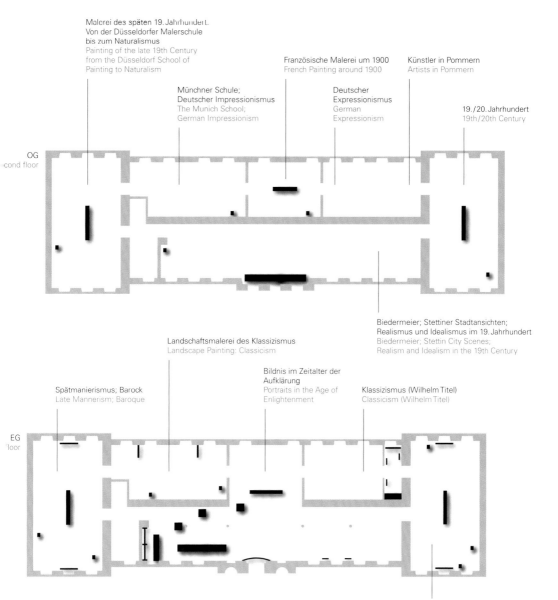

Malerei des späten 19. Jahrhundert.
Von der Düsseldorfer Malerschule
bis zum Naturalismus
Painting of the late 19th Century
from the Düsseldorf School of
Painting to Naturalism

Münchner Schule;
Deutscher Impressionismus
The Munich School;
German Impressionism

Französische Malerei um 1900
French Painting around 1900

Deutscher
Expressionismus
German
Expressionism

Künstler in Pommern
Artists in Pommern

19./20. Jahrhundert
19th/20th Century

OG
Second floor

Biedermeier; Stettiner Stadtansichten;
Realismus und Idealismus im 19. Jahrhundert
Biedermeier; Stettin City Scenes;
Realism and Idealism in the 19th Century

Landschaftsmalerei des Klassizismus
Landscape Painting: Classicism

Bildnis im Zeitalter der
Aufklärung
Portraits in the Age of
Enlightenment

Spätmanierismus; Barock
Late Mannerism; Baroque

Klassizismus (Wilhelm Titel)
Classicism (Wilhelm Titel)

EG
Floor

Kabinett (C. D. Friedrich, *Greifswalder
Marktplatz*); Malerei der Romantik
Display cabinets (C.D. Friedrich,
Greifswald Market Square), Romanticism

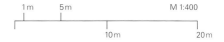

1 m   5 m   M 1:400

10 m   20 m

Auswahl der Wandfarben in der Gemäldegalerie: Idealer Hintergrund ist eine Wandfarbe, die dunkler ist als der hellste Punkt des auf ihr befindlichen Bildes. Die Lichter im Bild haben so durch ihre Kontrastwirkung mehr Tiefe – das Bild wirkt leuchtend.

Selecting the wall color in the painting gallery. The ideal background is a color that is darker than the lightest point on the respective painting. Through this contrast the light details have more depth – the painting is thus illuminated.

Kunstausstellungen
Art Exhibitions

Gemäldegalerie im Pommerschen Landesmuseum Greifswald
Art Gallery at the Pomeranian State Museum in Greifswald

Leiterin der Gemäldegalerie
Picture Gallery Director:
Dr. Birte Frenssen

Autoren / Kuratoren / Wissenschaftliches Team Authors / Curators / Research Team:
Mario Scarabis, Kai Kornow, Museologen Museologists, Dr. Michael Lissok, Prof. Bernfried Lichtnau, Dr. Gerd-Helge Vogel, Caspar-David-Friedrich-Institut, Universität Greifswald

Präsentationssystem für
Gemälde, die beidseitig, also
von vorne und hinten, betrachtet
werden sollen.
Gestelle aus Edelstahlrohren
unter Verwendung minimaler
Materialstärken erhalten den
leichten Gesamteindruck des
Raumes.

A presentation system for paintings, that are double sided – i.e.,
are viewed from the front and the
back – should be considered.
Frames made from stainless steel
tubing, in which the material has
a minimal thickness, slightly reflect the impression of the room.

Architektur Architecture:
Sunder-Plassmann Architekten, BDA
Ausstellungsgestaltung, Grafik- und
Corporate Design, Medienkonzeption
Exhibition Design, Graphic Design,
Corporate Design and Media Concept:
BERTRON SCHWARZ FREY

Entwurf Design:
Prof. Ulrich Schwarz, Aurelia Bertron
Ausführungsplanung
Planning and Execution:
Tomas Sturm

Lichtplaner Lighting Designer:
Dinnebier Licht
Einleuchten Lighting:
Ringo T. Fischer

Helle Räume, dezente Beleuchtung und eine klare Raumstruktur bringen die Gemälde zur Geltung. Die Enfilade der Gemäldegalerie knüpft an die einstige Raumstruktur des früheren Schulgebäudes an. Die Ästhetik einer Gemäldegalerie wird durch die folgenden Parameter entscheidend beeinflusst:
Hängung der Gemälde, Ausführung der Beschriftungen, Materialwahl bis hin zur Anfertigung von Museumsbänken.

Bright rooms with soft lighting compliment the paintings. The einfilade of the painting gallery connects to the rooms of the former school building. The aesthetics of an art gallery is evident in the hanging of the paintings, the design of the caption labels, and material selection right up to the model of the museum benches.

Foto auf Seite 107 Photo on page 107:
Juraij Lipták

Ein „pommerscher" Van Gogh, der bereits 1910 vom städtischen Museum in Stettin angekauft wurde. Das Bild entstand als eines der ersten Werke nach Van Goghs Übersiedlung nach Arles, wo er sich vor allem vom südlich strahlenden Licht und hier auch von den Winden des Mistrals beeindruckt zeigte.

A "Pomeranian" Van Gogh, purchased in 1910 by the municipal museum in Stettin. The picture was one of the first works by Van Gogh after he relocated to Arles, where he was especially impressed by the brilliant southern light as well as the mistral winds.

Wilhelm Titel
1784 – 1862

Drei Kinderbildnisse
1820, 1823
Pastellmalerei

Erworben durch die Bundeskunst-
sammlung

» ... das Gedeihn der
Kunst in Pommern ... «

60 Jahre. 60 Werke. Kunst aus der Bundesrepublik Deutschland 1949 bis 2009
60 Years. 60 Works. Art from the Federal Republic of Germany 1949 to 2009

Die Verfassung der Bundesrepublik war 2009 seit 60 Jahren in Kraft. Anlässlich dieses Jahrestages zeigte die Stiftung für Kunst und Kultur e.V. Bonn im Berliner Martin-Gropius-Bau die Ausstellung *60 Jahre. 60 Werke*. Präsentiert wurden 60 herausragende Arbeiten der Jahre 1949 bis 2009 von deutschen Künstlern, die das Kunstgeschehen national und international geprägt haben. Die Bandbreite der Werke reichte von Malerei und Grafik über Skulptur und Installation bis zur Fotografie. *60 Jahre. 60 Werke* zog Bilanz und erlaubte sich dabei durchaus auch einen subjektiven Blick auf die Kunstgeschichte. Jedes der 60 Werke stand für sich selbst und ermöglichte zugleich eine anschauliche Erfahrung der Zeit, in der es entstanden war. Die Geschichte der Bundesrepublik wurde am Beispiel ästhetischer Entwicklungen in der Bildenden Kunst erzählt. Dabei wurde das jeweils aktuelle Kunstgeschehen vor dem Hintergrund der politischen, gesellschaftlichen und kulturellen Ereignisse beleuchtet. Diese zeitgeschichtliche Einordnung war ein wesentlicher Bestandteil der Schau. Ziel war es, die Werke über die Medien Film, interaktive Info-Tische und „Zeitbilder" in den historischen Kontext ihrer Entstehungszeit einzubetten. Auf 60 Monitoren zeigten Filmzusammenschnitte die gesellschaftlichen und politischen Ereignisse jeweils eines Jahres. Interaktive Info-Tische, die sich inhaltlich mit jeweils einer Dekade befassten, informierten über die ausgestellten Werke und entsprechende Kunstströmungen und -ereignisse. 60 Kurzfilme aus Archivmaterial des WDR lieferten eine lebendige Chronik der Jahre 1949 bis 2009 und bebilderten die politische, gesellschaftliche und kulturelle Szene. Durch diese Kontextualisierung der Kunstwerke wurde eine Verbindung zwischen ihrer Entstehung und der Geschichte der Bundesrepublik hergestellt. Verantwortlich für die Konzeption und Auswahl der Werke zeichnete ein Kuratorium von Kunsthistorikern und Ausstellungsmachern, dem Prof. Dr. Götz Adriani, Dr. Robert

The year 2009 marked the sixtieth anniversary of the adoption of the constitution of the Federal Republic of Germany. To mark this anniversary the Foundation for Art and Culture Bonn presented the exhibition *60 Years. 60 Works* in Berlin's Martin-Gropius-Bau.
The exhibition presented sixty works produced between 1949 and 2009 by German artists who have shaped art at a national and international level. The scope of works ranged from painting and graphics to sculpture, installation, and photography. *60 Years. 60 Works* provided a retrospective that also allowed for a subjective view of the history of art over this period. Each of the sixty works stood for itself while at the same time providing an eloquent insight into the time in which it was created. The exhibition thus represented a telling of the history of the Federal Republic of Germany in terms of aesthetic developments in the fine arts, illuminating developments in the art world against the background of contemporaneous political, cultural, and social events.
Placing works in their historical context was an essential component of the show. The goal was to embed the works in the historical context of their creation using the media of film, interactive tables, and "documents" of the time. 60 monitors showed film montages charting the social and political events relating to each of the 60 years. Interactive tables, each of which was dedicated to one decade, provided information about the exhibited works and the respective currents, and events in the world of art. 60 short films made up of archival material from the German broadcaster WDR provided a vivid chronicle of the years from 1949 to 2009, covering developments in politics, society, and culture. As a result of this contextualization, a connection was generated between the artworks and the history of the Federal Republic. The exhibition concept and the selection of works was the responsibility of a curatorial board made up of the art historians and curators Prof. Dr. Götz Adriani,

Kunstausstellungen
Art Exhibitions

60 Jahre. 60 Werke. Kunst aus der Bundesrepublik Deutschland
60 Years. 60 Works. Art from the Federal Republic of Germany

Martin-Gropius-Bau Berlin
Niederkirchnerstraße 7
10963 Berlin

Autoren / Kuratoren / Wissenschaftliches Team Authors / Curators / Research Team: Prof. Dr. Götz Adriani, Dr. Robert Fleck, Prof. Dr. Siegfried Gohr, Prof. Peter Iden, Susanne Kleine, Ingrid Mössinger, Prof. Dr. Dieter Ronte, Dr. Frank Schmidt, Prof. Dr. h.c. Walter Smerling

Fleck, Prof. Dr. Siegfried Gohr, Prof. Peter Iden, Susanne Kleine, Ingrid Mössinger, Prof. Dr. Dieter Ronte, Dr. Frank Schmidt und Prof. Dr. h.c. Walter Smerling angehörten. *60 Jahre. 60 Werke* ging auf eine Initiative des Veranstalters Stiftung für Kunst e.V. Bonn und Deutschlands größter Tageszeitung BILD zurück, die als Medienpartner die Ausstellung begleitete. Hauptsponsor war das Energieunternehmen RWE. Ferner wurde das Projekt vom Innenministerium der Bundesrepublik Deutschland unterstützt. Die Ausstellungs- und Mediengestaltung erarbeiteten Prof. Joachim Sauter und sein Team von ART+COM, Berlin in Zusammenarbeit mit Prof. Ulrich Schwarz von BERTRON SCHWARZ FREY.

Walter Smerling

Dr. Robert Fleck, Prof. Dr. Siegfried Gohr, Prof. Peter Iden, Susanne Kleine, Ingrid Mössinger, Prof. Dr. Dieter Ronte, Dr. Frank Schmidt and Prof. Dr. h.c. Walter Smerling. *60 Years. 60 Works* was the result of an initiative by the organizer, the Foundation of Art and Culture Bonn, and Germany's biggest daily newspaper, BILD, which acted as the exhibition's media partner.
The main sponsor was the energy company RWE, and the project was also supported by the German Ministry of the Interior. The exhibition and media design was the result of a collaboration between Prof. Joachim Sauter and his team from ART+COM in Berlin and Prof. Ulrich Schwarz from BERTRON SCHWARZ FREY.

Walter Smerling

Ausstellungs- und Mediengestaltung
Exhibition and Media Design:
Prof. Joachim Sauter, ART+COM
Prof. Ulrich Schwarz,
BERTRON SCHWARZ FREY
Projektleitung Project Management:
Gert Monath, ART+COM

Zusammenstellung Kurzfilme
Short Film Compilation:
Dr. Heribert Schwan

Wechselausstellung Temporary Exhibition:
Ausstellungszeitraum
Exhibition Duration:
1. Mai bis 14. Juni 2009
May 1, 2009 until June 14, 2009

Die gestalterische Herausforderung bestand darin, die
Kunstwerke in den politischen
und kunsthistorischen Kontext
ihrer Entstehungszeit zu setzen
und damit die Geschichte der
BRD im Spiegel der Kunst
nachzuvollziehen. Hierfür wurden
zwei mediale Räume mit interaktiven Info-Tischen, „Zeitbildern"
und Filmwänden gestaltet,
die jeweils 30 Jahre Historie
aufbereiten.
Die „Zeitbilder" animierten den
Betrachter dazu, Bilder aus den
eigenen Erinnerungen hervorzu-
holen: Nur mit Bildunterschriften
versehene Schwarzbilder wiesen
auf allgemein bekannte historische Momentaufnahmen wie
z. B. Willy Brandts Kniefall hin
(siehe Seiten 118/119).
An den gegenüberliegenden
Wänden zeigten Monitore ein- bis
zweiminütige Kurzfilme, die für
jedes Jahr die wichtigsten Ereignisse aus Politik, Wirtschaft, Sport
und Kultur zusammenfassten
und das begehbare Panorama
vervollständigten.

In this instance the design challenge was to place the artworks
within their respective art-historical and political context, and
in a way that the history of the
Federal Republic of Germany was
mirrored in the works of art. Towards this end two media areas
were designed consisting of
interactive tables, actual pictures
from the era, and film projections
in which 30 years of history was
represented. The "Zeitbilder,"
or actual images from the era
encouraged the viewer to recall
images from their own memories: black and white captions
allude to well-known historical
snapshots such as Willy Brandt
kneeling down were (see pages
118/119). On opposite walls monitors showed one to two-minute
short films, summarizing the
most important events of each
year in politics, economy, sports,
and culture thus completing the
walk-in panorama.

Kunstausstellungen
Art Exhibitions

60 Jahre. 60 Werke. Kunst aus der
Bundesrepublik Deutschland
60 Years. 60 Works. Art from the Federal
Republic of Germany

Ausstellungsfläche Exhibition Area:
3 000 m²

116

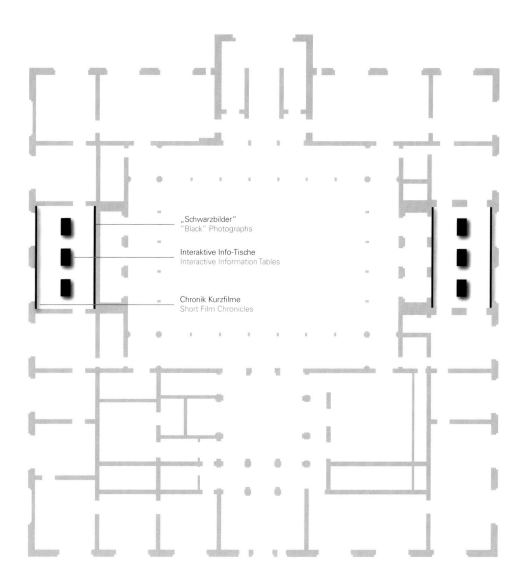

„Schwarzbilder"
"Black" Photographs

Interaktive Info-Tische
Interactive Information Tables

Chronik Kurzfilme
Short Film Chronicles

1 m   ca. M 1:500

5 m   10 m

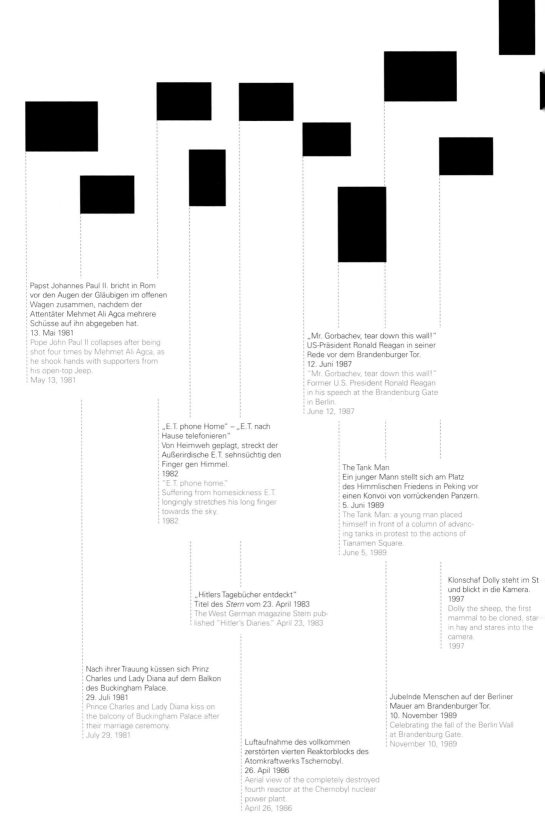

Papst Johannes Paul II. bricht in Rom
vor den Augen der Gläubigen im offenen
Wagen zusammen, nachdem der
Attentäter Mehmet Ali Agca mehrere
Schüsse auf ihn abgegeben hat.
13. Mai 1981
Pope John Paul II collapses after being
shot four times by Mehmet Ali Agca, as
he shook hands with supporters from
his open-top Jeep.
May 13, 1981

„Mr. Gorbachev, tear down this wall!"
US-Präsident Ronald Reagan in seiner
Rede vor dem Brandenburger Tor.
12. Juni 1987
"Mr. Gorbachev, tear down this wall!"
Former U.S. President Ronald Reagan
in his speech at the Brandenburg Gate
in Berlin.
June 12, 1987

„E.T. phone Home" – „E.T. nach
Hause telefonieren"
Von Heimweh geplagt, streckt der
Außerirdische E.T. sehnsüchtig den
Finger gen Himmel.
1982
"E.T. phone home."
Suffering from homesickness E.T.
longingly stretches his long finger
towards the sky.
1982

The Tank Man
Ein junger Mann stellt sich am Platz
des Himmlischen Friedens in Peking vor
einen Konvoi von vorrückenden Panzern.
5. Juni 1989
The Tank Man: a young man placed
himself in front of a column of advancing tanks in protest to the actions of
Tiananmen Square.
June 5, 1989

Klonschaf Dolly steht im St
und blickt in die Kamera.
1997
Dolly the sheep, the first
mammal to be cloned, star
in hay and stares into the
camera.
1997

„Hitlers Tagebücher entdeckt"
Titel des *Stern* vom 23. April 1983
The West German magazine Stern pub-
lished "Hitler's Diaries." April 23, 1983

Nach ihrer Trauung küssen sich Prinz
Charles und Lady Diana auf dem Balkon
des Buckingham Palace.
29. Juli 1981
Prince Charles and Lady Diana kiss on
the balcony of Buckingham Palace after
their marriage ceremony.
July 29, 1981

Jubelnde Menschen auf der Berliner
Mauer am Brandenburger Tor.
10. November 1989
Celebrating the fall of the Berlin Wall
at Brandenburg Gate.
November 10, 1989

Luftaufnahme des vollkommen
zerstörten vierten Reaktorblocks des
Atomkraftwerks Tschernobyl.
26. Apil 1986
Aerial view of the completely destroyed
fourth reactor at the Chernobyl nuclear
power plant.
April 26, 1986

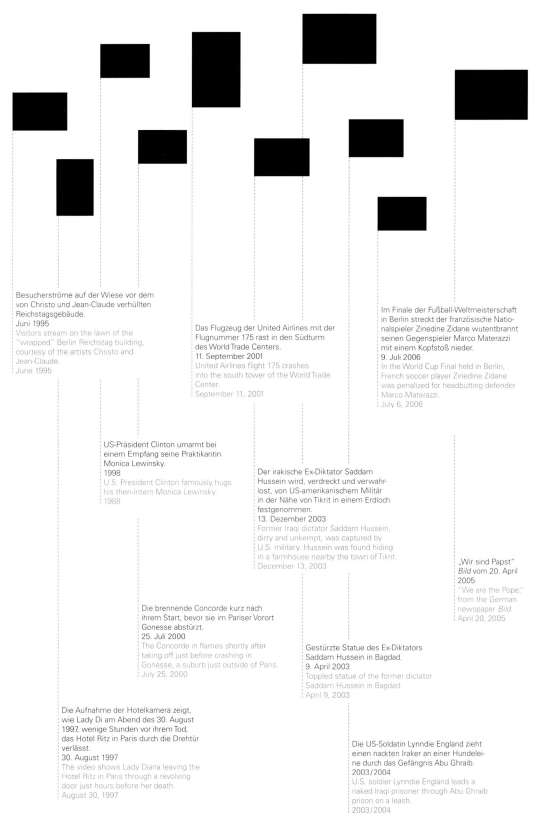

Besucherströme auf der Wiese vor dem
von Christo und Jean-Claude verhüllten
Reichstagsgebäude.
Juni 1995
Visitors stream on the lawn of the
"wrapped" Berlin Reichstag building,
courtesy of the artists Christo and
Jean-Claude.
June 1995

Das Flugzeug der United Airlines mit der
Flugnummer 175 rast in den Südturm
des World Trade Centers.
11. September 2001
United Airlines flight 175 crashes
into the south tower of the World Trade
Center.
September 11, 2001

Im Finale der Fußball-Weltmeisterschaft
in Berlin streckt der französische Natio-
nalspieler Zinedine Zidane wutentbrannt
seinen Gegenspieler Marco Materazzi
mit einem Kopfstoß nieder.
9. Juli 2006
In the World Cup Final held in Berlin,
French soccer player Zinedine Zidane
was penalized for headbutting defender
Marco Materazzi.
July 6, 2006

US-Präsident Clinton umarmt bei
einem Empfang seine Praktikantin
Monica Lewinsky.
1998
U.S. President Clinton famously hugs
his then-intern Monica Lewinsky.
1988

Der irakische Ex-Diktator Saddam
Hussein wird, verdreckt und verwahr-
lost, von US-amerikanischem Militär
in der Nähe von Tikrit in einem Erdloch
festgenommen.
13. Dezember 2003
Former Iraqi dictator Saddam Hussein,
dirty and unkempt, was captured by
U.S. military. Hussein was found hiding
in a farmhouse nearby the town of Tikrit.
December 13, 2003

„Wir sind Papst"
Bild vom 20. April
2005
"We are the Pope,"
from the German
newspaper Bild.
April 20, 2005

Die brennende Concorde kurz nach
ihrem Start, bevor sie im Pariser Vorort
Gonesse abstürzt.
25. Juli 2000
The Concorde in flames shortly after
taking off just before crashing in
Gonesse, a suburb just outside of Paris.
July 25, 2000

Gestürzte Statue des Ex-Diktators
Saddam Hussein in Bagdad.
9. April 2003
Toppled statue of the former dictator
Saddam Hussein in Bagdad.
April 9, 2003

Die Aufnahme der Hotelkamera zeigt,
wie Lady Di am Abend des 30. August
1997, wenige Stunden vor ihrem Tod,
das Hotel Ritz in Paris durch die Drehtür
verlässt.
30. August 1997
The video shows Lady Diana leaving the
Hotel Ritz in Paris through a revolving
door just hours before her death.
August 30, 1997

Die US-Soldatin Lynndie England zieht
einen nackten Iraker an einer Hundelei-
ne durch das Gefängnis Abu Ghraib.
2003/2004
U.S. soldier Lynndie England leads a
naked Iraqi prisoner through Abu Ghraib
prison on a leash.
2003/2004

Jeder der sechs berührungssensitiven Medientische dokumentierte eine Dekade Kunstgeschichte. Durch Antippen der Tischoberfläche konnten mehrere Besucher gleichzeitig weiterführende Informationen zu den ausgestellten Werken, Kunstströmungen und prägenden Ereignissen in der Kunstszene abrufen. An den gegenüberliegenden Wänden zeigten Monitore Kurzfilme, die für jedes Jahr die wichtigsten Ereignisse zusammenfassen.

Each of the six touch-sensitive media tables document a decade of art history. By touching the table's surface, visitors are simultaneously able to access further information on the exhibited works, art movements, and influential events in the art scene. On the opposite walls monitors show short films that summarize the main events for each year.

Kunstausstellungen
Art Exhibitions

60 Jahre. 60 Werke. Kunst aus der Bundesrepublik Deutschland
60 Years. 60 Works. Art from the Federal Republic of Germany

Gestaltung Interfaces und Wandgrafik
Interface Design and Wall Graphics:
Axel Pfänder, Arne Michel, Petra Trefzger, Mina Hagedorn
Medientechnische Planung
Media Technology Planning:
Stefan Helling, Stefanie Sturm
(alle ART+COM)

Grafik auf Seite 120, Fotos auf Seite 121
Graphics on page 120 and photos on page 121:
ART+COM

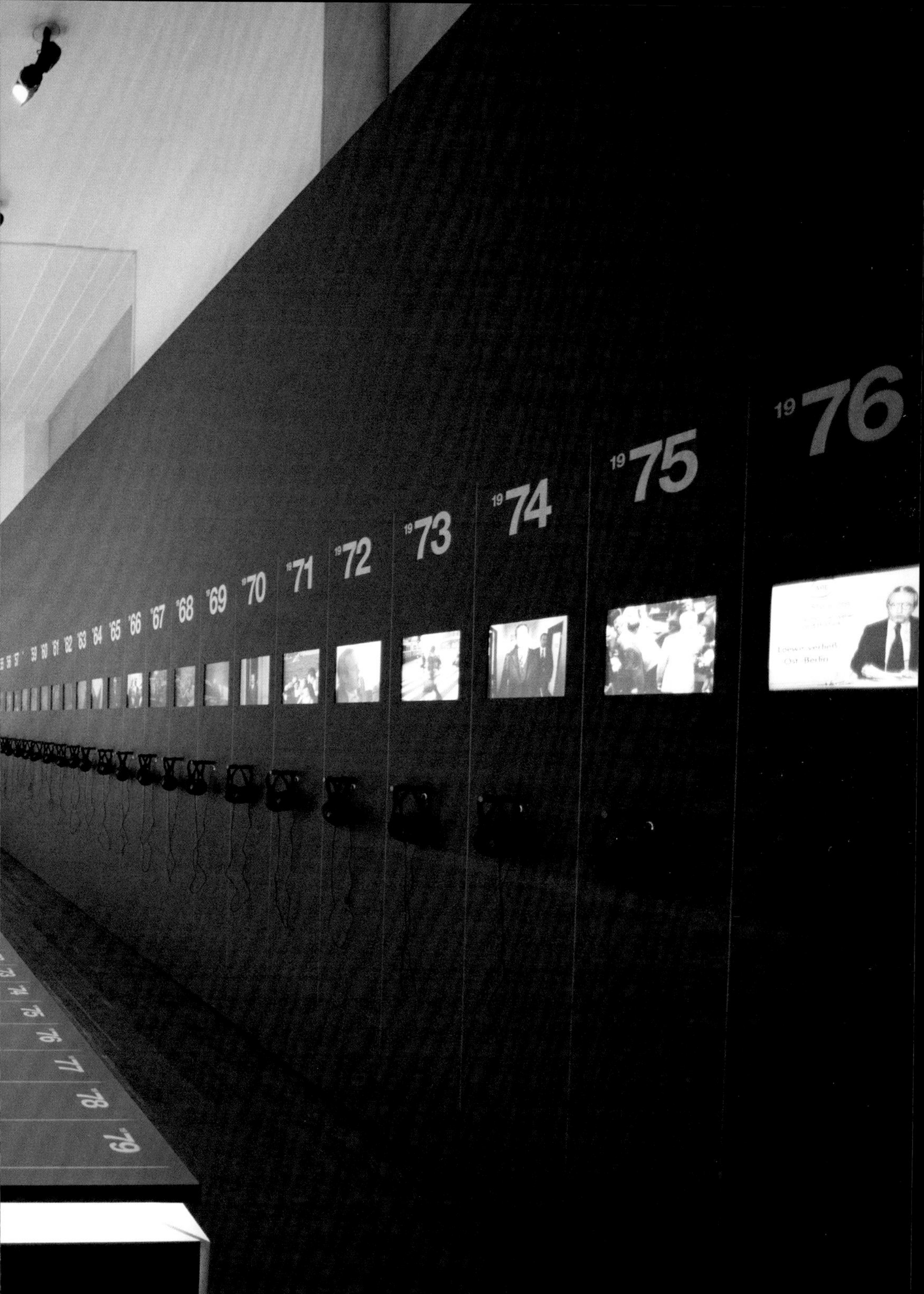

1976
1975
1974
1973
1972
1971
'70
'69
'68
'67
'66
'65
'64

19
59

19
60

¹⁹**61** ¹⁹**62** ¹⁹**63** ¹⁹**64** ¹⁹**65**

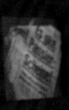

BAUDENKMÄLER, SCHLÖSSER, FREILICHTMUSEEN
HISTORICAL MONUMENTS, CASTLES, OPEN-AIR MUSEUMS

Das Ausstellen von Architektur stellt andere Anforderungen an Präsentation, Vermittlung und Vermarktung als das örtlich flexible Exponat. Es ist, als würde die Verpackung zum Inhalt. „Verpackung" ist dabei weiträumig zu betrachten: Landschaft, Stadtraum, Garten oder Blickbeziehung sind integraler Bestandteil. Zentrale Unterscheidungsmerkmale zum ortsungebundenen Exponat sind die materielle und funktionale Einbettung von Architektur in ihr Umfeld sowie die geschichtlichen und funktionalen Zusammenhänge zwischen Umgebung, Architektur und Ausstattung. Letztere können durch Berücksichtigung ihrer vielschichtigen Beziehungsebenen untereinander mit Hilfe eines Ausstellungskonzepts vermittelt werden.

Die Architektur als Exponat bildet typologisch zwei Hauptgruppen: das „Gesamtkunstwerk" und das „Einzelkunstwerk". Während beim Gesamtkunstwerk eine untrennbare Einheit – oft von Garten, Bauwerk, Inventar – besteht, ist das Einzelkunstwerk in der Architektur auf das Bauwerk selbst fokussiert. Beispiele sind der Park von Sanssouci und der Eiffelturm. Beim Einzelkunstwerk gibt es darüber hinaus eine Untergruppe, bei der die Architektur zwar selbst Exponat ist, aber eine Ausstellung beinhaltet, die nicht an das Bauwerk gebunden ist. Daher wird bei Schlössern zwischen „Museumsschlössern" und „Schlossmuseen" unterschieden. Sonderfälle sind Freilichtmuseen, die zum Zwecke der Ausstellung translozierter Bauwerke errichtet wurden und die museumstypologisch nichts anderes sind als eine Sammlungsausstellung unter freiem Himmel. Mahnmäler und Gedenkstätten erhalten durch museale Ausstellung oft eine Doppelfunktion. Als spezielle Ausprägung des Gesamtkunstwerks sind die großflächigen Denkmalensembles zu sehen, die oft ganze Altstädte umfassen. Deren Spezifizierungsmerkmal ist, dass Nutzung und Funktion nicht ausschließlich

Exhibiting architecture poses challenges in terms of presentation, communication, and marketing that differ from those usually associated with the presentation of exhibits that are flexible in terms of location. It is as if the "packaging" becomes the content. Packaging is of course being used in a very broad sense here, one that includes elements such as landscape, urban space, gardens, and visual connections. The central distinctions between architecture as exhibit and exhibits that are independent of location are based on the material and functional embedment of architecture in its environment, and the historical and functional interconnections between the surroundings, the architecture, and its infrastructure. The role of an exhibition concept may include communicating the multilayered interrelationships between the latter two.

In typological terms, architecture as exhibit can be divided into two main groups: the "synthetic artwork" – or *Gesamtkunstwerk* – and the "individual artwork." Whereas the synthetic artwork involves an indivisible unity – often comprising a garden, a building and its contents – the individual architectural artwork focuses on the structure itself. Examples include the Sanssouci Park and the Eiffel Tower. Moreover, the individual artwork includes a subgroup in which the architecture is itself an exhibit but additionally contains an exhibition that is not tied to the building. It is for this reason that a distinction is made between museum palaces and palace museums. Open-air museums represent special cases that involve the relocation of buildings and which, in terms of museum typology, constitute nothing more that the exhibition of collections in the open air. Monuments and memorials often take on a dual function in an exhibition context. A special form of the synthetic artwork can be found in the ensembles of historical monuments covering large areas, which often comprise entire historical town

museal sind. Diese grobe Einteilung lässt sich im Wesentlichen auch auf Garten- und Landschaftsarchitektur übertragen.

Wenn gebaute Umwelt zur Ausstellung wird, ist in der Regel Pflege und Vermittlung von Geschichte der Hintergrund für die Stilisierung der Architektur zum Exponat. Die Ursachen hierfür sind vielschichtig, sie können im politischen, wirtschaftlichen oder ästhetischen Kontext liegen. Die Frage, weshalb etwas zum Exponat wird, ist essenziell für das Ausstellungskonzept, denn die Hintergründe für den musealen Anspruch erweitern die Präsentations- und Vermittlungsmöglichkeiten oft erheblich, und meist erklärt sich ein Kunstwerk nicht von selbst.

Ausstellungsgestalter sind heute mit einem fast inflationär zu bezeichnenden Ausstellungswesen für Architektur konfrontiert. Die gebaute Umwelt wird als Wirtschafts- und Imagefaktor betrachtet, und über ihre Ausstellung wird „Architektur-Kultur" gefördert. Auch wachsendes Kultur- und Selbstbewusstsein führt zu Ausstellungen. Wenn auch die museale Qualifikation manchen Exponats diskussionswürdig sein mag, so ist doch entscheidend, wie das, was man hat, gezeigt und vermittelt wird. Architektur kann Nachfrage und Bedarf in ihrer Wechselwirkung extrem beeinflussen, ein Beispiel hierfür ist der „Bilbao-Effekt" des dortigen Guggenheim-Museums.

Die Herausforderung in der Ausstellungsgestaltung von Architekturexponaten beginnt im Außenraum, der oft selbst Ausstellungsstück ist. Im Gebäudeinneren setzt sich dies fort. In der präsentierten Innenarchitektur nebst Inventar müssen alle für die Nutzung notwendigen Funktionen untergebracht werden. Es gibt zentrale und dezentrale Lösungen, wenn mehrere Gebäude oder Freiflächen zur Verfügung stehen oder besonders große Anlagen für das Publikum zugänglich gemacht werden müssen.

Lange Zeit war der Außenraum oft mehr ein dienender Raum, und die Architekturausstellung begann erst mit der Fassade und setzte sich bestenfalls in den Innenräumen fort. Seit der Deutschen Einheit 1990 und den damit intensivierten großflächigen Er-

centers. Their key distinguishing feature is the fact that their use and function are not exclusively confined to the museological sphere. This typological division can generally be applied to landscape gardening and landscape architecture.

When a built environment becomes an exhibition, this is usually connected with the preservation and communication of a historical heritage. The reasons for this are diverse and can be primarily political, economic, or aesthetic. The question as to why something becomes an exhibit is essential for the exhibition concept since it often significantly informs and expands the possibilities for presentation and communication.

Today, exhibition designers are being confronted with an increasing demand for exhibitions focusing on architectural objects. The built environment is being increasingly regarded as an economic and image factor, and exhibiting it is seen as a means of promoting "architectural culture." A growth in cultural consciousness and self-confidence also leads to exhibitions. Given that the quality of some exhibits as exhibits is debatable, it is decisive how one shows and communicates what one has. Architecture can have a radical effect on the relationship between supply and demand, as illustrated by the "Bilbao effect" of the Guggenheim Museum.

The challenge for exhibition design presented by architectural exhibits begins in the external space, which is itself often an exhibit. This challenge continues into the interior of the building. All functions necessary to the exhibition need to be accommodated in the presented interior architecture and its fittings. In cases where several buildings or open spaces are available or particularly large areas need to be made accessible to the public, both centralized and decentralized solutions are possible. Previously it was often the case that the external area served as an auxiliary space, and the architectural exhibition began with the facade and continued into the interior spaces. Since German unification in 1990 and the associated implementation of greater measures to preserve large areas considered of historical value

haltungsmaßnahmen im Städtebau hat sich der museale Blickwinkel noch deutlicher auf das Umfeld ausgedehnt. Ein Trend ist, im internationalen Kontext durch das UNESCO-Weltkulturerbe geprägt, die zunehmende Großräumigkeit von Architektur und Landschaft als museal präsentiertes Exponat, in dem gleichzeitig ausgestellt, gelebt und gewirtschaftet wird. Für Ausstellungsgestalter ist es unausweichlich, sich dem Thema der Großräumigkeit musealer Präsentationen und damit der Vermischung von Nutzungen und Funktionen zu stellen und dies zum integralen Konzeptbestandteil zu machen. Flächenhaft angelegte „Architekturmuseen" oder „Kulturlandschaften" wie zum Beispiel das Elbpanorama in Dresden, Altstädte wie die von Bamberg, das Ruhrgebiet oder das mittlere Rheintal bedürfen eines komplexen übergeordneten Orientierungs-, Vermittlungs- und Ausstellungssystems, welches stufenweise bis zum Einzelexponat spezifiziert werden muss. Der klassische Museumsbau aus dem 18., 19. oder 20. Jahrhundert mit seiner Ausstellung wirkt angesichts dieser Dimensionen fast schon niedlich.

Die Zeitnot vieler Besucher ist ein großes Thema in Ausstellungskonzepten. In der Praxis kann dies bedeuten, dass unterschiedliche Informationstiefen sowie unterschiedliche Rundgänge und Führungen angeboten werden. Einerseits gibt es „Slow-Motion-Konzepte", andererseits auch sogenannte short tracks oder fast lines. Schon aus wirtschaftlichen Gründen müssen ein Shop-Stop und Coffee-Break ein integraler Ausstellungbestandteil sein. Die Zielgruppenorientierung ist wegen der zunehmenden Globalisierung der Besucher nicht nur polyglott auszurichten, sondern gleichzeitig auch individuell, interessenorientiert und vor allem schwerpunktorientiert. Manche Nationen bevorzugen Heidelberg und manche Neuschwanstein als architektonische Hauptattraktion in Deutschland. War vor wenigen Jahren behindertengerechte Architektur noch das beherrschende Thema, ist heute folgerichtig Barrierefreiheit angesagt, die deutlich facettenreicher und sinnvoller ist. Eine Ausstellungsgestaltung

within the context of urban development, the surroundings of architectural objects have increasingly become the subject of a museological perspective. Within an international context shaped by the UNESCO World Heritage Program, there is now a trend to present increasing expanses of architecture and landscape in museological terms, and to create zones that are simultaneously inhabited, exhibited, and economically valorized. Today exhibition designers can hardly avoid dealing with the challenge of creating museological presentations involving large external spaces, a task that involves blending uses and functions, and making this combination an integral part of the design concept. Extensive "architecture museums" and "cultural landscapes" such as the panorama along the River Elbe in Dresden, historical town center such as the one in Bamberg, the Ruhr area, and the Middle Rhine Valley require a complex orientation, information, and exhibition system that has to be specified in stages extending down to the individual exhibit. Compared with the dimensions involved in such projects, the classic museum building of the eighteenth, nineteenth, or twentieth century seems almost cute.

The fact that many visitors are subject to time pressure is an important theme in exhibition concepts. In practice this can mean that different routes, tours and levels of information are offered, with so-called short tracks or fast lines supplementing "slow motion" concepts. Shop stops and coffee breaks have now become integral exhibition elements – not least for economic reasons. When it comes to target-group orientation, the increasing globalization of the exhibition public, means that designers need to consider not only the multilingual aspect but also specific individual interests and thematic focuses. Some nationalities regard Heidelberg and others Neuschwanstein as Germany's major architectural attraction. Whereas disability-adapted architecture was the dominant theme a few years ago, today the emphasis is on accessibility and removing barriers, which is clearly a more sensible and multifaceted approach. An exhibition

Baudenkmäler, Schlösser, Freilichtmuseen
Historical Monuments, Castles, Open-air Museums

sollte sich mit der Tatsache auseinandersetzen, dass jeder Besucher in irgendeiner Form auf eine „Barriere" treffen kann. Es reicht schon aus, wenn die Landessprache nicht beherrscht wird, ein Kinderwagen oder Hund dabei sind oder kaum Zeit für den Museumsbesuch ist.

Bei Baudenkmälern, Schlössern und Freilichtmuseen steht die Präsentation der Geschichte im Vordergrund. Es sind Zeitreisen in die Vergangenheit, die oft gleichzeitig die Möglichkeit zur temporären Flucht aus dem Alltag eröffnen. Die Frage der Authentizität ist ein stetiges Diskussionsthema in der Architektur-Museologie. Soll die Geschichtsvermittlung authentisch oder ästhetisiert erfolgen? Es ist immer ein Verlust an Authentizität, wenn Geschichte zu sehr an den jeweiligen Zeitgeist angepasst und „wiederholt" wird. Das Vorstellungsvermögen der Besucher wird arg strapaziert, wenn Originales durch Nachbau von Verlorenem ersetzt wird und dann das verlorene Original zwecks Wahrung der Tatsachen anderweitig vermittelt werden muss. Der seit Jahren herrschende Drang nach Präsentation der „guten alten Zeit" nicht nur in den architektonischen Museumslandschaften Deutschlands ist aber auch ein ernst zu nehmendes Bedürfnis der Gesellschaft. Hier sind Ausstellungsplaner mehr gefordert denn je. Bei Architekturdenkmälern kann es im Sinne der Denkmalpflege nur darum gehen, Präsentation und Vermittlung stets aktuell und zeitgemäß zu halten, um das Exponat mit seinen Geschichtsschichten authentisch und materiell möglichst unverändert zu belassen. Das erfordert künftig eine Schwerpunktverschiebung bei den Akteuren. Statt materieller und funktioneller Anpassung der Baudenkmäler an den jeweiligen Zeitgeist wäre es zur Schonung der Denkmalsubstanz besser, die Gewichtung zunehmend auf die Vermittlung, also auf das Ausstellungskonzept zu legen und dieses regelmäßig zu aktualisieren. Es ist der Blickwinkel, der sich stetig ändert, nicht das Exponat.

Alfons Schmidt

design should take account of the fact that every visitor can encounter a "barrier" in one form or another. Such barriers can take the form of something as basic as being unable to speak the local language, having a baby carriage or a dog in tow, or having barely enough time to fit in a visit to a museum.

In the case of historical monuments, castles and open-air museums, the presentation of history is a key element. Such museological objects offer visitors a chance to travel back through time, a journey that often functions as a temporary escape from everyday routines. The question of authenticity is a constant theme of discussion in the field of architectural museology. Should the transmission of historical information place more emphasis on authenticity or aesthetic appeal? There is always a loss in terms of authenticity when history is adapted too much to the prevailing zeitgeist and "reenacted." Visitors' imaginations are placed under considerable strain when the original is substituted with a reconstruction of what has been lost and the facts pertaining to the lost original have to be conveyed elsewhere. The push to present the "good old days" is not only felt in Germany's architectural museum landscape but is a general societal need that has to be taken seriously. In this respect, exhibition planners are being challenged more than ever. Within the framework of the preservation of historical monuments, presentations and the transmission of information need to be kept up-to-date, and in keeping with the time in order to ensure the exhibit and its layers of history maintain an authenticity and remain as unchanged as possible in material terms. This means that in the future, exhibition planners will have to embrace shifts in thematic focus. Rather than adapting architectural monuments in material and functional terms to the prevailing zeitgeist, the preservation of the substance of monuments will be better served by placing increasing weight on the transmission of information, that is to say, on the exhibition concept, which will need to be constantly updated. It is the perspective that changes, not the exhibit.

Alfons Schmidt

Das Bauernhaus aus Aichelau im Freilichtmuseum in Beuren
The Farmhouse from Aichelau in the Beuren Open-air Museum

Ein jahrhundertealtes Bauernhaus erfährt in neuer Umgebung ungewohnte Wertschätzung. Sein Umzug ins Freilichtmuseum des Landkreises Esslingen in Beuren macht es möglich. Das Bauernhaus ist etwas Außergewöhnliches. Mit seinen rund 500 Jahren hat es ein stattliches Alter für ein Gebäude erreicht, das auf der rauen Alb Wind und Wetter trotzen musste. Vier Besonderheiten zeichnen das Konzept und die Gestaltung des Hauses aus:

Das Haus als begehbares Exponat
Aufgrund einer „neuen", besucherfreundlichen Wegeführung innerhalb des Gebäudes ergeben sich überraschende Einblicke in die Räume. Graue, moderne Laufstege aus Riffelblech führen durch das Haus und kennzeichnen Wege und Durchbrüche, die so im ursprünglichen Zustand nicht vorgegeben waren. Die neuen Durchbrüche zu den Räumen sind durch graue Stahlzargen gefasst. Die nicht originale Substanz zeichnet sich durch „neue" Materialien aus, beispielsweise in der Werkstatt, wo der Fußboden tiefer gelegt werden musste. So wurden originale Pfosten an der Unterseite mit einer Konstruktion aus Stahl versehen. Auch die Treppenaufgänge sind aus modernem, trittsicherem Baumaterial gefertigt. Ergänzungen an historischen Balken sind an der Einarbeitung neuer Hölzer zu erkennen.

Zeitschnitte:
1509/1511, 1663, 1824, 1949, 1984
Im Gegensatz zu den anderen Museumsgebäuden im Freilichtmuseum Beuren wird bei der Präsentation des Haupthauses kein einheitlicher Zeitschnitt festgelegt. Vielmehr werden unterschiedliche Zeitschnitte rekonstruiert und didaktisch aufgearbeitet. Schon von außen wird dieses Konzept augenfällig. Nord- und Ostfassade zeigen den Abbauzustand; Süd- und Westfassade die Zeit um 1824. Im Innern des Hauses erwartet die Besucher eine Zeitreise durch die 500-jährige Geschichte des Gebäudes. Interessante Baudetails aus verschiedenen

A centuries-old farmhouse is gaining an unaccustomed degree of attention in new surroundings. This is due to the fact that it has been moved from the Swabian Highland to the open-air museum in Beuren in the region of Esslingen. The farmhouse is extraordinary in the sense that it has withstood the rough highland winds and rains for about 500 years. Four features in particular distinguish the concept and design of the building:

The house as traversable exhibit
A "new" visitor-friendly pathway within the building provides visitors with surprising views into the various rooms. Gray, modern walkways made of corrugated sheet metal lead through the house, marking out paths and wall breakthroughs that were not part of the original structure. The new breakthroughs are supported by gray steel frames. "New" materials indicate where the original building substance has been altered, for example in the workshop, where the floor had to be lowered, necessitating the addition of a steel structure on the underside to support the original posts. The stairways are also made of modern, non-slip building material. New sections of wood indicate where reinforcements have been added to the original supporting beams.

Historical phases:
1509/1511, 1663, 1824, 1949, 1984
In contrast to the other museum buildings in the Beuren Open-Air Museum, the presentation of the main building is not based on a unitary historical phase. Instead, different phases have been reconstructed to provide visitors with an insight into the building's history. This concept is evident on the building's exterior. The northern and eastern facades show the state of the building when it was dismantled, while the southern and western facades show how it looked around 1824. The interior of the building takes visitors on a journey through the building's 500-year history. Interesting

Baudenkmäler, Schlösser, Freilichtmuseen
Historical Monuments, Castles, Open-air Museums

Das Bauernhaus aus Aichelau im Freilichtmuseum in Beuren The Farmhouse from Aichelau in the Beuren Open-air Museum

Freilichtmuseum Beuren
The Beuren Open-air Museum
In den Herbstwiesen
72660 Beuren

Museumsleiterin Museum Director:
Steffi Cornelius

Bauphasen wurden erhalten und verweisen auf den Gestaltungswillen der ehemaligen Bewohnerinnen und Bewohner und ihrer individuellen Lebensgeschichten, die sich im Gebäude spiegeln.

Neue Präsentation im Freilichtmuseum
In dem Haus, dem im Laufe seines Bestehens viele Umbauten widerfuhren, wird mit Hilfe verschiedener Medien „erzählt", was an Neuerungen im Bereich des Bauens stattfand, wer zum Zeitpunkt der Neuerung das Haus bewohnte und letztendlich, wie die Welt außerhalb Aichelaus aussah. Durch diese unterschiedliche Präsentation der sogenannten Zeitschnitte, können die Besucher in verschiedene Epochen eintauchen und sich über diese Zeitabschnitte informieren. Die Spanne reicht von der Erbauungszeit um 1509 bis 1511 über die Jahre nach dem Dreißigjährigen Krieg (1663) und die Hungerjahre nach 1817 bis in unsere Zeit. Der Zweite Weltkrieg mit seinen Folgen und das Haus im Zustand und der teilweisen Einrichtung seiner letzten Bewohnerin um 1984, der Witwe Barbara Knupfer, bilden das Ende der musealen Präsentation.

„Ein Haus zieht um"
Moderne Technik begegnet den Besuchern im Medienraum, der sich vor dem Abgang zum Gewölbekeller befindet. Die spektakuläre Umsetzung des Hauses, seine „Reise" nach Beuren und das Zusammenfügen im Albdorf im Freilichtmuseum Beuren wurde filmisch Schritt für Schritt dokumentiert. Manfred Schäffler-Wehnert begleitete den gesamten Ab- und Aufbau des Bauernhauses aus Aichelau. Aus mehr als 50 Stunden Filmmaterial hat er fünf Kurzfilme gemacht:
– Abbau Bauernhaus aus Aichelau
– Restaurierung in der Abbundhalle
– Translozierung Gewölbekeller
– Wiederaufbau im Freilichtmuseum Beuren
– Konservierung und Fertigstellung
Steffi Cornelius

details from the various building phases have been preserved and serve to illustrate the design ideas of the former occupants and their individual life stories, which are reflected throughout the building.

New presentation in the Open-air Museum
In the building, which has undergone many conversions in the course of its history, different media are used to "narrate" the various alterations to the structure, such as who was living there at the time of these renovations, and, finally, what was happening in the world outside Aichelau during these phases.
These different presentations of the so-called phases enable visitors to immerse themselves in different epochs and inform themselves about them. The scope of the presentation stretches from the original construction of the farmhouse between 1509 and 1511 to the years following the Thirty Years' War (1663) as well as the famine after 1817 and up to our own time. The Second World War and its consequences, and the house as it was in 1984, when it was occupied by its last inhabitant, the widow Barbara Knupfer, provide the themes marking the end of the presentation.

"A house moves house"
In the media room located in front of the stairs leading to the vaulted cellar, visitors encounter a display of modern technology. The spectacular relocation of the house, its "journey" to Beuren and its integration into the highland village in the Beuren Open-Air Museum is documented on film step by step. Manfred Schäffler-Wehnert documented the entire dismantling and reconstruction of the farmhouse from Aichelau and made five short films from a total of 50 hours of film material:
– Dismantling the farmhouse in Aichelau
– Restoration in the assembly hall
– Translocation of the vaulted cellar
– Reconstruction in the Open-air Museum
– Conservation and completion
Steffi Cornelius

Autoren / Kuratoren / Wissenschaftliches Team Authors / Curators / Research Team: Brigitte Haug, Ulrike Zimmermann, Karl Schmauder, Regina Gropper

Ausstellungsgestaltung Exhibition Design: BERTRON SCHWARZ FREY Entwurfsleitung Head of Design: Prof. Claudia Frey Ausführungsplanung Planning and Execution: Anja Kilian, Carina Ernst

Informationsgrafik, Medienoberflächen Schematic Design, Interactive Media Display: Christine Zecha, Katharina Tomaselli

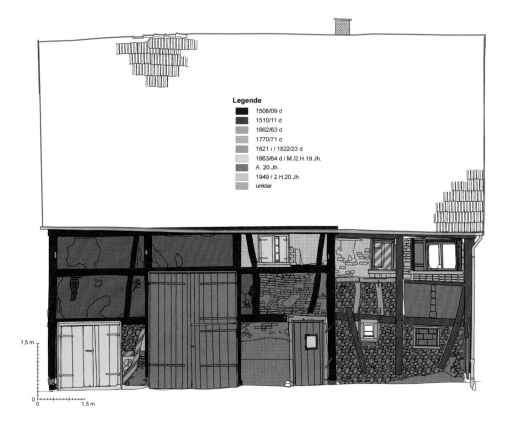

Legende
■ 1508/09 d
■ 1510/11 d
▨ 1662/63 d
▨ 1770/71 d
▨ 1821 i / 1822/23 d
▨ 1863/64 d / M./2.H.19.Jh.
▨ A. 20.Jh.
▨ 1949 / 2.H.20.Jh.
▨ unklar

1,5 m

0

0   1,5 m

| Baudenkmäler, Schlösser, Freilichtmuseen Historical Monuments, Castles, Open-air Museums | Dauerausstellung Permanent Exhibition Träger Supporting Institution: Landkreis Esslingen | Ausstellungsfläche Exhibition Area: Bauernhaus Farmhouse: 160 m² Ausgedinghaus retirement house: 20 m² |

Das Bauernhaus aus Aichelau im Freilichtmuseum in Beuren The Farmhouse from
Aichelau in the Beuren Open-air Museum

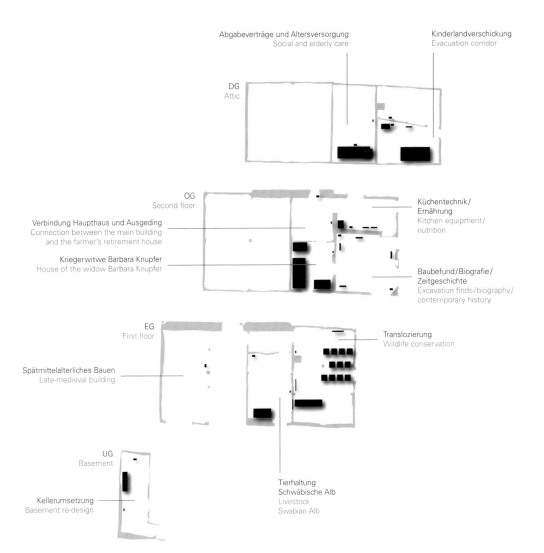

Abgabeverträge und Altersversorgung
Social and elderly care

Kinderlandverschickung
Evacuation corridor

DG
Attic

OG
Second floor

Küchentechnik/
Ernährung
Kitchen equipment/
nutrition

Verbindung Haupthaus und Ausgeding
Connection between the main building
and the farmer's retirement house

Kriegerwitwe Barbara Knupfer
House of the widow Barbara Knupfer

Baubefund/Biografie/
Zeitgeschichte
Excavation finds/biography/
contemporary history

EG
First floor

Translozierung
Wildlife conservation

Spätmittelalterliches Bauen
Late-medieval building

UG
Basement

Kellerumsetzung
Basement re-design

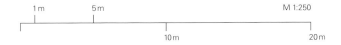

Tierhaltung
Schwäbische Alb
Livestock
Swabian Alb

1 m   5 m   M 1:250

10 m   20 m

Der historische Bestand jedes Raumes wird durch eine schmale Zeitleiste markiert. Ablesbar sind der aktuelle Zeitschnitt sowie wichtige Veränderungen in der Nutzung der Räume.
Die Typologie der Zeitleisten ermöglicht es, unterschiedliche Vermittlungsebenen zu integrieren: einfache Informationstafeln mit Text, Bild und Grafik, mit Drehelement oder Hörstation.

The historical significance of each room is indicated by a small-sized timeline. Up-to-date timelines as well as information detailing important changes in the way that each room was utilized is provided.
The typology of the timeline makes it possible to integrate the various teaching levels: basic information panels with a pivoting element display text, images and graphics, or contain an audio station.

Seit 1511 ist die Küche immer am selben Ort im Haus. Bis zu ihrer Modernisierung 1663 zieht der gesamte Rauch der Kochstelle frei über die zum Dachraum geöffnete Küchendecke ab. Die Rußspuren sind heute noch im Dachgebälk sichtbar. Um 1900 wurde ein geschlossener Kamin eingebaut.

Since 1511 the kitchen has remained in the very same location in the house. Until its renovation in 1663, the smoke from the cooking fire went up from the kitchen ceiling through an opening in the attic; the soot marks are still visible in the supportive beams. It wasn't until 1900 that a closed-style fireplace was installed.

Der Stall wurde 1824 eingebaut. Die kleinen Buchten weisen darauf hin, dass hier eine schmale, genügsame Rinderrasse gehalten wurde.
The stall was built in 1824. The small pens indicate that a small and resilient type of cows were kept.

Das Bauernhaus als Exponat und die kleinteilige Raumstruktur erlauben nur minimale gestalterische Eingriffe. Die Räume sind teilweise mit historischem Mobiliar ausgestattet, sodass sich zusätzliche Ausstellungselemente erkennbar unterscheiden sollen, ohne jedoch die spezielle Atmosphäre der Raumbereiche zu stören. Fundstücke und Exponate fügen sich fragmentarisch in das Gesamtbild des Raumes ein. Die Zeitleisten und Informationselemente sind reduziert in einheitlicher Farbigkeit gehalten. Die Farbe entspricht dem Corporate Design des Freilichtmuseums.

The farmhouse as an exhibit itself and the small-scale spatial structure allow for a minimal redesign. The rooms are partly decorated with historical furniture, so that additional exhibition elements appear distinguishable however, without disturbing the particular atmosphere of the rooms. Exhibits include artifacts and fragmentally spread into the overall concept of the room. The timeline and information elements are utilize a soft use of color. The color itself corresponds to the corporate design of the museum.

Rechte Seite oben:
In der Stube sind Wandfassungen aus vier unterschiedlichen Zeitschnitten von 1511 bis 1949 zu sehen. Das Leben der Bewohner und der gesellschaftspolitische Hintergrund der damaligen Zeit werden in digitalen Bildcollagen präsentiert.

Right top:
In the living room wall four timelines from 1511 until 1949 are on display. The everyday life of the residents and their respective sociopolitical backgrounds of the time are presented in digital collages.

Rechte Seite unten:
Vitrinenkommode im Schlafzimmer der letzten Bewohnerin mit Originalobjekten, Dokumenten und Fotos
Below right:
Display cases in the bedroom in which the original papers and photographs once belonging to the last inhabit are displayed.

Gartenkunst im Schloss Weikersheim
Garden Art in Weikersheim Palace

Anlass der Ausstellung war ein Jubiläum: 300 Jahre Barockgarten Weikersheim. Im Titel *Wasserkunst und Götterreigen. Geschichte und Entwicklung des Weikersheimer Schlossgartens* werden die Kernaussagen der Ausstellung bereits genannt. Die Ausstellung sollte an den Ausbau der Residenz ab 1708 erinnern, der vor allem der Anlage des Lustgartens und der städtebaulichen Neuordnung gewidmet war. Die Leitidee bestand in dem Versuch, sowohl den Duktus der Zeit – das Barock – wie regionale Einflüsse – Hohenlohe, fränkische Einwirkungen – verständlich zu ordnen.

Das wichtigste Objekt war und ist der an den Ausstellungsraum angrenzende Garten selbst. Die Möglichkeiten seiner Wahrnehmung sind medial wie mit Fragmenten der historischen Ausstattung (Tonvögelchen der Grotten, ein Stück der Wasserröhre, Pflanzenglocke, Baumkratzer) bereichert worden. Die barocke Gartenkultur sollte im Ansatz (be-)greifbar gemacht werden.

Eine übersichtliche thematische Ordnung (Chronologie, Skulpturen, Bepflanzung, Wasserkunst, Orangerie, Nutzung) erlaubt gerade in dem kleinen Raum eine Orientierung auf Wesentliches und Merkbares.

Auf einer zweiten Ebene, die gewissermaßen vom Besucher selbst aktiviert werden muss, werden pointiert und anschaulich exemplarische Ausschnitte der vergangenen Gartenkultur präsentiert.

Ein Blätterbuch und herausziehbare Karteikarten offerieren mit Pflanzenportraits (Blühzeitpunkt, mythologische Bedeutung, Herkunft und Verbreitung, Eigenschaften und Nutzung) vertiefte kulturgeschichtliche Einblicke in die zeitgenössische Gärtnerpraxis des Blumenschmucks und der Orangerie. Mehrere Gucklöcher ermöglichen einen Rückblick in verschiedene Etappen der Vergangenheit (perspektivische Ansichten aus unterschiedlichen Zeiten) und veranschaulichen damit das Phänomen des Wandels. In der Orangerie selbst wird als Außenstelle der Ausstellung die Gärtnerarbeit an ihrem tradierten Ort gewürdigt, indem Kultivie-

The occasion for installing this permanent exhibition was the 300th anniversary of Weikersheim's baroque gardens. The title, *Waterworks and Dance of the Gods. The History and Development of the Weikersheim Palace Garden*, already highlights the key focal points of the exhibition.

The exhibition commemorates the remodeling of the imperial residence that began in 1708 and primarily involved the construction of the pleasure garden and the refurbishment of the palace itself. The guiding idea was to locate these developments within the framework of the baroque period, and Hohenlohe and Franconian regional influences.

The most important object in this context was and is the garden itself, which borders the exhibition space. The range of ways of perceiving it has been extended by means of media installations as well as fragments of its historical trappings (clay birds from the grottos, a piece of water pipe, plant cloches, bark scrapers) which are designed to make Baroque garden culture more tangible.

A comprehensible thematic structure (chronology, sculptures, planting, waterworks, orangery, utilization) directs attention to essential and memorable aspects. A second level, which to some extent is activated by the visitors, presents vivid examples of the garden culture of the past.

A flip-book and a file of extractable index cards present plant portraits (flowering times, mythological significance, origin and distribution, qualities and uses) that offer cultural-historical insights into floral ornamentation and the uses of the orangery during this period. Peepholes provide a retrospective in different stages of the past (perspective views from different times) and thus illustrate the phenomenon of change. The exhibition continues in the orangery, where gardening work is presented in its traditional context, with transportable steles displaying information about cultivation and the protection of plants during the winter months. The connection to the orangery's

Baudenkmäler, Schlösser, Freilichtmuseen Historical Monuments, Castles, Open-air Museums	Staatliche Schlösser und Gärten Baden-Württemberg, Schlossverwaltung Weikersheim State Palaces and Gardens of Baden-Württemburg, Palace Weikersheim Marktplatz 11 97990 Weikersheim	Autoren/Kuratoren/Wissenschaftliches Team Authors/Curators/Research Team: Dr. Hartmut Troll, Dr. Carla Fandrey, Dipl.-Ing. Sophie von Schwerin, Andrea Steuble M.A., Joachim Stolz M.A.

rung und Überwinterung auf transportablen Stelen thematisiert werden. Die Verbindung zur wiedergewonnenen Funktion, die durch die Restaurierung 1997 möglich wurde, verleiht der Präsentation und ihrem Ort etwas Authentisches.

Das verwendete Bildmaterial bemüht sich, mit zeitgenössischen, möglichst lokalen und in jeder Themengruppe einheitlichen Quellen zu arbeiten. So wurden alle Blumenportraits mit Abbildungen aus den *Hortus Eystettensis* aus dem 17. Jahrhundert bebildert. Die Orangeriepflanzen und Gartenmotive zur gestalteten und geordneten Natur im Barock stammen allesamt aus dem Fundus der sogenannten Lambrisgemälde im Rittersaal des Weikersheimer Schlosses. Der Maler Thalwitzer versah dort ab 1715 die Lambris (Verkleidung des unteren Bereiches der Wandflächen) mit Ansichten bekannter französischer und deutscher Schlösser und Gärten, ferner die Laibungsnischen mit Portraits von Kübelpflanzen. Auf diese Weise wird das dargestellte Thema gewissermaßen mit der Wahrnehmung und Ästhetik der Zeit präsentiert.

Der Topos des Barockgartens, wie er mit der Anlage von Versailles festgelegt scheint, zeigt sich beispielhaft, aber auf dem Land im Detail durchaus anders als erwartet und sehr lebendig. Entscheidend war der Auftraggeber selbst: Graf Carl Ludwig von Hohenlohe-Weikersheim und seine persönliche und politische Konstellation. Sein Portrait steht zu Recht in der Mitte der Ausstellung und verbindet die verschiedenen gezeigten Facetten.

Die Ausstellungsgestaltung löst die Schwierigkeit der begrenzten Raumsituation mit einer modernen, aber auch zeitlosen Sprache, um damit dem Genius loci gerecht zu werden. Sie schafft gerade im Kleinen etwas Schönes, Inspirierendes und Charmantes.

Hartmut Troll

restored function made possible by the restoration carried out in 1997 lends this part of the exhibition and its location a particular authenticity.

The pictorial material used is based as far as possible on sources that date to the period in question, originate from the region, and are unified within each thematic group. For example, all flower portraits are illustrated with depictions from the *Hortus Eystettensis* from the seventeenth century. The plants in the orangery and the garden motives illustrating ideas of designed and ordered nature characteristic of the baroque all derive from the so-called *Lambrisgemälde*, or dado painting, in the banqueting hall of Weikersheimer Palace. Beginning in 1715, the painter Thalwitzer decorated the dado, the lower, paneled portion of the wall, with views of well-known French and German palaces and gardens, and the reveals with portraits of potted plants. In this way the thematic presentation also refers to the forms of perception and aesthetics of the time.

The topos of the baroque garden as defined by the Palace of Versailles is clearly exemplified here, but when viewed in detail on the land itself it appears different from what is to be expected and very much alive. A decisive influence on its creation was exercised by the client, Count Carl Ludwig von Hohenlohe-Weikersheim and his personal and political constellation. His portrait is rightly displayed in the middle of the exhibition and forms a link between its different facets.

The design of the exhibition deals with the difficulties presented by the limited spatial situation by using a modern yet timeless language in order to do justice to the genius loci. Working on a small scale, it creates something beautiful, inspiring, and charming.

Hartmut Troll

Ausstellungsgestaltung
Exhibition Design:
BERTRON SCHWARZ FREY
Entwurfsleitung Head of Design:
Prof. Claudia Frey
Grafik Graphic Design:
Katharina Tomaselli

Träger Supporting Institution:
Staatliche Schlösser und Gärten
Baden-Württemberg
State Palaces and Gardens of
Baden-Württemburg

Dauerausstellung Permanent Exhibition

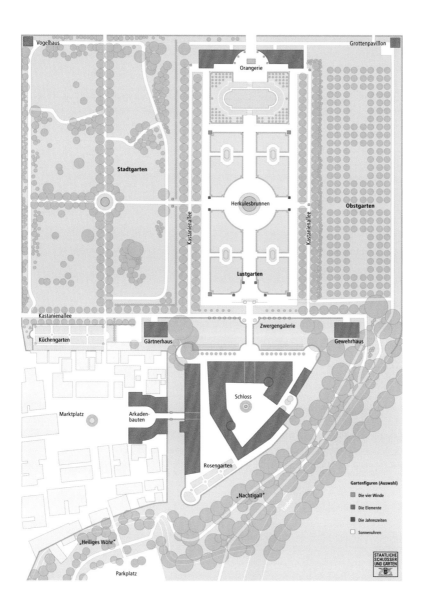

Vogelhaus

Grottenpavillon

Orangerie

Stadtgarten

Herkulesbrunnen

Obstgarten

Kastanienallee

Kastanienallee

Lustgarten

Kastanienallee

Küchengarten

Gärtnerhaus

Zwergengalerie

Gewehrhaus

Marktplatz

Arkaden-
bauten

Schloss

Rosengarten

Gartenfiguren (Auswahl)

Die vier Winde

Die Elemente

Die Jahreszeiten

Sonnenuhren

"Nachtigall"

Tauber

"Heiliges Wöhr"

Parkplatz

STAATLICHE
SCHLÖSSER
UND GÄRTEN

Baudenkmäler, Schlösser, Freilichtmuseen
Historical Monuments, Castles, Open-air
Museums

Gartenkunst im Schloss Weikersheim
Garden Art in Weikersheim Palace

Fotos Seiten 141/142
Photos pages 141/142:
Landesmedienzentrum BW

Ausstellungsfläche Exhibition Area:
120 m²

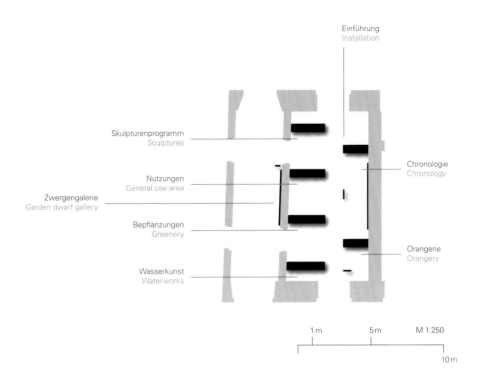

Einführung
Installation

Skulpturenprogramm
Sculptures

Nutzungen
General use area

Zwergengalerie
Garden dwarf gallery

Bepflanzungen
Greenery

Wasserkunst
Waterworks

Chronologie
Chronology

Orangerie
Orangery

1 m   5 m   M 1:250

10 m

Kultur Sammlung

Kultivieren · Überwinter · Pflanzensammlungen

Der Begriff «Orangerie» bezeichnet sowohl den Bestand exotischer Kübelpflanzen, als auch das Überwinterungshaus und den Platz der Sommeraufstellung.

Sammlungen von Orangeriepflanzen entwickelten sich seit dem 16. Jahrhundert zu einem unverzichtbaren Bestandteil europäischer Gartenkultur. Neben ihrer symbolischen Bedeutung und der vielseitigen Verwendbarkeit war der Wert der Orangeriepflanzen als Schmuck des Gartens einzigartig.

Dem barocken Grundprinzip der regelmäßigen Mischung von Pflanzen folgend, wurde bei der Aufstellung der Orangerie auf einen gleichmäßigen Wechsel unterschiedlicher Formen und Größen geachtet. Orangerien bestanden – neben den klassischen holzigen Kübelpflanzen – auch Blumen verschiedener Herkunft.

Für Weikersheim sind in einem Pflanzeninventar von 1745 vielerhand indianische Gewächse» und «800 Scherben mit Aurikeln und Nelken» erwähnt. Eine bemerkenswerte Kuriosität sind die 1745 vermerkten «20 Scherben mit Ingber». Ingwer war seit dem Mittelalter als Gewürz- und Heilpflanze verbreitet. Ihre ansehnliche Erscheinung hob sie wohl kurzfristig in den Stand einer Orangeriepflanze. 20 Jahre später

Baudenkmäler, Schlösser, Freilichtmuseen
Historical Monuments, Castles, Open-air Museums

Gartenkunst im Schloss Weikersheim
Garden Art in Weikersheim Palace

Während des Spaziergangs durch den Schlossgarten bekommt der Besucher über die Audioführung Informationen zum Figurenprogramm.
The visitor listens an audio guide that provides information on the statues, while walking through the garden.

Informationstafeln zur Pflege von Pflanzen und die Funktion der Orangerie
Labels provide information on plant care and on the function of the orangery.

Ein beeindruckendes Gesamtbild öffnet sich dem Besucher,
wenn er durch den Torbogen im
Schlosshof auf den Garten mit
Orangerie blickt. Die Ausstellung
im kleinen Gewölberaum ist Auftakt oder Abschluss des Garten-
spaziergangs. Aus dem Raum
dringen der Gesang von Vögeln,
Musik und die Klangkulisse
höfischer Gartenfeste nach
außen. Die in dieser Atmosphäre
präsentierten Themen, Bilder und
Objekte lassen in der Vorstellung
des Betrachters ein Bild von Leben und Arbeit im Garten zur Zeit
des 16. Jahrhunderts entstehen.

An impressive view is revealed to
the visitor when looking through
the archway in the courtyard towards the garden with orangery.
The exhibition in a small vaulted
room is found at either the beginning or conclusion of the garden
walk. The sound of singing birds,
music, and garden festivities can
be heard outside. The themes,
pictures, and objects presented
in this type of atmosphere allow
the visitor to imagine sixteenth-
century life and work in the
garden.

Über „Guckies" kann der Besucher auf
die Ansichten der Gartengestaltung
verschiedener Epochen zurückblicken.
Das Fenster daneben gibt die Sicht frei in
den aktuellen Garten.

Visitors to the garden can learn more
about the garden design of the various
eras by looking through a 3D viewer. The
nearby window provides beautiful views
of the present garden.

143

Die sechs Themenstationen falten sich als grünes Band durch den Raum und bilden eine leichte, bewegte Struktur. Exponate, Fundstücke, Vitrinen, Schubkästen, Blätterbücher und Textflächen fügen sich spielerisch in das Raumbild ein. Einen reizvollen Kontrast zu den in verschiedenen Grünschattierungen lackierten Präsentationsflächen bildet die rohe, unrestaurierte Wandfläche. Als zentrale Figur steht Graf Carl Ludwig von Hohenlohe-Weikersheim im Mittelpunkt. Im Hintergrund steht die Chronologie zur baulichen Entwicklung von Schloss und Gartenanlage. Aufgrund der großen Schwankungen von Temperatur und Feuchtigkeit im Ausstellungsraum wurden die Stationen aus Aluminiumblech gekantet und lackiert.

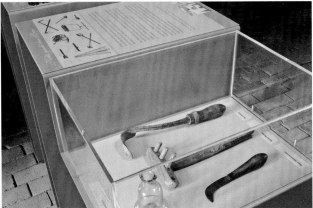

The six theme-based stations fold up as a green belt around the room and form a light, moving structure. Exhibits, artifacts, display cases, drawers, flip page books and text areas blend within the room in a playful way. It serves as a delightful contrast to the various shades of green painted spaces presentation areas against the raw, unrestored wall surface. Count Carl Ludwig von Hohenlohe-Weikersheim stands in the middle as the central figure. In the background is the chronology illustrating the structural development of the castle and gardens. Due to the large fluctuations of temperature and humidity in the exhibition space, the stations are made from edged sheet aluminum and painted.

Baudenkmäler, Schlösser, Freilichtmuseen
Historical Monuments, Castles, Open-air Museums

Gartenkunst im Schloss Weikersheim
Garden Art in Weikersheim Palace

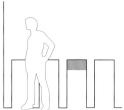

Tafel und vier Elemente, gleich groß
panel and four even elements

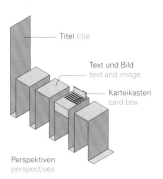

Titel title

Text und Bild
text and image

Karteikasten
card box

Perspektiven
perspectives

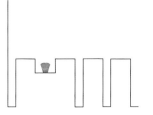

Tafel und vier Elemente, mit Vertiefung
für Objekte oder Vitrinen
panel and four elements with lower
parts for objects and cabinets

Exponat
exhibit

Seitenansichten
side views

Tafel und drei Elemente
panel and three elements

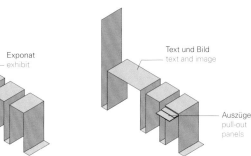

Text und Bild
text and image

Auszüge
pull-out
panels

Typologie des Präsentationssystems:
Titeltafel, Text- und Bildflächen, Auszüge
von Informationsflächen, Blätterbuch,
Exponatablage, Vitrine

The typology of the presentation system:
panel title, text and image areas, information excerpts, book, exhibit storage, and
cabinet

Leben auf der Ritterburg Life in the Knight's Castle

Das Burgmuseum auf Burg Guttenberg wurde im Jahr 1949 von meinem Großvater Gustav Freiherr von Gemmingen-Guttenberg geschaffen. Der Leitgedanke damals war, dass es zunehmend schwieriger wird, Burgen und Schlösser in privater Hand durch land- und forstwirtschaftlichen Besitz zu erhalten und dass deshalb Erträge aus dem Tourismus für den Unterhalt benötigt werden.

Das Museum auf Burg Guttenberg entwickelte sich nach verhaltenen Anfangsjahren sehr erfolgreich. Im Laufe der Jahre wurde die Ausstellung fortlaufend ergänzt und erweitert. 1997 reifte dann der Entschluss, die Museumskonzeption komplett nach dem Motto „Leben auf der Ritterburg" zu überarbeiten. Die Neugestaltung sollte nach modernen museumspädagogischen und -didaktischen Gesichtspunkten erfolgen. Im Ergebnis sollten Schulklassen wie Fachbesucher gleichermaßen angesprochen und begeistert werden. Neu an der Konzeption ist der chronologische „rote Faden" durch das Museum. Von der Gründungszeit der Burg bis hin in die Neuzeit spannt sich nun der Ausstellungsbogen – pro Epoche ein Ausstellungsraum, in welchem sich der Besucher mit den Fragen der jeweiligen Lebensumstände beschäftigen kann. Diese können lokal, regional oder auch überregionale Bezüge aufweisen. Darüber hinaus werden einzelne Bewohner der Zeit anekdotisch vorgestellt, ihr Leben und Tun wird auf einer Texttafel beleuchtet. Auf diese Weise wird „Geschichte zum Anfassen" ermöglicht. Die gezeigten Exponate stammen fast alle aus dem Fundus der unzerstörten Burg. Nur weniges wurde aus didaktischen Gründen ergänzt.

Die Holzbibliothek
Die Xylothek, eine Sonderform des Herbariums, erschienen gegen Ende des 18. Jahrhunderts, präsentiert sich in 93 Bänden. Jeder Band repräsentiert eine Baum- oder Buschart, die damals in unserer Region zu Hause war. Es handelt sich um

The museum in Guttenburg Castle was founded in 1949 by my grandfather Gustav Freiherr von Gemmingen-Guttenberg. At the time it was becoming increasingly difficult for the private owners of castles and old manor houses to maintain their properties through agriculture and forestry, and my grandfather's main motivation for establishing the museum was to bring in money for the castle from tourism.

Although business was slow in the early years, the museum subsequently proved extremely successful. Over the following years the exhibition was continually supplemented and expanded. In 1997 the decision was taken to completely rework the concept for the museum in accordance with the theme of "Life in the Knight's Castle," and to draw on the pedagogical and didactic approaches used in modern museum presentations. The aim was to create an exhibition that could appeal to and address both school classes and specialists in the field. One new aspect that can be seen today is the chronological "thread" that leads through the museum. The exhibition now forms an arc that spans the period from the construction of the castle to modern times – each epoch is given its own exhibition room in which visitors can explore the kind of living conditions that prevailed at the time. The material presented can refer to local, regional, or intra-regional circumstances. In addition, individual residents living during the respective period are presented anecdotally in the form of texts displayed on panels, thereby lending the exhibition a sense of living history. Almost all the exhibits on display were originally found in the castle itself, and only a few of them have been supplemented with objects from elsewhere for didactic reasons.

The wooden library
The xylotheque (herbarium), was compiled at the end of the eighteenth century in ninetythree volumes. Each volume represents a species of tree or bush that was native to our region at the time. The collection

Baudenkmäler, Schlösser, Freilichtmuseen Historical Monuments, Castles, Open-air Museums	Burgmuseum Burg Guttenberg Guttenburg Knight's Castle Burgstraße 1 74855 Haßmersheim-Neckarmühlbach	Autoren/Kuratoren/Wissenschaftliches Team Authors/Curators/Research Team: Christoph Freiherr von Gemmingen-Guttenberg, Silke Freifrau von Gemmingen-Guttenberg, Bernolph Freiherr von Gemmingen-Guttenberg, Landesstelle für Museumsbetreuung, Stuttgart
Leben auf der Ritterburg Life in the Knight's Castle		

ein komplett erhaltenes Kunstwerk mit interessanten Implikationen, da einige Arten heute nicht mehr vorkommen, einige heute vorkommende Pflanzenarten dagegen in der Bibliothek fehlen. Das Herbarium zeigt beispielhaft das im 18. und 19. Jahrhundert aufkommende naturwissenschaftliche Interesse, das sich in vielen Naturalien-Kabinetten und Skurrilitäten-Sammlungen niederschlägt.

Die Bibelsammlung

Das geistige Leben auf der Burg wird durch eine Sammlung deutschsprachiger Bibeln ab dem Jahr 1434 verdeutlicht – vorlutherische Bibelübersetzungen, die vor und kurz nach der Erfindung der Buchdruckerei gefertigt wurden. Zusammen mit einem Marienaltar aus der Spätgotik veranschaulicht dieser Teil der Ausstellung die intensive Beschäftigung der Burgbewohner mit religiösen Themen und die Problematik der Reformation im süddeutschen Raum.

Die Zinnfigurendioramen

Große Schaukästen mit zum Teil mehreren tausend Zinnfiguren dienen der Visualisierung unterschiedlichster Szenen aus dem Burgleben: Burgbelagerung, Reichsturnier, die Schlacht bei Wimpfen, die Belagerung Heidelbergs durch Tilly. Die Dioramen, die häufig mit Hilfe von (lichtschrankengesteuerten) Soundapplikationen ergänzt werden, sollen vor allem dem jungen, flüchtigen Betrachter bleibende Eindrücke vermitteln.

Die Ausstellung stellt insgesamt eine umfassende Kombination von Exponaten und eine schriftlich-grafische Erläuterung des Burglebens dar, die von einem Farbleitsystem und Soundapplikationen unterstützt wird. Zwei Kernaussagen, die sich in den einzelnen Räumen an den unterschiedlichsten Beispielen, Exponaten und Biografien ablesen lassen, sollen der Ausstellung entnommen werden:
Eine Burgromantik gab es nicht. Das alltägliche Leben auf den Stauferburgen war hart, entbehrungsreich, rustikal und ungesund, durchaus zu vergleichen mit dem Leben auf Bauernhöfen – nur eben in schützenden,

constitutes a completely preserved work of art with interesting implications, since several of the species are no longer found today, and a number of types of plants that now grow are absent from the collection. The herbarium provides a vivid example of the interest in the natural sciences developing in the eighteenth and nineteenth century, and its expression in cabinets devoted to natural phenomena and curiosities.

The bible collection
Religious life in the castle is witnessed by a collection of German-language Bibles, the first of which dates back to the year 1434 – pre-Lutheran Bible translations that were completed before and shortly after the invention of the printing press. Together with an Altar of Our Lady from the late gothic period, this part of the exhibition illustrates the intensive engagement of castle residents with religious themes, and the problem of the Reformation in southern Germany.

The tin figure dioramas
Large display cases featuring in some cases several thousand tin figures serve to create visual representations of diverse scenes from castle life: sieges, medieval tournaments, the Battle of Wimpfen, the siege of Heidelberg by the Count of Tilly. The dioramas, which are often supplemented by photo-sensor activated sound applications, are intended as a means of providing a lasting impression above all for young, fleeing visitors.

As a whole the exhibition presents a comprehensive combination of exhibits, and written and graphical explanations of castle life, which is supplemented by a color-coded system and sound applications. At the heart of the exhibition are two core statements, which are expressed in the individual rooms in a diverse range of examples, exhibits, and biographies. Life in the castle was anything but romantic. Everyday existence in the Staufer castles was hard, full of privations, rustic and unhealthy, and certainly comparable with life on the peasant farms – but enclosed in thick, protective walls.

Ausstellungsgestaltung
Exhibition Design:
BERTRON SCHWARZ FREY

Entwurf Design:
Prof. Ulrich Schwarz, Aurelia Bertron
Ausführungsplanung
Planning and Execution: Tomas Sturm
Grafik Graphic Design: Monika Richter

Dauerausstellung Permanent Exhibition

festen, dicken Mauern.

Das geistige Leben war trotz der widrigen Lebensumstände sehr reichhaltig. Man beschäftigte sich mit religiösen, philosophischen, juristischen, naturwissenschaftlichen und schöngeistigen Themen und unterhielt eine große Korrespondenz. Ein Austausch mit den bedeutendsten Köpfen der jeweiligen Epoche war gegeben.

Bernolph Freiherr von Gemmingen-Guttenberg

Despite the miserable living conditions intellectual life was extremely rich. Castle residents were interested in religious, philosophical, legal, scientific and aesthetic topics, and maintained an extensive body of correspondence. Clearly there was an exchange of ideas between the most significant thinkers of the respective epochs.

Bernolph Freiherr von Gemmingen-Guttenberg

Baudenkmäler, Schlösser, Freilichtmuseen Historical Monuments, Castles, Open-air Museums	Träger Supporting Institution: Privatmuseen Private Museums	Ausstellungsfläche Exhibition Area: ca. 300 m²
Leben auf der Ritterburg Life in the Knight's Castle		

Das Leben im 17., 18. und 19. Jahrhundert
Life in the 17th, 18th, and 19th century

2. OG
Third floor

OG
Second floor

Das Leben im 16. Jahrhundert
Life in the 16th century

EG
First floor

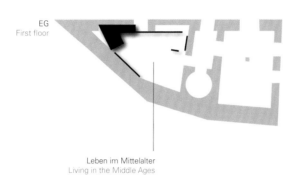

Leben im Mittelalter
Living in the Middle Ages

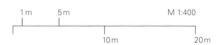

1 m   5 m   M 1:400

10 m   20 m

Große Schaukästen mit zum Teil mehreren tausend Zinnfiguren zur Visualisierung unterschiedlichster Szenen: Burgbelagerung, Reichsturnier, Schlacht bei Wimpfen usw.

Large display cases some of which contain several thousands pieces depicting various scenes such as castle sieges, empire tournaments and the Battle at Wimpfen.

Ausstellungsobjekte: Holzbibliothek, Zinnfigurendiorama und Bibliothek

Exhibits: wooden library, tin figure dioramas and library

Fotos Seiten 150/151 (Zinnfigurendiorama)
Photos on pages 150/151 (Tin Figure Dioramas):
Bernolph Freiherr von Gemmingen-Guttenberg

ARCHÄOLOGISCHE AUSSTELLUNGEN
ARCHEOLOGICAL EXHIBITIONS

Archäologische Ausstellungen boomen. Dies gilt für nahezu alle Epochen. Ob Neandertaler oder früher Homo sapiens, ob Steinzeitkulturen oder bronzezeitliche Grabfunde, Himmelsscheibe oder Goldhüte, ob Kelten oder Skythen, Römer oder Griechen, Langobarden oder Bajuwaren, mittelalterliche Klosterfunde oder Luthers Tischabfall, Moorleichen oder Totenkronen, Schlachtfelder oder Bombenschutt – alles wird zum Aufhänger für archäologische Ausstellungen. Auch die archäologische Arbeit selbst und die Geschichte des Faches wird immer häufiger zum Thema. Ausstellungen wie *Agatha Christie und der Orient*, *Lawrence von Arabien* oder jüngst *Das Große Spiel* haben Ausgrabungstätigkeit und Akteure zum Inhalt gehabt.

Was fasziniert die Besucher und Ausstellungsmacher? Das jeweilige Thema oder die Methoden der Archäologie? Eine eindeutige Antwort erscheint schwierig, aber es fällt auf, dass archäologische Ausstellungen ein Publikum erreichen, welches sich zum Beispiel von den Besuchern klassischer Kunstausstellungen deutlich unterscheidet. Es ist in der Regel jünger und gesellschaftlich vielfältiger. Dies ist wohl doch ein Indiz dafür, dass die Faszination wesentlich in der Arbeitsweise und Methodik des Faches begründet liegt.

Dieser Befund hat direkte Folgen für die Art der Ausstellungen. Lange Zeit haben insbesondere archäologische Dauerausstellungen ein Schattendasein geführt und sind bei Mehrspartenhäusern meistens in die Keller verbannt worden. Sie hatten sich in der Konkurrenz mit Kunstwerken zu behaupten. Auf diese Konkurrenz ist mit einer verstärkten Anpassung an die Methoden der Ausstellung historischer Kunstwerke reagiert worden. Das einzelne Objekt wurde vor weißem Hintergrund präsentiert und mit einer möglichst knappen Beschriftung versehen. Diese ästhetische, aber häufig kontextlose Präsentation galt als

Archeological exhibitions are booming. This applies to almost all historical epochs. Whether the subject is Neanderthals or early Homo sapiens, Stone Age cultures or Bronze Age grave finds, the Nebra sky disc or golden hats, Celts or Scythians, Romans or Greeks, Lombards or Baiuvarii, medieval cloister finds or the contents of Luther's wastepaper basket, bog bodies or death crowns, battlefields or bomb debris – all of them have proved fruitful themes for archeological exhibitions. We are also seeing archeological research itself and the history of the subject being made the theme of such presentations in an increasing number of cases. Exhibitions such as *Agatha Christie and the Orient*, *Lawrence of Arabia* and, most recently, *The Great Game*, all featured documentation of archeological digs and those working on them.

What is it about these types of exhibitions that is fascinating to those that visit them and those who are involved in their design? Is it the featured themes or the archeological process itself? It is difficult to provide an unambiguous answer. However, what is clear is that archeological exhibitions are now reaching an audience quite distinct from the segment of the general public that regularly attend traditional art exhibitions. In general this audience tends to be younger, and more socially diverse. This suggests that the fascination exerted by archeological exhibitions is fundamentally connected with the methods used in archeological research itself.

This has direct consequences for the character of exhibitions in this field. For a long time archeological exhibitions, particularly permanent ones, led a shadowy existence and, in the case of buildings that simultaneously housed several types of exhibitions, were usually consigned to the cellar. Archeological exhibits had to compete with artworks and, as a result, their presentation was strongly informed by the methods

Königsweg, um die Archäologie vom Image des Heimatmuseums mit seinen häufig liebevoll, aber selbstgestrickt wirkenden Darstellungsformen zu befreien. Die in nahezu jedem Stadtmuseum unverzichtbare Vorgeschichtsabteilung mit ihrer Mischung aus Modellen, Dioramen, Dokumentationsfotos, Kopien und Originalen sollte bei der Einrichtung größerer Dauerausstellungen überwunden werden. Doch es zeigte sich schnell, dass dieser Weg nicht erfolgreich ist. Archäologische Funde besitzen nur in wenigen Fällen die Aura eines großen Kunstwerkes. Ästhetisiert und in das Korsett strenger Architekturvorstellungen gezwängt, wird nur eine Seite des Exponates nachvollziehbar, die hinter ihm stehende Geschichte, die Informationen zu vergangenen Kulturen und Epochen, bleiben den meisten Besuchern verborgen.

Dabei wächst die Dichte der Informationen, die mit einzelnen Objekten verbunden sind, in einem Ausmaß, das vor wenigen Jahrzehnten nicht vorstellbar gewesen ist. Die modernen naturwissenschaftlichen Methoden haben zunächst mit Dendrochronologie und C14-Untersuchungen genaue Datierungen ermöglicht. Nun erhalten Skelettfunde von Menschen und Tieren aufgrund genetischer Analysen eine ganz neue Bedeutung. Die Isotopenanalyse lässt bereits Aussagen darüber zu, ob ein Mensch an dem Ort, an dem seine Gebeine entdeckt wurden, auch aufgewachsen ist oder ob er erst später in diese Region gelangte. Diese Methoden machen es, wie jüngst am Museum für Urgeschichte in Halle vorgeführt, schon jetzt möglich, aus einem archäologischen Fund einen Kriminalfall zu machen, bei dessen Erhellung „Profiler" des Landeskriminalamtes entscheidende Hinweise geben.

Die neuen naturwissenschaftlichen Methoden verändern vor allem auch die Kenntnisse von den frühesten Epochen der Menschheitsgeschichte. So hat sich unser Wissen über die Neandertaler erheblich vergrößert. Ein solcher Wissenszuwachs, der zudem stets im Fluss ist, verlangt auch eine Veränderung der Ausstellungsweise. Wegweisend ist zum Beispiel das Neandertalmuseum in Mettmann bei Düsseldorf gewesen, das als

characteristic of artwork presentations. The individual object was shown against a white background and supplied with a label that was kept as brief as possible. This type of aesthetic presentation, which was often devoid of context, was regarded as the best way of liberating archeology from the image of the local-history museum, and presentations that were often mounted with great care but tended to look rather "homemade." The establishment of larger permanent exhibitions was seen as a means of moving beyond the kind of prehistory section found in almost every city museum comprising models, dioramas, photographic documentation, and both copied and original objects. However, it soon became clear that such an aesthetically oriented approach was not successful in this context. Only a minority of archeological finds project the aura of an artwork. Aestheticizing and packaging exhibits in a framework defined by rigid architectural ideas limits the way they are comprehended; the history behind them, the information regarding past cultures and epochs, remains inaccessible for most visitors.

On the other hand, the amount of information associated with the individual objects is now growing to a degree that would have been unimaginable even a few decades ago. Precise dating has long been possible by means of dendrochronology, and carbon dating. Now genetic analysis is giving a whole new meaning to finds of human and animal skeletons. Isotope analysis makes it possible to determine whether an individual actually grew up at the location in which their bones were found or whether they only moved to the region at a later date. As recently shown by the Museum of Prehistory in Halle, these methods are already making it possible to treat archeological finds as criminal cases that can be solved with the help of police profilers.

The new scientific methods now available are above all providing us with a far greater insight into the earliest epochs of human history. For example, our knowledge of the Neanderthals has increased enormously. Such a growth in knowledge, which is constantly in flux, has created the need for

Themenmuseum mit sehr stark inszenierten Stationen entwickelt worden ist und den Besucher mit vielen interaktiven Elementen eigens einbezieht und ihm in Verbindung mit seiner eigenen Lebenswelt nachvollziehbar vermittelt, welche Informationen über den Neandertaler heute vorhanden sind.

Das Neandertalmuseum ist ein typisches Themenmuseum, das mit der Konzentration auf einen Fund und eine Fundstelle relativ einfach ein außergewöhnliches Profil gewinnen kann. Dies gilt auch für die vielen anderen an Ausgrabungsstätten entstandenen Museen, die immer dann besonders überzeugend präsentieren können, wenn die Verbindung zum Ort und dem, was dort geschehen ist, deutlich wird. Welche vielfältigen und auch unterschiedlich nah am archäologischen Befund entwickelten Wege dabei begangen werden können, demonstrieren die wechselnden Ausstellungskonzeptionen, mit denen der noch junge Museumsstandort in Kalkriese an die Varusschlacht anknüpft.

Aber auch die Landesmuseen haben sich in den letzten Jahren erheblich verändert. Mit der Denkmalschutzgesetzgebung ist seit den achtziger Jahren ein großer neuer Bedarf entstanden, da die damit verbundene Intensivierung der Grabungstätigkeiten auch die Notwendigkeit mit sich gebracht hat, die geborgenen Objekte zu präsentieren. Zwei Umsetzungen ragen dabei besonders heraus. Das Westfälische Museum für Archäologie wurde nach langen Diskussionen von Münster nach Herne verlegt. Dort sind die immer noch chronologisch gegliederten Exponate in eine begehbare Grabungslandschaft integriert worden. Die Methode Ausgrabung wird hier ganz bewusst zur Leitlinie der gesamten Gestaltung und die Frage nach dem Grund für die Attraktivität archäologischer Ausstellungen deutlich mit der Faszination Ausgrabung beantwortet. Eine übergreifende Darstellungsebene verbindet die vielen Einzelthemen, die sich aus der Vielfalt der Objekte und deren unterschiedlicher Zeitstellung ergeben.

Einen anderen Weg haben die Macher der Ausstellung in Halle gewählt. Die bisher eröffneten Abteilungen von der Steinzeit bis

a different approach to exhibitions. An excellent example is the Neanderthal Museum in Mettmann near Düsseldorf; it has been developed as a theme museum featuring carefully staged exhibits equipped with interactive elements that involve visitors in the presentations, and communicate current information on Neanderthals, which is comprehensible from a present-day perspective. The Neanderthal Museum is a typical theme museum, and shows how such an institution can relatively easily gain a profile by concentrating on a particular find at a particular location. This also applies to many other museums constructed at the sites of archeological digs, which are able to create particularly convincing presentations due to their clear connection with a site and what has occurred there. The many and diverse approaches that this proximity to an archeological find allows are illustrated by the changing exhibitions concepts employed by the museum in Kalkriese in Lower Saxony to present information on the Battle of Teutoburger Forest between Roman legions, and an alliance of Germanic tribes.

Established regional museums have also changed considerably in recent years. Since the 1980s German laws on the protection of historic sites have led to an increased need to present objects discovered as a result of more intensive archeological exploration. Within Germany, two changes in particular stand out. After a long period of discussion, the Westphalian Museum of Archeology was relocated from Münster to Herne, where the chronologically organized exhibits have been integrated into a traversable excavation site.

The excavation method has very consciously been made an organizing principle of the entire presentation, and the question as to the reason for the growing interest in archeological exhibitions has been clearly answered by foregrounding the fascination exerted by the excavation process. A comprehensive presentational format links the many individual themes emerging from the multiplicity of objects, and the different epochs from which they originate.

zur Bronzezeit zeichnen sich durch äußerst sorgfältige und detailgenaue Inszenierung der Objekte aus. Hervorragend ausgeleuchtete Einzelobjekte, große sorgfältige Montagen von Objektgruppen, Lebensbilder und Modelle ergeben eine schlüssige Gesamtdarstellung. Dabei wird die Ausstellung von den Erkenntnissen getragen, die aufgrund genauer wissenschaftlicher Analyse von Objektgruppen und Einzelexponaten vermittelt werden können.

Schon diese beiden Beispiele zeigen, dass archäologische Ausstellungen heute sehr vielfältig sein können. Die besondere Herausforderung besteht darin, jeweils die Besonderheit der eigenen Sammlung zu erkennen und auf ihr ein Vermittlungskonzept aufzubauen. Dieser Weg ist auch im Neuen Museum auf der Berliner Museumsinsel beschritten worden. Das Museum für Vor- und Frühgeschichte präsentiert dort seine umfangreiche und aus nahezu allen Teilen Europas stammende Sammlung. Gleichzeitig vermittelt schon das Museumsgebäude, dass auch die Geschichte eines Museums und seiner Objekte von Bedeutung ist. So ist der Sammlungsgeschichte der bereits 1850 für die Präsentation der „vaterländischen Altertümer" ausgemalte Saal gewidmet. Unter den Fresken der nordischen Götterwelt lässt sich lange über die Museumsgeschichte der Archäologie nachdenken, einer Disziplin, zu der jede Generation neue Zugänge gesucht hat. Unsere Zeit lässt eine große Vielfalt an Darstellungsformen erkennen, und es kann kein Zweifel bestehen, dass archäologische Ausstellungen noch weiter an Zahl und Bedeutung zunehmen werden.

Matthias Wemhoff

Exhibition designers in Halle have chosen a different approach. The sections covering the period from the Stone Age to the Bronze Age are notable for their extremely detailed, and accurate presentation of the exhibits. Excellently lit objects, large montages of object groups, illustrations, and models provide for a coherent overall presentation that is clearly based on knowledge gained from a precise scientific analysis of the object groups, and individual exhibits.

These two examples illustrate the kind of diversity found in contemporary archeological exhibitions. The particular challenge facing exhibition designers involves recognizing the specificity of individual collections, and tailoring a communication concept accordingly. This attention to detail is evident in the approach taken at the Neues Museum located on Berlin's Museum Island. The museum is devoted to prehistory and early history, and offers a comprehensive collection that originates from all over Europe. At the same time the museum building itself communicates the fact that the history of a museum, and its collection has its own significance. For instance, the main hall painted in 1850 for the presentation of "national antiquities" is devoted to the history of the collection. Visitors standing beneath the frescos portraying the world of the Nordic gods are invited to reflect on the history of archeology in the museum context, a discipline that each generation has sought new ways to access. At present we are seeing a wide variety of presentational forms unfolding, and there can be little doubt that archeological exhibitions will continue to grow in terms of numbers and significance.

Matthias Wemhoff

Schätze des Alten Syrien – Die Entdeckung des Königreichs Qatna
The Treasures of Ancient Syria – Discovery of the Kingdom of Qatna

Die altsyrische Königsstadt Qatna wurde bereits in den zwanziger Jahren des vergangenen Jahrhunderts entdeckt. Schon damals fand man Tontafeln, die den antiken Namen Qatna verrieten. Dennoch geriet die ca. 100 Hektar große Ruinenstätte in Vergessenheit. Seit 1999 gräbt dort eine internationale archäologische Kooperation, an der die Universität Tübingen unter der Leitung von Professor Dr. Peter Pfälzner, die Universität Udine unter der Leitung von Professor Dr. Daniele Morandi Bonacossi und der syrische Antikendienst unter der Leitung von Dr. Michel al-Maqdissi beteiligt sind.
2002 stieß die syrisch-deutsche Expedition im Palastbereich auf eine unterirdische Kammer, die den Zugang zu einer unberaubten Grabanlage freigab. In den Kammern konnten mehr als 2 000 Fundstücke sichergestellt werden. Nach der Bergung begann eine umfangreiche, Jahre dauernde Auswertung. 2009 war man so weit, dass die ersten Ergebnisse in der Großen Landesausstellung im Landesmuseum Württemberg in Stuttgart präsentiert werden konnten.
In der Ausstellung *Schätze des Alten Syrien – Die Entdeckung des Königreichs Qatna* sollten nicht nur die sensationellen Funde aus der Königsgruft, sondern auch die neuen Grabungsergebnisse aus dem Palastbereich und der Stadtanlage thematisiert werden. Das in der Ausstellung gezeigte Bild vom Aufstieg und Untergang des Stadtstaates Qatna sowie seiner Einbettung in die syrische Geschichte des 2. Jahrtausends v. Chr. vereinigt die Ergebnisse vieler Forschungsdisziplinen.
Es galt, dem Besucher auf einer Fläche von 1080 Quadratmetern in verständlicher Weise Zugang zur syrischen Bronzezeit, und somit zum Königreich Qatna zu verschaffen. Die packende Ausstellungsarchitektur wurde durch Medien wie Film, 3D-Animation und Tonstationen in ihrer narrativen Darstellung unterstützt. Raumüberschriften sowie Wand- und Objekttexte erläuterten die Themenkomplexe und ausgestellten Objekte. Ein deutscher oder englischer Audioguide

The ancient royal Syrian city of Qatna was already discovered in the 1920s and identified at the time by clay tablets bearing the city's name. The ruins, which stretch over some one hundred hectares, were subsequently forgotten for a number of decades. Then, in 1999, an international archeological team resumed excavations. This work remains ongoing and is being carried out by a group led by Professor Peter Pfälzner from the University of Tübingen, a group from the University of Udine led by Professor Daniele Morandi Bonacossi, and representatives of the Syrian Antiquities Mission led by Dr Michel al-Maqdissi.
In 2002, while excavating the site of city's palace, the Syrian-German expedition uncovered an underground chamber containing an undisturbed tomb. More than 2,000 artifacts were recovered from the chamber and, following the expedition, the group spent several years comprehensively evaluating them. In 2009, the first results of this process were presented in the Württemberg State Museum in Stuttgart.
The intention behind the exhibition *The Treasures of Ancient Syria – Discovery of the Kingdom of Qatna* was to present not only the sensational finds from the royal tomb, but also the new information yielded by the excavation of the palace site and the city complex. The exhibition's portrayal of the rise and fall of the Qatna city-state and its place in the history of Syria during the second millennium BC drew on a range of research disciplines.
The basic task facing the exhibition designers was to find a way of using the 1,080 square meter exhibition space that guided visitors in a comprehensible way into the Syrian Bronze Age and thus into the kingdom of Qatna. The result was a narrative presentation that supplemented the space's arresting architecture with media such as film, 3D animations, and audio stations. Information on the different thematic complexes and exhibited artifacts was also provided in the form of headings displayed at

Archäologische Ausstellungen Archeological Exhibitions	Landesmuseum Württemberg The Württemberg State Museum Schillerplatz 6, Altes Schloss 70173 Stuttgart	Gesamtleitung Project Coordinator: Prof. Dr. Cornelia Ewigleben, Direktorin Director Ulrich Volz, kaufmännischer Direktor Associate Director
Schätze des Alten Syrien – Die Entdeckung des Königreichs Qatna The Treasures of Ancient Syria – Discovery of the Kingdom of Qatna		

für Erwachsene sowie eine Kinderversion führten den Besucher durch die Präsentation. Kindgerechte Vitrinen, Trickfilm, Hörstation und Hands-on-Objekte integrierten eine eigene Vermittlungsebene für Kinder.

Es lag nahe, die Präsentation in vier Hauptbereiche zu strukturieren. Ein mächtiger Lehmwall gliederte die Ausstellung auch optisch in einen äußeren und inneren Bereich. Außerhalb des Walls erhielt der Besucher einen historischen Überblick über das 2. und 1. Jahrtausend v. Chr. in Syrien. Ein Kartenmorphing verdeutlichte die geografische Lage und die Entwicklung Qatnas und der zeitgleich existierenden Stadtstaaten und angrenzenden Reiche. Hochkarätige Exponate aus Qatna und den anderen Städten ermöglichten einen Vergleich des hohen Lebensstandards im 2. Jahrtausends v. Chr. in der Levante.

Jenseits des Walls empfing den Besucher eine helle Stadtarchitektur. Durch L-förmige Architekturelemente, die Gebäude der Stadt nachempfanden, wurde das zweite Hauptthema „Leben in Syrien im 2. Jahrtausend v. Chr." in verschiedene Bereiche gegliedert. Anhand einmaliger Exponate wurden folgende Themen dargestellt: häusliche Religiosität und Götterwelt, Diplomatie und Handel, Haus und Haushalt sowie Handwerk und Technik. Die Exponate wurden im Inneren der L-Elemente oder in Nischen präsentiert. Die Innenwände waren in einem dunklen Magentaton gehalten, der an die Farbe Purpur, ein wichtiges Handelsprodukt aus Qatna, erinnert. Bei der Auswahl der Objekte war zu berücksichtigen, dass sie ein möglichst umfassendes Bild des Lebens in einer altsyrischen Königsstadt vermitteln sollten.

Der Höhepunkt der Ausstellung war zweifelsohne der dritte Hauptteil „Zentrum der Macht". Am Ende der „Stadt" stand der Besucher vor einer monumentalen Palastarchitektur aus raumhohen Lehmziegelmauern mit einem mächtigen Tor. Eine gelbfarbene Markierung am Fußboden von der „Stadt" zum Palasttor unterstrich den Eindruck, die Akropolis zu erklimmen. Das Innere des Palastes war in mehrere Räume gegliedert, in denen die Zeugnisse des höfischen Lebens,

the entrances to the various rooms as well as texts mounted on the walls and adjacent to artifacts. Visitors could also make use of English and German audio guides for both adults and children. A specially integrated informational level for children included suitably designed display cases, animations, audio stations, and hands-on objects.

The nature of the material naturally lent itself to a presentation structured into four main sections. The exhibition was also divided visually into an exterior and interior area by a thick clay wall. Outside the wall, visitors were provided with an historical overview of Syria in the second and first millennium BC. A morphing map was used to show Qatna's location, illustrate its development, and identify the city-states and kingdoms also found in the region during this period. High-quality exhibits from Qatna and other cities in the region provided a comparative insight into the high standard of living generally prevailing in the Levant in the second millennium BC.

On the other side of the wall, visitors encountered a bright urban architecture. L-shaped architectural elements based on the buildings once making up the city were used to present the exhibition's second main theme, "Life in Syria in the Second Millennium BC," in a series of different segments. The unique exhibits provided by the Qatna excavation were grouped around the following themes: domestic religiosity and the divine sphere, diplomacy and commerce, housing and household, and handcrafts and technology. The exhibits were presented on the inner side of the L-shaped elements or in niches. The inner walls were colored in a dark magenta, recalling the crimson pigment that constituted one of Qatna's important trading commodities. An important criterion for the selection of exhibits was the extent to which they could contribute to a comprehensive portrayal of life in the ancient Syrian royal city.

The highpoint of the exhibition was undoubtedly the third main section "Center of Power." At the end of the "city" visitors found themselves standing in front of a monumental palace structure consisting of

Konzeption und wissenschaftliche Projektleitung Concept and Scientific Management:
Dr. Ellen Rehm (Leitung und Konzeption Management and Concept),
Dr. Erwin Keefer (Idee Idea)

Projektsteuerung Project Management:
Karin Birk (Leitung Supervisor),
Jan Warnecke
Wissenschaftliche Mitarbeiter Research Assistants:
Christiane Herb, Thomas Hoppe, Marc Kähler, Nina Willburger

Museumspädagogik Museum Education:
Tanja Karrer, Maria Rothhaupt-Kaiser

darunter die Tontäfelchen der königlichen Schreibstube, ausgestellt waren.

Als Erstes betrat der Besucher die große Säulenhalle. Eine der vier Zedernholzsäulen, die einst das Dach der 1 300 Quadratmeter großen Halle trugen, war real nachempfunden. Eine 3D-Animation setzte die angedeutete Palastarchitektur mit den mächtigen Säulen fort. Der Besucher gewann den Eindruck, durch die Säulenhalle zu wandeln, er sah Feuerbecken, das Palastheiligtum und gelangte so in den Thronsaal.

Der etwa um 1700 v. Chr. erbaute Palast gehörte mit 18 000 Quadratmetern zu den gewaltigsten seiner Zeit. Die Palastarchitektur wurde außerdem durch ein Modell fassbar. Eine Synchronisierung des Modells mit der 3D-Animation half bei der Orientierung. Mit Hilfe von LED-Leuchten im Modellboden wurde der Weg der „Kamera" durch den Palast aufgezeigt. Die 3D-Animation endete an dem Tor, das den Gang zur Gruft freigab. So wurde auch der Besucher in der nachempfundenen Palastarchitektur auf dieses „Tor" hingeführt. Die Ausstellungsfarbe änderte sich, ein Dunkelgrau bestimmte das Ambiente. Der Besucher gelangte durch einen mysteriös erleuchteten 10 Meter langen Gang, der den Eindruck vermittelte, in die Tiefe zu führen, in den Vorraum der Gruft. Hier stand er unmittelbar vor den

clay-brick walls reaching to the ceiling and an enormous gate. A path marked in yellow leading from the "city" to the palace gate underscored the impression of scaling the city's acropolis. The palace interior was divided into several rooms in which traces of courtly life were exhibited, including clay tablets from the royal scriptorium.

Visitors first entered the palace's imposing ceremonial hall, which featured a copy of one of the four main cedar-wood columns that once supported the roof over this 1,300 square meter space. The architectural features suggested by the exhibition space were presented in further detail in a 3D animation that provided visitors with an impression of walking through the hall with its towering columns, braziers, and palace shrine before entering the throne room.

The palace, which was built around 1700 BC and covered an area of 18,000 square meters, was one of the largest of its time. The exhibition also included a model of the original structure, which was synchronized with the 3D animation to help visitors orientate themselves. LED lighting in the floor of the model marked the path taken by the "camera" through the palace. The 3D animation ended at the gate opening onto a corridor leading to the tomb. Therefore, the reconstructed elements of the original palace

---

Fotos Königsfiguren, Tontafeln
Photos of royal statues and clay tablets:
Konrad Wita, Institut für die Kulturen des Alten Orients (IANES), Universität Tübingen

Die Statuen der Vorfahren
Der Eingang zur königlichen Gruft von Qatna wurde von zwei 85 Zentimeter hohen Statuen aus Basalt flankiert. Beide Figuren stammen aus dem 18./17. Jahrhundert v. Chr. und werden als königliche Ahnen gedeutet, denen geopfert wurde.

The Ancestor Statues
The entrance to the royal tomb of Qatna was flanked by two statues each 85 centimeters high and made of basalt. Both figures are from the 18th/17th century BC and are seen as royal ancestors which were subsequently sacrificed.

beiden Ahnenfiguren, die vor dem Eingang der Gruft als Grabwächter gefunden worden waren.

Die Sitte, die Toten unter dem Haus der Familie zu bestatten, war im Alten Orient nicht ungewöhnlich. Aus anderen syrischen Palästen sind ebenfalls Grüfte bekannt. In Qatna fand man zum ersten Mal einen aufwendig gearbeiteten Gang, der zur unberührten Gruft führte. Sie bestand aus einer Haupt- und drei Nebenkammern. Die Kammern waren mit Mobiliar und Grabbeigaben ausgestattet. In der Haupt- und in einer Nebenkammer stand je ein deckelloser Sarkophag, in dem Gebeine mehrerer Menschen lagen.

Die Ausstellungsarchitektur empfand den Grundriss der Gruft nach. Die Decke der Hauptkammer wurde durch vier Säulen gestützt und spiegelte so die große Halle im Palast wider. Zwei der Nebenkammern waren durch Nischen mit Großfotos der Kammern und 3D-Guckies mit Rekonstruktionen angedeutet. Ein „Taschenlampeneffekt" ließ den Besucher die spannende Entdeckung der Gruft miterleben. Genau wie bei der realen Auffindung zeigte ein Lichtkegel die steinernen Bänke mit einer Fülle von Gefäßen. Neben Keramik- und Steingefäßen gehörten auch Schmuck, darunter die goldenen Entenköpfe, Kleider-

architecture effectively guided the visitor to this "gate." Here the color of the exhibition surfaces changed, with a dark gray creating a different kind of ambience. Visitors passed along a mysteriously illuminated, 10-meter corridor, which created the impression of descending down into the tomb's vestibule. Here visitors found themselves standing directly in front of the two ancestral stone figures that had been found standing guard over the tomb during the excavation.

The practice of interring the dead underneath the building occupied by their families was not unusual in the ancient Orient. Tombs have also been found underneath other Syrian palaces. However, the discovery in Qatna of a carefully constructed corridor leading to an intact tomb remains unique. The tomb itself was composed of a main chamber and three subsidiary chambers, all containing furnishings and burial offerings. The main chamber and one of the subsidiary rooms each contained an open sarcophagus in which the bones of several people were found.

The exhibition architecture reflected the layout of the tomb. The roof of the main chamber was supported by four columns, thereby mirroring the palace's ceremonial hall. Two of the subsidiary chambers were represented in the form of niches contain-

Zierat in Form von Entenköpfen mit einer Hathormaske, 2. Hälfte des 2. Jahrtausends v. Chr. (detaillierte Beschreibung siehe Seite 174)
Ornaments in the form of ducks heads with a Hathor mask, second half of the second millennium BC (for a detailed description please see page 174)

Keilschrifttafeln aus der königlichen Schreibstube
Bei den Textfunden handelt es sich um Korrespondenz mit anderen Königen und Fürsten sowie um Rechts- und Verwaltungsurkunden.

Cuneiform tablets from the royal office
The text reveals correspondence with other kings and princes, as well as legal and administrative documents.

besatz, Waffen, Möbelzier, Rollsiegel und vieles mehr zu den geborgenen Kostbarkeiten. Die Funde spiegeln den Status der Besitzer wider oder dienten als Geschenke an die Götter.

Der Besucher verließ die Gruft und gelangte zum letzten Teil der Ausstellung: „Der Untergang von Qatna". Die Wandfarbe wechselte zu einem Dunkelblau. Der riesige Lehmwall war mit Brandspuren gezeichnet. Über den Wall hinweg erblickte er eine Flammenprojektion: Palastteile gingen in Flammen auf. Eine Karte verdeutlichte die Machtverhältnisse im 14. Jahrhundert v. Chr. in Syrien. Das Mittani-Reich hatte an Macht verloren, und die expandierenden Hethiter konnten sich von Norden her ausbreiten. Von Süden drangen die Ägypter bis an die Grenzen Qatnas vor.

Als einzige Objekte im Raum wurden zwei Tontafeln präsentiert. Diese Tafeln enthalten einen Hilferuf des Königs von Qatna an den ägyptischen Pharao, der ihm gegen die Hethiter zur Seite stehen sollte. Der eindringliche Hilferuf des Königs Akizzi wurde als Keilschrift-Animation groß an die Wand projiziert und von einem Sprecher in Akkadisch und Deutsch vorgetragen. Der Pharao kam Akizzi nicht zur Hilfe. Die Hethiter eroberten um 1340 v. Chr. Qatna und ließen den Palast in Flammen aufgehen. Der Besucher verließ die Ausstellung durch den „brennenden Palast".

Eintragungen im Besucherbuch wie „wunderschöne Exponate", „erstklassige Infotafeln" oder „eine einzigartige, hervorragend präsentierte Ausstellung" belegen, dass die archäologische Erforschung Qatnas, die herausragenden Funde und die erzählende Ausstellungsarchitektur eine gelungene Symbiose darstellten, die nahezu 120 000 Besucher erfreute.

Karin Birk

ing large-format photos and 3D viewers presenting reconstructions. A "flashlight effect" was used to recreate the sense of excitement associated with the discovery of the tomb. A light cone revealed stone benches supporting a rich array of vessels. Apart from these ceramic and stone vessels, the excavation also yielded a range of precious jewelry, which included golden duck's heads, garment trimmings, weapons, furniture adornments, and cylinder seals. These finds represented the status of their original owners or as gifts to the gods.

Upon leaving the tomb, visitors moved on to the last part of the exhibition, "The Decline of Qatna." The color of the walls changed to a dark blue, and the giant clay wall was marked by traces of fire. Beyond the wall visitors could see a projection of flames engulfing parts of the palace. A map showed the power relations prevailing in Syria during the fourteenth century BC. The power of the Mittani kingdom had declined, which enabled the Hittites to expand their sphere of influence from the north. Meanwhile, the Egyptians advanced from the south to Qatna's borders.

The only artifacts presented in this room were two clay tablets on which a plea for help against the Hittites from the king of Qatna to the Egyptian pharaoh is inscribed. This urgent plea by King Akizzi was projected onto the wall in cuneiform script and read over a speaker in Akkadian and German. The pharaoh did not come to Akizzi's aid and around 1340 BC the Hittites overran Qatna and burned the palace. It was through this "burning palace" that visitors left the exhibition.

The exhibition attracted almost 120,000 visitors and entries made in the visitors' book such as "wonderful exhibits," "first-class information panels" and "a unique, excellently presented exhibition" confirmed that a successful symbiosis was achieved between the archeological study of Qatna, the outstanding finds it has produced, and the narrative provided by the architecture of the exhibition.

Karin Birk

Archäologische Ausstellungen
Archeological Exhibitions

Schätze des Alten Syrien – Die Entdeckung des Königreichs Qatna
The Treasures of Ancient Syria – Discovery of the Kingdom of Qatna

Fotos Seiten 159 und 161
Photos pages 159 and 161:
Hendrik Zwietasch / Peter Frankenstein, Landesmuseum Württemberg
The Württemberg State Museum

Ausstellungsfläche Exhibition Area: 1 080 m²

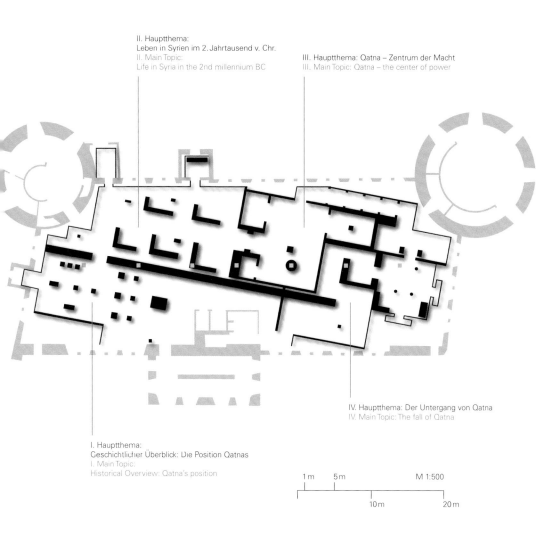

II. Hauptthema:
Leben in Syrien im 2. Jahrtausend v. Chr.
II. Main Topic:
Life in Syria in the 2nd millennium BC

III. Hauptthema: Qatna – Zentrum der Macht
III. Main Topic: Qatna – the center of power

IV. Hauptthema: Der Untergang von Qatna
IV. Main Topic: The fall of Qatna

I. Hauptthema:
Geschichtlicher Überblick: Die Position Qatnas
I. Main Topic:
Historical Overview: Qatna's position

1 m   5 m   M 1:500

10 m   20 m

Blick in den Gang zur Grabkammer mit Resten der Lehmziegelmauern. Um die Grabungsfläche feucht zu halten, wurde der Grabungsschnitt mit Plastikfolien abgedeckt. Die Ausstellungsgestaltung greift die Anmutung der Lehmziegelarchitektur auf.

A view of the entrance to the burial chamber with the remains of the chamber walls constructed of mud brick. In order to keep the excavation area moist the excavation trench was covered with plastic sheeting. The exhibition design incorporates elements of loam brick architecture.

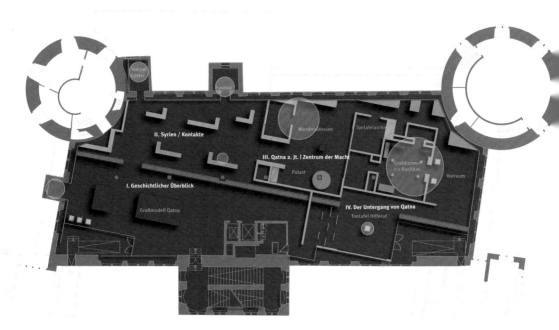

Archäologische Ausstellungen
Archeological Exhibitions

Schätze des Alten Syrien – Die Entdeckung des Königreichs Qatna
The Treasures of Ancient Syria – Discovery of the Kingdom of Qatna

Träger Supporting Institution:
Landesmuseum Württemberg
The Württemberg State Museum
Foto Photo:
Carlos Maria Lopez Martinez

Unten: Verortung der Themen / Inzenierungen im Grundriss
Below: Location of topics / Floorplan staging

Das Thema entwickelt sich über die räumlich-inhaltliche Gliederung: Einleitung, Aufstieg, Höhepunkt, Niedergang, Katastrophe.
Jedes neue Ereignis baut auf dem vorhergehenden auf. So führt der Rundgang von außen nach innen, vom Hellen ins Dunkle, von der Weite in die Enge der Grabkammer. Ziel ist die Darstellung des Zusammenhangs von Handlung, Ort und Zeit. Der Ausstellungsrundgang beginnt mit einem monumentalen Nachbau der Festungsmauer und führt zum dramaturgischen Höhepunkt der Ausstellung, in die Enge der Grabkammer. Stilmittel der Präsentation ist die mediale Verstärkung sowie die immaterielle Schaffung dreidimensionaler Räumlichkeit, die die Präsentation der sensationellen Funde in den Mittelpunkt stellt.

The theme evolves over a thematic-spatial context: introduction, rise, climax, fall, and disaster. Every new event builds on the previous one; the tour will start from the outside in, from light to dark, from the vastness into the narrowness of the burial chamber. The aim is to present the context in terms of acts, place, and time. The exhibition tour begins with a monumental replica of the fort wall, and ends at the dramatic climax of the exhibition – in the narrowness of the burial chamber. The presentation's stylistic devices depended upon the media presence as well as the immaterial creation of a three-dimensional space in which the presentation will focus on the sensational discoveries.

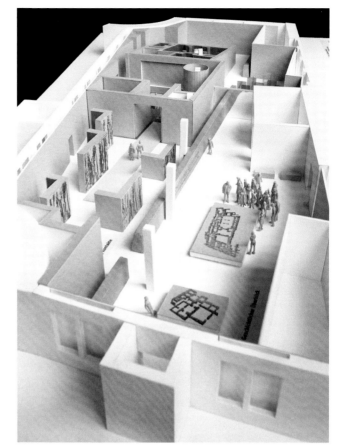

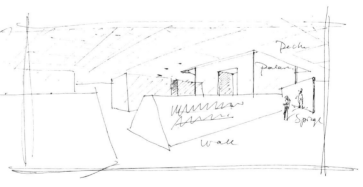

Ausstellungsgestaltung
Exhibition Design:
BERTRON SCHWARZ FREY
Entwurf Design Concept:
Prof. Claudia Frey, Prof. Ulrich Schwarz,
Aurelia Bertron
Ausführungsplanung
Planning and Execution:
Anja Kilian, Christian Schmutz

Grafik Design, Medienoberflächen
Graphic Design, Interfaces:
Aurelia Bertron, Marie Lauenroth
3D-Rekonstruktionen/Animationen
3D Reconstruction/Animation
Faber Courtial
Licht Lighting:
Ringo T. Fischer

Wechselausstellung Temporary Exhibition:
Ausstellungszeitraum
Exhibition Duration:
17. Oktober 2009 bis 14. März 2010
October 17, 2009 until March 14, 2010

Fläche Basisfarbe Lehm
Flächen Erdton
Flächen Erdton dunkel
Exponathintergrund schwarz
Rückwände | Infoflächen dunkelblau
Rückwände | Infoflächen blau
Akzent Grafik | Typografie hellblau
Akzent Grafik | Typografie rost
Akzent Grafik | Typografie gelb
Akzent Fläche goldgelb (Materialoptik)
Akzent Grafik | Typografie weiß

vor **3000** Jahren   vor **2000** Jahren   vor **1000** Jahren   vor **800** Jahren

Archäologische Ausstellungen
Archeological Exhibitions

Schätze des Alten Syrien – Die
Entdeckung des Königreichs Qatna
The Treasures of Ancient Syria – Discovery
of the Kingdom of Qatna

Die Farbigkeit der Texttafeln passt
sich dem jeweiligen Umfeld an. Die
gewählten Schriften sind größer als es
in Ausstellungen üblich ist. Dadurch soll
die Monumentalität der Bauten zum
Ausdruck gebracht werden.

The color of the text panels have been
coordinated to their respective environment. The selected writings are larger
than what is usually seen in exhibitions.
It serves as an expression of the monumentality of the buildings.

Die Farben leiten sich aus der Landschaft und Umgebung der Grabungsstätte ab. Zum Einsatz kommen sandig-braune Erde als Basiston und ein sonniges Gelb als Akzentfarbe. Großbilder bespielen die Außenwände der Ausstellungselemente, die Innenseiten tragen Vitrinen und Informationen.

The colors are derived from the landscape and region surrounding the excavation site. Sandy brown earth is used as foundation shade and a sunny yellow as an accent color. Large-format pictures of the exhibition elements are projected onto the outside while on the inside are display case and information.

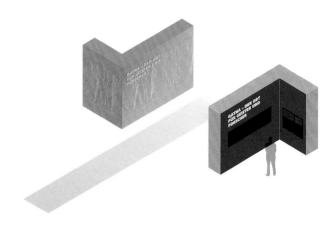

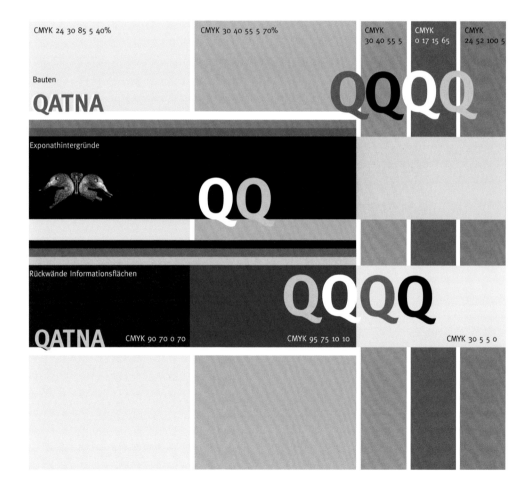

CMYK 24 30 85 5 40%

Bauten

QATNA

CMYK 30 40 55 5 70%

CMYK 30 40 55 5

CMYK 0 17 15 65

CMYK 24 52 100 5

Exponathintergründe

Rückwände Informationsflächen

QATNA CMYK 90 70 0 70

CMYK 95 75 10 10

CMYK 30 5 5 0

Themenüberschriften werden als Bestandteil der Bauten reliefartig, konkav und konvex ausgeführt. Die Textfelder sind vertieft in die Ausstellungswände eingelassen, um die Dreidimensionalität hervorzuheben.

Subject headings are designed as part of the buildings as a relief, concave and convex. The text fields are embedded in the exhibition walls in order to highlight their three-dimensionality.

Archäologische Ausstellungen
Archeological Exhibitions

Schätze des Alten Syrien – Die
Entdeckung des Königreichs Qatna
The Treasures of Ancient Syria – Discovery
of the Kingdom of Qatna

Fotos Seiten 166, 168–174, 176 f.
und 179–181 Photos pages 166, 168–174,
176 f. and 179–181
Hendrik Zwietasch / Peter Frankenstein,
Landesmuseum Württemberg
The Württemberg State Museum

Zentralperspektive auf den Palast Qatnas
(Rendering und Umsetzung)
Central perspective of the Qatnas Palace
(Rendering and Implementation)

166

Hinter einem bis auf Augenhöhe reichenden Wall erheben sich architektonisch wirkende Bauten als Referenz auf die machtvolle Anlage der Stadt Qatna. Sie symbolisieren von außen Stadt und Gebäude, von innen dienen sie als funktionale Ausstellungsmöblierung für die Präsentation von Objekten in eingebauten Vitrinen, integrierten Medien und Rekonstruktionen.
Der Weg führt über eine zentralperspektivisch betonte Achse in den Palast, dessen Lehmmauern auch in der Ausstellung machtvoll erscheinen. Die ursprüngliche Größe und Funktion der Palasträume werden medial erfahrbar. Eine raumgreifend projizierte 3D-Animation erzeugt eine bewegte Raumillusion (siehe Seite 170 ff.).

Behind a wall which reaches to eye level architectural-like buildings rise acting as a symbol to the powerful system of the city Qatna. From outside they symbolize the city and buildings, while from the inside they serve as functional exhibition furniture in which the presentation of objects in the built-in display cabinets are held as well as integrated media and reconstructions. In the palace itself the route leads through a central-perspective emphasized axis, and whose adobe walls appear powerful also within the exhibition. The original size and function of the palace rooms are experienced through utilizing various media. An expansive projected 3D animation creates an illusion of moving space (see page 170 ff.).

Eröffnungsbild, erstes Panorama auf die Bauten, die in ihrer architektonischen Kubatur ein Symbol für die Stadtanlage darstellen.
The opening image, the first panorama of the buildings in which their architectural cubature is representative as a symbol of the city.

Die Säule durchbricht als optische Illusion die Decke. Die Lichtführung lässt den Eindruck von einfallendem Tageslicht entstehen.
The column breaks through the ceiling as an optical illusion. The lighting creates the impression of a natural incident light.

SCHÄTZE D

DIE ENTDECKUNG

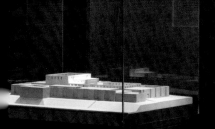

DER PALAST VON QATNA
THE PALACE OF QATNA

AUFRISS DES KÖNIGSPALASTES VON QATNA

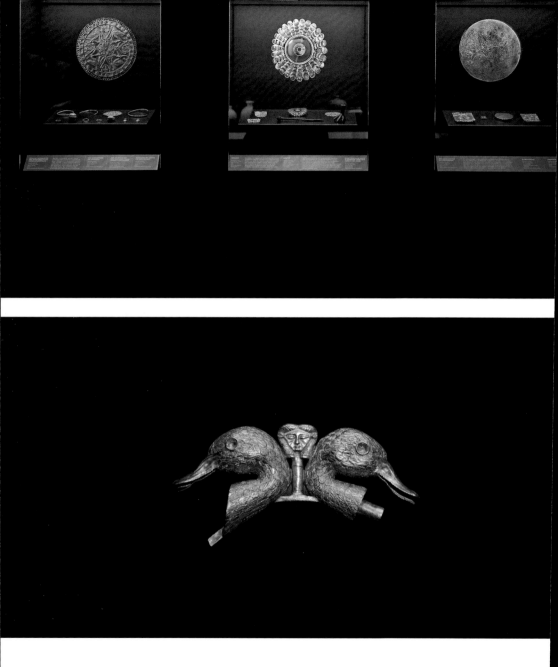

Archäologische Ausstellungen
Archeological Exhibitions

Schätze des Alten Syrien – Die
Entdeckung des Königreichs Qatna
The Treasures of Ancient Syria – Discovery
of the Kingdom of Qatna

Die aus Gold gegossenen Entenköpfe,
die aus der Königsgruft stammen, gehö-
ren mit zu den Meisterwerken syrischer
Kunst. Trotz der Parallelen zur ägyptischen
Kunst sind die Entenköpfe ein syrisches
Erzeugnis des 2. Jahrtausends v. Chr.

The ducks heads were cast from gold
and originate from the royal tomb; they
belong to the masterpieces of Syrian
art. Despite the similarities to Egyptian
art the ducks heads are indeed a Syrian
product from the 2nd millennium BC.

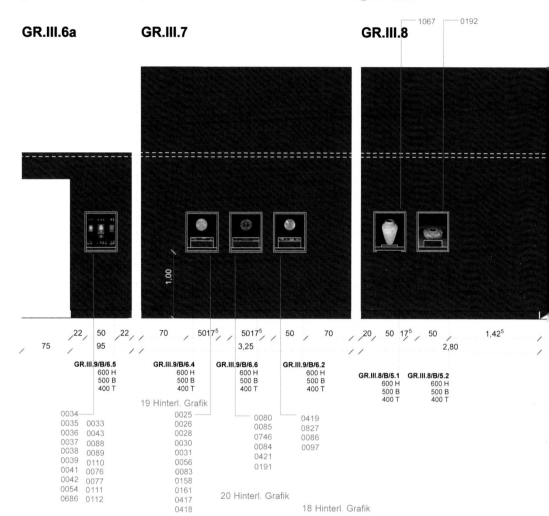

GR.III.6a

GR.III.7

GR.III.8

1067   0192

1,00

22	50	22	70	5017^5	5017^5	50	70	20	50 17^5	50	1,42^5
75	95			3,25					2,80		

GR.III.9/B/6.5		GR.III.9/B/6.4	GR.III.9/B/6.6	GR.III.9/B/6.2	GR.III.8/B/5.1	GR.III.8/B/5.2
600 H		600 H	600 H	600 H	600 H	600 H
500 B		500 B	500 B	500 B	500 B	500 B
400 T		400 T	400 T	400 T	400 T	400 T

19 Hinterl. Grafik

0034		0025	0080	0419
0035	0033	0026	0085	0827
0036	0043	0028	0746	0086
0037	0088	0030	0084	0097
0038	0089	0031	0421	
0039	0110	0056	0191	
0041	0076	0083		
0042	0077	0158		
0054	0111	0161		
0686	0112	0417		
		0418		

20 Hinterl. Grafik

18 Hinterl. Grafik

Die Präsentation aus dem Dunklen heraus bringt die meist kleinen Exponate besonders gut zur Geltung. Eine punktuelle, fokussierte Lichtführung lässt die Objekte vor dem Hintergrund schwebend erscheinen.

The presentation against a pure black background brings out the most of small exhibits – and usually to their advantage. A selective, focused lighting makes it appear as if the objects are floating in front of the background.

Höhepunkt der Ausstellung ist die Entdeckung der Grabkammer in szenischer Umsetzung durch mediale Verstärkung. Runde Taschenlampen-Lichtkegel tasten den Raum ab und projizieren ein virtuelles Bild der Gruft mit Schatten der Opferhandlungen. Die Größe der nachgebauten Grabkammer entspricht den Originalmaßen.

The highlight of the exhibition is the discovery of the burial chamber which is a staged and strengthened utilizing media. Round beam flashlights scan the room and project a virtual image of the tomb with shadows of the sacrificed. The size of the replica burial chamber was constructed according to its original dimensions.

Archäologische Ausstellungen
Archeological Exhibitions

Schätze des Alten Syrien – Die Entdeckung des Königreichs Qatna
The Treasures of Ancient Syria – Discovery of the Kingdom of Qatna

178

Vorherige Seite:
Wächterfiguren flankierten den Eingang zur Grabkammer in der Ausstellung. Der Ahnenkult war in der Levante weit verbreitet. Opfer vor den Statuen waren ein Weg, um mit den Ahnen in Kontakt zu treten. Die verstorbenen Vorfahren wurden wie Götter verehrt und um Beistand gebeten.

Previous Page:
In the exhibition guardian figures flanked the entrance to the burial chamber. Ancestral worship was widespread in Levant. Placing offerings before the statues were a way to establish contact with the ancestors. The dead ancestors were revered as gods and asked for help.

Das letzte Ausstellungssegment inszeniert den Untergang Qatnas. Der Weg führt von innen wieder nach außen. Der Fokus liegt auf zwei einzelnen Tontafeln, die in der Raummitte in ihrer Bedeutung überhöht inszeniert sind. Es ist der Höhepunkt des Dramas, die Katastrophe, der ungehörte Hilferuf des Königs von Qatna (siehe Seiten 180/181). Die Faszination entsteht aufgrund der die „Lesbarkeit" der Keilschrift durch mediale Übersetzung.

The last segment exhibition stages the fall of Qatna. The path again leads from the inside to the outside. The focus is on two separate clay tablets, which are positioned in the middle of the room in order to underscore their importance. The drama's climax has been reached; the catastrophe ensues as the cry for help issued by the king of Qatna goes unanswered (please see pages 180/181). The fascination is the result of the "readability" of cuneiform through a form of media-based translation.

Alamannenmuseum Weingarten – Ein neues Museum für einen alten Fundplatz
Alemanni Museum Weingarten – A new museum for an old find site

Von 1952 bis 1957 wurden in Weingarten 801 Gräber aus der Zeit vom 5. bis zum frühen 8. Jahrhundert freigelegt. Es handelt sich bei diesem Reihengräberfeld um einen der bedeutendsten Fundplätze Südwestdeutschlands. In den siebziger Jahren hat die Stadt im Kornhaus eine Dauerausstellung für die Funde aus dem Gräberfeld eingerichtet. Der Zuwachs an wissenschaftlichen Erkenntnissen und der Bedarf ihrer didaktischen, zeitgemäßen Vermittlung führten zu der Entscheidung, die Ausstellung neu zu gestalten.
Da die ungefähr 5000 Fundstücke des Gräberfeldes sich im Eigentum der Stadt befinden, war für die Ausstellungsmacher die einmalige Gelegenheit gegeben, die schönsten und aussagekräftigsten Exponate aus den Magazinbeständen für die Ausstellung auszuwählen. Wichtigste Vorgabe war die Schaffung von Themenstationen, die Einblicke in den Lebensalltag der damaligen alamannischen Bevölkerung geben sollten. Schon bald kristallisierten sich zehn Themen heraus: Grabung, Forschung, Geschichte der Alamannen, Handwerk, Tracht und Waffen der Männer, Tracht und Schmuck der Frauen, Glaube und Volksfrömmigkeit, Handel und Verkehr, Metallhandwerk sowie Abschiedsrituale. Die Themenstationen wurden durch jeweils eine Stele mit einem aussagekräf-

Between 1952 and 1957, 801 graves dating from the fifth to the eighth century were found in Weingarten, making it one of the most significant archeological finds in Southwestern Germany. In the 1970s, a permanent exhibition of the artifacts from the grave field was established in the town's historic "Grain House." In 2008 the exhibition was completely redesigned in response to the increase in scientific knowledge and the need to convey it in a didactic, contemporary fashion.
The approximately 5,000 artifacts recovered from the grave field are the property of the city of Weingarten, which meant that the exhibition designers were given a unique opportunity to select the most striking and expressive objects from the museum's repository for the new exhibition. The most important task in the design process was to establish thematic stations that provided insights into the everyday lives of the Alemanni people during this period. A study of the material quickly yielded ten major themes: the dig, research, history of the Alemanni, craftwork, men's clothing and weapons, women's clothing and jewelry, religion and beliefs, trade and commerce, metal crafts and funerary rituals. Each thematic station is marked by a stele featuring a particularly significant exhibit. The

Archäologische Ausstellungen
Archäologische Ausstellungen

Alamannenmuseum Weingarten
Alemanni Museum Weingarten
Karlstraße 28
88250 Weingarten

Fotos Photos:
Yvonne Mühleis, Regierungspräsidium Stuttgart, Landesamt für Denkmalpflege (Goldblattkreuze) Stuttgart Regional Council, Office for the Preservation of Historical Monuments, Johannes Volz (Scheibenfibel Disc fibula)

tigen Leitexponat gekennzeichnet, das mit einem kurzen Leittext den Einstieg in das jeweilige Thema darstellt. Als zweite Informationsebene dient eine mit jeder Stele korrespondierende, für das jeweilige Thema individuell gefertigte Vitrine mit Exponaten, die sich teilweise unter Klappen verbergen. Besucher, die weitere Informationen über ein Thema haben möchten, können auf einer dritten Informationsebene Exponate in Schubladen entdecken, die sich in den Vitrinen befinden.

Zu den herausragenden Stücken der Ausstellung zählen zwei Goldblattkreuze aus dem Frauengrab 615. Sie weisen darauf hin, dass die Bestattete schon Kontakt mit dem Christentum hatte. Beigaben im Grab mit magischem oder amulettartigem Charakter wie Zierscheibe und Bergkristallkugel zeigen jedoch, dass sie in einer synkretistischen Glaubenswelt lebte. Beide Kreuze wurden erst kurz vor der Bestattung aus sehr dünn ausgewalztem Gold gefertigt, auf ein Tuch aufgenäht und auf das Gesicht der Toten gelegt.

Die Beleuchtung in dem Ausstellungsraum richtet sich punktuell auf die Vitrinen und die Stelen, um eine Stimmung zu erzeugen, die die Wertigkeit der Exponate hervorhebt. Ein wichtiger Teil der Planung war von Anfang an, eine eigene Ebene für junge Besucher

second informational level is constituted by an adjacent display case that addresses the respective theme and featuring exhibits some of which are concealed by removable covers. Visitors seeking more information on a particular theme can find further exhibits in drawers – the third informational level – contained in the display case.

Two gold-leaf crosses from find 615, a woman's grave, are among the exhibition's most outstanding pieces. They indicate that the interred individual already had contact with Christianity. However, other grave artifacts such as phalerae and quartz spheres, which seem to have functioned as magical objects or amulets, show that this woman lived in a world of syncretistic beliefs. Both crosses were manufactured from very thinly rolled gold shortly before the burial and were sewn onto a cloth that was laid on the face of the deceased.

The lighting in the exhibition space is designed to project shafts of illumination onto the display cases and the steles in order to create an atmosphere that emphasizes the value of the exhibits. From the beginning, an important part of the planning process was to create a dedicated level for young visitors in order to make early medieval life more comprehensible for this visitor group. Every display case features

Goldblattkreuze
Zwei Goldblattkreuze aus dem Frauengrab 615. Sie geben Hinweise auf den christlichen Glauben der Bestatteten.
Gold-leaf crosses
Two gold-leaf crosses from a woman's grave (find 615) seem to indicate that the deceased held to Christian beliefs.

Goldscheibenfibel
Goldscheibenfibel aus Grab 615. Handwerklich einmaliges Stück. Schauseite mit fünf runden Almandinen auf gewaffelter Goldfolie verziert. Nadelhalter auf der Rückseite als Eberkopf gestaltet.

Golden disc fibula
Golden disc fibula from grave 615. A unique piece of craftwork. Visible side decorated with five round almandines on rippled gold foil. Back side features a pin holder shaped as a boar's head.

zu schaffen, um das Leben des frühen Mittelalters für diese Besuchergruppe besser begreifbar zu machen. In jede Vitrine wurde eine Kinderstation integriert, die Texte für Kinder enthält. Darüber hinaus soll der Nachwuchs vor allem durch Aktivitäten motiviert werden: Kinder können u.a. Texte in Runenschrift schreiben oder mit Keramik basteln.

Die Besucher der Dauerausstellung, vor allem auch Kinder, sollen durch ein vielfältiges Medienangebot über den Stand der Alamannenforschung sowie das Alltagsleben der Alamannen informiert werden. Zusammenfassend lässt sich sagen, dass die Neugestaltung des Alamannenmuseums in Weingarten nicht nur eine Anpassung an heutige Besuchergewohnheiten bietet. Vielmehr ist eine ganz neue Darstellung der Kultur der Alamannen entstanden, die wissenschaftlich aktuell mit neuen didaktischen Möglichkeiten vermittelt wird.

Rolf Schaubode

an integrated station containing texts for children. In addition, emphasis has been placed on motivating children through activities such as writing texts in runes and making ceramics.

The permanent exhibition offers a diverse range of media presentations designed to inform visitors, including and above all children, about the state of current research into the Alemanni and their everyday life. In summary it can be said that the new design of the Alemanni Museum in Weingarten not only offers a form more suited to the viewing habits of today's visitors. The result is in fact a completely new type of presentation of Alemanni culture, which is conveyed in a way that incorporates its scientific underpinnings as well as current didactic possibilities.

Rolf Schaubode

Archäologische Ausstellungen
Archeological Exhibitions

Alamannenmuseum Weingarten
Alemanni Museum Weingarten

Dauerausstellung Permanent Exhibition
Träger Supporting Institution:
Stadt Weingarten
The town of Weingarten
Foto Photo:
Achim Mende

Ausstellungsfläche Exhibition Area:
ca. 200 m²

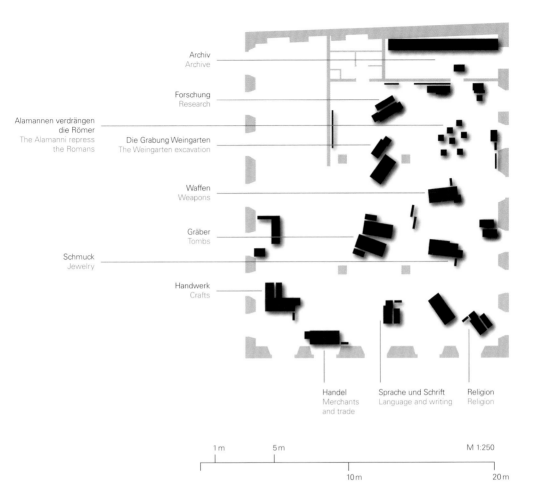

Archiv
Archive

Forschung
Research

Alamannen verdrängen
die Römer
The Alamanni repress
the Romans

Die Grabung Weingarten
The Weingarten excavation

Waffen
Weapons

Gräber
Tombs

Schmuck
Jewelry

Handwerk
Crafts

Handel
Merchants
and trade

Sprache und Schrift
Language and writing

Religion
Religion

1 m   5 m   M 1:250

                              10 m

                                                               20 m

Zehn Themenstationen zur Geschichte der Alamannen richten sich mit archäologischen Spielstationen besonders an junge Besucher. Die Topografie des Gräberfelds als Forschungszone ist Ideengeber und Matrix für das Raumbild und die Anordnung der Ausstellungsinhalte.
Auf den ersten Blick ragen die Stelen mit den Leitobjekten aus dem Vitrinenfeld. Die Vertiefungsebenen und Spielstationen erschließt sich der Besucher sukzessive. Der Rundgang gleicht der Entdeckungstour durch eine Grabungslandschaft.

Ten theme-based stations archaeological game stations on the history of the Alemanni were especially aimed towards appealing to young visitors. The topography of the burial ground as a research area provided the ideas served as a matrix for the room's spatial concept and the arrangement of the exhibition content. At first glance it seems as if the stelae protrude outward with the objects from the display cases. The depth and game stations are gradually revealed to the visitors. The tour is similar to that of a discovery through an excavation landscape.

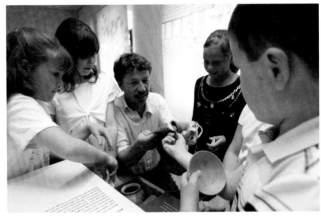

Autoren/Kuratoren Authors/Curators:
Rolf Schaubode, Uwe Lohmann
Wissenschaftliches Team Scientific Team:
Prof. Dr. Claudia Theune-Vogt,
Universität Wien The University of Vienna,
Constanze Cordes

Ausstellungsgestaltung
Exhibition Design:
BERTRON SCHWARZ FREY
Entwurfsleitung Head of Design:
Prof. Claudia Frey
Ausführungsplanung: Planning and
Execution: Cathrin Runge

Spielstationen in der Dauerausstellung:
mit Grabungswerkzeug selbst Objekte
freilegen, Materialien zum Anfassen und
Quiz zu den Grabungsfunden
Hands-on Exhibition Stations:
Utilizing the excavation tools visitors are
able to discover objects as well as touch
the materials and learn more through
quizes.

Diese Spitze einer Lanze nahm der Mann a...
Grab 244 mit auf den Weg ins Toten...
Seine Familie bestattete ihn m...
Raubzüge, persönliche...
damals das Alltag...
die Vorstell...
Zu...

Inszenierte Leitobjekte aus dem umfangreichen Objektfundus setzen inhaltliche Themenschwerpunkte. Die Wirkung der Exponate unterschiedlichster Materialität ist dabei ein wichtiger Aspekt. Das helle Graublau der Exponathintergründe hebt farbige Exponate, Knochen- und Keramikfragmente sowie goldene Schmuckstücke ebenso gut hervor wie dunkle Metallbeschläge. Das Grundprinzip des Kommunikationskonzepts ist eine enge Verknüpfung von Objekt und Informationsvermittlung. Die den Exponaten direkt zugeordneten Textebenen einerseits und die auf jeder Inhaltsebene stattfindende Kommentierung durch Originalobjekte andererseits schaffen ein komplexes Bild des Fundplatzes.

Objects from the extensive artefacts serve as the basis for the thematic areas. The effect of various exhibits materiality is an important aspect. The light blue-gray background of the exhibit highlights colorful exhibits, bone and pottery fragments, and gold jewelry pieces as well as dark, metal fittings. The basic principle of the communication approach is a close link between the object and supplying information. on The one hand the exhibits directly allocate various levels of text-absed information while simultaneously providing commentary with original objects at each content level creates a complex picture of the excavation site.

Archäologische Ausstellungen
Archeological Exhibitions

Alamannenmuseum Weingarten
Alemanni Museum Weingarten

Fotos auf den Seiten 186–195
Photos on pages 186–195:
Johannes Volz

Die junge Frau aus Grab 511 bekam diese
Gewandspangen wahrscheinlich, als sie 12 oder
13 Jahre alt war. Wir nennen sie wegen ihrer
Form heute »Bügelfibeln«.

In Männergräbern lagen selten Ringe oder
Armreifen, Frauengräber aber sind meistens mit
Schmuck ausgestattet oder mit schönen Fibeln,
die das Gewand verschlossen.

Man fand es damals offenbar sehr wichtig,
die Verstorbene für das Jenseits in eine schöne
Tracht zu kleiden, damit auch dort ihr Status
deutlich erkennbar war. Meistens trug die Tote
aber nur eine Kette oder Ohrringe, denn die
Ausstattung mit Fibeln und Schmuck konnten
sich nur wenige leisten.

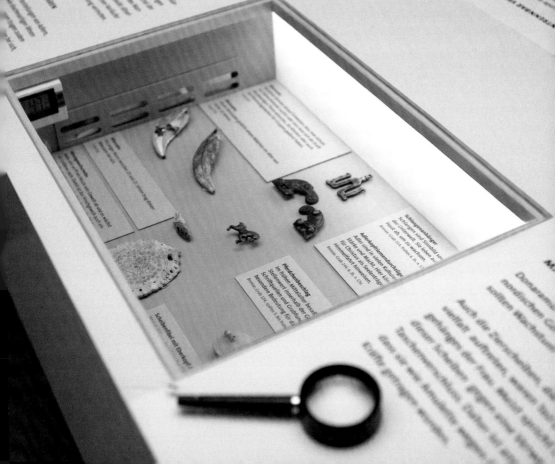

GESCHICHTSAUSSTELLUNGEN
HISTORICAL EXHIBITIONS

Geschichte ist „in"! Nicht nur im Fernsehen boomen seit Jahren Geschichtsdokumentationen, auch historische und kulturgeschichtliche Museen und Ausstellungen können in Deutschland auf rapide steigende Besucherzahlen verweisen.

Nach Angaben des Instituts für Museumsforschung stiegen die Besucherzahlen in historischen und archäologischen Museen im Jahr 2009 um 9,8 Prozent und in kulturgeschichtlichen Spezialmuseen um 5,4 Prozent.[1] Damit stehen sie vor allen anderen Museumsarten mit deutlichem Abstand an der Spitze. Rechnet man die meist (kultur-) geschichtlich angelegten Sammlungen der Schloss- und Burgmuseen mit dazu, so stellen Geschichtsmuseen im weitesten Sinne 39,3 Prozent des aktuellen Ausstellungspublikums,[2] obwohl sie quantitativ nur ein Viertel aller Museen und Ausstellungshäuser des Landes umfassen. Sie sind damit landesweit zu wichtigen kulturellen und touristischen Standortfaktoren geworden. Dabei driften sowohl die Inhalte als auch die musealen Charakteristika der unter dem Sammelbegriff „historische Ausstellungen" vereinten Expositionen nach wie vor weit auseinander. Neben den klassischen Präsentationen regionaler und lokaler Geschichte – die in der Regel in zu ihr gehörenden historischen Gebäuden gezeigt werden und dadurch eine zusätzliche Authentizität erhalten – haben in den letzten zwei Jahrzehnten verstärkt thematische Sonderausstellungen zu nationalen (kultur-)geschichtlichen Themen an Bedeutung gewonnen. Eine Bindung an die Jubiläen konkreter historischer Ereignisse („Anlassausstellungen") wie an den Ort ihres Geschehens ist dabei nicht immer Voraussetzung. Was ebenso zählt, ist die Attraktivität des Themas und dessen musealer Aufbereitung. Der historische Bogen wird weit gespannt: Er reicht von den alten Germanen über die deutschen Kaiser bis in die Neuzeit und die unmittelbare Gegenwart.

History is in! In the last several years not only have we seen a boom in historical documentaries on television, in Germany museums and exhibitions devoted to history, and cultural history have been recording rapidly growing attendance numbers. According to figures compiled by the Institute for Museum Research, attendance numbers reported by historical and archeological museums in 2009 increased by 9.8 percent over the previous year, and by 5.4 percent at museums that specialize in cultural history.[1] These figures place cultural history oriented museums above all other types of museums. If attendance figures for the collections held by Germany's palace museums are added to these numbers – which for the most part are devoted to cultural history – then historical museums are now attracting 39.3 percent of overall exhibition attendance,[2] although they constitute only a quarter of all museums, and exhibition spaces in the country. These institutions are thereby making a significant contribution to the enhancement of cultural identity as well as becoming important tourist attractions throughout Germany.

However, it should be considered that the range summarized by the collective concept of "historical exhibitions" remains an extremely diverse one. Apart from classic presentations of regional and local history – which as a rule are shown in historical buildings that lend an extra sense of authenticity – the last two decades have also seen an increase in the role of national cultural historical themes as the focus of special exhibitions. Moreover, such exhibitions do not necessarily have to rely on a link to the anniversaries of specific historical events, or the locations of such events. Equally important is the interest awakened by the chosen theme, and the character of the presentation. The historical span covered by such exhibitions is a broad one, and stretches from the ancient Germanic peoples, to the

---

Historische Ausstellungen
Historical Exhibitions

[1] In: *Statistische Gesamterhebung an den Museen der Bundesrepublik für das Jahr 2009. Materialien aus dem Institut für Museumsforschung*, Heft 64, Berlin 2010, S. 20. Die Besuche in historischen und archäologischen Museen werden hier gemeinsam erfasst.

[1] In: *Statistische Gesamterhebung an den Museen der Bundesrepublik für das Jahr 2009. Materialien aus dem Institut für Museumsforschung*, vol. 64 (Berlin, 2010): p. 20. This publication records visits to both historical and archeological museums.

Ihnen allen gemeinsam ist der Versuch einer populären und breite Besucherschichten ansprechenden Präsentation. Für dieses potenzielle Massenpublikum sollen möglichst viele Anknüpfungspunkte bereitgestellt werden, ohne jedoch die wissenschaftliche Grundierung der jeweiligen Expositionen außer Acht zu lassen. Für das 1994 in Bonn eröffnete Haus der Geschichte der Bundesrepublik Deutschland, das für sein Konzept bereits ein Jahr später mit dem Museumspreis des Europarates ausgezeichnet wurde, warb programmatisch ein Plakat mit dem Satz „Geschichte ist *war* langweilig!", wobei das Wörtchen *„war"* von Kinderhand eingefügt worden ist.

Diesem Anspruch versuchen heute viele historische Ausstellungen und Museen gerecht zu werden, indem sie – wie etwa das 2010 in Essen neu eröffnete Ruhr-Museum – ein breites Panorama an Objekten in ihre Schau integrieren, die die engen Grenzen traditioneller historischer Ausstellungen weit hinter sich lassen. Sie beziehen geologische Funde ebenso selbstverständlich in die Vermittlung von Geschichte mit ein wie archäologische Artefakte, naturwissenschaftliche Objekte wie auch künstlerische Werke und Inszenierungen. Und längst halten sich in solchen Expositionen „große Geschichte" und „Alltagsgeschichte" selbstredend die Waage. Eine für die Region in hohem Maße authentische bauliche Hülle – im Fall des Ruhr-Museums ist es die ehemalige Kohlenwäsche der auf der Welterbeliste der UNESCO stehenden Zeche Zollverein – sorgt zudem oft dafür, dass das „Gehäuse", in dem Geschichte vermittelt wird, nicht nur architektonische Zutat, sondern selbst ein sprechendes geschichtliches „Zitat" ist.

Zentrales Anliegen der überwiegenden Mehrheit der (kultur-)historischen Museen und Ausstellungen ist heute – neben der Vermittlung von Bildung – eindeutig die Identitätsstiftung durch Geschichte. Diese kann sich auf regionale Identitäten ebenso beziehen wie, im vereinigten Deutschland, zunehmend auch auf eine übergreifende nationale Identität. So wurde nicht zuletzt in den 1990 wieder entstandenen ostdeutschen Bundesländern sowohl durch die Ein-

German emperors, to the modern period, and finally to the immediate present. However, they all have the common goal of creating presentations that are able to appeal to a broad cross-section of the public. Exhibitions need to provide this potential mass public with as many points of reference as possible while, at the same time, taking into account the scholarly nature of the material presented. A brief example of this combined approach can be seen in a poster used to advertise the Haus der Geschichte der Bundesrepublik Deutschland (House of History of the Federal Republic of Germany), which opened in 1994, and one year later was awarded the Council of Europe Museum Prize. The poster featured the sentence, "History is was boring!" with the word "was," written in a child's handwriting.

Today many museums and exhibitions devoted to historical themes are attempting to meet this challenge by integrating a broad spectrum of objects into their displays, which extend well beyond the narrow boundaries of traditional historical exhibitions – as in the case of the Ruhr Museum that opened in Essen in 2010. Curators now approach their subjects more comprehensively, and include not only archeological artifacts, but also geological finds, scientific objects, and works of art. Moreover, it has now become an established practice to accord equal status to world historical events, and the history of everyday life. Entire buildings representing authentic aspects of the history of a region are now often included in presentations of history. This is particularly evident in the case of the former coal washing plant housing the Ruhr Museum at the Zollverein Coal Mine Industrial Complex, which has been recognized by UNESCO as a World Heritage Site. Here, the housing is much more than an architectural addition, but is in actuality an integral part of the history being conveyed.

Clearly a central element of the approach taken by the great majority of cultural history museums today – apart from education – is the formation of identity through history. This can relate to regional identities

---

[2] Das entspricht rund 42 Millionen Besuchen im Jahr 2009.
[2] This amounts to some 42 million visits in 2009.

[3] Das Konzept des Pommerschen Landesmuseums umfasst sowohl die Erd- und Landesgeschichte als auch eine Gemäldegalerie, während sich die Landesmuseen von Sachsen-Anhalt, Sachsen und Brandenburg allein auf Vorgeschichte bzw. Archäologie konzentrieren. Das Landesmuseum Thüringen bezieht seinen besonderen Charakter dagegen von dem barocken Residenzschloss Heidecksburg in Rudolstadt, in dem es untergebracht ist.

[3] The Pomeranian State Museum combines exhibitions on geology and regional history with a painting gallery, while the state museums of Saxony-Anhalt, Saxony and Brandenburg are devoted to prehistory and/or archeology. On the other hand, the Thuringian State Museum has a very particular character due to its location in the baroque Heidecksburg Palace in Rudolstadt.

richtung von Landesmuseen (wie etwa das Pommersche Landesmuseum Greifswald)[3] als auch mit Hilfe repräsentativer kulturhistorischer Landesausstellungen (wie etwa die Ausstellung *Otto der Große, Magdeburg und Europa* 2001 in Magdeburg)[4] gezielt ein breiteres historisches Fundament für die verschüttete Identität der Sachsen, Sachsen-Anhaltiner, Thüringer, Brandenburger und Bewohner Mecklenburg-Vorpommerns gelegt, reichte die in der DDR vermittelte Geschichtsperspektive doch oftmals kaum über die Arbeiterbewegung des 19. und 20. Jahrhunderts bzw. die Zeit des Bauernkrieges hinaus. Erst in den achtziger Jahren hatte der „Arbeiter- und Bauernstaat" zögerlich begonnen – auch mit Hilfe großer Ausstellungen –, Luther und die Reformation in Deutschland oder Friedrich II. und das Preußentum für das eigene Geschichtsverständnis zu „entdecken".

Die relativ späte Gründung des Hauses der Geschichte Baden-Württembergs (1992 erstmals mit einer Ausstellung hervorgetreten, seit 2002 in einem eigenen Gebäude in Stuttgart beheimatet) als erstes seiner Art in der Bundesrepublik[5] belegt zugleich, dass auch in den alten Bundesländern die Potenzen musealer Präsentationen für die Stiftung regionaler Identitäten lange Zeit unterschätzt wurden. Strittig waren sie im regionalen Rahmen dagegen kaum, während sie im nationalen Zusammenhang – im In- wie Ausland – lange Zeit kritisch beäugt wurden. Insbesondere wenn es sich dabei um die museale Hinterfragung der von Deutschland im 20. Jahrhundert ausgelösten beiden Weltkriege und ihrer katastrophalen Folgen für die Menschen in ganz Europa handelt. Hier war man, wie das Beispiel der *Wehrmachtsausstellung* belegt (1995–99 und 2001–04 als Wanderausstellung in 45 Orten gezeigt[6]), über 50 Jahre nach dem Ende des Zweiten Weltkrieges im eigenen Land immer noch schnell mit dem Vorwurf der „Diffamierung der Deutschen"[7] bei der Hand. Heftige nationale wie internationale Diskussionen lösten auch die Bemühungen des Bundes der Vertriebenen aus, mit einem „Zentrum gegen Vertreibung" zugleich eine ständige Präsentation der

as well as to a comprehensive national identity. Reunified Germany during the 1990s provides a good example in this respect. In the federal states formerly constituting the GDR, a number of state museums were established (such as the Pomeranian State Museum in Greifswald)[3] and a number of large exhibitions focusing on cultural history were mounted (such as the 2001 exhibition *Otto the Great, Magdeburg and Europe in Magdeburg*)[4] with the specific aim of providing a broader historical foundation in regard to the identities of the inhabitants of Saxony, Saxony-Anhalt, Thuringia, Brandenburg, and Mecklenburg-Western Pomerania. The historical perspective cultivated in the GDR period had often not extended far beyond the workers' movements of the nineteenth and twentieth century and/or the Peasants' Revolt. It was only in the 1980s that the East German "Workers and Peasants' State" slowly began – also by means of large-scale exhibitions – to discover the significance of Luther and the German Reformation, and Friedrich II and the age of Prussian dominance in terms of its own historical heritage.

The relatively late establishment of the House of History in the south-western German state of Baden-Württemberg (it held its first exhibition in 1992, and is located in its own building in Stuttgart since 2002), the first history museum of its kind in Germany,[5] shows that even in Western Germany the importance of museum presentations for regional identity was long underestimated. Instances in which such regionally based presentations were developed have rarely attracted controversy. By contrast, exhibitions based around national identity were long regarded critically, particularly when it came to the analysis of the two world wars triggered by Germany in the twentieth century, and their catastrophic consequences for people throughout Europe. For instance, even fifty years after the end of the Second World War, the *Wehrmachtsausstellung* (German Army exhibition), a traveling exhibition presented in 1995–99 and 2001–04 in forty-five locations,[6] was accused of "defaming the Germans."[7] Vehement

---

[4] Weitere Landesausstellungen widmeten sich Sachsen im Europa der Reformationszeit (Torgau 2004), dem Land der Residenzen (Thüringen 2004), der Himmelsscheibe von Nebra (Halle 2005), Elisabeth von Thüringen (Eisenach 2007) oder aktuell der mittelalterlichen Handelsstraße Via Regia (Görlitz 2011).

[4] Other regional exhibitions include Saxony in Europe during the Reformation (Torgau 2004), Land of Residences (Thuringia 2004), The Forged Sky (Halle 2005), Elisabeth of Thuringia (Eisenach 2007) and Via Regia, an exhibition currently being shown in Görlitz focusing on the medieval road used above all by traders.

[5] Das dezentrale Haus der Bayerischen Geschichte wurde zwar bereits 1983 gegründet, veranstaltet aber Ausstellungen in ganz Bayern (bisher über 200).
[6] The "House of Bavarian History" was already founded in 1983. Since this time it has presented guest exhibitions in over two hundred locations in Bavaria.

Vertreibungsgeschichte der Deutschen nach 1945 zu errichten. Sie wurden durch die von dem „Zentrum" 2006 in Berlin veranstaltete Ausstellung *Erzwungene Wege* noch weiter angefacht. Eine andere Ausstellung zum Thema, die unter dem Titel *Flucht, Vertreibung, Integration* ein halbes Jahr zuvor im Haus der Geschichte in Bonn (und anschließend auch in Berlin und Leipzig) präsentiert wurde, zeigte dagegen angemessene Wege auf, sich dem strittigen Thema mit musealen Mitteln zu nähern. Auf ihrer Basis wird nun in Berlin, durch eine unselbstständige Stiftung innerhalb des Deutschen Historischen Museums, ein „sichtbares Zeichen" dazu errichtet werden.

Das Deutsche Historische Museum war 2010/11 auch Veranstalter der Ausstellung *Hitler und die Deutschen. Volksgemeinschaft und Verbrechen*, die mit über einer Viertelmillion Besuchern bewies, welch großes Interesse an der Auseinandersetzung mit dem Nationalsozialismus in Ausstellungen hierzulande vorhanden ist, auch wenn es in diesem Fall für die Besucher oft mehr zu lesen als zu sehen gab.

Spektakuläre historische Themen werden aktuell auch in anderen Medien, insbesondere in Film und Fernsehen (Stichwort: Doku-Dramen), immer wieder erfolgreich aufbereitet. Die große Resonanz, die diese medialen Geschichtspräsentationen finden, (ver)führt Kuratoren und Gestalter von historischen Ausstellungen partiell dazu, immer stärker Show-Effekte und spielerische Elemente in ihre Konzepte mit einzubeziehen. Stark im Wachsen begriffen sind in historischen Ausstellungen ebenfalls der Einsatz medialer und interaktiver Elemente – selbst bei der musealen Aufbereitung älterer Epochen, aus denen keine medialen Zeugnisse übermittelt sind. In diesem Umfeld die Balance zwischen Streben nach (immer mehr) Attraktivität und Seriosität zu halten wird eine der zentralen Herausforderungen an historische Ausstellungen in den nächsten Jahren bleiben.

Bernd Lindner

national and international discussions were also triggered by the efforts of the German Federation of Expellees (BdV) to establish a Center against Expulsions, and a permanent exhibition of the history of the expulsion of Germans after 1945. This reaction was further fomented by the exhibition *Erzwungene Wege* (Coerced Paths) mounted by the "center" in Berlin in 2006. By contrast, an exhibition on the same subject entitled *Flucht, Vertreibung, Integration* (Flight, Expulsion, Integration), which was shown six months before in the House of History in Bonn (and subsequently in Berlin and Leipzig) pointed to more appropriate ways of dealing with this theme in a museum context. This exhibition has provided a basis for the decision by an independent foundation to establish a visible symbol dedicated to this theme within the German Historical Museum.

In 2010/11 the German Historical Museum also organized the exhibition *Hitler and the Germans. Nation and Crime*, which was seen by over a quarter of a million visitors, proving that there is a great interest in Germany in exhibitions dealing with National Socialism, even though in this case there was often more for visitors to read than to actually see.

Currently, historical themes are also significantly represented in other media, particularly film and television (in the latter case especially in the form of docudramas). The widespread response that these historical presentations are attracting is partially leading (or seducing) curators, and designers of historical exhibitions to increasingly integrate "show" effects, and playful elements into their concepts. On a more general level, media and interactive elements are also increasingly finding their way into historical exhibitions – even in exhibitions devoted to long-ago eras in which such media did not exist. Given the availability of such tools, maintaining a balance between the aspiration to (ever greater) attractiveness while assuring a level of seriousness, will remain one of the central challenges for history exhibitions in the coming years.

Bernd Lindner

---

⁶ Die Ausstellung wurde vom Hamburger Institut für Sozialforschung erarbeitet und war heiß umstritten. Wissenschaftler warfen ihr u.a. unpräzise Quellenangaben einzelner Fotografien vor. 1999 zurückgezogen, wurde sie durch eine unabhängige Historikerkommission überprüft und zeigte danach mehr Text- und weniger Bilddokumente.

⁶ The exhibition was put together by the Hamburg Institute of Social Research. Its first version attracted particular controversy. It was accused of imprecise information on the origin of several of the photographs used. In 1999 the organizers withdrew the exhibition, and it was examined by an independent historical commission. The second version subsequently included more textual, and less pictorial documents.

⁷ „Wie Deutsche diffamiert werden", in: *Bayernkurier* vom 22. Februar 1997.
⁷ "Wie Deutsche diffamiert werden, in: *Bayernkurier*," February 22, 1997.

Pommersches Landesmuseum Greifswald:
14 000 Jahre Pommern – eine Ausstellung zur Geschichte einer Region
The Pomeranian State Museum in Greifswald: Fourteen Thousand Years
of Pomerania – An Exhibition Devoted to the History of a Region

1996 gründeten die Bundesrepublik Deutschland, das Land Mecklenburg-Vorpommern, die Hansestadt Greifswald, die Universität Greifswald, die Stiftung Pommern Kiel sowie die Pommersche Landsmannschaft die Stiftung Pommersches Landesmuseum. Die Stiftung hat mehrere Aufgaben: „Vergangenheit und früheres Leben sowie Geschichte, Kunst und Kultur der (…) Provinz Pommern (…) [zu] bewahren und dokumentieren", „in besonderer Weise einen Beitrag zur Verständigung und Versöhnung mit der Republik Polen und ihren Menschen" zu leisten sowie „die historischen Verbindungen Pommerns zu den Anrainerstaaten der Ostsee, namentlich zu Schweden und Dänemark, wieder sichtbar und lebendig werden [zu] lassen".
2005 wurde das Museum eröffnet. In der Abteilung Landesgeschichte werden auf 1 700 Quadratmeter die Entwicklung der Landschaft, Kultur und Leben, die große Politik, aber auch die kleinen Besonderheiten der Region erfahrbar gemacht.
Ein „Pommersches Landesmuseum" kann vor dem Hintergrund der wechselvollen Geschichte Pommerns nur in enger Kooperation mit polnischen und skandinavischen Einrichtungen agieren. So arbeiten im Wissenschaftlichen Beirat und den Stiftungsgremien auch Vertreter dieser Länder.
Mehrere Fragen mussten vor Beginn der Arbeit am Konzept geklärt werden: Welches Ordnungsprinzip wählen? Welchen geografischen Raum abdecken? Wann anfangen und wann aufhören?
Mit einem chronologischen Rundgang haben wir uns für eine klassische Präsentationsform entschieden: Zeitenübergreifende Darstellungen anhand ausgewählter Themen, wie sie in jüngster Zeit mehrfach umgesetzt worden sind, können reizvoll sein. Wir glauben jedoch, dass der klassische Weg für die Besucher letztlich gewinnbringender ist, da

The Pomeranian State Museum Foundation was established in 1966 by the Federal Republic of Germany, the State of Mecklenburg-Vorpommern, the Hanseatic city of Greifswald, the University of Greifswald, the Pomerania Kiel Foundation, and the Pomeranian Territorial Association. The many tasks performed by the foundation include "preserving and documenting the past, former life, history, art and culture of … the Province of Pomerania … making a special contribution to achieving reconciliation and good relations with the Republic of Poland and its inhabitants," and "illustrating and bringing to life the historical links between Pomerania and the states bordering the Baltic, particularly Sweden and Denmark." The museum was opened in 2005. The Department of Regional History, which has been assigned 1,700 meters of floor space, is not only devoted to the culture, life, landscape, and major political developments in the region, but also presents many Pomeranian particularities. In view of Pomerania's diverse history, a regional museum can only act in close cooperation with Polish and Scandinavian institutions. As such, representatives of both these countries work on its advisory board and the foundation's committees.
Several questions had to be clarified before we could begin working on the concept: Which organizational principle should be used? Which geographical region should be covered? When should the exhibition start and end?
We selected a traditional presentational form based on a chronological tour of the exhibition. The theme-based presentations of recent years, especially those that span across historical periods can be attractive, however we nevertheless believe that, in the end, a traditional approach brings greater benefits to visitors since it is linked to a familiar organizational pattern. Accounts that jump from one period to the next are

---

Historische Ausstellungen
Historical Exhibitions

Pommersches Landesmuseum
Greifswald Pomeranian State Museum
in Greifswald
Rakower Straße 9
17489 Greifswald

Direktor Director:
Dr. Uwe Schröder
Autoren / Kuratoren / Wissenschaftliches
Team Authors / Curators / Research Team:
Dr. Uwe Schröder, Dr. Stefan Fassbinder,
Heiko Wartenberg, Birte Launert,
Bettina Pfaff

er an vertraute Ordnungsmuster anknüpft. Zeitenspringende Darstellungen verwirren oft. Der Rundgang versammelt unmittelbar nebeneinander Gemälde, kunstgewerbliche und alltagsgeschichtliche Objekte, Archivalien, Münzen usw. Wir sind überzeugt, dass nur so ein Bild einer Epoche entsteht. Die Einbeziehung archäologischer Funde bis in die jüngsten Zeitabschnitte hinein ist noch ungewöhnlich.

Bei der Wahl des chronologischen Startpunktes kamen z. B. das erste Auftreten des Menschen um 12 000 v. Chr. oder das Auftauchen des Namens „Pommern" in den Schriftquellen in Frage. Da sich die Kulturgeschichte einer Region nicht unabhängig von den physischen Gegebenheiten entwickelt, beginnt unser Rundgang noch früher mit einer Abteilung zur Entstehung der Landschaft und wird mit dem Wegfall der Grenzkontrollen nach dem Beitritt Polens zum Schengener Abkommen 2007 enden.

Sobald man sich mit der Darstellung regionaler Geschichte in schriftlose Zeiten begibt, stellt sich die Frage nach der Abgrenzung des Territoriums. In der Steinzeit gab es noch kein „Pommern". Wir haben uns aus pragmatischen Gründen entschieden, die preußische Provinz Pommern als Arbeitsgebiet zu wählen.

Nach diesen Vorentscheidungen mussten die Themen ausgewählt werden. Ein Museum ist kein begehbares Geschichtsbuch. Vollständigkeit kann auch nicht annähernd erreicht werden und wäre sehr ermüdend. Wir entscheiden deshalb nach drei Kriterien, die nicht immer alle erfüllt sein müssen:

1. Historische Bedeutung:
Wenn die Geschichte Pommerns erzählt wird, muss auch der Zweite Weltkrieg behandelt werden.

2. Pommersche Besonderheiten:
Der Dreißigjährige Krieg betraf ganz Mitteleuropa. Aber nur in Pommern landete der schwedische König Gustav II. Adolf 1630 mit seiner Flotte.

3. Exponatlage:
Ein Museum wird über die Präsentation originaler historischer Objekte definiert. Text, Grafik, Modelle, Rauminszenierungen und Medien haben nur unterstützende Funktion.

often confusing. Our tour presents paintings, applied art, everyday historical objects, archival materials, and coins right next to each other. We are convinced that this is the only way to allow a coherent picture of an era to emerge. It is still quite unusual to include archaeological finds, especially in the most recent periods.

Various points in time seemed possible as chronological starting points for the exhibition: the arrival of humankind around 12,000 BC, such as the first mention of the word "Pomerania" in written sources. However, since the cultural history of a region does not develop independently of physical conditions, our tour begins even earlier, in a section devoted to the origins of the landscape. It ends with the lifting of the border controls after Poland entered into the Schengen Agreement in 2007.

When exhibition designers consider how to portray regional history in periods before writing, they confront the question of how to demarcate a territory. Pomerania did not yet exist during the Stone Age. So, for pragmatic reasons, we chose the Prussian Province of Pomerania as the focus of our work.

After making these preliminary decisions, we had to select the subject areas. A museum is not a history book that people can step into. Museums cannot even come close to providing a complete account of history – this would be tiresome anyway. For this reason we based our decisions on three criteria – though all three did not always need to be met at the same time:

1. Historical significance:
When the history of Pomerania is told, the Second World War must be considered as well.

2. Pomeranian peculiarities:
The Thirty Years' War affected all of Central Europe, but it was only in Pomerania that the Swedish king Gustav II Adolf landed his fleet in 1630.

3. Exhibits: A museum is defined by the fact that it presents original historical objects. Texts, graphics, models, spatial presentations, and media play only a supporting role. Due to this focus on exhibits, other fields

Architektur Architecture:
Gregor Sunder-Plassmann

Ausstellungsgestaltung, Grafik- und Corporate Design, Medienkonzeption
Exhibition Design, Graphic Design, Corporate Design and Media Concept:
BERTRON SCHWARZ FREY

Entwurfsleitung Head of Design:
Prof. Ulrich Schwarz
Ausführungsplanung
Planning and Execution: Anja Kilian
Ausstellungsgrafik Graphic Design:
Aurelia Bertron

Diese Orientierung an den Exponaten lässt z. B. Ideen- oder Verfassungsgeschichte in den Hintergrund treten. Auf der anderen Seite rechtfertigen attraktive Exponate manches historisch weniger relevante Thema. Bei der Wahl der Präsentationsformen ist die extreme Heterogenität des Publikums zu beachten: Vom Heimatforscher über Badeurlauber, die vor Regen flüchten, bis hin zur unfreiwillig anwesenden Jugendgruppe. Da wir möchten, dass alle das Haus zufrieden verlassen, bieten wir verschiedene Zugänge zu den historischen Themen an: attraktive Exponatpräsentationen, klassische Modelle – sogar Zinnfiguren-Dioramen –, humorvolle Bildergeschichten, Rauminstallationen, Filme, selten neue Medien, spielerische Präsentationen, haptische und akustische Erlebnisse usw.

Noch größer ist die Herausforderung bei den Texten. Diese müssen kurz, allgemeinverständlich, frei von Fremdwörtern und Fachbegriffen, aber dennoch fachwissenschaftlich korrekt, präzise und lehrreich sein. Zudem wünschen sich Besucher klare Aussagen: „Wie war es denn nun im Mittelalter?" Die Diskussion verschiedener Thesen ist ebenso ausgeschlossen wie ergänzende Informationen in Fußnoten. Die Herausforderung für den Textautor besteht darin, sich erst das ganze Wissen zu einem Thema anzueignen, um es dann in wenigen Sätzen unter Beachtung der genannten Kriterien wiederzugeben. Wer zum Beispiel einmal versucht hat, ein Thema wie das mittel-

such as the history of ideas and constitutional history recede into the background. On the other hand, attractive exhibits may justify many topics that have less historical relevance.

We also had to consider the audience's extreme heterogeneity when selecting the presentational forms. Visitors range from local historians to seaside vacationers seeking to escape rainy weather to youth groups who do not come voluntarily. Because we want all our visitors to be satisfied with their visit to the museum, we offer different ways of learning about the historical subjects: attractive exhibits, traditional models (even dioramas of tin figures), amusing picture stories, spatial installations, films, playful presentations, as well as tactile and aural experiences. Only rarely do we use new media.

Texts pose an even greater challenge. They must be short, comprehensible to a general audience, and free of foreign words and specialized terms. At the same time, they must be scientifically precise, correct, and instructive. In addition, visitors want clear messages: "What was life like in medieval times?" There is no room to discuss different theses or provide supplementary information in footnotes. Authors face the challenge of first having to learn all there is to know about a subject, and then presenting this knowledge in just a few sentences taking into account the aforementioned criteria. For example anyone who has tried

---

Goldring von Peterfitz/ *Piotrowice*, 500–600 n. Chr.
Der Ring aus 1,8 kg Gold wurde wahrscheinlich als Opfergabe an die Götter im Moor versenkt. Nach seiner Auffindung um 1900 zierte er einen Pferdewagen, dann eine Gaststätte als „Messing"-Ring.

Gold ring by Peterfitz/ *Piotrowice* between 500–600 AD
The ring was made out of 1.8 kilograms of gold, and was probably sunk in the moor as an offering to the gods. After its rediscovery in 1900 it first graced a horse and wagon, and then a restaurant as a "brass ring."

Croy-Teppich, Peter Heymanns, Stettin 1554
Der Teppich aus der Regierungszeit Herzog Philipps I. (1532–1560) ist ein Bekenntnis zur Reformation und zugleich ein Denkmal der engen Verbundenheit des sächsischen und pommerschen Fürstenhauses.

alterliche Ablasswesen Besuchern ohne kirchlichen Hintergrund zu erläutern und dabei weder den Blickwinkel der Zeit noch heutige Wertungen außer Acht zu lassen – ganz zu schweigen vom Verzicht auf konfessionelle Polemik –, weiß, was ich meine. Diese Aufgabe wird oft unterschätzt.

Ein regionalgeschichtliches Museum steht noch vor einer weiteren Herausforderung. Einerseits kommen Besucher – z. B. Schulklassen –, für die ein Thema wie „Die mittelalterliche Stadt" Neuland ist. Diese fordern allgemeine Informationen. Auf der anderen Seite haben wir Besucher, die schon lange wissen, was eine mittelalterliche Stadt auszeichnet, und bei uns erfahren möchten, wie die spezifisch pommersche Entwicklung verlief. Wir haben uns für ein mehrstufiges Textsystem entschieden.

1. Leittexte: fünf bis acht pro Abteilung (z. B. Mittelalter), zwei bis vier kurze Sätze.
2. Haupttexte: ein bis fünf pro Thema (bzw. Leittext), ein bis drei kurze Absätze.
3. Exponattexte: standardisierte Informationen zu allen Exponaten, ab und zu weitere Erläuterungen mit maximal zwei Sätzen.
4. Texte an allen Abbildungen, Modellen usw., die neben dem Titel auch zwei bis drei erläuternde Sätze umfassen können.
5. Historische Zitate, auch als Gestaltungsmittel einsetzbar.
6. Gelegentlich zusätzliche Informationen, meist umfangreiche Faktensammlungen. Diese Texte sind verborgen, z. B. in einer Schublade.

to explain a subject such as the medieval system of indulgences to visitors without a religious background, or who has attempted to include past perspectives and present-day values – while avoiding denominational polemics – knows what I am talking about. The difficulty of the task is often underestimated.

A museum of regional history like ours faces an additional challenge. On the one hand, it is visited by groups such as school classes for whom topics like "The Medieval City" is new ground; they require general information. On the other hand, it attracts people who are familiar with the special features of a medieval city and come to learn more about specific Pomeranian developments. To meet these needs we selected a multistage text system.

1. Overarching texts: Five to eight per department (e.g., Middle Ages), consisting of two to four short sentences.
2. Main texts: One to five per subject (or overarching text), consisting of one to three short paragraphs.
3. Exhibit texts: Standardized information about all the exhibits, occasionally with additional explanations no more than two sentences long.
4. Texts about all the images, models, etc., which may include two to three explanatory sentences in addition to the title.
5. Historical quotes that are sometimes used as design elements.

Croy Tapestry, Peter Heymann,
Stettin 1554
The tapestry from the reign of Duke
Philip I (1532–1560) is a commitment to
the Reformation and also a remembrance
of the closeness of the Saxon and
Pomeranian royal houses.

Kürassierhelm mit Durchschlagsloch,
1620/1670
Ein Helm bot Schutz, doch das Gewicht
der Rüstung und der Hitzestau machten
das Kämpfen und Marschieren oft zur
Qual; und kugelsicher war sie auch nicht.

Cuirassier's helmet with puncture,
1620/1670
A helmet offered protection, but the
weight of the armor and the heat
accumulation while fighting and marching
often made wearing them quite unpleasant; and it also was not bulletproof.

So ist es uns gelungen, eine große Fülle an Informationen anzubieten, ohne dass sie den Besucher erschlagen. Gerade die Exponat- und Abbildungstexte sind dabei hilfreich. Allerdings ist der Aufwand, mehrere tausend Objekte zu beschriften und rechtzeitig zu kalkulieren hoch. Bei vielen Exponaten muss erst wissenschaftlich gearbeitet werden, um wirklich Aussagen zur Datierung, Herkunft, Nutzung usw. machen zu können. Das Gleiche gilt für historische Zitate, die sich gelegentlich bei näherer Überprüfung als gut erfunden erweisen. Mit zahlreichen Schaubildern, Texten, Modellen usw. haben wir uns für einen didaktischen Ansatz entschieden. Der Besucher soll durchaus etwas über Pommern lernen. Dass dabei möglichst alle Sinne angesprochen werden müssen, ist eine alte, aber nicht überholte Maxime. Da die meisten Besucher in ihrer Freizeit unser Haus aufsuchen, sogar Geld dafür ausgeben, muss das Lernen so gestaltet werden, dass es zu einem gerne wiederholten Erlebnis wird. Kognitives und ästhetisches Erleben müssen sich gegenseitig stützen. Es entspricht dabei unserem Selbstverständnis, dass die Exponate im Mittelpunkt stehen. Es gibt eine „Aura des Originals", die wir sowohl fördern als auch nutzen möchten. Didaktik und Gestaltung sind dafür verantwortlich, dass diese Aura erfahren, im Augenblick als beglückend empfunden und günstigenfalls noch lange nachhallt und -wirkt.

Stefan Fassbinder

6. Occasionally additional information, mostly in the form of comprehensive collections of facts that are hidden from view, e.g. in a drawer.

This system has enabled us to provide a large amount of information without overwhelming our visitors. The exhibit and image texts are particularly helpful. On the other hand, it is important to give ample consideration to just how much time is needed to create texts for several thousand objects. Many exhibits require research work in order to determine the date, origin, and use of an object. The same applies to historical quotations, which occasionally turn out to be entirely fictitious when they are checked.

We decided to take an educational approach that makes use of numerous charts, texts, and models. We want our visitors to learn something about Pomerania. Engaging all the senses is an old but not outdated principle. Since most of our visitors come to the museum in their spare time – even spending money on admission – we must structure learning in such a way that it is an experience that they want to repeat. Cognitive and aesthetic experience must be mutually supportive. These goals reflect our understanding of our work as being focused on the exhibits. There exists an "aura of the original" that we would like to promote and utilize. Education and design ensure that this aura is experienced and perceived as uplifting and that, in the ideal case, it lives on and resonates for a long time to come.

Stefan Fassbinder

Historische Ausstellungen
Historical Exhibitions

Pommersches Landesmuseum
Greifswald The Pomeranian State
Museum in Greifswald

Dauerausstellung Permanent Exhibition
Träger Supporting Institution:
Stiftung Pommersches Landesmuseum
The Pomeranian State Trust
Foto Photo:
Armin Wenzel

Ausstellungsfläche Exhibition Area:
1 900 m²

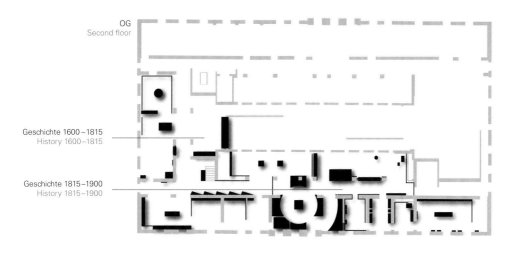

OG
Second floor

Geschichte 1600 – 1815
History 1600–1815

Geschichte 1815–1900
History 1815–1900

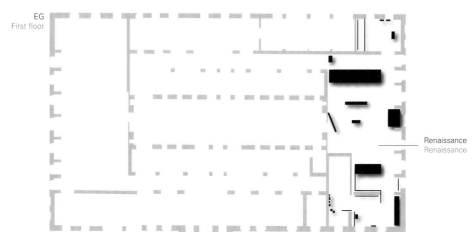

EG
First floor

Renaissance
Renaissance

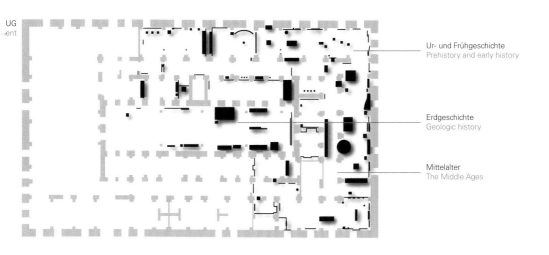

UG
ent

Ur- und Frühgeschichte
Prehistory and early history

Erdgeschichte
Geologic history

Mittelalter
The Middle Ages

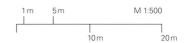

1 m   5 m   M 1:500

10 m   20 m

Farbkonzept

Das Farbkonzept für das Pommersche Landesmuseum folgt nicht der gängigen Systematik der farblichen Codierung von Themen oder Abteilungen. Vielmehr stellt es atmosphärische Anforderungen in den Fokus der Gestaltung. Die Festlegung der Farben für die einzelnen Gebäude und Ausstellungsteile erfolgte unter Berücksichtigung der Bestandsfarben mit dem Ziel, die Eleganz der Architektur zu unterstreichen. So entstand ein komplexes Farbklima, das das Gebäude als Ganzes behandelt und alle Ausstellungskomponenten mit einbezieht.
Der Rundgang beginnt im Untergeschoss, einem Gewölbekeller. Eine starke Farbgebung setzt hier Akzente und trennt die sehr unterschiedlichen Themengebiete. Im Erdgeschoss und in der anschließenden Gemäldegalerie bildet eine reduzierte, auf die Kunstpräsentation abgestimmte Farbpalette den Hintergrund für die Exponate.
Die kabinettartigen Räume im Obergeschoss und Ausstellungssegmente, die Aspekte des Wohnens, Lebens und Arbeitens behandeln, sollten „eingerichtet" wirken. Die darauf abgestimmten Farben berücksichtigen auch die Tageslichtpräsentation in diesem Bereich.

The Color Scheme

The color scheme for the Pomeranian State Museum does not follow the usual scheme of color coding the topics or departments. Rather, the focus is placed on the atmospheric design requirements. The selection of the colors for the different buildings and parts of the exhibition took into account the component colors with the aim to emphasize the elegance of the architecture. The result was a complex color scheme that treats the building as a whole – inclusive of all the exhibition components. The tour begins in the basement which is a vaulted cellar; here strong overtones and coloring accent the area which serves to separate the different exhibition themes. On the ground floor and the adjoining art gallery a reduced color palette was selected in order to match it to the colors of the exhibition background in which the works are presented. The cabinet-like spaces in the first floor and exhibition areas that have to do with living, everyday life, and work should look as if they are "lived in." The selected colors were coordinated to complement the natural lighting in this area.

OG 2nd floor Keim 9482	S 757 kobaltblau/cobalt bl

| J 70 sahara/sahara |
| EG First floor Keim 9482 |

Gemäldegalerie Art Gallery Brillux 4104 Pflaume 1:30	Brillux 57.06.09	Brillux 57.06.09
Seidenbespannung/covering of silk	Seidenbespannung/covering of silk	Leder schwarz/leather black

Bestand Kellergewölbe/Stein
existing construction: vault of basement/stone

S 631 neptunblau/neptune blue

Historische Ausstellungen
Historical Exhibitions

Pommersches Landesmuseum
Greifswald The Pomeranian State
Museum in Greifswald

Ausstellungsbauten und Informationsflächen in abgestimmten Farbabstufungen

Exhibition buildings and information areas in coordinated shades of color

S 139 tiefschwarz / dark black	S 2 taubenblau / dove blue	S 95 weiß / white

B 34 anthrazit / anthracite

EG
First floor
Keim 9493

7.06.09

fgrün / sedge green	F 5 ginstergelb / broom yellow	E 8 gelborange / orange	S 139 tiefschwarz / dark black

Nextel-Farbpalette für Ausstellungsbauten
Keim classic für Wandanstriche
Brillux für Wandanstriche
Weiß geschlämmte Eiche
Schwarzes Kernleder

Nextel color palate for exhibition
constructions and showcases
Keim classic wall paint
Brillux wall paint
white matte oak
black saddle leather

Die Illustrationen zeigen den gleichen Inhalt auf vollkommen verschiedene Weise und richten sich damit an verschiedene Zielgruppen.

The illustrations depict the same content in a completely different way and are thereby directed to different target groups.

Historische Ausstellungen
Historical Exhibitions

Pommersches Landesmuseum
Greifswald The Pomeranian State
Museum in Greifswald

Bildnachweis Illustration:
Flemming Bau, Ralph Kaiser

Foto Photo:
Juraij Lipták

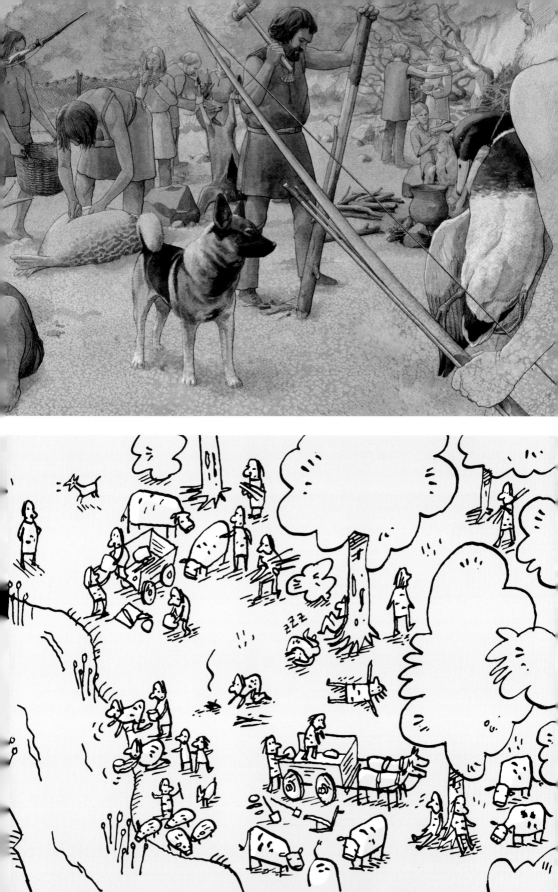

Die Exponate beziehen ihre Wirkung durch die Art der Präsentation in Sondervitrinen mit speziell auf das Exponat abgestimmter Beleuchtung. Den Gesamteindruck bestimmt jedoch die Architektur des Gewölbes, in die sich die Ausstellung harmonisch einfügt.

The exhibits relate their effects through the way in which they are presented, namely in special showcases with special lighting specifically selected for the exhibition. However, the vault's architecture determines the overall impression in which the exhibition is harmoniously included.

Historische Ausstellungen Historical Exhibitions	Lichtplaner Lighting Designer: Dinnebier Licht Einleuchten Lighting: Ringo T. Fischer	Ausstellungsbau Exhibition Construction: Arthur Jaschek GmbH & Co. KG
Pommersches Landesmuseum Greifswald The Pomeranian State Museum in Greifswald		

ommern im Umbruch

Die Materialwahl kontextualisiert und konnotiert die ausgestellten Objekte. Eine Wandbespannung aus Rohseide als Hintergrund für ein relativ kleines und ohne besondere Präsentation unscheinbar wirkendes Gemälde hebt zusammen mit der fokussierten Beleuchtung den Wert besonders hervor.
Die Abtrennung eines thematisch definierten Teils der Ausstellung in Form eines mit Eichenpaneelen ausgeschlagenen Kabinetts definiert den Raum als eigenständige Einheit.

The material selection contextualizes and connotes the exhibited objects. A wall fabric made of raw silk fabric as a background for a relatively small and seemingly unimpressive painting raises the value with the use of focused lighting.
The separation of a thematically defined part of the exhibition in the form of an oak paneled and lined cabinet further defines the space as a separate entity.

Maria an der Fensterbank, Umkreis Quentin Massys (um 1465–1530), Niederlande, um 1510
Das Bild aus dem Wolgaster Schloss diente als Andachtsbild und Zeugnis der Kunstsinnigkeit Herzog Philipps I.

Virgin and Child (1510), style of Quentin Massys (c.1465–1530), The Netherlands
The Andachtsbild (Christian devotional painting) originates from the Wolgast Castle and signifies Duke Philip's interest in the arts.

Zwischen 1580 und 1605 schufen wenigstens drei bisher unbekannte Künstler die Portraits von sieben Töchtern und Gemahlinnen der pommerschen Herzöge.
Between 1580 and 1605 at least three previously unknown artists painted the portraits of the seven daughters and wives of the Pomeranian Duke.

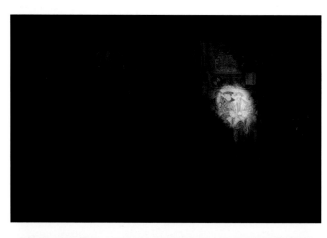

Im Museum geht es darum, dass Objekte Geschichten erzählen. Das Zentrum der Ausstellung bestimmt der 6,80 Meter lange und 4,32 Meter hohe Croy-Teppich, der wegen seiner Qualität als einzigartiges kulturhistorisches Zeugnis der Reformation gilt. Zu sehen sind die Familie des pommerschen Herzogs und die des kursächsischen Fürstenhauses, in der Mitte der predigende Martin Luther und im Hintergrund die Reformatoren Philipp Melanchthon und Johannes Bugenhagen. Der Teppich gibt Anlass, verschiedene Geschichten zu erzählen: „Ernst Bogislaw verfasst sein Testament", „Ob eine sächsisch-pommersche Ehe glücklich enden kann", über „Eine pommersche Prinzessin" oder über „Das Loch im Teppich".
Erzählt werden diese Geschichten von dem an die Auswahl gekoppelten Audioguide.
Eine spezielle Lichtinstallation beleuchtet die auf dem Teppich abgebildeten Bilder synchron zu der erzählten Geschichte.

In a museum objects that tell stories are found. The center of the exhibition is dominated by a Croy tapestry measuring 6.8 meters long and 4.32 meters high which due to its high quality serves as a unique cultural and historical witness of the Reformation. On display are the families of the Pomeranian Duke and the Saxon Royal House; in the middle a preaching Martin Luther and in the background the reformers Philipp Melanchthon and Johannes Bugenhagen. The tapestry tells different stories: "Ernst Bogislaw writing his will," "Whether a Saxon-Pomeranian marriage can end happily," "A Pomeranian princess," or "A hole in the tapestry." The stories are told through an audio guide; a special light installation illuminates the images depicted on the tapestry that corresponds to the story.

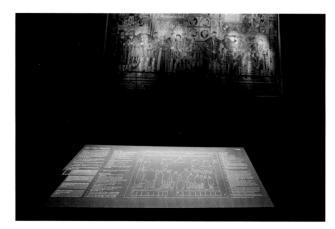

Historische Ausstellungen
Historical Exhibitions

Pommersches Landesmuseum Greifswald The Pomeranian State Museum in Greifswald

Croy Teppich, Stettin 1554, des niederländischen Künstlers Peter Heymann
Croy tapestry, Stettin 1554, from the Dutch artist Peter Heymann

Seite 224 f. Page 224 f.:
Vitrine zum Thema Dreißigjähriger Krieg
Display case from the Thirty Years' War exhibit

Das interaktive Exponat vermittelt spielerisch, wie die Landvermessung funktionierte. Über eine Winkelfunktion lässt sich die Entfernung eines Objektes ermitteln. Mit Hilfe des Lasers oder über Kimme und Korn kann dann der jeweilige Winkel abgelesen und errechnet werden.

The interactive exhibit playfully provides information on topics such as how land surveying is done. Visitors are able to determine the distance of an object through a trigonometric function. Either with the help of the laser or through notch and bead sights the corresponding angle is read and subsequently calculated.

Fotos Photos:
WHITEvoid interactive art & design

Von A bis Z: Die Vitrine enthält viele, sehr unterschiedliche Ausstellungsstücke, die alle Facetten des Kunsthandwerks repräsentieren. Wären alle Objekte gleichzeitig sichtbar, so entstünde ein Eindruck der Unordnung. Die Aufteilung in durch Klappen verschlossene Segmente macht die Präsentation interessanter und bezieht die Besucher mit ein.

From A to Z: The cabinet contains many, very different exhibit objects that represent all facets of the arts. If all the objects were visible at one time the impression of disorder would prevail. By dividing it into segments that are closed by flaps the presentation is made more interesting and enticing to the visitors.

Stralsunder Fayencen, 1767/1790
Die Stralsunder Fayencemanufaktur gehörte zu den führenden Einrichtungen Europas.
Stralsund Faience, 1767/1790
The Stralsund fiaence factory belonged to one of the leading institutions in Europe.

Schädel eines rauchenden Soldaten (1678/1715), Tonpfeifen (1600/1800), Stralsund
Der schwedische Soldat hatte wohl ständig eine Pfeife im Mund. Das hinterließ tiefe Spuren an den Zähnen.

A smoking soldier's skull (1678/1715), clay pipes (1600/1800), Stralsund
The Swedish soldier probably always had a pipe in his mouth; the constant smoking left behind deep marks on the teeth.

„Einer, der studiert, muss notwendig viel Tabak rau[chen]
damit die Geister nicht verloren gehen, oder dass sie anfang[en]
umzulaufen, weshalb der Verstand ... wieder möge erwec[ken]
worauf alles klar und deutlich dem Geiste überliefer[t]
Zwanzig Pfeifen an einem Tag zu rauchen, ist nicht z[u]

Johann Ignatius Worb Beintema van Peima, Tabacologia, 1690

Tabak

Der Tabak kam aus Amerika nach Europa. Anfangs meist geschnupft,
18. Jahrhundert das Rauchen langer Tonpfeifen durch. Studenten bev[orzugten]
besonders lange, mit Bändern verzierte Pfeifen, die bis zum Boden re[ichten]
Um den Bedarf zu decken, wurde auch in Pommern Tabak angebaut.
In Greifswald gab es 1708 drei Tabakspinner.

Tonpfeifen, 1600/1800
Fundort: Stralsund

Pfeifenreiniger in Pferdeform, 1700/1730
Fundort: Stralsund

Schädel eines Pfeife rauchenden Soldaten, 1678/1715
Fundort: Stralsund

Der schwedische Soldat hatte wohl ständig eine Pfeife im Mund.
Das hinterließ tiefe Spuren an den Zähnen.

Student rauch[t]

U

Z

C
.
G

S

R
.

E

J   L   N   [?]   F

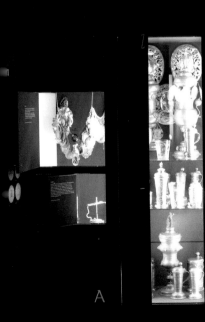

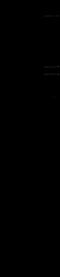

A

M   H   I

Der Schornstein
raucht

Sommer

„Jetzt ist die Zeit,
und Stunde da,
wir ziehen nach Amerika!"

einmal will
glücklich leben,
s sich auf die Reis'
ach Brasilien begeben!"

Das Königreich Württemberg. 1806–1918 Monarchie und Moderne
The Kingdom of Württemberg 1806–1918: Monarchy and Modernity

Am 1. Januar 1806 wurde Württemberg zum Königreich erhoben, am 30. November 1918 verzichtete der letzte württembergische König auf die Krone. Aus Anlass des 200-jährigen Jubiläums der Erhebung im Jahr 2006 behandelte die Große Landesausstellung *Das Königreich Württemberg. 1806–1918 Monarchie und Moderne* diese 112 ereignisreichen Jahre. Mit der historischen Ausstellung wurde der neue Wechselausstellungsraum des Landesmuseums Württemberg eröffnet, der im dritten Obergeschoss der Dürnitz im Alten Schloss in Stuttgart seinen Platz gefunden hat.

Den Ausgangspunkt der Ausstellung bildeten die territorialen Veränderungen zu Beginn des 19. Jahrhunderts, die aus dem kleinteiligen Flickenteppich den Flächenstaat Württemberg entstehen ließen. Leitmotiv war die Darstellung der grundlegenden Neuerungen in Politik, Wirtschaft, Kultur und Gesellschaft, die das Land teilweise bis heute prägen. Als Weg in die Moderne wurden diese Entwicklungen, quasi als Motto, schon im Untertitel der Ausstellung angesprochen. In dem nur durch zentrale Stützen gegliederten Ausstellungsraum galt es, die Themen in einer Art zu verorten, zusammenzufassen und zu strukturieren, die den Besuchern einen leicht verständlichen Zugang ermöglichte. Die gestalterische Lösung bestand in einem Rundgang mit zwei deutlich voneinander abgesetzten Teilen: Der erste folgte einem chronologischen Aufbau und stand unter dem Titel „Von der Monarchie zur Republik", der zweite war thematisch gegliedert und trug die Überschrift „Vom Agrarland zur Industriegesellschaft".

Den Auftakt bildeten die Kroninsignien – Krone und Szepter – und der Thron, umgeben von den Staatsportraits der vier Könige, die in den 112 Jahren regierten. Im Anschluss wurden diese Monarchen in einer Abfolge von vier Räumen vorgestellt. Hier standen das Selbstverständnis des jeweiligen Königs, sein persönliches Umfeld aber auch seine individuellen Vorlieben und Eigenarten im Vordergrund. Die Gestaltung

The kingdom of Württemberg was established on January 1, 1806 and lasted until November 30, 1918, when the last king abdicated. The exhibition *The Kingdom of Württemberg 1806–1918: Monarchy and modernity* was organized to mark the 200th anniversary of the kingdom's establishment and charted the 112 eventful years of its existence. This historical exhibition was also the first to be mounted in the Württemberg State Museum's new space for temporary exhibitions on the third floor of the *Dürnitz* (main hall) in Stuttgart's *Altes Schloss* (old castle).

The exhibition's point of departure was the territorial changes taking place at the beginning of the nineteenth century that led to the emergence of the unified territorial state of Württemberg. A leitmotif of the presentation was the fundamental political, economic, cultural, and social changes that occurred during this period and that in part continue to shape the region's identity today. As indicated by the exhibition's subtitle, these developments were interpreted as marking Württemberg's transition into the modern age.

The basic task facing the exhibition's designers was to find a way of using an exhibition space articulated only by central supports that would enable them to position, integrate, and structure these themes so as to make them easily accessible for visitors. The design solution they arrived at consisted in a tour made up of two distinctly separate parts. The first was structured chronologically and entitled "From Monarchy to Republic," while the second was organized thematically and entitled "From Farmland to Industrial Society."

The beginning of the tour through the exhibition was marked by the royal insignia – crown und scepter – and the throne, which were framed by official portraits of the four kings who ruled during the 112 years of the kingdom's existence. From there visitors moved through a sequence of four spaces in which they were introduced to

Historische Ausstellungen
Historical Exhibitions

Das Königreich Württemberg. 1806–1918
Monarchie und Moderne
Kingdom of Württemberg 1806–1918:
Monarchy and Modernity

Landesmuseum Württemberg
The Württemberg State Museum
Schillerplatz 6
70173 Stuttgart

Gesamtleitung Project Coordinator:
Prof. Dr. Cornelia Ewigleben,
Direktorin Director

der Kabinette schuf allein durch Anlage und Farbgebung eine dem jeweiligen Zeitstil gemäße Atmosphäre. Ohne in Konkurrenz zu den Objekten zu treten, vermittelte sich auf diese Weise die kühle Strenge des Empire bei König Friedrich ebenso wie der Hang zum Exotischen bei König Wilhelm I. Wurde der König Karl gewidmete Bereich mit dem historistischen Mobiliar aus Russland vom Repräsentationsbedürfnis seiner Gattin, der Zarentochter Olga, dominiert, so wirkte der Raum für König Wilhelm II., den letzten württembergischen König, nüchtern und unauffällig. Er entsprach damit ganz dem Bild, das die Bevölkerung seinerzeit von „Württembergs geliebtem Herrn" hatte. Parallel zu dieser eher ästhetisch narrativ bestimmten Abfolge war ein Bogen gespannt, der den Besuchern die herausragenden historischen Ereignisse jener Jahre in einer kontinuierlichen Darstellung mit Objekten und erklärenden Texten vermittelte. Diese didaktische Übersicht wurde mit den Kriegen ab 1806 eingeleitet und mit dem Ersten Weltkrieg beendet. Ein Ausstellungsbereich zu den Vereinheitlichungen im Königreich Württemberg, zu dessen Eingliederung ins Deutsche Kaiserreich bis hin zum Untergang infolge der Revolution von 1918, begleitete diese Chronologie.

Als bewusste Zäsur und räumliches Scharnier in der Darstellung der beständigen Entwicklung erschien im ersten Ausstellungsteil eine zentrale Einheit, die dem Land und seiner Bevölkerung gewidmet war.
Ein von diesem Bereich aus begehbares Kabinett war jenen Bürgern vorbehalten, die trotz aller staatlichen Versuche, soziale Maßnahmen zur Bekämpfung der Armut einzuleiten, auswanderten und ihr Glück in anderen Ländern suchten. In Ermangelung von Originalobjekten wurde in dieser Einheit mit Reproduktionen gearbeitet, die in der Vergrößerung und gezielten Anpassung an die räumliche Situation effektvolle Wirkungen erzielten. Sowohl die Präsentation als auch die gewählte Form der Reproduktion machte deutlich, dass es sich hier nicht um Originale handelte.
Der erste Ausstellungsteil endete mit einem kleinen Raum, in dem Alltagsgegenstände

each of these monarchs. The focus here was on the self-conception of the respective ruler, his personal surroundings, and his individual preferences and idiosyncrasies. The design of the display cabinets, their construction and coloring, already conveyed an atmosphere in keeping with the style of the period under consideration. As a result, while the exhibits themselves remained the focus of the exhibition, the framework in which they were presented also contributed to communicating, for example, the cool austerity that characterized the rule of King Friedrich and the penchant for the exotic associated with the reign of King Wilhelm I. Whereas the area devoted to King Karl, with its lavish Russian furnishings, was dominated by the sense of prestige cultivated by his wife Olga, the Russian tzar's daughter; the space dedicated to King Wilhelm II, the last king of Württemberg, was characterized by an atmosphere of sobriety and understatement, corresponding to Wilhelm's popular image at the time as "Württemberg's beloved gentleman."

Parallel to this sequence organized around aesthetic and narrative concepts, the exhibition also spanned across the period in the form of a continuing presentation of artifacts and explanatory texts providing insights into the outstanding historical events associated with this epoch. This didactic overview began with the wars fought from 1806 onwards and ended with the First World War. This chronology was further supplemented by an exhibition area devoted to the unification of the kingdom of Württemberg, its integration into the German empire, and its collapse as a result of the German Revolution of 1918.

The first part of the exhibition included a centrally located section dedicated to the region and its population, and conceived as a caesura and a point of spatial articulation within the presentation of Württemberg's ongoing development. A cabinet that visitors could walk into was dedicated to those members of the population who, in spite of all attempts by the state to introduce social changes to combat poverty, emigrated in order to try their luck elsewhere. Due to a

| Konzeption und wissenschaftliche Leitung Concept and Scientific Management: Dr. Rainer Y, Dr. Fritz Fischer | Ausstellungsorganisation und wissenschaftliche Mitarbeit Exhibition Organization and Scientific Research: Dr. Edith Neumann | Wechselausstellung Temporary Exhibition: Ausstellungszeitraum Exhibition Duration: 22. September 2006 bis 4. Februar 2007 September 22, 2006 until February 4, 2007 |

und persönliche Erinnerungsstücke einen sentimentalen Rückblick auf die Könige und Königinnen boten. In ironischer Brechung orientierte sich die Gestaltung dieses Bereichs an sakralen Reliquienkammern. Ziel dieses ersten Ausstellungsteils war es, den Besuchern einen sehr komprimierten historischen Überblick zu geben, der mit unterschiedlichen Blickwinkeln und Erzählformen arbeitete und daher verschiedensten Interessen gerecht werden konnte. Als Hinweis auf die allgemeinen technischen Errungenschaften im 19. Jahrhundert wurde in diesem Ausstellungsabschnitt exemplarisch das Medium Bild eingesetzt, dessen Entwicklung sich von gemalten Portraits über Fotografien bis zum Stummfilm verfolgen ließ. Die Ausstellungsgestaltung war wesentlicher Teil der Interpretation, indem sie beispielsweise Objekte und Ausstellungsbereiche allein durch Platzierung und Kontext so begreifbar machte, dass die jeweils beabsichtigte Aussage deutlich wurde. Plakative Überschriften erleichterten darüber hinaus Zuordnung und Orientierung.

Die zweite Ausstellungshälfte setzte mit einem Raum ein, der die Anmutung einer Gemäldegalerie hatte. Als Pendant zu den vier Königsportraits am Anfang des ersten Teils waren auch hier vier Gemälde, allerdings mit Figurengruppen, zu sehen. Sie

lack of original artifacts, this section featured reproductions, which were enlarged and specifically positioned within the space to enhance their effect. Both the presentation and the form of reproduction underlined the fact that the artifacts were not the true originals.

The first part of the exhibition concluded with a small space in which everyday items and personal keepsakes offered a sentimental view of the kings and queens of Württemberg. An ironic twist was added by the design of this space, which recalled a chamber used to store sacred relics.

The aim of this first part of the exhibition was to give the visitors a very condensed historical overview, one that worked with different perspectives and narrative forms and thus appealed to a wide range of interests. To underscore the technological achievements of the nineteenth century, this section also focused on the development of the image as a medium, from the painted portrait to photography and silent film. Again, the design of the exhibition was fundamental to the interpretation being presented, with artifacts and sections positioned and contextualized in a way that clearly underscored the intended statement. Compelling titles were also used as an aid to classification and orientation.

Die Krone des Königreichs Württemberg
Als Herrschaftszeichen und Symbol der 1806 errungenen Königswürde war die Krone zentraler Bezugspunkt der Ausstellung.

The crown of the Kingdom of Württemberg
The crown serves as a secular sign of power and symbol of the 1806 kingship and therefore a central point of reference within the exhibition.

Kronprinzessin Olga von Württemberg (1822–1892)
Das Bild zeigt die nachmalige Königin von Württemberg, deren Schönheit gerühmt wurde, als anmutige Erscheinung von hoheitsvoller Unnahbarkeit. Das Portrait wurde 1856 bei Franz Xaver Winterhalter in Auftrag gegeben.

vertraten den Klassizismus, die Genremalerei, den Realismus und den Beginn der Abstraktion. Schlaglichtartig wurde anhand der Kunstentwicklung das sich im Verlauf des 19. und frühen 20. Jahrhunderts radikal verändernde Menschenbild dargestellt. Diese bewusst plakativ gestaltete Einheit lebte gerade von der konzisen Reduzierung.

Der Duktus der sich daran anschließenden thematischen Bereiche setzte sich deutlich von dem des ersten Teils der Ausstellung ab. Den Inhalten angepasste Raumbilder, die ganz unterschiedliche Assoziationen erlaubten und deren Gestaltung sehr viel stärker auch mit grafischen Elementen und Reproduktionen arbeitete, waren hier in einer freieren Struktur in eine Abfolge gebracht. So bildete beispielsweise ein Brötchen aus den Hungerjahren von 1816/17 den Einstieg zur Abteilung über die Entwicklung der Landwirtschaft, und bei der Darstellung der neuen Mobilität wurde mit raumgreifenden, bewegten Bildern in Form von historischem Filmmaterial gearbeitet. Die akustische Einblendung von Alarmsignalen entsprach den ausgewählten Objekten, die vom Posthorn über die Automobilhupe bis zur Fahrradklingel reichten.

Die Einheiten zur Gewerbeförderung und zur Industrialisierung führten zu einem „Schaufenster", das die neue Welt des

The second part of the exhibition began with a space that suggested a painting gallery. The four royal portraits that marked the beginning of the first section were emulated by another four paintings, though in this instance featuring groups of figures and respectively representing classicism, genre painting, realism, and the beginning of abstraction. This "snapshot" of the development of pictorial art illustrated the radical changes undergone by the image of the human being over the course of the nineteenth and early twentieth centuries. The effectiveness of this impressively designed section was based not least on its minimalist character.

The thematic segments that followed exhibited a very different character from the first part of the exhibition. The images created to address the respective themes, which evoked diverse associations and made much more use of graphic elements and reproductions, were arranged in a more loosely structured sequence. For example, a bread roll from the famine years of 1816/17 was used to mark the entrance to a section devoted to the development of agriculture, and a segment on the new mobility made use of expansive, moving images taken from historical film material. Exhibits were also accompanied by their characteristic

Princess Olga of Württemberg
(1822–1892)
The picture depicts what subsequently became the Queen of Württemberg – initially well-known for her beauty; though here her once-graceful likeness has been replaced by a more majestic aloofness. The portrait was commissioned in 1856 by Franz Xaver Winterhalter.

Das Plakat *Ausstellung für Elektrotechnik und Kunstgewerbe* für die Stuttgarter Ausstellung von 1896
Inbegriff des Fortschrittsglaubens

The exhibition poster for the Stuttgart Engineering, and Art Design Exhibition of 1896
The epitome of a total belief in progress

Warenkonsums präsentierte. Bereiche, die sich mit den Lebensverhältnissen der Arbeiter und des Bürgertums beschäftigten, schlossen sich an. Ein besonderer Schwerpunkt war dem Kulturleben gewidmet: Der bürgerliche Salon, Vereinsgründungen, das neue Presse- und Verlagswesen oder die Entstehung von Museen machten deutlich, dass mit dem sich herausbildenden Wirtschafts- und Bildungsbürgertum neuartige Institutionen in dessen Verantwortung entstanden sind. Städtebauliche Entwicklungen wurden am Beispiel Stuttgarts aufgezeigt. Am Ende des zweiten Teils stand die Frage nach der württembergischen Identität. Die Entstehung von Trachten- und Heimatvereinen, der Bau des Ulmer Münsterturms und der Kult um Eberhard im Bart bildeten hier einige der Facetten.

Der Rundgang endete mit einem historischen, aus Zeppelin und Flugzeug aufgenommenen Film, der aus der Zeit um 1920 stammt. Der Blick auf Württemberg aus der Vogelperspektive, noch ohne die Zerstörungen durch den Zweiten Weltkrieg, bildete einen betont emotionalisierenden Abschluss.

Die Darstellung wurde durch ein „Pantheon des schwäbischen Geistes" ergänzt, das den Dichtern des Landes gewidmet war und das sich aus Platzgründen auf einem anderen Stockwerk befand. Aber auch weitere Ausstellungsräume des Landesmuseum Württemberg waren thematisch auf den Gegenstand „Königreich Württemberg" abgestimmt worden, sodass das ganze Haus in diese Große Landesausstellung eingebunden war.

Rainer Y

acoustic signals, such as post horns, car horns, and bicycle bells. The sections dedicated to the promotion of commerce and industrialization led to a "display window" presenting the new world of commodity consumption. This was in turn connected with areas dealing with the living conditions of the workers and the bourgeoisie. A particular focus was given to cultural life. References to the bourgeois salon, citizens' associations, the founding of newspapers and publishing houses, and the establishment of museums made it clear that the formation of a new economic middle class and associated intelligentsia also led to the emergence of new institutions. Urban development during the period was also shown using Stuttgart as an example.

The last section of the exhibition's second part took into consideration the question of a Württemberg identity. The emergence of associations devoted to traditional forms of dress and local history, the construction of the Ulm Minster steeple, and the cult around Eberhard I of Württemberg all formed facets of this segment.

The tour ended with a historical film taken from a zeppelin and an airplane in the 1920s. This bird's eye view of Württemberg prior to the destruction wrought by the Second World War provided an emphatically emotional conclusion.

The presentation was supplemented by a "Pantheon of the Swabian Mind" dedicated to the region's writers, which was located on another floor due to a lack of space. For the duration of the exhibition, the theme of the "Kingdom of Württemberg" also featured in other spaces within the Württemberg State Museum, with the result that the entire museum complex was integrated into this major state exhibition.

Rainer Y

Historische Ausstellungen
Historical Exhibitions

Das Königreich Württemberg. 1806–1918
Monarchie und Moderne
Kingdom of Württemberg 1806–1918:
Monarchy and Modernity

Träger Supporting Institution:
Landesmuseum State Museum

Ausstellungsfläche Exhibition Area:
Ausstellung Exhibition: 1 000 m²
Kinderausstellung Children's Exhibition:
120 m²

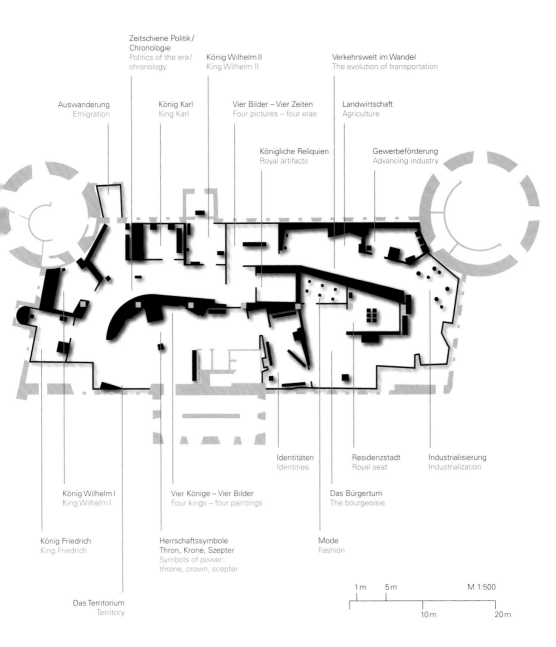

Auswanderung
Emigration

Zeitschiene Politik/
Chronologie
Politics of the era/
chronology

König Karl
King Karl

König Wilhelm II
King Wilhelm II

Vier Bilder – Vier Zeiten
Four pictures – four eras

Königliche Reliquien
Royal artifacts

Verkehrswelt im Wandel
The evolution of transportation

Landwirtschaft
Agriculture

Gewerbeförderung
Advancing industry

Identitäten
Identities

Residenzstadt
Royal seat

Industrialisierung
Industrialization

König Wilhelm I
King Wilhelm I

Vier Könige – Vier Bilder
Four kings – four paintings

Das Bürgertum
The bourgeoisie

König Friedrich
King Friedrich

Herrschaftssymbole
Thron, Krone, Szepter
Symbols of power:
throne, crown, scepter

Mode
Fashion

Das Territorium
Territory

1 m   5 m   M 1:500

10 m   20 m

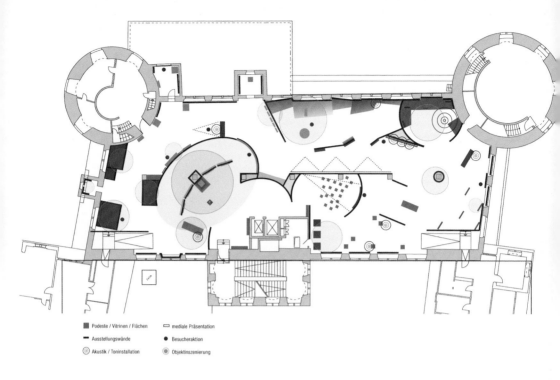

Die Grundidee der Ausstellungsgestaltung definiert für jeden
Themenbereich Räume und Bereiche mit eigener Atmosphäre.
Um die Fülle an Themen mit den
dazugehörenden Exponaten zu
strukturieren, wurde ein System
aus Ausstellungswänden, Vitrinen und Podesten entwickelt.
Die Modelle dienen dazu, die
Proportionen des Entwurfes zu
erproben.

The basic idea of the exhibition
design defines for each theme
rooms and areas each with their
own atmosphere. In order to
better organize and structure
the plethora of topics with the
respective exhibit, a system of
exhibition walls, display cases
and pedestals were designed.
The models were utilized to test
the proportions of the design.

Historische Ausstellungen
Historical Exhibitions

Das Königreich Württemberg. 1806–1918
Monarchie und Moderne
Kingdom of Württemberg 1806–1918:
Monarchy and Modernity

Wissenschaftliche Mitarbeiter
Research Assistants:
Dagmar Bayer M.A., Dr. Christoph
Bittel, Thomas Brune M.A., Nicole
Deisenberger M.A., Andrea Hartl M.A.,
Dr. Sabine Hesse, Dr. Ulrich Klein, Viktoria
Klutmann M.A., Frank Lang M.A.,
Dr. Irmgard Müsch, Dr. Annette Schmidt,

Dr. Gustav Schöck, Dr. Heike Schröder,
Leo von Stieglitz M.A.
Projektsteuerung Project Management:
Jan-Christian Warnecke, Georg Schnepper
Kinderausstellung Children's Exhibition:
Karin Birk M.A., Maria Rothhaupt-Kaiser,
Melanie Jakob

Ausstellungsgestaltung
Exhibition Design:
BERTRON SCHWARZ FREY

Entwurfsleitung Head of Design:
Prof. Claudia Frey
Ausführungsplanung
Planning and Execution: Cathrin Runge
Grafik Graphic Design: Alexander Hartel

Wettbewerbsentwurf
Competition entry

Im ersten Ausstellungsraum öffnet sich dem Besucher eine repräsentative Szene, die mit den großen Staatsportraits der vier Könige die Entwicklung von der Monarchie zur Moderne veranschaulicht.

In the first exhibition room a representative scene greets the visitor in which the full-length state portraits of the four kings illustrates the development of the monarchy to modernity.

Historische Ausstellungen
Historical Exhibitions

Das Königreich Württemberg. 1806–1918
Monarchie und Moderne
Kingdom of Württemberg 1806–1918:
Monarchy and Modernity

Fotos Seiten 244–246
Photos pages 244–246:
Hendrik Zwietasch/Peter Frankenstein,
Landesmuseum Württemberg

Fotos Seiten 250–253 und 255–263
Photos pages 250–253 and 255–263:
Hendrik Zwietasch

zu Ludwigen und ... , Hohenberg und ...
Schmiedefeld, Sontheim, Hohenberg und ...
Herr zu Heidenheim, Justingen, Rottweil, Heilbronn,
Hall, Aldorf und Adelmannsfelden ꝛc. ꝛc.

entbieten allen Unsern lieben und getreuen Dienern und Unterthanen
Unsere Königliche Gnade.

Licht Lighting:
Ringo T. Fischer

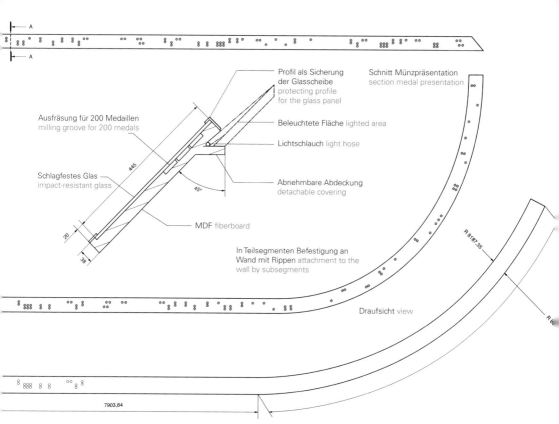

Profil als Sicherung
der Glasscheibe
protecting profile
for the glass panel

Schnitt Münzpräsentation
section medal presentation

Ausfräsung für 200 Medaillen
milling groove for 200 medals

Beleuchtete Fläche lighted area

Lichtschlauch light hose

Schlagfestes Glas
impact-resistant glass

Abnehmbare Abdeckung
detachable covering

445

45°

20

36

MDF fiberboard

In Teilsegmenten Befestigung an
Wand mit Rippen attachment to the
wall by subsegments

R 8187,35

Draufsicht view

7903,84

Geschichte vermittelt sich meist chronologisch anhand von Jahreszahlen, zugeordneten Fakten und herausragenden Ereignissen. Um dies greifbar zu machen, helfen Objekte, die mit der Zeit ihrer Entstehung in Verbindung gebracht werden. Besonders interessant wird die Vermittlung von Geschichte, wenn die ausgewählten Objekte selbst zum Bedeutungsträger werden. Im abgebildeten Beispiel erklärt sich die Chronologie mittels Münzen und Medaillen.
Die Präsentation kommt durch die eingefrästen runden Flächen ohne weitere Befestigung aus. Gesichert werden die Objekte durch eine aufgesetzte Glasplatte.

History is usually conveyed on a chronological basis utilizing facts and figures, and facts associated with outstanding historical events. In order to makes these events more tangible it is helpful to provide objects in conjunction with the time of their origination. Teaching history is particularly interesting when the selected objects themselves become symbolic. In the illustrated example coins and medals are used to explain the chronology. The presentation is fitted with in-cut rounded surfaces in which it is not necessary to mount the coins; the objects are further secured by a fitted glass top plate.

Historische Ausstellungen
Historical Exhibitions

Das Königreich Württemberg. 1806–1918
Monarchie und Moderne
Kingdom of Württemberg 1806–1918:
Monarchy and Modernity

Haus-in-Haus-Präsentationen zeigen zum Beispiel das Wohnen und den zeittypischen Einrichtungsstil in einem originalgetreu nachgebildeten Raum. Dazu fehlt jedoch in den meisten Fällen der Platz. Wohnräume in Kabinetten als Raumeinblick zu inszenieren, bietet hier die Möglichkeit, einzelne Exponate als Versatzstücke auszustellen. Das räumliche Gesamtbild entsteht durch große hinterleuchtete historische Raumansichten, die durch seitliche Spiegel eine tiefenräumliche Illusion erzeugen.

For example "house within a house" presentations show the living and the typical contemporary décor in a room that has been faithfully recreated. It is usually a lack of space that poses a problem for these type of exhibits. Living spaces presented as an arrangement in a display cabinet offers the possibility to display an exhibit as a "prop." The overall spatial image is created by large backlit historical space views that creates a spacial illusion of depth within the room through the use of side mirrors.

Wand 8 B wall 8 B   Wand 7 B wall 7 B   Wand 10 A wall 10 A

Historische Ausstellungen
Historical Exhibitions

Das Königreich Württemberg. 1806–1918
Monarchie und Moderne
Kingdom of Württemberg 1806–1918:
Monarchy and Modernity

svitrine
lay cases

Wand 10 B wall 10 B

Sicherheitsvitrine
safety display cases

Wand 9 A wall 9 A

Wand 8 B wall 8B

Kabinett König Wilhelm I. –
der „träumende König"
Inszenierung der privaten Räumlichkeiten
in der „Wilhelma"

The display cabinet of King Wilhem I:
"The dreaming king"
Staging of the provare quarters in the
"Wilhelma"

Jeder Ausstellungsbereich erhält ein auf die Exponate abgestimmtes Farbklima, das die Wirkung der Objekte unterstreicht. Dabei sind im Ablauf der Ausstellung einige Bereiche kräftiger, andere wiederum dezent und neutraler gehalten.

Each area of the exhibition is assigned a color scheme that has been coordinated to the exhibits, and which underlines the theme and the relevance of the objects. As a result certain areas of the exhibition require brighter colors while in other areas the colors are kept neutral and discreet.

Historische Ausstellungen
Historical Exhibitions

Das Königreich Württemberg. 1806–1918
Monarchie und Moderne
Kingdom of Württemberg 1806–1918:
Monarchy and Modernity

Kabinett König Karl – „Regent mit mildem Szepter"
Höfische Repräsentation

Display cabinet: King Karl – "Regent with a mild scepter"
Royal representation

Die Exponate stehen für die verschiedenen Ausstellungsthemen und vermitteln sich durch Inszenierung als großes Gesamtbild.

The exhibits represent the various exhibition themes and convey the larger-picture through their staging.

Kabinett Mode im 19. Jahrhundert
Display cabinet: 19th-century fashion

Kabinett König Wilhelm II. –
der „jagende König"
Display cabinet: King Wilhem II –
"the hunting king"

„Die Industrialisierung Württembergs war ein dynamischer Prozess, der mehr und mehr alle und alles erfasste. Er veränderte das Land und brachte Wohlstand und Armut, Arbeit und Frust, Chancen, Freiheiten, Rechte und die bunte und farbige Warenwelt."

„The industrialization of Württemberg was a dynamic process that more and more covered each and everything. It changed the country and brought with it prosperity and poverty, work and frustration, opportunities, freedoms, rights, and the bright and colorful world of commodities."

Historische Ausstellungen
Historical Exhibitions

Das Königreich Württemberg. 1806–1918
Monarchie und Moderne
Kingdom of Württemberg 1806–1918:
Monarchy and Modernity

Thema Industrialisierung
Schlüsselobjekte repräsentieren
verschiedene Fabrikationszweige.

Industrialization
Key objects represent the various
manufacturing sectors.

Die Themen Industrialisierung, Gewerbeförderung und Mobilität sind als technische Entwicklungen eng miteinander verzahnt. Für das Bild der rasenden Entwicklung mit steigender Geschwindigkeit steht die collagenartig gestaltete synchronoptische Wand mit aufprojizierten Bildern von Eisenbahnen, Autos, Flugzeugen, Rädern und Telefonapparaten als Synonym für die Moderne.

The themes of industrialization, economic development, and mobility are closely linked as technical developments. In order to paint a portrait of the rapid development and the ever increasing speed of technological advances a collage-like presentation in which images of trains, cars, planes, bicycles, and telephones as symbols of modernity are projected on the wall.

Historische Ausstellungen
Historical Exhibitions

Das Königreich Württemberg. 1806–1918
Monarchie und Moderne
Kingdom of Württemberg 1806–1918:
Monarchy and Modernity

260

Synchronoptische Darstellung mit
Objekten zum Thema „Verkehrswelt im
Wandel"

A synchronoptic representation of
objects on the evolution of the "World of
Transportation"

Das oberste Stockwerk des
Turmes bietet den Rahmen für
ein „Pantheon des Schwäbischen
Geistes", gewidmet den bedeu-
tenden Dichtern und Denkern des
Landes. Die Inszenierung bedient
sich moderner audiovisueller und
akustischer Medien.

The top floor of the tower
provides the setting for the
"pantheon of Swabian spirit,"
devoted to the great poets
and thinkers of the region. The
production makes use of modern
audio-visual and audio media.

Historische Ausstellungen
Historical Exhibitions

Das Königreich Württemberg. 1806–1918
Monarchie und Moderne
Kingdom of Württemberg 1806–1918:
Monarchy and Modernity

262

Pantheon des Schwäbischen Geistes
Audiovisuelle Installation

Pantheon of the Swabian spirit
An Audiovisual installation

Neues Klostermuseum in Ulm-Wiblingen
The New Monastery Museum in Ulm-Wiblingen

Das ehemalige Benediktinerkloster Wiblingen wurde 1093 von den Grafen Hartmann und Otto von Kirchberg gegründet. Das heutige barocke Erscheinungsbild der Klosteranlage wurde im 18. Jahrhundert geprägt. Die Arbeiten an der barocken Kirche und an den Klosteranlagen waren noch nicht vollendet, als das Kloster 1805 aufgehoben wurde. Um die zentral gelegene frühklassizistische Klosterkirche erstreckt sich die symmetrische Anlage, deren südwestlicher Flügel erst Anfang des 20. Jahrhunderts vollendet wurde.

Von überragender kunsthistorischer Bedeutung ist der berühmte Bibliothekssaal, der von führenden Künstlern des 18. Jahrhunderts ausgestattet wurde. Seit 2006 besitzt die Anlage mit dem „Museum im Konventbau" einen weiteren Anziehungspunkt für Besucher. Einst beherbergte die an den prunkvollen Bibliothekssaal angrenzende Raumflucht im zweiten Obergeschoss die ehemaligen Gästeappartements des Klosters. Hier wird heute zum ersten Mal die Geschichte des Klosters und seiner Gebäude aus einem neuen, ungewohnten Blickwinkel in ansprechender, moderner Gestalt präsentiert. Vor allem die weltlichen Aspekte des klösterlichen Lebens, die finanzielle Seite der Klosterherrschaft und Klosterwirtschaft, nicht die spirituellen

The former Benedictine monastery in Wiblingen was founded in 1093 by the counts Harmann and Otto von Kirchberg. The baroque appearance of the monastery complex dates from the eighteenth century, and work on the baroque church and the monastery buildings had still not been completed when the monastery was closed in 1805. An early classicist monastery church is positioned at the center of the symmetrical complex, the southwestern wing of which was only completed at the beginning of the twentieth century.

The famous library hall is of particular significance in art-historical terms and was decorated by leading artists of the eighteenth century. Since 2006 the monastery museum has provided a further attraction for visitors and is located in the wing adjacent to the magnificent library hall on the second floor, once the site of the monastery's guest apartments.

Here the history of the monastery and its buildings is presented from a new and unusual perspective in an appealing, modern design. Rather than concentrating on the religious aspect, the new museum focuses above all on the worldly facets of monastery life, the financial dealings of its leadership, and the monastery economy. The tension between secular power and spiritual mis-

Historische Ausstellungen
Historical Exhibitions

Neues Klostermuseum in Ulm-Wiblingen
The New Monastery Museum in
Ulm-Wiblingen

Kloster Ulm-Wiblingen
Ulm-Wiblingen Monastery
Schlossstraße 38
89079 Ulm

Zwei Flügel eines spätgotischen Altares
Vermutlich stammen die beiden um
1500 durch den Meister von Sigmaringen vollendeten Gemälde aus der
alten Klosterkirche. Dargestellt sind die
Heiligen Antonius Eremita und Fridolin
von Säckingen.

Aspekte, werden im neuen Museum thematisiert. Die Spannung zwischen weltlicher Herrschaft und geistlicher Sendung zieht sich als roter Faden durch die Ausstellung. Interaktive Stationen und audiovisuelle Präsentationen laden die Besucher zu einer individuellen Spurensuche ein.

Die Hinführung zum Museumsbereich beginnt bereits außerhalb des Gebäudes durch Hinweistafeln und eine große Metallinitiale. Im Treppenhaus wird die Hinleitung ebenso fortgesetzt wie auf dem Flurbereich, der zum Kassenraum und Klostershop führt. Eine abgedunkelte „Zeitschleuse" empfängt die Besucher nach dem Durchqueren des Kassenraumes und lotst sie mit einer Collage aus Klängen und Bildern in die vergangene, facettenreiche Welt der barocken Klosterherrschaft.

In den angrenzenden Räumen werden folgende Bereiche thematisiert: Spiritualität und Herrschaft, Klosterstaat und Klosterherrschaft, Klosterwirtschaft und Finanzen, Wallfahrt, Bau- und Kunstgeschichte, Säkularisation und nachklösterliche Zeit, Wissenschaft und Schule. Im Bibliothekssaal und auf dem Flur, der wieder zum Ausgang führt, wird die Zeit des Klosters als Kaserne Wiblingen dargestellt. Nur wenige Ausstattungsstücke des einst so prächtigen Klosters haben sich bis heute erhalten.

sion is a theme running through the exhibition, and interactive stations and audiovisual presentations invite visitors to embark on an individual search for traces of how this tension was played out.

Visitors are directed towards the museum area outside the building by information panels and large metal initials. The route to the museum continues to be indicated in the stairwell and the vestibule leading to the cash desk and the monastery shop. After passing the cash desk, a darkened "time lock" featuring a collage of sounds and images leads visitors into a past, multi-faceted world ruled by baroque monasteries.

The rooms making up the museum itself present different themes: spirituality and power, monastery state and monastery rule, monastery economy and finances, pilgrimage, building and art history, secularization and the post-monastery period, scholarship and schooling. In the library hall and the vestibule leading to the exit, the period is presented in which the monastery was used as a military barracks.

Only a few of the decorative pieces that once adorned this magnificent abbey have been preserved. Numerous didactic exhibition elements in all the rooms, including stations with audio-texts, help to fill these gaps and make the history of the abbey

Two panels of a late Gothic altar
The two paintings completed in 1500 by the Master of Sigmaringen probably are from the old monastery church. The paintings depict St. Anthony and St. Fridolin of Säckingen.

Kruzifix
Das um 1510 im Umkreis der Michel-Erhart-Werkstatt entstandene Kruzifix hing früher in der Sakristei der Klosterkirche. Die qualitätvolle Arbeit verweist sowohl auf das spirituelle Leben im Kloster als auch auf die zentrale Rolle des Ulmer Raumes für die gotische Schnitzkunst.

The Crucifix
The crucifix crafted in 1510 from the circle of the Michel Erhart workshop was previously hung in the sacristy of the monastery church. The high quality craftsmanship is a testament to both the spiritual life in the monastery and the central role of the Ulm region in Gothic wood carving.

Zahlreiche didaktische Ausstellungselemente in allen Räumen, darunter auch Stationen mit Hörtexten, schließen diese Lücke und machen die Klostergeschichte lebendig. So zeigt eine interaktive Karte die allmähliche Vergrößerung der Wiblinger Klosterherrschaft im Laufe der Jahrhunderte, ihren Zuwachs an Besitz und Rechten, bis sie zu einem kleinen Territorium angewachsen war. Wie detailliert die Beziehungen zwischen Kloster und Untertanen geregelt waren, verdeutlichen die ausgestellten Urkunden. Damit sie besser zu lesen sind, befinden sich neben ihnen deckungsgleiche Übertragungen. In einer Audiovision kann der Besucher die Entwicklung der Klosteranlage von der Romanik bis zum abschließenden Bau des Klausur-Südflügels durch das württembergische Militär 1915–1917 miterleben. Stelen mit Informationen zu Baumeistern, Künstlern und Kunsthandwerkern vertiefen diesen Bereich. Die Forschungen der Mönche werden im Wortsinn durch faksimilierte Blätter und ganze Bücher greifbar, die zum Blättern aus dem Regal genommen werden dürfen. Wer will, kann sich an einem Schreibpult auch selbst als Klosterschüler versuchen. Mit der neu konzipierten Audioguide-Führung können sich die Besucher in der ehemaligen Klosterbibliothek individuell durch den Saal bewegen und sich ganz nach Wunsch und in eigenem Tempo die detailreichen Fresken und Skulpturen erklären lassen.

Gabriele Kleiber

come alive. For example, an interactive map shows the gradual expansion of the Wiblingen monastery's power over the centuries and the increase in its property and rights to the point where it became a small territory in its own right. Exhibited documents illustrate how far-reaching the relationships between the monastery and its subjects were, and they are accompanied by clearly legible reproductions of their contents. An audiovisual presentation provides visitors with an insight into the development of the monastery complex from the Romanesque period to the construction of the southern wing by the Württemberg military between 1915 and 1917. This area is supplemented by steles displaying information on the master builders, artists, and artisans associated with the monastery.

The research carried out by monks is presented on facsimiles of individual sheets and entire books, which can be taken out of their shelves. Visitors are also invited to sit at a desk once occupied by pupils of the monastery school.

The new audio-guide for the exhibition allows visitors to explore the former monastery library individually while listening to explanations of the detailed frescos and sculptures at a tempo of their own choosing.

Gabriele Kleiber

Historische Ausstellungen
Historical Exhibitions

Neues Klostermuseum in Ulm-Wiblingen
The New Monastery Museum in Ulm-Wiblingen

Träger Supporting Institution:
Staatliche Schlösser und Gärten Baden-Württemberg
State Palaces and Gardens of Baden-Württemburg

Ausstellungsfläche Exhibition Area:
Dauerausstellung Permanent Exhibition:
450 m²
Flure Corridor: 250 m²
Bibliothekssaal Library Hall: 270 m²

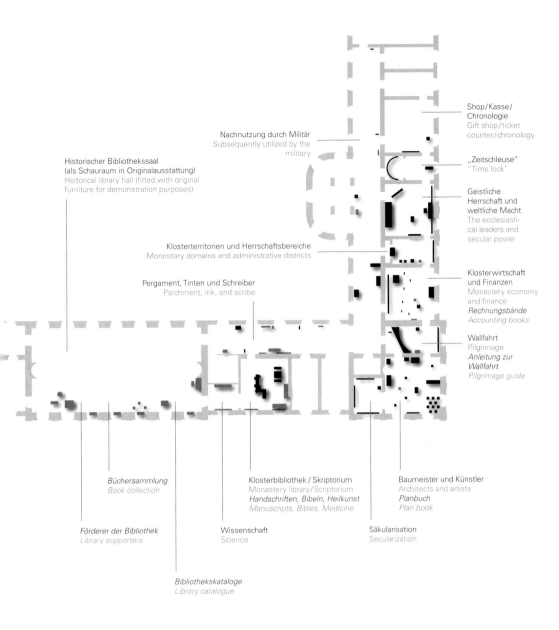

Nachnutzung durch Militär
Subsequently utilized by the
military

Shop/Kasse/
Chronologie
Gift shop/ticket
counter/chronology

„Zeitschleuse"
"Time lock"

Historischer Bibliothekssaal
(als Schauraum in Originalausstattung)
Historical library hall (fitted with original
furniture for demonstration purposes)

Geistliche
Herrschaft und
weltliche Macht
The ecclesiasti-
cal leaders and
secular power

Klosterterritorien und Herrschaftsbereiche
Monestary domains and administrative districts

Klosterwirtschaft
und Finanzen
Monastery economy
and finance
Rechnungsbände
Accounting books

Pergament, Tinten und Schreiber
Parchment, ink, and scribe

Wallfahrt
Pilgrimage
Anleitung zur
Wallfahrt
Pilgrimage guide

Büchersammlung
Book collection

Klosterbibliothek / Skriptorium
Monastery library/Scriptorium
Handschriften, Bibeln, Heilkunst
Manuscripts, Bibles, Medicine

Baumeister und Künstler
Architects and artists
Planbuch
Plan book

Förderer der Bibliothek
Library supporters

Wissenschaft
Science

Säkularisation
Secularization

Bibliothekskataloge
Library catalogue

1 m   5 m   M 1:500

10 m   20 m

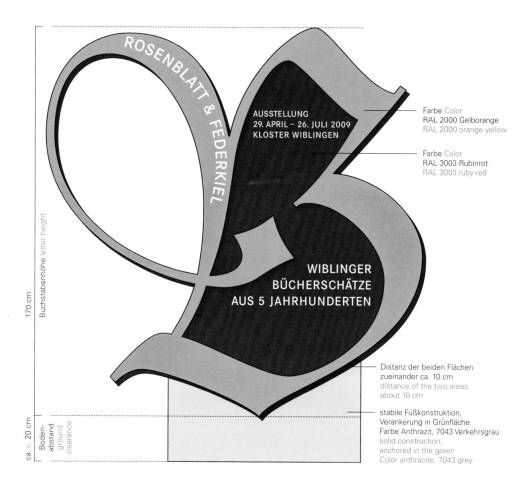

ABCDEFGHIJKLMN OPQRSTUVW

ROSENBLATT & FEDERKIEL

AUSSTELLUNG
29. APRIL – 26. JULI 2009
KLOSTER WIBLINGEN

WIBLINGER
BÜCHERSCHÄTZE
AUS 5 JAHRHUNDERTEN

170 cm | Buchstabenhöhe letter height

ca. c. 20 cm | Boden-abstand ground clearance

Farbe Color
RAL 2000 Gelborange
RAL 2000 orange yellow

Farbe Color
RAL 3003 Rubinrot
RAL 3003 ruby-red

Distanz der beiden Flächen
zueinander ca. 10 cm
distance of the two areas
about 10 cm

stabile Fußkonstruktion,
Verankerung in Grünfläche
Farbe Anthrazit, 7043 Verkehrsgrau
solid construction,
anchored in the green
Color anthracite, 7043 grey

Historische Ausstellungen
Historical Exhibitions

Neues Klostermuseum in Ulm-Wiblingen
The New Monastery Museum in
Ulm-Wiblingen

Dauerausstellung Permanent Exhibition
Wechselausstellung Temporary Exhibition

Eröffnung Opening:
März 2006 March 2006

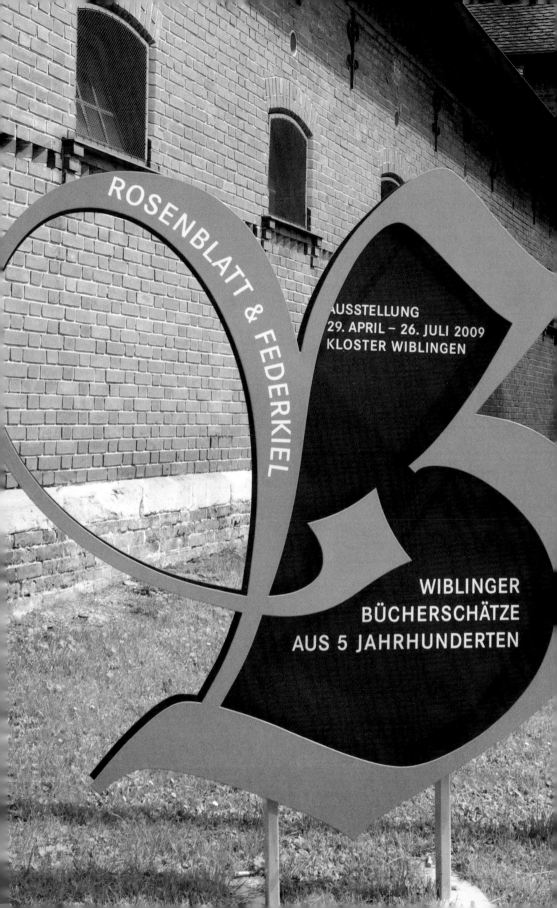

ROSENBLATT & FEDERKIEL

AUSSTELLUNG
29. APRIL – 26. JULI 2009
KLOSTER WIBLINGEN

WIBLINGER
BÜCHERSCHÄTZE
AUS 5 JAHRHUNDERTEN

In der Sonderausstellung „Rosenblatt und Federkiel. Wiblinger Bücherschätze aus fünf Jahrhunderten" leiten Themeninseln durch 500 spannende Jahre Wiblinger Bücher- und Bibliotheksgeschichte. Sie widmen sich der mühsamen Herstellung der Handschriften, den Formen mittelalterlicher Bild- und Textauslegung wie auch Bibliothekaren, Archivaren und Besuchern der Wiblinger Bibliothek des 18. Jahrhunderts.

In the special exhibition "Rose Petal and Quill, Wiblingen's five centuries of book treasures" theme areas take the visitor through 500 years of exciting Wiblingen book and library history. The exhibition is dedicated to the often labor intensive production of manuscripts – the forms of medieval text and pictorial interpretation to as well as librarians, archivists and visitors to the Wiblingen library of the 18th century.

Historische Ausstellungen
Historical Exhibitions

Neues Klostermuseum in Ulm-Wiblingen
The New Monastery Museum in
Ulm-Wiblingen

Ausstellungszeitraum Wechselausstellung
Exhibition Duration Temporary Exhibition:
29. April bis 26. Juli 2009
April 29, 2009 until July 26, 2009

Besonders lichtempfindliche Ausstellungsstücke werden in Vitrinen mit Deckeln aufbewahrt. Sobald der Deckel geöffnet wird, schaltet sich eine schwache Beleuchtung ein. Damit wird die auf das Objekt auftreffende Lichtmenge enorm begrenzt.

Particularly light-sensitive exhibit objects are kept in glass cases with covers. Once the lid is opened the object is automatically softly illuminated. Thus, the enormous amount of light striking the object is limited. This system limits the large amounts of light that are usually used to illuminate an object.

Historische Ausstellungen
Historical Exhibitions

Neues Klostermuseum in Ulm-Wiblingen
The New Monastery Museum in
Ulm-Wiblingen

Gesamtleitung Coordination:
Dr. Gabriele Kleiber
Autoren/Kuratoren/Wissenschaftliches
Team Authors/Curators/Research Team:
Dr. Raimund Waibel, Freier Historiker
Elke Valentin M.A.

Ausstellungsgestaltung
Exhibition Design:
BERTRON SCHWARZ FREY

Besonders hervorzuheben sind die farbig gefassten barocken Stuckdecken, die durch abgetönte Wandfarben eine leuchtende Wirkung erzielen.
Das Beleuchtungssystem erlaubt eine indirekte Ausleuchtung und den Verzicht auf unter Putz verlegten Stromkabeln.

In order to especially highlight the color sculpted baroque stucco ceiling subtly tinted wall colors were used resulting in a illuminating color effect.
The lighting system allows for an indirect lighting and the decision not to use the power cables underneath the plaster.

Eine abwechslungsreiche Raumfolge sorgt für unterschiedliche Stimmungen. Im Vordergrund steht in einigen Räumen die Objektinszenierung, in anderen Klang oder Medien.

The varied room sequences provide for a unique ambience.
In certain areas the object, the staging or setting of the exhibition object, is in the foreground while in others sound or media serves as the main theme.

Entwurfsleitung Head of Design:
Prof. Claudia Frey
Ausführungsplanung
Planning and Execution: Cathrin Runge
Grafik Graphic Design: Alexander Hartel

Fotos Seiten 272/273
Photos pages 272/273:
Martin Duckek

Fotos Seite 265
Photos page 265:
Gesa Bernges, Dr. Felix Muhle

Zwischen Himmel und Erde – Klöster und Pfleghöfe in Esslingen
Between Heaven and Earth – Monasteries and Pfleghöfe in Esslingen

Es war in Esslingen kein Geheimnis, dass die ehemalige Reichsstadt am mittleren Neckar auf eine reiche klösterliche Vergangenheit zurückblicken kann. Doch es ist auch für Kenner der Esslinger Geschichte eine Überraschung, was die Forschungen zur Vorbereitung dieser Ausstellung ergeben haben: In keiner anderen in der Größe vergleichbaren deutschen Stadt gab es im 13. Jahrhundert eine ähnliche Dichte von Bettelordensklöstern wie in Esslingen. Wird noch die sehr hohe Zahl von Wirtschaftshöfen geistlicher Institutionen hinzugezählt, die in Esslingen „Pfleghöfe" genannt werden, rechtfertigt sich das Projekt *Zwischen Himmel und Erde – Klöster und Pfleghöfe in Esslingen* beinahe von selbst. Es handelt sich nicht nur um eine stadtgeschichtliche Episode, sondern um ein Phänomen von überregionaler Relevanz.

Struktur der Ausstellung

Die Ausstellung fand vom 27. September 2009 bis zum 31. Januar 2010 in der Franziskanerkirche sowie im gesamten Stadtraum statt. Den thematischen Schwerpunkt bildete die Zeit des Mittelalters. Dementsprechend standen kirchliche Objekte, städtische und kirchliche Urkunden sowie Bücher vom 12. bis 16. Jahrhundert im Vordergrund.
In den Räumen vor dem Kirchenchor wurde die Geschichte der Stadt in mittelalterlicher Zeit erläutert. Ein zentraler Aspekt war der große Reichtum der Reichsstadt Esslingen, der die vielen Bettelorden veranlasste, sechs Klöster in der Stadt zu bauen. Die Baugeschichte der einzelnen Klöster und ihre Bedeutung für die Stadt wurden ausführlich behandelt. Außerdem wurden die elf Pfleghöfe auswärtiger Klöster vorgestellt – eine außerordentlich große Anzahl. Alle wurden von Klöstern betrieben, die nicht von Bettelorden geführt wurden, zum Beispiel von Zisterziensern oder Benediktinern, aber auch von anderen Orden. Schon in diesem Bereich wurden zur Illustration der Themen einige Objekte gezeigt. Im teilweise noch erhaltenen Lettnerbereich

It is well known that monasteries have played an important role in the history of Esslingen, a former imperial city in Germany's Central Neckar region. However, the research conducted in preparation for this exhibition revealed information that surprised even those well versed in Esslingen's history. During the thirteenth century, no other German city of a comparable size contained as many monasteries run by mendicant orders. Moreover, the city also contained a significant number of Wirtschaftshöfe, or as they are known in Esslingen, Pfleghöfe – urban premises used to conduct legal and commercial business with the city in which they were located that belonged to religious institutions. This historical constellation is not only of interest as an episode in the city's history but as a phenomenon of interregional significance, and it provided the basis for the exhibition *Between Heaven and Earth – Monasteries and Pfleghöfe in Esslingen.*

Structure of the Exhibition

The exhibition took place from September 27, 2009 to January 31, 2010. It was presented across the entire city area, with Esslingen's Franciscan church providing a major venue. The central thematic focus of the exhibition was the medieval period and particular emphasis was accordingly placed on church artifacts, city and church documents, and religious books dating from the twelfth to the sixteenth century.
Esslingen's medieval history was presented in the space in front of the church's choir gallery. A central aspect was the enormous wealth enjoyed by the imperial city of Esslingen during this period, which led to the establishment of six monasteries by mendicant orders in the city. The history of the construction of the individual monasteries and their significance for Esslingen was given comprehensive treatment. The exhibition also presented the eleven Pfleghöfe owned by outside monasteries – an unusually large number for one town. All of them were run

Historische Ausstellungen
Historical Exhibitions

Klöster und Pfleghöfe in Esslingen
Monasteries and Pfleghöfe in Esslingen

Städtische Museen Esslingen
Municipal Museums of Esslingen
Hafenmarkt 7
73728 Esslingen am Neckar

Gesamtleitung Coordination:
Dr. Kirsten Fast
Autoren/Kuratoren/Wissenschaftliches
Team Authors/Curators/Research Team:
Christian Rilling M.A., Dr. Martin Knauer,
Dr. Joachim Halbekann, Dr. Iris Holzwart-Schäfer

wurde das Sujet „Klöster und Pfleghöfe" dann detailliert vorgestellt. Es ging um die Stadt als Bezugsrahmen für die kirchlichen Bauten, um die Themen Betteln und Armut, Wirtschaft, Bildung und Wissenschaft – und um die Architektur der Bauten.

Der Hauptraum der Ausstellung, der Kirchenchor aus der Mitte des 13. Jahrhunderts, war vor allem wegen der vielen in situ erhaltenen Objekte wichtig. Eine unermesslich große Zahl von Objekten in den mittelalterlichen Klöstern und Pfleghöfen in Esslingen, und natürlich nicht nur da, ist während der Reformation und der Säkularisation verlorengegangen. So waren wir sehr froh, im Chor der Franziskanerkirche ausstellen zu können, wo neben dem bedeutendsten Schatz der Kirche, den Glasfenstern, auch noch Totenschilde, Epitaphien, Sakristei- und Tabernakelnischen sowie Wandmalereien vorhanden sind. Das Hauptthema der Ausstellung, „Das spirituelle Leben, die Andacht und die Mystik" wurde im Chor präsentiert. Es war in folgende Themenbereiche unterteilt: „Frauenklöster als Zentren der Mystik", „Ausstattung der Esslinger Klosterkirchen", „Stifter und Stiftungen", „Predigt", „Seelsorge" und „Stundengebet und Messe". Gerade hier wurden sehr viele wertvolle Leihgaben aus deutschen Klöstern, Museen und Privatsammlungen gezeigt. Im letzten Raum der Ausstellung, der Sakristei, konnte vor allem anhand von Funden auf dem Gelände des ehemaligen Karmeliterklosters in Esslingen der Gegenstand „Alltag im Kloster" behandelt werden.

Die Ausstellung in der früheren Franziskanerkirche war indes nur ein Teil des Projekts. Ein Stadtrundgang mit Begleitheft führte zu dem noch weitgehend erhaltenen Dominikanerkloster St. Paul und zu den Standorten der früheren Augustiner-, Karmeliter-, Klarissen- und Dominikanerinnen-Klöster ebenso wie zu den zum Teil erhaltenen elf Pfleghöfen. Das Programm wurde durch Vorträge, Lesungen, musikalische Veranstaltungen, Führungen und Exkursionen zu den Themen der Ausstellung abgerundet.

Neben dem Einführungsbereich der Ausstellung befand sich ein großer museumspädagogischer Raum. Dort wurden regelmäßig

by non-mendicant orders, including Cistercian and Benedictine communities, and this part of the exhibition featured a number of artifacts related to this subject.

The area around the partially preserved rood screen featured a more detailed presentation on the theme of "Monasteries and Pfleghöfe." This part of the exhibition looked at the city as a frame of reference for church buildings and addressed themes such as begging and poverty, education and scholarship, and economic activity – as well as the architecture of the buildings themselves.

The main space used for the exhibition, the choir gallery dating from the middle of the thirteenth century, was significant above all due to the many artifacts preserved there in situ. During the Reformation, an enormous number of objects originally located in medieval monasteries and Pfleghöfe were lost – in Esslingen and of course elsewhere as well. We were therefore extremely pleased to have the opportunity to exhibit in the Franciscan church's choir gallery, which contains not only the church's most significant treasure, its stained glass windows, but also death shields, epitaphs, sacristy and tabernacle niches and murals. The major theme of the exhibition, "Spiritual Life, Devotions and Mysticism," was presented in the choir gallery and divided into the following topics: "Nunneries as Centers of Mysticism," "Furnishings of the Esslingen Monastery Churches," "Sponsors and Endowments," "Homily," "Pastoral Care," and "Liturgy of the Hours and Mass." This part of exhibition featured a large number of valuable loans from German monasteries, museums, and private collections.

The last exhibition space, the sacristy, was devoted to the theme of "Everyday Monastery Life," which was presented using primarily finds from the site of the former Carmelite monastery in Esslingen. The exhibition in the early Franciscan church was only one part of the project. A city tour, for which a specially printed guidebook was produced, led to the largely preserved Dominican monastery of St. Paul and to the locations of former Augustinian, Carmelite, Sisters of St. Clare, and Dominican cloisters

Ausstellungsgestaltung Exhibition Design:
BERTRON SCHWARZ FREY
Entwurfsleitung Head of Design:
Prof. Claudia Frey
Grafik Graphic Design: Christine Zecha
Ausführungsplanung Planning and
Execution: Sebastian Scheller

Ausstellungszeitraum Exhibition Duration:
27. September 2009 bis 31. Januar 2010
September 27, 2009 until January 31,
2010

Wechselausstellung Temporary Exhibition

Führungen und Mitmachprogramme für Kinder angeboten. Außerdem zeigten wir Filme zum klösterlichen Leben heute und hatten am Wochenende häufig Mönche und Nonnen aus Klöstern in Baden-Württemberg zu Besuch, die auch durch die Ausstellung führten. Wichtig für das Thema war, dass die Ausstellung in einem mittelalterlichen Kirchengebäude stattfinden konnte. Sowohl der historische Wert dieses Gebäudes als auch die ästhetische Qualität sollte sich den Besuchern mitteilen. Bei Befragungen wurde dieses auch bestätigt.

Wir kamen mit nur wenigen Kopien aus – einige Kunstwerke konnten nicht verliehen werden, was auch an den schwer zu erfüllenden Klimaauflagen der Leihgeber lag. Die ausgeliehenen Skulpturen, Gemälde, Bücher, Archivalien und kirchliche Objekte mussten größtenteils in Klimavitrinen gezeigt werden. Erwartungsgemäß stellten wir fest, dass gerade die Objekte im Kirchenraum besonders wahrgenommen wurden, sicherlich ein Zusammenspiel dieser Ausstellungsstücke mit ihrem „ehemaligen" Standort. Gerade hier hielt sich das Publikum besonders lange auf und „meditierte" im Chorgestühl oder las in dem Begleitbuch zur Ausstellung. Eine weitere Besonderheit der Ausstellung, die sechs Hörstationen, fand im Chorraum außergewöhnliche Beachtung.

as well is to the eleven, partly preserved Pfleghöfe. The overall program also included lectures, readings, musical events, guided tours, and excursions based on the themes of the exhibition.

A large room adjacent to the entrance to the exhibition functioned as the event's pedagogical headquarters. Here, regular guided tours and participatory programs were offered for children. We also used the space to show films on monastery life today, and to introduce monks and nuns visiting on weekends from cloisters in Baden-Württemberg, who also acted as exhibition guides. It was important for the theme that the exhibition could take place in a medieval church building, since this meant that visitors were directly confronted with the historical value and aesthetic qualities of such structures.

Most of the exhibits were original pieces – a number of artworks could not be borrowed due to the climatic conditions required for their display. The majority of the sculptures, paintings, books, archival materials, and church artifacts lent to the exhibition had to be displayed in climate-controlled display cabinets. As expected, we found that objects displayed inside the church drew particular attention, no doubt due to the interplay between these exhibits and their

Historische Ausstellungen
Historical Exhibitions

Klöster und Pfleghöfe in Esslingen
Monasteries and Pfleghöfe in Esslingen

Fotos Photos:
Peter Frankenstein, Hendrik Zwietasch, Landesmuseum Württemberg The Württemberg State Museum, Städtische Museen Esslingen, Stadtmuseum im Gelben Haus Municipal Museum of Esslingen, City Museum in the "Gelbes Haus"

Die Weiler Pietà, 1471, Landesmuseum Württemberg, Stuttgart
Das einzige (nicht ortsfeste) künstlerische Ausstellungsstück, das sich aus den Esslinger Klöstern erhalten hat. Eine große Skulptur als Beispiel der Frömmigkeits-Praxis in spätmittelalterlichen Frauenklöstern Süddeutschlands.

Die Grundfarben der Ausstellung, Rot und Lila, standen jeweils für die Bereiche Kirche und Pfleghof. Entsprechend waren die Ausstellungssegmente gestaltet, und auch die Grundfarben der Texttafeln waren Rot und Lila – ein Gestaltungselement, das die grauen und beigefarbenen Mauern belebte und von den Besuchern positiv registriert wurde. In gleicher Weise wurde das Farbschema auch bei dem Rundgang durch die Stadt gestaltet.

Es war uns wichtig, dass mit dem Ausstellungsprojekt sowohl für auswärtige Besucher als auch für die Esslinger selbst die mittelalterliche Bedeutung der Stadt besonders betont wird. Die Ausstellung weckte durch die vielen Werbeplakate und durch den nicht zu übersehenden Rundgang natürlich im ganzen Stadtraum Aufmerksamkeit. Da viele der Klosterkirchen nicht mehr erhalten sind und vor allem deren Einrichtung zerstört ist, haben wir mit diesem Projekt Erwachsenen und Kindern die historische, kunsthistorische und wirtschaftliche Bedeutung Esslingens in der Zeit vom 13. bis zum 15. Jahrhundert nahegebracht. Ein weiterer wichtiger Gedanke war, herauszuarbeiten, was hinter dem weitgehend unbekannten Begriff „Pfleghof" steht.

"former" location. Visitors spent a particularly long time in this part of the exhibition, "meditating" in the choir stalls or reading their exhibition guidebooks. Six audio stations, a further feature of the exhibition located in the choir gallery area, also drew a great deal of visitor interest.

The basic colors used for the exhibition, red and mauve, represented the spheres of the church and Pfleghof respectively. The design of the different exhibition segments also made use of these colors, with red and mauve also featured on the information panels – a design element that enlivened the gray and beige-colored walls and received positive reactions from visitors. The same color scheme was also used for the tour through the city.

It was important for us that the exhibition project emphasized the medieval significance of the city, both for Esslingen's inhabitants and visitors. Posters advertising the exhibition and the conspicuously marked tour route drew attention throughout the city. Many of the monastery churches have not been preserved, and in those that have the original infrastructure and fittings have been destroyed. One of this project's most important goals was therefore to provide both adults and children with a greater sense of Esslingen's historical, cultural-

The *Weiler Pietà* (1471), State Museum Württemberg, Stuttgart
The only (movable) artistic exhibit object, which has been obtained from the Essling monasteries. A large sculpture serves as an example of the practice of piety in late-medieval convents in Southern Germany.

Glasmalereien der Esslinger Franziskanerkirche, 1325/30
Die Farbverglasungen der Esslinger Kirchen gehören zu den bedeutendsten deutschen Glasmalereien des frühen 14. Jahrhunderts. Sie sind in Form, Harmonie und Komposition einzigartig und technisch perfekt gearbeitet.

Stained glass of the Franciscan church in Esslingen, 1325/30
The colored glass of the Esslingen churches are amongst the most important examples of German stained glass of the early 14th century. They are unique in their harmony and composition, and the craftsmanship is technically perfect.

Ausstellungsgestaltung

Da die Ausstellung nicht im Museum, sondern in einer schwer zu bespielenden Kirche stattfand, waren die Erwartungen an die Ausstellungsgestalter sehr spezifisch. Die Idee der Gestaltung beruht auf kräftigen Farben und sorgfältiger Lichtgestaltung. Die konservatorischen Bedingungen in den Kirchenräumen sind problematisch. Die Ausstellung wurde im Winter gezeigt, und Temperatur und Luftfeuchtigkeit entsprachen nicht dem bei diesen wertvollen Objekten gebotenen Standard. So musste mit Klimavitrinen gearbeitet und sehr genau auf die Klimawerte geachtet werden.

Die Inszenierung in einem Kirchenraum ist besonders delikat, weil natürlich viel mehr als in den für Ausstellungen konzipierten Museumsräumen Rücksicht auf historische und kunsthistorische Bedingungen eines mittelalterlichen Raumes genommen werden muss. Der große, sehr hohe Raum wurde in verschiedene Bereiche unterteilt und die in situ befindlichen Objekte in großer Höhe, wie die Kirchenfenster und die Wandmalereien, mussten dem Besucher nahegebracht werden. Ferner durften die Wände nicht für Beschriftungen verwendet werden. Die gefundenen Gestaltungslösungen zeigen beispielhaft, wie unter den gegebenen Bedingungen eine Ausstellung geschaffen werden kann, die auf ein großes Publikumsinteresse stößt.

Kirsten Fast

historical, and economic significance in the period from the thirteenth to the fifteenth century. Another important aim was to explore the largely unknown concept of the Pfleghof.

Exhibition Design

Since the exhibition was not located in a museum but in a far less flexible church space, the expectations placed on the exhibition designers were very specific. The concept for the design was based on the use of striking colors and careful lighting. Protecting exhibits displayed in church interiors is problematic. The exhibition was shown in winter, and the temperature and level of humidity exceeded the limits prescribed for these valuable artifacts. As a result climate-controlled display cases had to be used and carefully monitored.

Staging an exhibition in such a church interior also presents particular challenges because a great deal of consideration has to be given to the historical and art-historical character of the medieval space. The large, extremely high space was divided into different areas, and original in situ artifacts positioned high up the walls, such as windows and murals, needed somehow to be brought closer to the visitor. In addition, the walls could not be used for labeling. The design solutions that were devised provide an excellent example of how, given such conditions, an exhibition can be mounted that attracts the interest of a broad public.

Kirsten Fast

Historische Ausstellungen
Historical Exhibitions

Klöster und Pfleghöfe in Esslingen
Monasteries and Pfleghöfe in Esslingen

Träger Supporting Institution:
Städtische Museen Esslingen,
Stadtarchiv Esslingen
Municipal Museum of Esslingen and the
Esslingen City Archives

Ausstellungsfläche Exhibition Area:
ca. c. 600 m²

Spirituelles Leben, Andacht
und Mystik
Spiritual life, contemplation
and prayer, and mysticism

Alltag im Kloster
Daily life in the monastery

Klöster und Pfleghöfe
Monastery and Pfleghöfe

Reformation und Nachleben
The Reformation and aftermath

Historische Einführung
Historical introduction

1 m   5 m   M 1:400

10 m   20 m

Eine räumliche Besonderheit bietet der
Ausstellungsort. Das Gemeindehaus
wurde in den 1920er-Jahren direkt an den
noch bestehenden Lettner und nachfol-
genden Chorraum der Franziskanerkirche
angebaut. Im mittleren Raum treffen so
zwei bauliche Epochen aufeinander.

A special feature of the exhibition space:
the community center was constructed
in the 1920th years utilizing the existing
choir screen and choir room next to
the Franciscan Church. In this way, two
architectural eras collide in the middle of
the room.

Seelsorge Klausur
Frömmigkeit

Die Spiritualität
der Bettelorden

Grafikwand graphic panel

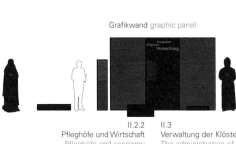

II.2.2
Pfleghöfe und Wirtschaft
Pfleghöfe and economy

II.3
Verwaltung der Klöster und Pfleghöfe
The administration of the Monasteries
and Pfleghöfe

II.2.1
Mutterklöster der Pfleghöfe
The Maternal Monasteries
of the Pfleghöfe

II.1
Die Stadt als
Bezugsrahmen
The City as a
frame of reference

Grafikwand graphic panel

III.1
Lettner
Choir Screen

II.4.1
Betteln, Armut, Armenfürsorge
Begging, poverty and poor relief

II.4.2
Bildung und Wissenschaft
Education and scholarship

II.4.3
Architektur der Bettelorden
The architecture of the
mendicant orders

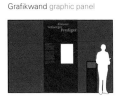

II.4.4
„Geist", „Predigt", „Seelsorge"
"Spirit," "Homily," "Pastoral Care"

Historische Ausstellungen
Historical Exhibitions

Klöster und Pfleghöfe in Esslingen
Monasteries and Pfleghöfe in Esslingen

Mittelalterliche Figur des Hl. Sebastian
A statue of St. Sebastian from
the Middle ages

Die Segmente der Ausstellungswände
stehen je nach Raumsituation zusammen
oder auch einzeln, z.B. als Blickpunkt in
den Lettnernischen.
The segments of the exhibition walls
stand either separately or together
depending on the room situation as seen
here, for example, in the choir screens.

280

Geistliche Herrschaft und weltliche Macht sind zwei Pole, die das Handeln der Klöster bestimmte – ein Gegensatz, der zu einem kräftigen Farbkontrast von Rot und Violett inspirierte. Zudem schaffen die markanten Farben eindeutige Blickpunkte und stimmige Hintergründe für die mittelalterlichen Exponate sowie eine durchgängige Gestaltungslinie in den heterogenen Räumlichkeiten des historischen Bestands.

Ecclesiastical authority and secular power are two areas that are handled by the monasteries – a contrast that inspired a strong red and violet color contrast. Moreover, the striking colors create unique focal points and are consistent backgrounds for the medieval exhibits as well as a consistent design concept in the heterogeneous areas of the historic holdings.

Die Beleuchtung und Inszenierung der Exponate wurden direkt in die Ausstellungselemente integriert.

The lighting and arrangement of the exhibition objects are directly integrated into the exhibition elements.

Epitaph
für Hans von Stetten
(Anfang 15. Jahrhundert)

Die Bildtafel zeigt Maria mit dem Kind und die heilige
Barbara, die einen Kelch mit Hostien trägt. Zu Füßen
Marias kniet der Stifter. Eine ausführliche Bildunter-
schrift verrät mehr über die Person und den Todestag
dieses Stifters:
„Anno 1404 ... starb der frumm und vest Hans von Stetten, Edelknecht ..."
Er starb am Mittwoch, dem 11. November (Namenstag
des heiligen Martini) im Jahre 1404.

Die Bildtafel sollte nicht nur an den Stifter erinnern.
Auch der Konvent wurde dadurch auf die Verpflichtung
hingewiesen, die er dem Stifter gegenüber eingegangen war. In einer Stiftungsurkunde wurde festgelegt,
dass regelmäßig Messen für den Verstorbenen zu lesen
sind.

... Epitaph hing vermutlich ursprünglich in der
... Frauenkirche.

Kunstwerke, die sich im Chor-
raum an nicht zugänglichen
Stellen befinden, sind eine
besondere Herausforderung für
die Ausstellungsgestaltung.
Mittelalterliche Fresken, Epitaphe
und Gemälde werden an den
Informationspulten erklärt
und können ebenso wie das
Figurenprogramm der farbigen
Glasmalereien mit Ferngläsern im
Detail betrachtet werden.

Artworks that are found in the
choir room in inaccessible areas
are a particular challenge to the
exhibition design. Medieval fres-
coes, epitaphs, and paintings are
clarified at the information desks,
and can be seen in detail through
binoculars such as the figures in
the stained glass windows.

Historische Ausstellungen
Historical Exhibitions

Klöster und Pfleghöfe in Esslingen
Monasteries and Pfleghöfe in Esslingen

Ausstellungselemente halten Abstand
zum historischen Bauwerk. Sakrale Musik
erfüllt den Chorraum akustisch und
atmosphärisch.

Exhibition elements are kept at a distance
from the historic building. Sacred music
fills the choir room acoustically and
atmospherically.

Besitzungen
Privilegien
Reichsstadt

**Die Stadt als Bezugs-
rahmen für Klöster und
Pfleghöfe**

Jüdisches Museum Berlin – Deutsche und Juden zugleich
The Jewish Museum Berlin – German and Jewish at the Same Time

Im Mittelpunkt des im Jahr 2005 neu eröffneten Kapitels der Dauerausstellung stehen das Selbstverständnis deutscher Juden im 19. Jahrhundert und die äußeren Bedingungen, die dieses Selbstverständnis prägten. Eine dieser Bedingungen war der Prozess der rechtlichen Gleichstellung. Erst 1871 wurde die Gleichstellung in der Verfassung des Deutschen Reiches festgeschrieben – nach jahrzehntelangen Debatten über die „Judenfrage". In einer Hörstation stellen wir Argumente von Gegnern und Fürsprechern der Emanzipation einander gegenüber. Diese Argumente erinnern auch an Diskussionen, die heute über Fragen der Integration von Migranten und der deutschen Staatsbürgerschaft geführt werden.

Die Fortschritte der Emanzipation und die Öffnung der Gesellschaft im 19. Jahrhundert machten es möglich, dass sich die Juden die Kultur und Lebensweise ihrer Umgebung aneigneten und Deutsche wurden. Eine Minderheit bemühte sich um vollständige Assimilation und ließ sich taufen.

Die Anhänger der zionistischen Bewegung sprachen gegen Ende des Jahrhunderts von einer nationalen jüdischen Identität und unterstützten den Aufbau eines jüdischen Gemeinwesens in Palästina. Die Mehrheit der deutschen Juden fühlte sich dem Judentum und der deutschen Nation und Kultur

The new section of the permanent exhibition, which opened in 2005, focuses on the self-image of German Jews in the nineteenth century, and the external conditions that shaped this self-image. One of the determinants was the process of legal emancipation. After decades of debate about the "Jewish question," legal equality for Jews was finally set forth in the Constitution of the German Empire in 1871. An audio station presents the arguments of both the opponents and supporters of emancipation, which call to mind current discussions of the integration of migrants, and the awarding of German citizenship.

The progress of emancipation and the opening of society in the nineteenth century enabled Jews to adopt the culture and lifestyle of their environment, and become German. A minority of Jews attempted to assimilate completely and had themselves baptized. In the late nineteenth century, the followers of the Zionist movement spoke of a national Jewish identity and supported the establishment of a Jewish commonwealth in Palestine. The majority of German Jews felt strong ties to both Judaism, and the German nation and culture. "As I myself am both German and Jewish at the same time," wrote Johann Jacoby, "the Jew in me cannot become free without the German; nor the

Historische Ausstellungen
Historical Exhibitions

Jüdisches Museum Berlin
The Jewish Museum Berlin
Lindenstraße 9–14
10969 Berlin

Portrait Albertine Mendelssohn Bartholdy, geb. Heine (1814–1879), als Braut
August Theodor Kaselowsky (1810–1890), Berlin, 1835, Öl auf Leinwand

zugehörig. „Wie ich selbst Jude und Deutscher zugleich bin", schrieb Johann Jacoby, „so kann der Jude in mir nicht frei werden ohne den Deutschen und der Deutsche nicht ohne den Juden". Doch die Hoffnung auf gesellschaftliche Anerkennung erwies sich als trügerisch. Wenige Jahre nach der Gründung des Deutschen Reiches forderten die Anhänger des modernen Antisemitismus die Rücknahme der Emanzipation.

Vier Formen des jüdischen Selbstverständnisses werden in diesem Raum der Dauerausstellung vorgestellt: der Patriotismus deutscher Juden, die politische Linke am Beispiel von Karl Marx und Ferdinand Lassalle, die Taufe und der Zionismus. Dem deutschen Dichter Heinrich Heine wird am Ende der Präsentation ein besonderer Platz eingeräumt. Denn in seiner Person spiegelt sich die deutsch-jüdische Problematik der Zeit: Das romantische Gedicht *Die Loreley* machte Heine als deutschen Dichter weltberühmt. Mit 27 Jahren ließ er sich taufen – und bereute diesen Schritt später. Jede Form von Nationalismus lehnte er ab: Dem „Brechpulver" Deutschland kehrte er 1831 den Rücken und zog nach Paris.

Maren Krüger

German free without the Jew." However, the hope for social recognition proved illusory. Just a few years after the German Empire was founded, the supporters of a modern anti-Semitism demanded that equal rights be repealed.

This section of the permanent exhibition introduces four aspects of Jewish self-identity: the patriotism of German Jews, leftwing politics (based on the examples of Karl Marx and Ferdinand Lassalle), baptism, and Zionism. At the end of the presentation, a special exhibit is devoted to the German writer Heinrich Heine, who reflected the German Jewish problems of his age. Heine's romantic poem *Die Loreley* made him famous worldwide as a German poet. He was baptized when he was twenty-seven – only to regret taking this step later in life. Rejecting all forms of nationalism, Heine turned his back on "nauseating" Germany in 1831, and moved to Paris.

Maren Krüger

Gestaltungskonzept

Daniel Libeskind hat das Projekt Jüdisches Museum Berlin „Between the Lines" (Zwischen den Linien) genannt, weil es sich für ihn dabei um zwei Linien, zwei Strömungen von Gedanken, Organisation und Beziehungen handelt. Die eine Linie ist gerade und in Fragmente zersplittert, die andere windet sich und setzt sich unendlich fort.[1]

In der Dauerausstellung liegt dem neu gestalteten Segment „Deutsche und Juden zugleich" derselbe Gedanke zugrunde: das Verfolgen von zwei Linien. Architektur und Ausstellung als jeweils eigenständige Gestaltungselemente in adäquatem Zusammenspiel von Bau und Einbau.

Der komplexen Architektur werden einfache, geometrische Formen gegenübergestellt. Libeskinds Formensprache zu imitieren war in jedem Fall ausgeschlossen. Die Atmosphäre der Ausstellung soll dem Gebäude Raum lassen, einladend sein, Ausblicke ermöglichen und Assoziationen wecken.

Design Concept

Daniel Libeskind called his design for the Jewish Museum Berlin "Between the Lines" because it focuses on two lines – or two currents of thought, organizational forms, and types of relationships. One line is straight and divided into fragments, the other is tortuous and continues infinitely.[1] The newly designed section of the permanent exhibition, entitled "German and Jewish at the Same Time," is based on the same idea of following two lines, epitomized by the architecture and the exhibition as independent design elements in an effective interplay between structure and installation. The complex architecture is contrasted with simple, geometric forms. A mere emulation of Libeskind's formal vocabulary was ruled out from the start. The exhibition was designed to make the building welcoming, open up views, and spark associations.

[1] Daniel Libeskind, *Erweiterung des Berlin Museums mit Abteilung Jüdisches Museum*, Berlin 1992, S. 58.
[1] Daniel Libeskind, *Erweiterung des Berlin Museums mit Abteilung Jüdisches Museum* (Berlin 1992): p. 58.

Fotos Seiten 287/288
Photos pages 287/288:
Jens Ziehe, JMB Berlin

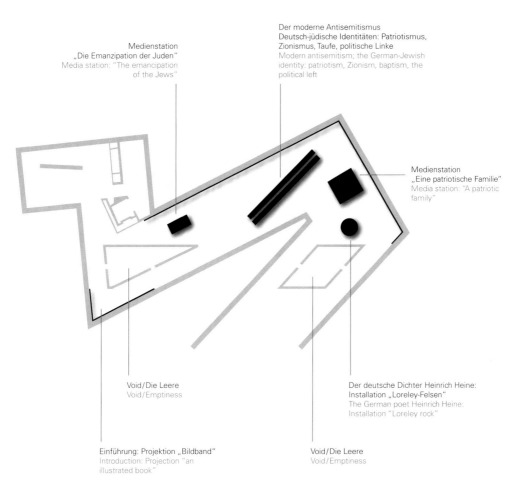

Medienstation
„Die Emanzipation der Juden"
Media station: "The emancipation
of the Jews"

Der moderne Antisemitismus
Deutsch-jüdische Identitäten: Patriotismus,
Zionismus, Taufe, politische Linke
Modern antisemitism; the German-Jewish
identity: patriotism, Zionism, baptism, the
political left

Medienstation
„Eine patriotische Familie"
Media station: "A patriotic
family"

Void/Die Leere
Void/Emptiness

Der deutsche Dichter Heinrich Heine:
Installation „Loreley-Felsen"
The German poet Heinrich Heine:
Installation "Loreley rock"

Einführung: Projektion „Bildband"
Introduction: Projection "an
illustrated book"

Void/Die Leere
Void/Emptiness

1 m   5 m   M 1:400

10 m

Für die Zerrissenheit deutsch-
jüdischer Identität, das Wider-
sprüchliche, Gegensätzliche, aber
auch das Verbindende steht die
durch einen Lichtspalt geteilte
monumentale Wand. Sie verdeutlicht das „Zusammen-und-
doch-Getrennt".

The inner turmoil of German-Jewish identity, often contradictory
and opposed, but also unifying is
represented by a separating gap
of light in the monumental wall;
highlighting the idea of "together
yet separate."

Historische Ausstellungen
Historical Exhibitions

Jüdisches Museum Berlin
The Jewish Museum Berlin

Träger Supporting Institution:
Bundesrepublik Deutschland
The Federal Republic of Germany

Autoren/Kuratoren/Wissenschaftliches
Team Authors/Curators/Research Team:
Martina Lüdicke, Maren Krüger,
Jana Reimer

baptized and it doesn't help me
GETAUFT und es hilft mir nichts

Ausstellungsgestaltung und Medienkonzeption Exhibition Design and Interfaces: BERTRON SCHWARZ FREY Entwurf: Head of Design: Prof. Ulrich Schwarz, Aurelia Bertron Grafik Design Graphic Design: Aurelia Bertron

Ausführungsplanung Planning and Execution: SchielProjekt GmbH Fotos Photos: Volker Kreidler Medienproduktion Media Production: Christopher Bauder whitevoid, Till Beckmann, Christopher Fröhlich, Simon Krahl, Stephen Lumenta, Lisa Rave

Dauerausstellung Permanent Exhibition: Eröffnung Opening: 28. April 2005 April 28, 2005

Bedingt durch die architektonischen Gegebenheiten erschien es zweckmäßig, dem Besucher einen visuellen und akustischen Anreiz zu bieten, ihn durch bewegte Bilder in die Ausstellung hineinzuziehen. Die von rechts nach links vorbeiziehenden Abbildungen erzeugen durch ihre unterschiedliche Geschwindigkeit die Illusion einer räumlichen Staffelung auf verschieden entfernten Ebenen. Näher liegende Objekte bewegen sich dabei schneller als weiter entfernt liegende – eine Wahrnehmungserfahrung, die man z. B. vom Blick aus einem fahrenden Zugabteil kennt.
Die ausgestellten Objekte stehen als Schlüsselobjekte für die darzustellenden Themen, ihr kunsthistorischer Wert ist für die Präsentation von nachgeordneter Bedeutung.
Durchblicke stellen inhaltliche Bezüge her, wie zum Beispiel den Zusammenhang zwischen dem Patriotismus deutscher Juden und dem Zionismus.

Due to the architectural features it seemed appropriate to offer the visitor a visual and acoustic stimulus in which it is possible to drag along the moving exhibition images. The illustrations, which pass from right to left, through their varying speeds create an illusion of spatial positioning on different distant levels. Objects that are near move faster than objects that are farther away – a perceptional experience that is usually experienced if looking from a moving train.
The exhibition objects are displayed as key objects for their respective themes, their art-historical value is of secondary importance for the presentation. Perspectives provide conceptual connections such as the relationship between the patriotism of German Jews and Zionism.

Historische Ausstellungen
Historical Exhibitions

Jüdisches Museum Berlin
The Jewish Museum Berlin

Vitrinen mit den Schlüsselobjekten zu den Themen Taufe, Zionismus und Patriotismus
Taufgeschirr der Familie Mendelssohn, Spendenbüchsen des Jüdischen Nationalfonds, Mannschaftshelm

Display cases contain key objects concerning themes such as baptism, Zionism, and patriotism
Baptism wares from the Mendelssohn family, collection boxes belonging to the National Jewish Funds, and a military helmet

292

ERINNERUNGS- UND GEDENKSTÄTTEN
MEMORIALS AND COMMEMORATIVE SITES

Erinnern und Gedenken sind en vogue. Kulturwissenschaftler sprechen seit geraumer Zeit von einem Memory Boom, der die deutsche und internationale politische Kultur prägt und mit ihr auch die jeweilige Museumslandschaft. Überall finden sich Gedenkzeichen und Erinnerungsstätten – oder Gedenkstätten und Erinnerungszeichen. Die Verwendung der beiden Begriffe ist inzwischen so inflationär, dass die Definitionen immer austauschbarer werden und die Einrichtungen, die sie bezeichnen, in einer Melange von Assoziationen zu verschwimmen drohen.

Erinnern und Gedenken zählen zu den ältesten menschlichen Kulturtechniken. Beide sind stets sozial bedingt. Vergangenheit kann immer nur in den Rahmenbedingungen einer kulturellen Gegenwart rekonstruiert werden. Die Tradierung historischer Ereignisse ist also immer von den sozialen Kontexten abhängig, in die sie eingebettet werden. Nicht das, was passiert, ist für die Repräsentation im Gedächtnis entscheidend, sondern vielmehr, wer etwas zu welchem Zweck erinnert.

Das älteste tradierte Medium jeder Mnemotechnik ist die Verräumlichung. In allen Kulturen und in allen Epochen waren und sind Orte, ob als konkrete topografische Räume, topologische Symbole oder memoriale Medien von herausragender Bedeutung – sei es als imaginierte Räume in der antiken rhetorischen Kunstform der *ars memoria*, sei es als durch Grenzen markierte politische Räume, sei es als zu Zeichen erhobene semiotisierte Räume wie heilige Landschaften, Denkmäler, Gedenkstätten oder Museen. An diesen „Erinnerungsorten" gerinnt Vergangenheit zu symbolischen Figuren. Sie werden als Subjekte wahrgenommen, denen ein eigenes Vergegenwärtigungspotenzial von Vergangenheit innewohnt. Gleichzeitig fungieren Erinnerungs- oder Gedächtnisorte aber auch als Objekte, die mit Erinnerungszuschreibungen bewusst aufgeladen werden.

Remembrance and commemoration are in vogue. For some time now, cultural scholars have been referring to a "memory boom," one that is shaping German and international political culture, and in the process museum landscapes in general. It seems that we are now finding memorial signs and commemorative sites – or memorial sites and commemorative signs – everywhere. These terms are being so overused that their definitions are becoming increasingly interchangeable, and the objects they designate are blurring into a mélange of associations.

Remembrance and commemoration are among the oldest aspects of human culture; both are always socially conditioned. The past can only be reconstructed within the framework of a cultural present. The transmission of historical events is therefore always dependent on the social context in which it is embedded. It is not what happens that is decisive for representation in memory, but rather who is remembering and for what purpose.

The oldest mnemonic technique is that of spatialization. In all cultures and all epochs there were and are sites – concrete topographical spaces, topological symbols, or memorial media – invested with a special significance, whether in the form of imagined spaces in the ancient rhetorical art of the *ars memoria*, political spaces marked by borders, or semiotized spaces such as sacred landscapes, memorials, commemorative sites, and museums. At these "sites of remembrance" the past congeals into symbolic figures, which are perceived as subjects in which there inheres a potential for a visualization of the past. At the same time, sites of remembrance or commemoration also function as objects that are consciously loaded with memory ascriptions.

Communication about the past, the social framework, the culturally available semiotic system, and materializations of memories

Die Kommunikation über die Vergangenheit, die sozialen Rahmen, die kulturell vorhandenen Zeichensysteme sowie die Materialisierungen der Erinnerungen durchdringen und bedingen sich wechselseitig. Bei Erinnerungsorten und Gedenkstätten haben wir es mit Symbolkontexten zu tun, die hochgradig diskursiv überlagert sind, und zwar sowohl alltagshermeneutisch wie auch durch politische Zuschreibungen. Dadurch werden Assoziationsressourcen transportiert, die einer beständigen Aktualisierung unterliegen.

Erinnerungsorte verfügen demnach über vielfältige Sinnpotenziale, die von den Bedeutungszuschreibungen derjenigen abhängen, die über diese sprechen und schreiben, sie besuchen – und natürlich auch ganz maßgeblich von jenen, die sie konzipieren und gestalten.

permeate and condition one another. In the case of memorials and commemorative sites we are dealing with symbolic contexts that are discursively overlaid both in terms of everyday hermeneutics and by political ascriptions. In this way associative resources are transported that are being constantly updated.

As a result, sites of remembrance have diverse signification potentials that are dependent on ascriptions of meaning by those who speak and write about them, visit them – and of course by those who conceive and design them.

**Erinnerung ausstellen
Ehemalige Konzentrationslager als moderne zeithistorische Museen?**

1. Szenografie:
Ausgestellte Tatorte

Am 16. April 1945, fünf Tage nach der Befreiung des Konzentrationslagers Buchenwald, wurden auf Anordnung des Kommandeurs der 3. U.S. Army, General Patton, knapp 1 000 Bürger Weimars dazu gezwungen, Leichenberge anzusehen, die aus toten Häftlingen errichtet worden waren. Ein Teil dieser Leichenstapel war aus den Leibern nach der Befreiung Verstorbener neu aufgehäuft worden. Den Zwangsbesuchern sollte ein möglichst authentischer Eindruck von den Verhältnissen im Lager gegeben werden. Diese Extrempraktik wurde allerdings schon wenige Tage später wieder eingestellt – weniger aus Pietätsgründen als vielmehr aus der Erkenntnis heraus, dass außer der Lagerwirklichkeit selbst keine geeigneten Repräsentationsformen dieser Massenverbrechen zur Verfügung standen.

**Exhibiting Memory
Former concentration camps as modern museums of recent history?**

Scenography 1: Exhibited crime scenes

On April 16, 1945 five days after the liberation of the Buchenwald Concentration Camp, on the orders of US Third Army Commander General Patton, the inhabitants of Weimar (numbering about 1,000) were forced to view the pile of corpses of former camp inmates. Some of these piles were new and made up of the bodies of those who had died since the camp had been liberated. These forced visits were intended as a way of conveying as authentic an impression as possible of conditions in the camp. However, this extreme strategy was abandoned after only a few days – less out of a perceived need to respect the dead than a recognition that, aside from the realities of the camp, no adequate form of representation for these mass crimes existed.

2. Szenografie:
Ehemalige Lager als Museen

Im Jahr 1947 verabschiedete der polnische Sejm ein Gesetz, das die Lagergelände in Auschwitz, Majdanek und Stutthof zu staatlichen Museen erklärte. Die Lagergelände sollten als Corpus Delicti, als Beweise für die dort begangenen Verbrechen, für immer erhalten werden. Gleichzeitig wurden große Nationaldenkmäler und auch Ausstellungen geplant. Diese ersten Ausstellungen in ehemaligen Konzentrationslagern entstanden stets in einem eindeutigen politischen und nationalen Sinnstiftungskontext und wurden vor allem ergänzend zu monumentalen Denkmalsanlagen konzipiert.
Die ersten – national-kommunistischen – Ausstellungen in Auschwitz und Majdanek, aber auch das 1949 entstandene Ghetto Fighters' House in Nordisrael und das 1954 eingerichtete Museum des Widerstandes auf dem Gelände des ehemaligen KZ Buchenwald stehen exemplarisch für diesen frühen Typus der Nachkriegsausstellung. Und dies sowohl im inhaltlichen Narrativ wie in der musealen Konzeption. Gezeigt wurden vor allem Artefakte, die auf den Terror der SS verwiesen, Instrumente der Tortur, oftmals nicht im Original, sondern aus der noch frischen Erinnerung rekonstruiert – so wie die frühen Leichenstapel in Buchenwald. Diese Schau von Verbrechenswerkzeugen wurde oftmals mit erhaltenen Sachzeugnissen von ehemaligen Häftlingen, Relikten und Reliquien, Häftlingskleidung, Schuhen und Devotionalien kontrastiert. Es waren Schauen, die das Grauen authentisierten.

3. Szenografie:
Erkämpfte Ausstellungen

Die erste bedeutende Dauerausstellung in einer KZ-Gedenkstätte in der Bundesrepublik wurde erst 1965 in Dachau eröffnet. Sie war eine direkte Reaktion auf Versuche, die nationalsozialistischen Verbrechen zu leugnen und zu relativieren. Folglich war sie auch eine dezidiert politische Ausstellung. Ziel der konzeptionell und gestalterisch Verantwortlichen war vor allem die Präsentation von

Scenography 2:
Former camps as museums

In 1947, the lower house of the Polish parliament, the Sejm, passed a law according the sites of the camps in Auschwitz, Majdanek, and Stutthof the status of state museums. It was decreed that as corpus delicti, as evidence of the crimes committed there, these sites should be forever preserved. At the same time, plans were made to erect large national monuments as well as exhibitions. These first exhibitions in former concentration camps were created in a context clearly loaded with political and national meaning, and were conceived above all as supplementing monumental memorial sites.
The first (national-communist) exhibitions in Auschwitz and Majdanek, along with the Ghetto Fighters' House built in northern Israel in 1949 and the Museum of Resistance erected in 1954 on the site of the former Buchenwald Concentration Camp, are all representative examples of this early type of postwar exhibition, both in terms of their thematic narratives as well as their museological concepts. The exhibits primarily consisted of artifacts that were representative of the regime of terror cultivated by the SS – instruments of torture that were often reproductions constructed on the basis of recent memory – such as the piles of corpses in Buchenwald. Such tools of horrific crimes were often contrasted with material relics of former prisoners such as religious artifacts, prison uniforms, shoes, and devotional objects. These were exhibitions that served to authenticate the horrific events that had taken place.

Scenography 3:
Hard-won exhibitions

The first significant permanent exhibition on a concentration camp site in West Germany was opened in Dachau in 1965, and was a direct reaction to attempts to deny and underplay National Socialist crimes. As a consequence, it was also a decidedly political exhibition. The aim of those responsible for the exhibition concept and design was

Beweisen und das Auslösen eines emotionalen Schocks. Großfotos inszenierten den Terror der SS gegenüber den Häftlingen. Die Ausstellung folgte – ebenso wie die Lager- und Leichenbesichtigung in Buchenwald – dem Modus der Konfrontation und Rekonstruktion. Parallel zur Ausstellung ließ das internationale Dachau-Komitee zwei Baracken in Appellplatznähe rekonstruieren.

4. Szenografie:
„Aktive Museen" und Dokumentationen

Die Dachauer Ausstellung aus dem Jahr 1965, die über fast zwei Jahrzehnte die einzige Ausstellung in einer KZ-Gedenkstätte der Bundesrepublik war, steht prototypisch für das Verständnis von NS-Ausstellungen im Land. Diese Haltung wurde in den achtziger Jahren besonders populär und lässt sich in einzelnen Einrichtungen bis heute besichtigen. Im gesellschaftlichen Klima der achtziger Jahre entstanden an unzähligen Orten sogenannte Geschichtswerkstätten und Gedenkstätteninitiativen. Relikte von KZ-Außenlagern, Kriegsgefangenenlagern und NS-Täterorten wurden entdeckt und freigelegt. Stets wurde auch die Forderung nach bislang fehlenden historischen Informationen zu diesen Orten erhoben. Hierbei eigneten sich einzelne Initiativen bewusst den Museumsbegriff an, etwa der heute noch bestehende Geschichtsverein „Aktives Museum Berlin". Element der Aneignung war aber gleichzeitig auch eine Abgrenzung gegenüber „klassischen" Geschichtsmuseen. Man definierte „Aufklärung" nicht als Kulturgut, sondern in einem politisch-moralischen Sinn. Entscheidend war nicht die Frage des *Wie* von Ausstellungen, sondern des *Ob*. Ausstellungen in Gedenkstätten waren zu dieser Zeit *Dokumentationen*, also Text-Bildschauen, eine Sonderform historischer Ausstellungen.

primarily to present evidence, and to trigger an emotional shock. Large-format photographs showed the terrorization of inmates by the SS. Like the enforced inspections of the camp and corpses in Buchenwald, the key methods of the exhibition were confrontation and reconstruction. Parallel to mounting the exhibition, in addition the international Dachau Committee had two barracks reconstructed close to the camp's roll-call area.

Scenography 4:
"Active museums" and documentations

The Dachau exhibition created in 1965 remained the only exhibition at a West German concentration camp memorial site for nearly two decades, and represents a prototype of the kind of approach that developed in exhibitions focusing on Nazi crimes. It was an approach that became particularly popular in the 1980s and its influence is still evident in a number of institutions today. The social climate of the 1980s led to the establishment of numerous so-called history workshops and memorial site initiatives. An increasing number of relics from satellite complexes associated with concentration camps, prisoner-of-war camps, and other sites of Nazi crimes were discovered, and demands were voiced for more historical information pertaining to these sites to be made available. In this context, some initiatives consciously adopted a museological approach, such as the "Active Museum" initiative in Berlin, which still exists today. At the same time, such initiatives sought to formulate a concept of museum presentation that was distinct from that of the "classic" historical museum. They defined the concept of "Enlightenment" not in a cultural and historical sense, but rather in a political and moral one. The decisive question for them was not the "how" of exhibitions but rather the "if." Exhibitions at memorial sites at this time were documentations comprising displays of pictures and text – a special form of historical exhibition.

5. Szenografie:
Ehemalige Lager als moderne
zeithistorische Museen

Scenography 5:
Former camps as modern museums of
contemporary history

Mit der deutschen Wiedervereinigung wurden auch die geschichtspolitischen Narrative beider deutscher Staaten renovierungsbedürftig. Unter dem Motto „KZ-Gedenkstätten als moderne zeithistorische Museen" begann eine Professionalisierung der historisch-fachwissenschaftlichen, der pädagogisch-didaktischen, aber auch der museologischen Arbeit in den KZ-Gedenkstätten. Die 1995 neu eröffnete Ausstellung in der KZ-Gedenkstätte Buchenwald bezog sich in ihrem inhaltlichen und ästhetischen Ausdruck direkt auf die vormalige DDR-Ausstellung, indem sie Exponate, Artefakte, Fotos und Texte im Gestus eines Archivs, einer Art negativer Schausammlung präsentierte. In Sachsenhausen entschied sich der wissenschaftliche Beirat dezidiert für ein dezentrales Ausstellungskonzept mit Themeninseln. Inhaltlich bedeutsam war nicht nur eine perspektivische Differenzierung des Themas Konzentrationslager, sondern auch eine kritische Selbstreflexion der Nachnutzungs- und „Gedenkstättengeschichte", die sich in neuen Ausstellungen zur Rezeptionsgeschichte nach 1945 niederschlug. Mittlerweile sind auch in den Gedenkstätten in Dachau, Neuengamme, Bergen-Belsen und Flossenbürg neue Ausstellungen eröffnet worden, die sich sehr offensiv und selbstbewusst als moderne zeithistorische Museen begreifen.

With the reunification of Germany also came a perceived need to recast the historical-political narrative of both German states. Under the banner of "concentration camp memorial sites as modern museums of contemporary history" a campaign was launched to professionalize historical-scholarly, pedagogical-didactic, and museological work at concentration camp memorial sites. In terms of its content and aesthetic character, the new exhibition opened at the Buchenwald Concentration Camp memorial site in 1995 referred directly to the previous GDR exhibition in the sense that it presented artifacts, photos, and texts in a form recalling an archive. In Sachsenhausen the advisory board decided for a distinctly decentralized exhibition concept using thematic islands. This exhibition was informed not only by a differentiation of perspectives on the concentration camp theme, but also by a process of critical self-reflection on the subsequent use of the site and "memorial site history," an approach that has since been reflected in new exhibitions on "reception history" since 1945. In the meantime, new exhibitions have also been opened at the memorial sites in Dachau, Neuengamme, Bergen-Belsen, and Flossenbürg that have been clearly conceived as modern museums of contemporary history.

Gedenkstätten als Museen?
Interventionen und Reflexionen

Memorial Sites as Museums?
Interventions and Reflections

Das Ausstellen der Verbrechen an den ehemaligen Tatorten selbst verdeutlicht den fundamentalen Bruch mit den Präsentations-, Auratisierungs- und Authentisierungswünschen, welche die Entwicklungsgeschichte europäischer Museen seit ihren Ursprüngen begleitet. Seit den rekonstruierten Leichenbergen in Buchenwald bewegen sich alle Versuche, Gerinnungs-

The exhibition of crimes at their original sites in itself represents a fundamental break with the presentation, auratization and authentication aims that have accompanied the developmental history of European museums since their beginnings. Ever since the piles of corpses were reconstructed in Buchenwald, all attempts to find forms for a multifaceted expression of realities in

und Ausdrucksformen der Lagerwirklichkeit zu finden, im Spannungsfeld von Fakt und Fiktion, von Moral und Musealisierung. KZ-Gedenkstätten sind multiple Orte. Sie sind Schädelstätten, Friedhöfe, Generationenorte, Freilichtmuseen, Lernorte, Quellen – für die Zeit des Konzentrationslagers und für die Zeit des Umgangs mit ihnen während der letzten Jahrzehnte. KZ-Gedenkstätten haben aber eine weitere und zunehmend wichtigere Funktion: Sie sind auch Museen. Diese Definition stellt das Konzipieren von Ausstellungen vor besondere Herausforderungen. Es geht heute weniger um die Authentisierung des Grauens, sondern um seine reflexive und diskursive Darstellung, Inszenierung und Kommentierung. Die große Aufgabe von Ausstellungen in KZ-Gedenkstätten besteht darin, Geschichte und Geschichtsprozesse in ihrer Komplexität lesbar zu gestalten, Akteure zu benennen, Perspektivwechsel herzustellen und ohne vordergründiges Moralisieren Empathie mit den Opfern zu ermöglichen.

Die Geschichte von Ausstellungen in KZ-Gedenkstätten in der Bundesrepublik ist eine Geschichte ihres jahrzehntelangen Erkämpfens und ihrer ideologiekritischen und selbstreflexiven Neukonzeption nach der Wiedervereinigung. Es gilt, dieses aufklärerische Potenzial zu bewahren und immer wieder zu erneuern, gerade auch was die Rezeptionsgeschichte der Lager betrifft. Sollte dies gelingen, wären KZ-Gedenkstätten mit ihren Ausstellungen nicht nur Sonderformen von Museen, deren museologische Satisfaktionsfähigkeit von klassischen Geschichtsmuseen bisweilen noch immer in Frage gestellt wird. Sie hätten hinsichtlich der Präsentation historischer Prozesse vielmehr Avantgarde-Charakter.

Jörg Skriebeleit

the camp have operated within a tension between fact and fiction, moralization and musealization.

Concentration camp memorial sites are multiple sites. They are modern Golgothas, cemeteries, sites of family histories, open-air museums, places of learning, and historical sources – both for the period of the concentration camps themselves and for the following decades of dealing with their historical existence. However, concentration camps have a further and increasingly important function: they are also museums.

Defining them in this way presents the conceptualization of exhibitions with particular challenges. The issue today is not so much one of providing authentic proof of the horrors that occurred there as of generating a reflexive and discursive presentation of as well as commentary on these horrors. The great task facing exhibitions at concentration camp memorial sites consists in making history and historical processes decipherable in all their complexity, in naming actors, providing changes in perspective, and facilitating empathy with the victims without superficial moralization.

The history of exhibitions at concentration camp memorial sites in Germany is a history of a decades-long struggle to establish them, and their ideology-critical and self-reflexive reconception following reunification. They have a potential to enlighten that which needs to be conserved and repeatedly renewed, particularly in relation to the history of the reception of the camps. If they succeed in this endeavor, concentration camp memorial sites and their exhibitions will become more than merely special forms of museums whose capacity to function at a museological level is still occasionally questioned by classic historical museums. In terms of their presentation of the historical process they could in fact acquire an avant-garde character.

Jörg Skriebeleit

Was bleibt – Nachwirkungen des Konzentrationslagers Flossenbürg
What Remains – The Aftermath of the Flossenbürg Concentration Camp

„Wo geht's hier zum Lager?" So fragen viele Besucher der KZ-Gedenkstätte Flossenbürg. Auf den ersten Blick finden sich fast keine Spuren des früheren Konzentrationslagers. Eine Straße führt durch das Gelände, an einem Hang steht eine Wohnsiedlung. Aus dem Wald ragt ein einzelner Wachturm auf. Was ist vom ehemaligen Lager geblieben? Was geschah nach 1945 mit den Tätern? Wo blieben die Überlebenden? Welche Rollen spielte Flossenbürg in der Erinnerung, was wurde vergessen, wessen wurde gedacht? Unter dem Titel *Was bleibt – Nachwirkungen des Konzentrationslagers Flossenbürg* widmet sich eine Dauerausstellung seit Oktober 2010 diesen vier Leitfragen. Als erste Ausstellung in einer KZ-Gedenkstätte befasst sie sich ausschließlich mit den über 60 Jahren nach dem Ende des „Dritten Reichs".
Eine der vielen Herausforderungen bestand darin, die speziellen Entwicklungen vor Ort in die (deutsche) Zeitgeschichte einzubetten. Die Beseitigung der baulichen Reste des Lagers, der milde Umgang mit den Tätern, die späte Anerkennung der Opfer –, all dies ist nicht ohne die historischen Entwicklungen zu verstehen. Nicht ohne die große Politik, den Kalten Krieg und die beiden deutschen Staaten, aber auch nicht ohne soziale und kulturelle Entwicklungen. Die gewandelte Einstellung gegenüber gesellschaftlichen Minderheiten, die kritische Erforschung der Heimatgeschichte, Bücher wie das *Tagebuch der Anne Frank* und Filme wie *Schindlers Liste* seien stellvertretend genannt.
Die vier Leitthemen „Täter", „Überlebende", „Erinnerung" und „Ort" waren das Ergebnis einer langen Diskussion innerhalb des Ausstellungsteams, das ausschließlich aus Beschäftigten der Gedenkstätte bestand. Um diese Leitthemen über 60 Jahre hinweg verfolgen zu können und zugleich die Bezüge zur Zeitgeschichte zu verdeutlichen, war ein Raumkonzept nötig, das auf 400 Quadratmetern die Komplexität der Geschichte zeigt, ohne die Besucher zu erschlagen.
Der räumliche Entwurf nimmt die Situation der Besucher ernst, von denen die meisten

"How do you get to the camp?" This is a question asked by many visitors to the Flossenbürg Concentration Camp memorial site. At first glance there seem to be few traces left of the former camp. A road runs through the site and a housing development occupies one of its slopes. A single watchtower stretches up out of the forest. What is left of the former camp? What happened after 1945 to the perpetrators of the crimes committed here? And what of the survivors? What role does Flossenbürg play in memory, what has been forgotten, who is commemorated? Since October 2010 a permanent exhibition entitled *What Remains – The Aftermath of the Flossenbürg Concentration Camp* has explored these four key questions, focusing exclusively on the sixty years since the end of the "Third Reich."
One of the particular challenges for such a project entails the integration of specific local developments into the broader recent German history. The removal of the structural remains of the camp, the mild treatment of the perpetrators of crimes committed there, the belated recognition of the victims – all this can only be understood in the context of broader historical developments. These include the prevailing political atmosphere, the Cold War and relations between the two German states, but also social and cultural developments such as changing attitudes to social minorities, critical research of local history, books such as the *Diary of Anne Frank*, and films such as *Schindler's List*.
The four key themes of the exhibition, "Perpetrators," "Survivors," "Memory," and "Site," were the result of a long discussion within the exhibition team, which was composed exclusively of individuals working at the memorial site. In order to be able to pursue these themes across a time span of sixty years while at the same time illuminating connections to include contemporary history, a spatial concept was required that could show the complexity of this history in

Erinnerungs- und Gedenkstätten
Memorials and Commemorative Sites

Was bleibt – KZ-Gedenkstätte Flossenbürg What Remains – The Flossenbürg Concentration Camp

KZ-Gedenkstätte Flossenbürg
The Flossenbürg Concentration Camp
Gedächtnisallee 5–7
92198 Flossenbürg

Gesamtleitung Coordination:
Dr. Jörg Skriebeleit
Projektkoordination Project Manager:
Ulrich Fritz, Johannes Ibel

zuvor das ehemalige Lagergelände oder die Dauerausstellung zur Geschichte des KZ Flossenbürg gesehen haben dürften und die damit eine Fülle von Informationen in Text und Bild zu verarbeiten haben.

In der neuen Ausstellung betreten sie ein Foyer, in dem ausgewählte Zitate von Besuchern der Gedenkstätte, von Überlebenden und Anwohnern abwechselnd auf die Wände projiziert werden. „Ich habe von Dachau und Auschwitz gehört, aber nie von Flossenbürg", „Es sollte nicht immer auf Kosten der Flossenbürger gehen", „Die Landschaft kann ja nichts dafür" – mit diesen anonymen Statements sollen die Besucher eingestimmt und neugierig gemacht werden. Der eigentliche Ausstellungsraum thematisiert zuerst die Befreiung des KZ Flossenbürg am 23. April 1945. Mit der Befreiung durch die Alliierten endete die unmittelbare Verfolgung der Häftlinge – sie ist der notwendige Beginn der im Folgenden dargestellten Ereignisse.

Der gut überschaubare Raum besteht aus zwei klar getrennten Bereichen: einer regelmäßigen Anordnung von Vitrinen im Raum – über einigen von ihnen hängen lampenartige Audio-Elemente – sowie einer großen Wand mit Monitoren. Die doppelte Gliederung erschließt sich auf zwei Ebenen. An der Rückwand des Küchengebäudes ist hinter jeder Vitrinenreihe ein Leitthema zu lesen: „Täter", „Überlebende", „Erinnerung", „Ort". An der Monitor-Wand geben große Jahreszahlen die chronologische Abfolge der Ausstellung vor, von 1945 bis in die Gegenwart.

Die Vitrinen präsentieren Objekte in Kombination mit Abbildungen und Text. Die meisten besitzen nicht die selbstverständliche Aura von Gegenständen, die von Häftlingen gemacht oder benutzt wurden und nun in Ausstellungen zur KZ-Geschichte zu sehen sind. Hier findet man eher unscheinbare Dinge, Objekte, die schwer zu entziffern sind. Eines davon ist ein Gipsmodell des Bildhauers Wilhelm Vierling von 1948. Es zeigt zwei Männer mit nacktem Oberkörper: Ein Stehender hilft einem Sitzenden auf. Die Steinwerkzeuge weisen darauf hin, dass beide Männer Häftlinge

a space measuring 400 square meters without overwhelming visitors with information. The spatial design takes into account the fact that most visitors will already have seen the former camp area or the permanent exhibition on the history of the Flossenbürg Concentration Camp itself, and in the process will have had to absorb a considerable degree of information in the form of texts and pictures.

In the new exhibition visitors enter a foyer featuring alternating wall projections of statements by visitors to the memorial site, survivors, and local residents. "I've heard of Dachau and Auschwitz but never of Flossenbürg," "It shouldn't be at the expense of Flossenbürg residents," "It's not the landscape's fault" – these anonymous statements are intended as a means of drawing in visitors and making them curious.

The initial section of the exhibition space deals with the liberation of the Flossenbürg Concentration Camp on April 23, 1945. Liberation by the Allies meant the end of direct persecution of the inmates, and it marked the beginning of the series of events that are subsequently presented. The space consists of two clearly divided zones, one constituted by regularly arranged display cases – lamp-like audio elements have been installed over several of them – and the other by a large wall with monitors. The dual structure can be accessed on two levels. On the back wall of the former kitchen building one of the key themes is displayed behind each row of display cases: "Perpetrators," "Survivors," "Memory," and "Site." Large dates displayed on the monitor wall indicate the chronological sequence of the exhibition – from 1945 until the present. The display cases present objects in combination with pictures and texts. Most of these objects do not have the kind of aura one tends to expect from artifacts made and used by prisoners that are now presented in exhibitions on the history of the concentration camps. As a rule these objects are rather inconspicuous and difficult to decipher. One is a plaster model by the sculptor Wilhelm Vierling from 1948. It shows two men with naked torsos: one

Wissenschaftliches Ausstellungsteam
Scientific Exhibition Team:
Anja Fritz, Ulrich Fritz, Kathrin Helldorfer, Johannes Ibel, Annette Kraus, Dr. Christa Schikorra, Dr. Alexander Schmidt, Dr. Jörg Skriebeleit

Weitere Mitarbeit Collaboration:
Anna Andlauer, Eva Bracke, Thomas Muggenthaler, František Nachlinger, Jeanette Toussaint
Wissenschaftlicher Fachbeirat
Scientific Advisory Committee:
Prof. Wolfgang Benz, Wulff E. Brebeck, Prof. Michael Brenner, Dr. Gabriele Camphausen, Michel Clisson, Charles

Dekeyser, Prof. Eberhardt Dünninger, Prof. Rudolf Endres, Dr. Karola Fings, Dr. Renate Höpfinger, Uwe Neumärker, Dr. Oskar Schneider, Miloš Volf, Dr. Jens-Christian Wagner, Dr. Celina Wojnarowicz, Dr. Jürgen Zarusky

des KZ Flossenbürg darstellen sollen. Der Entwurf betont die gegenseitige Hilfe und Unterstützung der Gefangenen. Er diente als Bestandteil einer Kreuzigungsgruppe in der Kapelle „Jesus im Kerker". Die dortige Ausführung in Lindenholz, die erst ein Jahr später angebracht wurde, zeigt nun aber ein anderes Bild. Aus dem Helfenden wird ein Schlagender, der eine Peitsche schwingt – vielleicht ein Kapo, also ein etwas privilegierter Funktionshäftling. Der am Boden kauernde Geschlagene versucht, seinen Kopf zu schützen. Statt gegenseitiger Hilfe zeigt das Altarbild nun Schikane und Terror. So inszeniert die Altargruppe ein lange verbreitetes Vorurteil: In Flossenbürg waren nur Verbrecher eingesperrt, die sich dort gegenseitig das Leben zur Hölle machten. Die Außenwelt konnte sich mit dieser Erzählung aus ihrer Mitverantwortung entlassen.

Im Lauf der Zeit veränderten sich die Formen und Inhalte der Erinnerung an Flossenbürg. Prominente Gefangene wie Admiral Canaris wurden gewürdigt und wieder vergessen. Der gemeinsam mit Canaris ermordete Dietrich Bonhoeffer wurde seit den achtziger Jahren fast zu einem evangelischen Heiligen. Verfolgte Gruppen wie die Sinti und Roma wurden erst spät in das Gedenken einbezogen. Die Objekte, Bilder und Texte der Ausstellung zeigen diese Entwicklungen anhand von Flossenbürger Beispielen, die mit der Zeitgeschichte in Beziehung gesetzt werden. So wird deutlich, dass Flossenbürg häufig stellvertretend für Deutschland bzw.

of the figures is standing and helping the other up. Their stone work tools indicate that both men are inmates of the Flossenbürg Concentration Camp. The piece emphasizes the help and support inmates offered one another. It once served as part of a crucifixion group in the "Jesus in Prison" chapel. A sculpture in linden wood, which was added one year later, shows a different image. Here the standing figure is wielding a whip – perhaps a capo or another privileged prisoner functionary. The man he is beating cowers in the ground trying to protect his head. Rather than mutual help, the altar image shows victimization and terror. The altar group thus refers to the long-held belief that all the inmates in Flossenbürg were criminals who basically inflicted their suffering on one another. It was a narrative that relieved the outside world of its responsibility for what occurred in the camp.

Over time the ways in which Flossenbürg was remembered changed both in terms of form and content. Prominent prisoners such as Admiral Canaris were honored and then again forgotten. Since the 1980s, on the other hand, Dietrich Bonhoeffer, who was murdered with Canaris, has been revered almost as a Lutheran saint. It took a considerable amount of time for some persecuted groups, such as the Sinti and Roma, to be commemorated at all. The objects, pictures, and texts in the exhibition illustrate these developments using concrete Flossenbürg

die Bundesrepublik steht – aber auch, dass der Ort in der Oberpfalz den Zeitläufen bisweilen hinterherhinkte.

Am unmittelbarsten verdeutlicht sich die Gleichzeitigkeit der Ereignisse auf den 27 Monitoren der Medienwand, die in sich eine Art „Gesamtkunstwerk" bildet. Zu sehen sind (neben den orientierenden Jahreszahlen und Periodisierungen) drei Darstellungs-Modi, die alle ohne Ton ablaufen. Die Hauptrolle spielen Filmclips mit Bezug zum Komplex „Flossenbürg" – Filmaufnahmen der amerikanischen Befreier vor Ort, eine Fotofolge zur Errichtung von KZ-Friedhöfen mit Opfern der Todesmärsche, aber auch Zeitungsartikel zum Prozess gegen Iwan Demjanjuk in München, der nach seiner Dienstzeit im Vernichtungslager Sobibor Wachmann in Flossenbürg war. Durch die unterschiedliche Länge der Filmclips entstehen immer neue Konstellationen und Gegenüberstellungen historischer Sachverhalte. Wechselwirkungen gibt es aber auch mit den Vitrinen.

Der zweite Modus besteht aus kurzen Texten, die an die Rezeption des Nationalsozialismus erinnern: Das Erscheinen des Buchs *Der SS-Staat* von Eugen Kogon wird hier ebenso genannt wie der Auschwitz-Prozess in Frankfurt am Main oder die Einweihung des Holocaust-Mahnmals in Berlin. Beim dritten Modus erscheinen 27 Fotos auf den Monitoren: Der Siegesjubel der deutschen Nationalmannschaft bei der Fußball-WM 1954, der Sprung eines Solda-

examples, which are placed in the context of broad contemporary historical events. In this way it becomes clear that Flossenbürg has often been representative of wider developments in Germany and the Federal Republic – but also that sometimes this site in the Upper Palatinate region has failed to keep abreast of the temper of the time. The simultaneity of certain events is most clearly illustrated by the twenty-seven monitors on the media wall, which form a kind of "synthetic artwork." Along with dates and periodizations, it involves three modes of presentation, all of which function without sound. The main role is played by film clips referring to the "Flossenbürg" complex – films of American liberators at the camp, a photo series showing the construction of concentration camp graveyards with victims of the death marches, as well as newspaper articles on the trail of Ivan Demjanjuk in Munich, who, after working in the Sobibor extermination camp, was a guard in Flossenbürg. As a result of the different lengths of the film clips, and the interconnections between the film material and the themes explored in the display cases, new constellations and juxtapositions of historical material are constantly being generated. The second mode is comprised of short texts that recall the reception of National Socialism. This material refers to a diverse range of subjects, such as the publication of the book *The SS State* by Eugen Kogon, the Auschwitz court case in Frankfurt am

Beinkiste für Umbettungen, um 1958
An ossuary for reburial c. 1958

Hemd von Lieutenant Samuel Goldstein, 357. Infanterieregiment, der an der Befreiung des KZ Flossenbürg beteiligt war.
Shirt of Lieutenant Samuel Goldstein of the 357th Infantry Regiment who was involved in the liberation of the Flossenbürg Concentration Camp.

Dauerausstellung Permanent Exhibition
Eröffnung Opening:
Oktober 2010 October 2010

ten über den Stacheldraht beim Bau der Berliner Mauer, eine Demonstration gegen Atomkraft in den achtziger Jahren – viele der Abbildungen sind Ikonen, vielfach bekannt aus Geschichtsbüchern und Medien. All diese Ereignisse der Zeitgeschichte betten die Geschichte des ehemaligen Lagers in das Weltgeschehen ein.

Was bleibt – Nachwirkungen des Konzentrationslagers Flossenbürg ist eine ambitionierte Ausstellung, die den Besuchern große Freiheiten lässt, aber auch erhebliche Eigenleistungen abverlangt. Die präsentierte Geschichte erzählt sich nicht von selbst, der Besucher muss sie sich erschließen. Die Ausstellung belohnt ihn dafür mit neuen Erkenntnissen und dient anderen Historikern hoffentlich als Inspirationsquelle für weitere Projekte dieser Art.

Ulrich Fritz

Main, and the dedication of the Holocaust Memorial in Berlin. This series concludes with twenty-seven photos shown on the monitors: the German football team celebrating following its victory at the 1954 World Cup, a soldier leaping over the barbed wire dividing east and west during the building of the Berlin Wall, and an anti-nuclear demonstration in the 1980s – many of these images are iconic and have often featured in history books and the media, and they serve to embed the history of the former concentration camp in world events.

What Remains – The Aftermath of the Flossenbürg Concentration Camp is an ambitious exhibition, one that allows visitors considerable scope in the way they approach the material while also requiring a significant level of individual engagement. Visitors' efforts in this regard are rewarded with new insights into historical events, and it is hoped that the exhibition will inspire other historians to pursue further projects of this kind.

Ulrich Fritz

Gestaltungskonzept[1]
Die Vergegenständlichung der Zeit durch den Raum

Was bleibt ist eine Ausstellung zur Nachkriegsgeschichte des ehemaligen KZ Flossenbürg. Sie stellt die Fortsetzung der bestehenden Dauerausstellung „Konzentrationslager Flossenbürg 1938–1945"dar. Das Gestaltungskonzept fragt danach, wie Ort und Raum sich auf die Erinnerung auswirken, und versucht, das Phänomen Zeit visuell abzubilden. Grundlegend sind dabei zwei Aspekte:
– der Raum als Mittel zur Strukturierung von Geschichte
– der Raum als Mittel zur Memorierung von Geschichte
Einerseits wird die Erinnerung mit Orten und Gegenständen verknüpft, andererseits ist der Raum ein Beziehungsgefüge, das weniger der Erinnerung als der Informationsvermittlung und gleichsam als Erkenntnisinstrument dient.

Räumliche Beziehungen können abstrakte inhaltliche Beziehungen auf klare Weise

Design Concept[1]
The objectification of time through the space *What Remains* is an exhibition on the post-war history of the former Flossenbürg concentration camp. It represents the continuation of the already existing permanent exhibition "Flossenbürg Concentration Camp 1938–1945." The design concept asks how place and space affect the memory, and tries to visually depict the phenomenon of time. There are two basic aspects:
– Space as a means of structuring history
– Space as a means of memorizing history
On the one hand, the memory of places and objects will be linked together, while on the other space is a structure of relationships, that serves memory to a lesser extent than the provision of information and, simultaneously serving as a cognitive instrument.
Spatial relationships can illustrate abstract substantive relationships in a clear manner. In this sense we can understand the space as an independent medium.

Erinnerungs- und Gedenkstätten
Memorials and Commemorative Sites

Was bleibt – KZ-Gedenkstätte Flossenbürg What Remains –The Flossenbürg Concentration Camp

[1] Vgl. Ulrich Schwarz: „Gestaltungskonzept", in: *Was bleibt – Nachwirkungen des Konzentrationslagers Flossenbürg. Katalog zur Dauerausstellung*, Göttingen 2011, S. 14–17.

[1] See Ulrich Schwarz: „Gestaltungskonzept", in: *Was bleibt – Nachwirkungen des Konzentrationslagers Flossenbürg. Katalog zur Dauerausstellung*, Göttingen 2011, p. 14–17.

veranschaulichen. In diesem Sinne kann man den Raum als eigenständiges Medium verstehen.

Gestaltung ist Haltung

Wir beschäftigen uns bei der Aufgabe der Ausstellungsgestaltung mit der Gegenwart der Vergangenheit. Thematisch behandelt die Ausstellung die Nachwirkungen des Konzentrationslagers Flossenbürg, also die Geschichte von 1945 bis heute.
Die Geschehnisse im ehemaligen KZ Flossenbürg sind zweifellos der Vergangenheit zuzuordnen. In einem modernen, zeitgemäßen Verständnis geht es nicht nur darum, an diese Vergangenheit zu erinnern, mit dem Ziel, dass diese Betrachtung dann in einem wiederholten „Nie wieder" mündet. Vielmehr gilt es, Erkenntnisse aus der Beschäftigung und Auseinandersetzung mit dieser Vergangenheit zu ziehen. Es stellt sich die Frage, wie sie rezipiert wird, wie die Geschichte auf die Gegenwart einwirkt. Eine weitere grundsätzliche Überlegung gilt der der Ästhetik des Ekels. Gräuel üben eine eigenartige und fragwürdige Anziehungskraft aus. Es gibt Situationen, in denen man den Blick nicht abwenden kann. Das Abbild des Schrecklichen, Abscheulichen wirkt anziehend und abstoßend zugleich. Die explizite Darstellung von Leichen bedeutet einen Tabubruch. Doch die abschreckende Wirkung von Gräueldarstellungen ist fraglich. Im Angesicht des bis dahin Unvorstellbaren baut der Betrachter aus Selbstschutz eine innere Distanz auf. Die in vielen Dokumentationen dargestellten Vorgänge der Massenvernichtungen haben zweifellos stattgefunden. Die schonungslose Konfrontation mit Bergen abgemagerter Leichen stellt jedoch noch nicht per se eine heilende Schocktherapie dar. Im Zusammenhang mit diesen Überlegungen haben wir andere Gedenkstätten hinsichtlich ihrer Gestaltungselemente analysiert und die Frage gestellt, ob es einen einheitlichen, erkennbaren Formenkanon für Gedenkstätten gibt. Was ist die Syntax des Gedenkstätten-Designs? Und wie weit darf man sich davon entfernen, ohne Gefahr zu

Design is Attitude

We are engaged in the task of designing the exhibition with the presence of the past. Thematically, the exhibition dealt with the aftermath of the Flossenbürg Concentration Camp, that is the history from 1945 until the present. The events in the former Flossenbürg Concentration Camp are undoubtedly attributable to the past. In a modern, present-day understanding it's not just about remembering that past, it is rather the intent of "never again." Rather, it is important to draw lessons from the discussion and engagement with this past. Thought, this raises the question of how it is received as history affects the present. Another fundamental consideration is the aesthetic of the repellent act. Atrocities exert a unique and questionable attraction. There are situations in which one can not avert their eyes. The image of atrocities and vileness is attractive and repulsive at the same time. The explicit representation of corpses is a taboo. But the deterrent effect of depictions of atrocities is questionable. Confronted with the unimaginable the viewer builds an inner distance from these atrocities as an act of self-protection. The processes shown in many documentaries of mass exterminations have without a doubt taken place. The relentless confrontation with mounds of emaciated corpses does not represent a healing shock therapy per se. Together with these considerations, we have analyzed other memorials in terms of design elements and asked the question, of whether there is a single, identifiable form for memorials. What is the syntax of the memorial design? And how far can you remove it, without running the risk of designing an inappropriate representation of the topic?

So much can be found on the general characteristic style of memorials: The canon is characterized by functional text-image configurations with a strictly documentary character and strict chronological order. Although the basic representations represent a credible reality, however, these are

laufen, eine dem Thema unangemessene Darstellung zu entwerfen?

So viel kann zum allgemeinen Duktus von Gedenkstätten festgestellt werden: Der Kanon ist gekennzeichnet durch funktionale Text-Bildanordnungen mit strikt dokumentarischem Charakter und streng (chrono-) logischer Anordnung. Die gängigen Darstellungen repräsentieren zwar in glaubwürdiger Weise die Realität, jedoch handelt es sich dabei überdeutlich um eine abgeschlossene Vergangenheit.
Das Wagnis, eingetretene Wege zu verlassen, neue Vermittlungsformen zu suchen und damit vielleicht sogar zu provozieren, sind die Wissenschaftler in Flossenbürg bewusst eingegangen. Bekannte Muster und Wahrnehmungsgewohnheiten werden aufgebrochen, um bestehende Erwartungshorizonte zu erweitern. Das Wesen des Neuen liegt in einem Medienkonzept, das zwar die klassische Triade von Objekt, Text und Bild beibehält, jedoch die gängigen Vermittlungsformen dekonstruiert.

Das klassische Drama als Vorlage

Der Entwurf sucht neue Wege der Vermittlung von Geschichte und verlässt den bestehenden Formenkanon der deutschen Gedenkstätten-Landschaft. Die Ausstellung ist wie ein klassisches Drama gegliedert – mit Prolog und Epilog.
Im Foyer bezieht eine raumgreifende Medieninstallation die Besucher ein.
Der Hauptteil durchbricht mit seiner Darstellungsform gängige Wahrnehmungsmuster – ein neues Medienformat arbeitet mit der Verfremdung von bewegtem Bild und Ton. Die ausgestellten Objekte konfrontieren die Besucher mit originalen Tondokumenten. Am Ende gibt die Ausstellung den Blick frei auf das Zentrum des Geschehens und bietet Raum zur Reflexion. Ziel der Gestalter ist es, zur Auseinandersetzung anzuregen und das Gestern mit dem Heute und Morgen in Beziehung zu setzen.

clearly representative of a closed past. The research team in Flossenbürg have often mindfully chosen to risk leaving the well-worn path in order to search for new forms of communication and perhaps even to encourage such forms. These well-known perception and habit patterns were broken in order to expand existing horizons of expectation. The essence of the new approach is a media concept which, while retaining the classic triad of object, text, and image, simultaneously deconstructs the common forms of communication.

The classical drama as a template

The design concept seeks new ways of teaching history and leaves the existing canon of German memorial landscape. The exhibition is structured like a classic drama – with a prologue and epilogue. In the foyer, an expansive media installation involves the visitors. The main part breaks with its usual form of presentation patterns of perception – a new media format uses the alienation of moving pictures and sound. The exhibition objects confront visitors with the original sound recordings. Lastly, the exhibition provides a view of the center and provides the visitor a space for reflection. The aim of the designers is to stimulate debate, and to place together yesterday with today and tomorrow.

Erinnerungs- und Gedenkstätten Memorials and Commemorative Sites	Träger Supporting Institution: Stiftung Bayerische Gedenkstätten Bavarian Memorial Trust	Ausstellungsfläche Exhibition Area: 1 000 m²
Was bleibt – KZ-Gedenkstätte Flossenbürg What Remains – The Flossenbürg Concentration Camp		

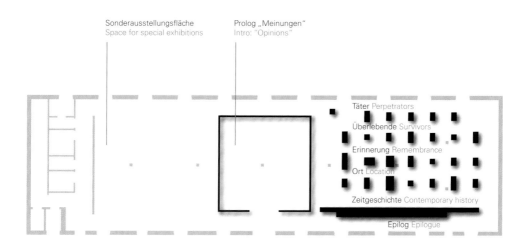

Sonderausstellungsfläche
Space for special exhibitions

Prolog „Meinungen"
Intro: "Opinions"

Täter Perpetrators
Überlebende Survivors
Erinnerung Remembrance
Ort Location
Zeitgeschichte Contemporary history
Epilog Epilogue

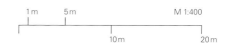

1 m   5 m   M 1:400
                    10 m   20 m

Das Ausstellungsprojekt beschreibt die Möglichkeiten einer künstlerisch-gestalterischen Übersetzung von geschichtsbezogenen Archiven in medial erfahrbare, räumliche Museografien. Das Interface, die Benutzeroberfläche des Archivs ist der Raum. Er fungiert als Denkmodell und Erkenntnishilfe. Die räumliche Anordnung macht Beziehungen und Zusammenhänge lesbar.
Chronologisch gliedert sich die Geschichte in definierbare Zeit-Phasen:

The exhibition project outlined the possibilities of an artistic and creative translation of historical archives in the media-related experiential, and spatial museography. The interface, or rather the user interface of the archive is the room. It serves as a model for knowledge and understanding. The spatial arrangement makes relationships and connections visible.
The story is divided chronologically into definable time periods:

Phase 1	Frühjahr 1945	Schwellensituation Befreiung
Phase 2	Sommer 1945–1950	Übergang und Neuordnung
Phase 3	1950–1958	Schlussstrich und Integration
Phase 4	1958–1970	Verdrängen und Vergessen
Phase 5	1970–1980	Selektives Erinnern
Phase 6	1980–1995	Umstrittene Wiederentdeckung
Phase 7	1995–2010	Hinterlassenschaften

Phase 1	Spring 1945	Threshold situation liberation
Phase 2	Summer 1945–1950	Transition and reorganization
Phase 3	1950–1958	Drawing the line and integration
Phase 4	1958–1970	Repress and forget
Phase 5	1970–1980	Selective memory
Phase 6	1980–1995	Controversial rediscovery
Phase 7	1995–2010	Legacies

Diese Darstellungsform ist chronologisch, in Zeitschnitten, linear angeordnet und entspricht damit den gängigen Gliederungsformen. Neu ist eine zusätzliche Gliederung in thematische Handlungsstränge, die sowohl für sich als auch in ihren Beziehungen zueinander durch ihre Verortung im Raum ablesbar werden:
– Täter
– Überlebende
– Erinnerung
– Ort
Das Archiv bietet dazu jeweils Exponate unterschiedlicher Ausprägung:
– Bilder, Fotografien
– Gegenstände
– Schriftstücke
– Zeitzeugenberichte
– Tondokumente

This presentation is chronological, in time periods, arranged linearly and corresponds to the usual forms of organization. A new component is the additional organization into thematic areas; the thematic areas are organized according to their location within the space:
– Perpetrators
– Survivors
– Memory
– Place
The archive provides these additional components to the exhibits in varying degrees:
– Pictures, photographs
– Personal items
– Documents
– Eyewitness reports
– Sound recordings

Erinnerungs- und Gedenkstätten
Memorials and Commemorative Sites

Was bleibt – KZ-Gedenkstätte Flossenbürg What Remains – The Flossenbürg Concentration Camp

Ausstellungsgestaltung
Exhibition Design:
BERTRON SCHWARZ FREY

Entwurf Head of Design:
Prof. Ulrich Schwarz, Aurelia Bertron, Prof. Claudia Frey
Ausführungsplanung Planning and Implementation: Carina Ernst
Grafik Design Graphic Design:
Aurelia Bertron, Marie Lauenroth

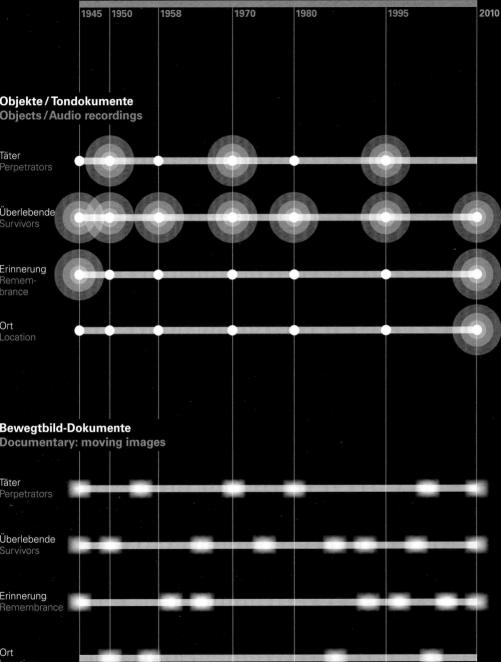

	1945	1950	1958	1970	1980	1995	2010

Objekte / Tondokumente
Objects / Audio recordings

Täter
Perpetrators

Überlebende
Survivors

Erinnerung
Remem-
brance

Ort
Location

Bewegtbild-Dokumente
Documentary: moving images

Täter
Perpetrators

Überlebende
Survivors

Erinnerung
Remembrance

Ort

Originale Objekte belegen die Geschichte und bieten thematische Bezüge. Die Präsentation erfolgt klassisch, in jeweils auf das Objekt abgestimmten Vitrinen. Die Objektpräsentationen sind teilweise mit Audio-Installationen kombiniert, die Originaltexte über gerichtete Lautsprecher abspielen. Die Hördokumente haben ebenso wie originale Objekte authentischen Charakter.

Original objects accompany the story and provide thematic reference points. The classic presentation presents the objects in matching display cases. The object presentations are partly combined with audio installations and play the original texts on outward facing speakers. Audio recording have an authentic character just as the original objects themselves.

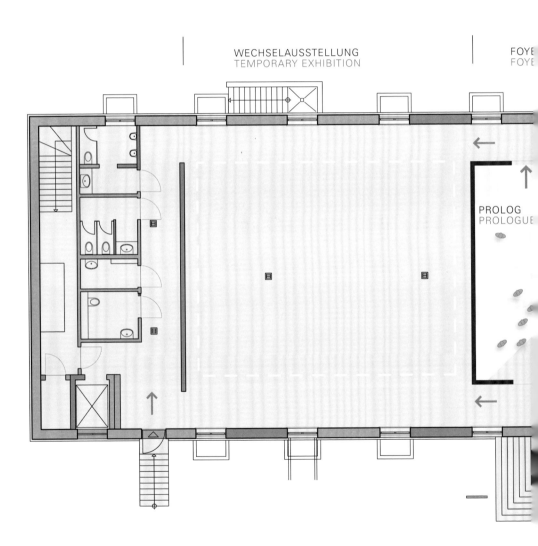

WECHSELAUSSTELLUNG
TEMPORARY EXHIBITION

FOYE
FOYE

PROLOG
PROLOGUE

Erinnerungs- und Gedenkstätten
Memorials and Commemorative Sites

Was bleibt – KZ-Gedenkstätte
Flossenbürg What Remains – The
Flossenbürg Concentration Camp

Die Ausstellung ist in der ehemaligen Häftlingsküche des KZ Flossenbürg angesiedelt. Das Bauwerk wurde 1939 errichtet und war eines der wenigen massiven Steingebäude im Häftlingsbereich.

The exhibition is located in the former prisoner's kitchen of the Flossenbürg Concentration Camp. The building was built in 1939 and was one of the few massive stone buildings in the prisoner's area.

Tondokumente werden in Bezug auf ihre Eignung für Ausstellungspräsentationen als problematisch eingeschätzt; die Geräuschkulisse wird als störend empfunden. Die Idee der neuen Ausstellung ist, vor allem die Überlebenden zu Wort kommen zu lassen. Die verfügbaren Tondokumente repräsentieren als O-Ton-Dokumente sowohl die Zeitschnitte als auch die unterschiedlichen inhaltlichen Bezüge. Diese so entstandene Struktur stellt die Blaupause für den Grundriss der Ausstellungsgestaltung dar.

Audio recordings are assessed as problematic in terms of their suitability for exhibition display; the noise is bothersome. The idea of this new exhibition is above all to allow the survivors to speak. The available audio recordings represent the original sound-documents and a representation of the era as well as the different referenced content. This resulting structure provides the blueprint for the layout of the exhibition design.

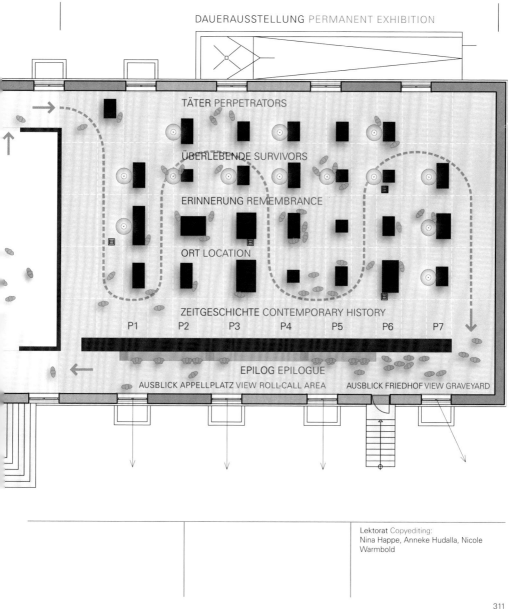

DAUERAUSSTELLUNG PERMANENT EXHIBITION

TÄTER PERPETRATORS

ÜBERLEBENDE SURVIVORS

ERINNERUNG REMEMBRANCE

ORT LOCATION

ZEITGESCHICHTE CONTEMPORARY HISTORY

P1   P2   P3   P4   P5   P6   P7

EPILOG EPILOGUE

AUSBLICK APPELLPLATZ VIEW ROLL-CALL AREA   AUSBLICK FRIEDHOF VIEW GRAVEYARD

Lektorat Copyediting:
Nina Happe, Anneke Hudalla, Nicole Warmbold

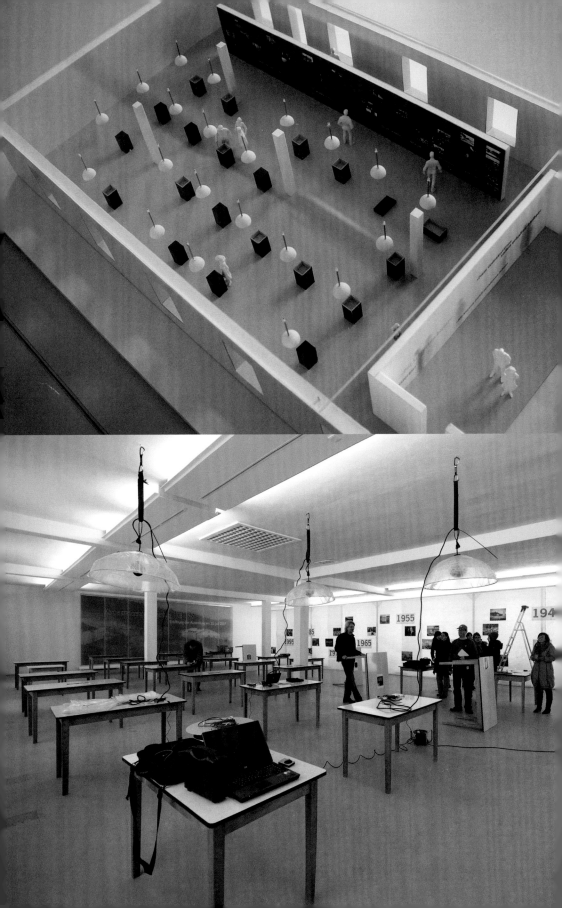

Eine räumliche Erzählform

An Stelle eines strikten Nach-
einanders steht ein strukturiertes
Nebeneinander von Informationen
und Vermittlungsformen, das
Bezüge erkennen und Schlüsse
zulässt. Die Wissensaneignung
leistet das Publikum autonom.
Eine Reihenfolge ist nicht vorgegeben. Die klare, übersichtliche Anordnung der einzelnen
Ausstellungselemente – Vitrinen,
Hörstationen und synchronoptische Medienwand – bietet jedoch
jederzeit und an jeder Stelle eine
zeitliche und thematische Orientierung und Zuordnung.
Dieser neue Ansatz begreift das
Denken als offenes System,
mit dem Ziel, Erkenntnis durch
Lesbarkeit von Zusammenhängen
zu erreichen.

A spatial narrative

Rather than a strict sequence
a structured juxtaposition of
information and forms of communication are used that allow
for connections and conclusions.
The audience is able to acquire
knowledge on their own accord.
A specific order is not predetermined. The clear, concise arrangement of the individual exhibition
elements – display cases, audio
stations and synchronoptic media
walls – offers at any time and any
place a temporal and thematic
orientation and classification.
This new approach considers the
mind as an open system with
the aim to achieve recognition
through a readability of contexts.

Wettbewerbsmodell, 1:1 Stellprobe
Competition entry, 1:1 example

Jury Gestaltungswettbewerb
Design Competition Jury:
Wulff E. Brebeck, Peter Brückner,
Elisabeth Bücherl-Beer, Dr. Gabriele
Camphausen, Ulrich Fritz, Rikola-Gunnar
Lüttgenau, Dr. Jörg Skriebeleit

Planungsphase Planning Phase

Erinnerungs- und Gedenkstätten
Memorials and Commemorative Sites

Was bleibt – KZ-Gedenkstätte
Flossenbürg What Remains – The
Flossenbürg Concentration Camp

Baumaßnahmen, Planung und Bauleitung
Construction, Planning and Construction
Site Management:
Elisabeth Bücherl-Beer, Klaus Koch,
Roland Wellert, Christian Denz, Hans
Zierer, Lothar Völkl, Staatliches Bauamt
Amberg-Sulzbach State department of
planning and building inspection Amberg-
Sulzbach

Rendering aus Wettbewerbsbeitrag
Rendering from Competition entry

Im Foyer werfen Projektoren Zitate von Besuchern und Bürgern an die Wände. Das projizierte Zitat bleibt für eine gewisse Zeit präsent, bevor es dann wieder verschwindet. Der Besucher sieht seinen eigenen Schatten und setzt sich so selbst in Beziehung zu den Zitaten.

The projector in the foyer projects quotes from visitors and citizens onto the walls. The projected quote remains for a few moments before it disappears. The visitor is able to see their own shadow in relation to the quote.

Lichtplanung Lighting Design:
Ringo T. Fischer
Englische Textfassung
English Version:
Patricia Szobar

Ausstellung Exhibition

was bleibt | what remains

Nachwirkungen des Konzentrationslagers Flossenb
The Aftermath of the Flossenbürg Concentration Ca

KZ-Gedenkstätte
Flossenbürg

STIFTUNG
BAYERISCHE GEDENKSTÄTTEN

Die Landschaft
kann nichts da[...]
die ist ja nicht böse.

Es sollte nicht immer
zu Lasten der Flossenbürger
gehen.

I will go back home,
I will give them
a message of the things
I saw here and felt here.

Die Medienwand ist klassischen Ausstellungstafeln überlegen; sie bietet auf relativ begrenztem Raum, autoaktiv gesteuert, drei verschiedene Modi:
Modus A: Ort, Erinnerung, Überlebende, Täter – bewegte Bilder mit unmittelbarem Bezug zu Flossenbürg;
Modus B: Text – Ereignisse aus der Rezeptionsgeschichte des Nationalsozialismus in der Bundesrepublik und der DDR;
Modus C: Bild – Ikonen zur Zeitgeschichte nach 1945.

A media wall in contrast to a classic exhibition panel is an excellent option in that within a relatively limited space three various automated modes are offered:
Mode A: place, memory, survivors, perpetrators – moving images directly relating to Flossenbürg;
Mode B: texts – events from the history of reception of National Socialism in Germany and the GDR;
Mode C: images – icons of contemporary history since 1945.

Erinnerungs- und Gedenkstätten
Memorials and Commemorative Sites

Was bleibt – KZ-Gedenkstätte Flossenbürg What Remains – The Flossenbürg Concentration Camp

Medienproduktion, Filmschnitt
Film Production and Editing:
WHITEvoid interactive art & design:
Christopher Bauder, Christian Perstl, Sylvia Steinhäuser

Audioproduktion Sound Production:
Bayerischer Rundfunk, Studio Regensburg: Thomas Muggenthaler

STEVEN SPIELBERG, SCHINDLERS LISTE

Der Film basiert auf der Geschichte des Unternehmers Oskar Schindler, der 800 jüdische Zwangsarbeiter rettete. Die Hollywood-Produktion findet weltweit ein Millionenpublikum.

1993

STEVEN SPIELBERG, SCHINDLER'S LIST

The film was based on the story of the industrialist Oskar Schindler, who saved 800 Jewish forced laborers. Millions around the world saw the Hollywood production.

ÜBERGANG UND NEUORDNUNG   RESTORATION AND ACCLIMATION

Erinnerungs- und Gedenkstätten
Memorials and Commemorative Sites

Was bleibt – KZ-Gedenkstätte
Flossenbürg What Remains – The
Flossenbürg Concentration Camp

326

Gesprochene Sprache erzeugt beim Zuhörer ein eigenes, inneres Bild und beglaubigt außerdem, zum Beispiel bei Berichten von Zeitzeugen, die abstrakten, historischen Darstellungen. Akustische Medien sind auch im besonderen Maße dazu geeignet, Emotionen zu erzeugen. Kaum jemandem kommen beim Anblick eines Bildes oder beim Lesen eines Textes Tränen – dagegen lösen Musik und erzählte Geschichten starke Emotionen in uns aus. Das „Hinsehenmüssen" bei Abbildungen des Gräuels wird ersetzt durch „Hinhörenmüssen". Das Abstoßende und Distanzierende wird ersetzt durch das Verständnis und das Erzeugen von Empathie.

Spoken language creates a private, inner image for the listener, and further authenticates eyewitness accounts when detailing abstract, historical accounts. Acoustic media are also to a certain extent particularly suitable to generate emotion. Few people come to tears at the sight of a picture or reading a text – on the other hand, listening to music and telling stories often evokes strong emotions in us. The "must see" with images of atrocity is replaced by "must hear." The repellent and distanced is replaced by an understanding and empathy.

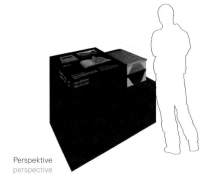

Perspektive
perspective

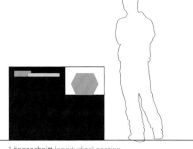

Längsschnitt longitudinal section

Draufsicht view

Seitenansicht links side view left

Frontansicht front view

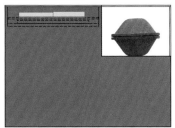

Seitenansicht rechts side view right

Draufsicht view

Erinnerungs- und Gedenkstätten
Memorials and Commemorative Sites

Was bleibt – KZ-Gedenkstätte
Flossenbürg What Remains – The
Flossenbürg Concentration Camp

Entwurf und Ausführungsplanung
Vitrine „Friedhofsruhe"
Exponate: Beinkiste, Bücher als Grafik
über Beinkiste, Foto als Grafikfläche

Design and Execution of the display case
"Graveyard Peace"
Exhibit objects: Ossuary, illustrated
books about ossuaries, photograph as a
graphic area

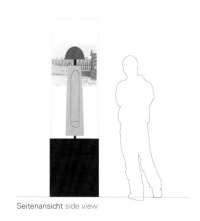

Seitenansicht side view

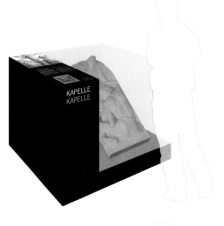

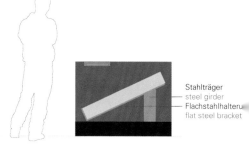

Stahlträger
steel girder
Flachstahlhalteru
flat steel bracket

Erinnerungs- und Gedenkstätten
Memorials and Commemorative Sites

Was bleibt – KZ-Gedenkstätte
Flossenbürg What Remains – The
Flossenbürg Concentration Camp

Vitrinenkatalog von oben nach unten:
Oben: Befreiung; Exponate: Helm, Hemd,
Foto Begrüßungsbanner;
Mitte: Christliche Sinnstiftung; Exponate:
Gipsmodell, Foto als Grafikfläche;
Unten: Wohnort Lager; Exponate:
Bebauungsplan in Schublade, Luftbild als
Wackelbild.

Display catalogue from top to bottom:
Above: Liberation; Exhibits: helmet, shirt,
photo, welcoming banner;
middle: Christian Inspiration; Exhibits:
plaster model, photo as a graphic space;
below: Living area; Exhibits: development
plan in drawer, aerial view as a shifting
image.

Funde im ehemaligen Lagergelände, 2000–2010

Artifacts from former concentration camp grounds, 2000–2010

BESTRAFUNG ODER BEGNADIGUNG
PUNISHMENT AND PARDON

SPÄTFOLGEN
AFTERMATH

ZEUGENSCHAFT
BEARING WITNESS

BEGRENZTE ANERKENNUNG
LIMITED RECOGNITION

KAMPF UM ENTSCHÄDIGUNG
STRUGGLE FOR COMPENSATION

COLD WAR OVER THE

**Gefälschter Ausweis von Max Koegel,
ohne Datum**
National Archives, Washington D.C.

Der letzte Kommandant des KZ Flossenbürg,
Max Koegel, taucht bei der Auflösung des
Lagers unter. Er wird jedoch am 26. Juli 1946
von amerikanischen Soldaten gefasst. Am Tag
danach erhängt er sich im Untersuchungs-
gefängnis.

**Forged identification card belonging
to Max Koegel, undated**
National Archives, Washington D.C.

The last Commandant of the Flossenbürg
camp, Max Koegel, went into hiding at the
time of the camp's dissolution of the camp.
He was captured by American soldiers on
June 26, 1946. The day after, he hanged
himself in the remand prison.

Der ehemalige Häftlingspfleger
im Krankenrevier, Carl Schrade,
identifiziert angeklagte SS-Männer,
Dachau 1946
Private source

Carl Schrade, a former prisoner
who had been assigned sick bay
duty at Flossenbürg, identifies
accused SS men, Dachau 1946
Private source

Der ehemalige Häftlingsschreiber
Miloš Kučera erläutert die Arbeit in
der Lagerverwaltung, Dachau 1946
National Archives, Washington D.C.

Miloš Kučera, a former prisoner who
had been assigned record keeping
tasks, explains the activities of the
camp administration, Dachau 19
National Archives, Washington D.C.

Dokumentation über das
KZ Flossenbürg, 3. US-Armee,
1945 (Nachbau)
National Archives, Washington D.C.

Bereits kurz nach der Untersuchungskommis-
sionen in Flossenbürg SS-Dokumente
gesichert und ausgewertet. Diese vier
Bände sind ein zentrales Beweismittel
im Dachauer Flossenbürg-Prozess.

Documentation on the Flos
concentration camp, 3rd U
1945 (reproduction)
National Archives, Washington D.C.

American investigation
secured and evaluate
in Flossenbürg soon
These four volumes
of evidence in the F
in Dachau

VERFOLGUNG
DER TÄTER

Nach Kriegsende entziehen sich viele Täter der drohenden Strafe
durch Flucht, manche sogar durch Selbstmord. In Dachau klagt ein
amerikanisches Militärgericht 52 SS-Angehörige und Funktionshäftlinge
KZ Flossenbürg an. Das Verfahren dauert von August 1946 bis
1947. Der Prozess stützt sich auf Aussagen ehemaliger Häftlinge
reiches Belastungsmaterial. Viele Urteile werden später
25 Haftstrafen.

TÄTER

PERPETRATORS

ÜBERLEBENDE

VERDRÄNGTE SCHULD
SUPPRESSED GUILT

SPÄTE ERMITTLUNGEN
LATER INVESTIGATIONS

Naturwissenschaften in Ausstellungen zu vermitteln ist das Ziel vieler Einrichtungen. Die Wege, die sie dabei beschreiten, sind jedoch sehr unterschiedlich. Neben den technischen und naturkundlichen Museen sind in jüngerer Zeit vor allem Science Center entstanden, die eigenständiges und spielerisches Experimentieren mit naturwissenschaftlichen Phänomenen in den Vordergrund des Ausstellungsbesuches stellen.

In den letzten Jahren entwickelten sich daneben auch diverse Mischformen, sodass sich ein breites Spektrum an naturwissenschaftlichen Ausstellungen etabliert hat.

Im klassischen Sammlungsmuseum werden Artefakte und Objekte gesammelt. Die Sammlungen dienen neben Ausstellungszwecken auch der Forschung. Meist wird den Museumsbesuchern in Dauer- und Sonderausstellungen ein Teil der Objekte präsentiert, der Kontext ihres Vorkommens und ihrer Bedeutung werden dokumentiert. Allerdings arbeiten nur noch wenige Museen traditionell, vielmehr kombinieren viele Häuser ihre Objekte mit interaktiven Elementen. So unterscheidet Friedman (2010) naturwissenschaftliche Museen erster und zweiter Generation.[1] Demnach sind die Museen der ersten Generation die klassischen Sammlungsmuseen des 19. Jahrhunderts, während die zweite Generation zu Beginn des 20. Jahrhunderts entstanden ist. Das Deutsche Museum in München ist eines der prominentesten Beispiele und Vorreiter dieser Kategorie. Seit seinem Gründungsjahr 1903 wurden hier Phänomene durch das Museumspersonal vorgeführt und Knopfdruckexponate zur Aktivierung von Experimenten den Besuchern zur Verfügung gestellt.

Einen völlig neuen Typus stellen die Science Center dar, welche Friedman als dritte Generation naturwissenschaftlicher Museen bezeichnet. Mit dem Exploratorium in San Francisco wurde das erste Science Center

Presenting the natural sciences at exhibitions is the goal of many institutions, but they take very different approaches. In addition to technology and natural history museums, the institutions that have been established in recent years include a large number of science centers that make independent, playful experimentation with scientific phenomena a focus of exhibition visits. A variety of hybrid forms have also emerged, widening the spectrum of scientific exhibitions organized today.

In traditional "collecting" museums, the focus is on compiling artifacts and objects. The collections are used for exhibition purposes, and are also the subject of research. In most cases, a variety of objects are presented to museum visitors in permanent and special exhibitions, which document their original contexts and their meanings. Yet only a few museums take this traditional approach today. Many institutions combine objects with interactive elements. With an eye on these developments, Friedman (2010) distinguishes between first- and second-generation science museums:[1] first-generation museums are the traditional collecting museums of the nineteenth century, while the second-generation museums are those that were established in the early twentieth century. The Deutsches Museum in Munich is one of the most prominent examples, and a pioneer in this latter category. Ever since the museum was founded in 1903, scientific phenomena have been demonstrated by staff, and push-button exhibits have invited visitors to activate experiments themselves.

Science centers are an entirely new type of institution, one that Friedman calls the third generation of science museums. The Exploratorium, the first such center, was established in San Francisco in 1969. Here the educational principle is based on interaction with scientific phenomena. All the exhibits encourage visitors to try their

[1] Alan J. Friedman: „The evolution of the science museum", in: *Physics today*, Oktober 2010, www.physicstoday.org.

[1] Alan J. Friedman, "The Evolution of the Science Museum," in *Physics Today*, October 2010, www.physicstoday.org.

im Jahr 1969 gegründet. Hier wurde die Interaktion mit naturwissenschaftlichen Phänomenen zum didaktischen Prinzip erhoben. Alle Exponate fordern die Besucher zum Experimentieren auf. Die Interaktion beschränkt sich nicht auf Knopfdruck und Kurbeldrehung, sondern ermöglicht die Manipulation verschiedener Parameter. Das eigene Experimentieren, die „Schönheit des Phänomens", wie Michel Junge es 2005 genannt hat[2], und die Einbeziehung aller Sinne sollen eine vertiefte Auseinandersetzung mit wissenschaftlichen Hintergründen auslösen.

Doch auch bei den Science Center gibt es mittlerweile viele Facetten. In Deutschland orientieren sich phæno, Spektrum und Phänomenta deutlich am Exploratorium. Ihre Ausstellungen bieten grobe thematische Zuordnungen und eine reduzierte Raumgestaltung, um nicht vom eigentlichen Phänomenerleben abzulenken. Universum, Experimenta und Dynamikum strukturieren ihre Ausstellungen stärker und bieten den Besuchern durch inszenatorische Elemente Kontext an. Das Mathematikum schränkt das weite Themenspektrum der Science Center zugunsten einer thematischen Spezialisierung ein. Auch Themenhäuser wie das Klimahaus und das Welios (Wels, Österreich) fokussieren sich auf ein Thema. Ihre Ausstellungen sind von multimedialen Ansätzen und ausgeprägten Raum-in-Raum-Inszenierungen bestimmt.

Insgesamt gesehen spannen die Ausstellungen des klassische Sammlungsmuseums und des Science Centers im Stile des Exploratoriums ein Spektrum an verschiedensten Ausstellungsformen auf. Ihre Vielfalt wird sich durch neue Technologien und Techniken wohl auch in Zukunft weiter differenzieren. Entscheidend bei der Entwicklung neuer oder der Weiterentwicklung bestehender Ausstellungen ist das selbst definierte, didaktische Konzept. Es führt die Ausstellungsmacher unweigerlich in das Spannungsfeld zwischen Objekt, Phänomen und multimedialer Möglichkeit.

Tobias Wolff

hand at experiments. The interaction is not confined to pushing a button or turning a crank; it involves manipulating a wide variety of parameters. This idea of experimenting on one's own – exploring the "beauty of the phenomenon," as Michel Junge put it in 2005[2] – is supposed to lead to a deeper engagement with scientific phenomena, as is the involvement of all the senses.

But science centers now have many different facets. The centers in Germany – phæno, Spektrum and Phänomenta – borrow heavily from the Exploratorium. Their exhibitions feature roughly defined thematic categories, and a streamlined spatial design that does not distract from the actual experience of the phenomena. Universum, Experimenta, and Dynamikum give their exhibitions a clearer structure and use presentational elements to provide context for the viewers. The Mathematikum limits the wide range of science center topics in the interest of thematic specialization. Theme-based centers such as the Klimahaus and the Welios (located in Wels, Austria) focus on a single topic. Their exhibitions are characterized by multimedia approaches, and distinct room-in-room presentations.

Overall, the exhibitions at both traditional collecting museums and Exploratorium-style science centers offer a range of different exhibition forms. They will probably become even more nuanced in the future as a result of new technologies and techniques. The self-defined educational concept plays a pivotal role in developing new and enhancing existing exhibitions. This concept inevitably draws the exhibition organizers into the tensions between object, phenomena, and multimedia possibilities.

Tobias Wolff

[2] Michel Junge: „Lernen am Phänomen", in: Physik in unserer Zeit, 36. JJ., Nr. 4, 2005, S. 192–193.

[2] Michel Junge, "Lernen am Phänomen," in Physik in unserer Zeit, 36, vol. 4 (2005): pp. 192–193.

Planetarium Zeiss Zeiss Planetarium

Auf der Pariser Weltausstellung 1937 war das »Universal-Großplanetarium« von Carl Zeiss Jena eine Attraktion. 60 Jahre später nahm im Palais de la Découverte ein völlig neuer Projektor den Vorführbetrieb auf. Er zeichnet sich durch die außergewöhnliche Qualität aus, mit der der Sternenhimmel wiedergegeben wird. Die Inszenierung ist ebenfalls neu. War der Projektionssaal bisher in Brauntönen gehalten, wird er nun in ein galaktisches Nachtblau getaucht. Der historische Projektor wird im Zentrum des Saals präsentiert. Das Gestaltungskonzept folgt der Leitidee, Dinge sichtbar zu machen, die für das menschliche Auge allein nicht wahrnehmbar sind.

Das Thema Astronomie vermittelt sich den Besuchern über speziell gestaltete Ausstellungselemente und Medien. Zwei 3 x 3 Meter große, linsenförmige Informationskörper wurden entwickelt, die zu den Themen Planetarien, Astronomie und Optik informieren und auch auf wesentliche Kompetenzen der Firma Zeiss hinweisen: auf ihre Leistungen in der Weltraumtechnologie, aber auch auf die Qualität ihrer optischen Produkte.

Gestaltungsmerkmale

Die Themen eröffnen sich über intuitives Vorgehen. Der Besucher erschließt sich die Inhalte aktiv ohne umfangreiche Erklärungen. Dies stellt hohe Anforderungen an Entwurf und Planung von mechanischen und elektronischen Ausstellungselementen. Haltbarkeit und Wartungsfreundlichkeit sind vorrangige Gestaltungskriterien. Anders als bei musealer Objektpräsentation sind die Exponate nicht Schaustücke, sondern Dinge, die zwar durchaus als Unikate geschaffen wurden, die aber nicht in einer Vitrine vor dem Zugriff geschützt sind, sondern offen präsentiert werden und zum Benutzen einladen. Alle Sinne werden einbezogen, der lebendige Ausstellungscharakter animiert zum Mitmachen.

One of the big attractions at the Paris World Exhibition in 1937 was the Universal Large-dome Planetarium produced by Carl Zeiss Jena. Sixty years later a completely new projector was installed in the Palais de la Découverte that is renowned for the extraordinary quality of its rendering of the starry sky. The presentation is also new. Whereas the projection auditorium was previously painted in brown tones, it now features a galactic night blue. The historic projector is positioned in the center of the auditorium. The design concept is based around the idea of making things visible that the human eye alone cannot perceive.

The theme of astronomy is communicated to the visitor via specially designed exhibition elements and media. Two 3 x 3 meter lens-shaped information stations have been developed that address the themes of planetariums, astronomy, and optics as well as providing information on the work of the Zeiss firm, its achievements in the field of space-related technology and the quality of its optical products.

Design features

Visitors are encouraged to intuitively explore the presented themes, actively accessing content without the aid of detailed explanations on how to proceed. This approach places considerable demands on mechanical and electronic exhibition elements, and durability and ease of maintenance constitute primary design criteria. Unlike in the case of the presentation of objects in the museum context, the exhibits are not simply there to be looked at. While they are unique, they are not protected by display cases but are rather presented openly, and for direct use. The vital character of the exhibition engages all the senses and animates visitors to get involved.

Science Center Science Center Planetarium Zeiss Zeiss Planetarium	Palais de la Découverte Palais de la Découverte Avenue Franklin Delano Roosevelt 75008 Paris Frankreich	Ausstellungsfläche Exhibition Area: 200 m²

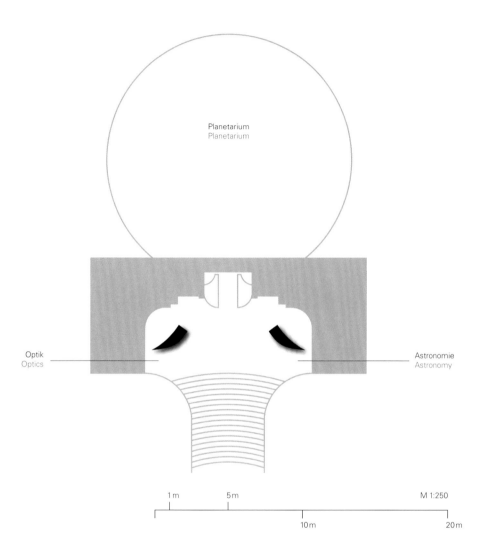

Planetarium
Planetarium

Optik   Astronomie
Optics   Astronomy

1 m   5 m   M 1:250

                                            10 m   20 m

Zwei gigantische Ausstellungs-
körper in Form von riesigen
Linsen dienen als Informationsträger für analoge und interaktive
Hands-on-Elemente, die
spielerisch wissenschaftliche
Inhalte auch für jüngere Besucher
„übersetzen". Die zentralperspektivisch angeordneten
Ausstellungselemente, der Einbe-
zug des Treppenaufgangs und die
intensive Farbgestaltung setzen
den Eingang zum Planetarium
dramatisch in Szene.

Two gigantic exhibition structures
in the form of large lenses serving as an information medium for
analog and interactive hands-on
elements that playfully "translate"
scientific content for younger
visitors.
The central perspectively arranged exhibition elements,
the inclusion of the stairway,
and the intense colors make
for a dramatic entrance into the
planetarium.

Science Center
Science Center

Planetarium Zeiss Zeiss Planetarium

Kooperationspartner für die Realisation
Implementation cooperation partners:
MPRA Communication Maurel Phélizon
Réalisateurs et Associés, Paris

Agentur Agency:
Michael Conrad & Leo Burnett.
Christoph Barth, Frankfurt

| Ausstellungsgestaltung Exhibition Design: BERTRON SCHWARZ FREY Entwurf Design: Prof. Ulrich Schwarz, Wolfgang Sattler Aurelia Bertron, Prof. Claudia Frey, Birgit Kölz | Fotos Photos: Daniel Osso | Dauerausstellung Permanent Exhibition 220 000 Besucher jährlich 220,000 visitors annually |

Das Science Center Medizintechnik von Otto Bock – Begreifen was uns bewegt
The Otto Bock Science Center Medical Technology – Discover What Moves Us

500 Quadratmeter bilden zwischen dem Brandenburger Tor und dem Potsdamer Platz eine offene Bühne der Medizintechnik für jedermann. Hier lädt eine Ausstellung interessierte Laien wie auch Experten dazu ein, spielerisch etwas über das Besondere im scheinbar Selbstverständlichen zu erfahren. Die kostenlos zugängliche Ausstellung wird durch das Medizintechnikunternehmen Otto Bock HealthCare ermöglicht.

Die Devise auf den drei Etagen des Science Center lautet: Ausprobieren erwünscht! Hier sind die Besucher aktiv gefordert – ob sie multimedial einen Faden durch ein Nadelöhr stecken, um ihr Fingerspitzengefühl zu testen, oder einen Balanceakt in 250 Metern Höhe über eine reißende Schlucht unternehmen, um ihren Gleichgewichtssinn auf die Probe zu stellen. Die Geheimnisse, die hinter unseren Bewegungen stecken, werden auf einem interaktiven Tisch erkundet. Wer mag, wirft einen Blick unter die Haut und erlebt so das fein abgestimmte Zusammenspiel seiner Knochen, Muskeln, Sehnen und Nerven. Und wer in die Zukunft schauen möchte, kann auf seinem Rundgang sein individuelles statistisches Krankheitsrisiko in 20 Jahren errechnen und sich über Krankheitsbilder informieren.

Neben dem Gezeigten ist auch das Zeigen selbst ein Inhalt der Ausstellung. Die kreative Wissensvermittlung ist die Aufgabe der 15 speziell geschulten Science Guides, die auf den Ausstellungsebenen und in Führungen Hintergründe zu den Exponaten erläutern und Informationen zum Unternehmen Otto Bock geben.

Das vom Initiator, Professor Hans Georg Näder, zur Eröffnung als „Experiment" bezeichnete Projekt gilt heute mit über 280 000 Besuchern als feste Größe in der Berliner Ausstellungslandschaft.

Alexandra Grossmann

Between Berlin's Brandenburg Gate and Potsdamer Platz a 500-square-meter area has been transformed into a stage for the presentation of medical technology in a way that is accessible to everyone. The exhibition invites both amateurs and experts to experience something about the peculiar character of what seems self-evident. The free exhibition has been made possible by the medical technology firm Otto Bock HealthCare.

The motto of the exhibition, which extends over three floors, is: Try it out yourself! Visitors are actively encouraged to take a hands-on approach to the multimedia environment, whether by threading a virtual needle to check their manual dexterity, or performing a balancing act 250 virtual meters above a raging torrent to test their sense of balance. An interactive table provides an opportunity to explore the secrets behind our movements, taking the observer under the skin and exposing the finely tuned interplay of bones, muscles, sinews, and nerves. Those who would like to look into the future have the possibility of calculating their statistical risk of illness in twenty years and learning more about disease patterns.

Visitors are encouraged not only to explore exhibits themselves but also to learn about them from fifteen specially trained Science Guides who provide background information on the exhibits and explain the workings of the firm of Otto Bock.

The project, which was described as an "experiment" by Otto Bock's initiator, Professor Hans Georg Näder, when he opened the exhibition in June 2009, has now been visited by 280,000 people and become an established fixture in Berlin's exhibition landscape.

Alexandra Grossmann

Science Center
Science Center

Otto Bock Science Center Medizintechnik Berlin The Otto Bock Science Center Medical Technology
Ebertstraße 15a
10117 Berlin

Ausstellungsfläche Exhibition Area: 500 m²
Fotos Seiten 347, 354 Photos pages 347, 354:
diephotodesigner

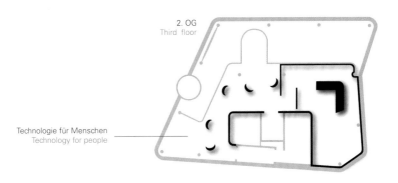

2. OG
Third floor

Technologie für Menschen
Technology for people

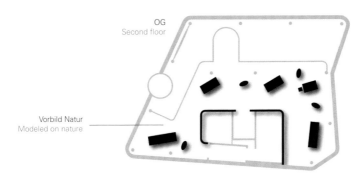

OG
Second floor

Vorbild Natur
Modeled on nature

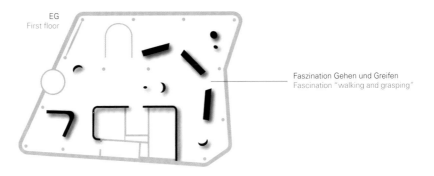

EG
First floor

Faszination Gehen und Greifen
Fascination "walking and grasping"

1 m   5 m   M 1:400

10 m   20 m

Der Wiederaufbau
durch Max Näder
Rebuilding by Max Näder

Max Näder beginnt in Duderstadt mit dem
Neuaufbau des Unternehmens. Er muss bei
Null anfangen, denn einzig das Vertrauen der
Kunden ist der Familie erhalten geblieben.

Max Näder starts rebuilding the company in
Duderstadt. He has to start over from scratch,
since all the family is left with is the confidence
of their customers.

Die bewegten 50er Jahre
Erste Tochter in den USA
The turbulent 50s
First branch in the USA

Die schwierigen Nachkriegsjahre erfordern Improvisation und
Durchhaltevermögen. In den folgenden Jahrzehnten ist die
Familien- und Firmenhistorie an markanten Wendepunkten
auch ein Spiegelbild der deutsch-deutschen Geschichte.

The difficult post-war years require improvisation and
staying power. Over the following decades, the family
and company history mirrors German-German history
at significant turning points.

Max Näder kehrt von seiner ersten USA-Reise zurück.
Max Näder returns from his first trip to the USA.

-1945
Im Zweiten Weltkrieg schränken die Nationalsozialisten
die unternehmerische Selbstbestimmung stark ein.
Orthopädische Aufträge werden zentralisiert vom Staat
vergeben. Otto Bock wird als kriegswichtiger Betrieb
eingestuft und darf weiter produzieren.

Entrepreneurial independence is severely restricted by
the national socialist government during World War II.
Orthopaedic contracts are centrally awarded by the
government. As Otto Bock is an industry that provides
war materiel with orthopaedic fittings, the company is
permitted to continue production.

Kopiermaschine für Holzprothethe
Turning machine for wood compounds

1946
Max und Marie Näder gründen in Duderstadt die
„Zweigstelle Nord", die in der britischen Besatzungs-
zone den Vertrieb und die Beschaffung von Rohmate-
rialien im Westen regelt, soll. In Königsee wirken
unter sowjetischer Besatzung die Reparationsfor-
derungen zunehmend erdrückend.

Max and Marie Näder found the "North Branch" in
Duderstadt in the British zone of occupation in
order to handle sales and the procurement of raw
materials from the west. Demands for separations
under Soviet occupation in Königsee are becoming
increasingly oppressive.

1948
In Königsee werden der Firmenbesitz und das
Privatvermögen der Familie entschädigungslos
enteignet. Auch Otto Bock zieht nun nach Duderstadt. Dort ermöglichen die Voraussetzungen von
guten Kunden den Aufbau einer neuen Produktion.

The company assets, as well as the private property
of the family in Königsee, are expropriated without
compensation. Otto Bock now also moves to Duderstadt. Here prerequisites by major customers support
the construction of a new production facility.

Otto Bock Brief, 1952
Otto Bock letter, 1952

1952
Der Rohstoff Holz wird Mangelware. Max Näder
experimentiert mit Polyurethan-Schäumen und führt
Plastsohle aus Kunststoff in die Praktik ein. 1953,
kurz nach dem Tod des Firmengründers, geht daraus
die „Otto Bock Kunststoff" hervor, die heute auch für
die Auto- und Möbelindustrie ein führender Anbieter
von Schaumstoffen und Schaumsystemen ist.

Wood becomes scarce as a raw material. Max Näder
experiments with polyurethane foams and introduces
plastic components in prosthetics. In 1953, shortly
after the death of the company founder, his innovative
thinking leads to the birth of "Otto Bock Kunststoff"
which is now also one of the leading suppliers of
foams and foam systems for the automotive and
furniture industries.

Die erste Längsschneidemaschine für Schaumstoffe
The first long-slicing cutter for foam materials

1958
Die Internatio...
gründet in T...
Auslandigem...
einen Hand...
Geschäftsfüt...

International business begins – Max Näder...
the first Otto Bock foreign branch in...
USA. This start is sealed by a handsha...
Vereinbarungen who becomes the comm...

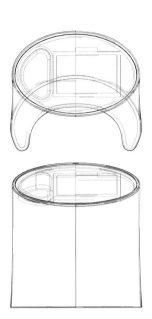

Architektur Architecture:
Gnädiger Architekten (Rolf Gnädinger),
Christoph Claus
Generalplaner und Ausstellungsgestaltung
General Planner and Exhibition Design:
ART+COM in Zusammenarbeit mit Otto
Bock HealthCare GmbH

Szenografische Konzeption
Scenographic Design:
Prof. Ulrich Schwarz in Zusammenarbeit
mit ART+COM in cooperation with
ART+COM

Medienkonzept, interaktive Insze-
nierungen und Interfacedesign Media
Concept, Interactive Installations and
Interface Design:
ART+COM

Blick unter die Haut

Muskeln | Sehnen | Nerven | Knochen | Gelenke | Bänder | Schalten

Die Handfläche

Das unterste Glied der Finger wird ausschließlich von Muskeln bewegt, die in der Hand liegen. Diese entspringen an den Mittelhandknochen oder an den langen Sehnen der Unterarmmuskeln. Alle Glieder der Finger sind so im Bewegungsablauf miteinander verkoppelt.

English

Die Drehung der Hand

Schalten

Bei einer Prothese wird die Drehung der Hand von einem Motor am Handgelenk gesteuert. Die Drehbewegung, die beim natürlichen Arm durch das Überkreuzen von Elle und Speiche ermöglicht wird, geschieht hier direkt im Handgelenk.

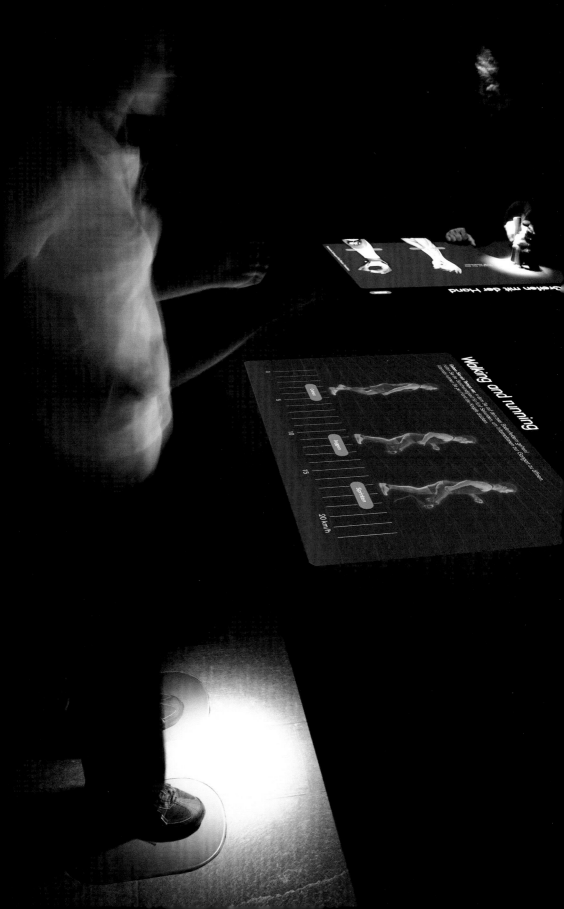

Auf 450 Quadratmetern vermitteln interaktive Medienstationen, wie die komplexe menschliche Motorik funktioniert und wie die Natur als Vorbild für hochentwickelte technische Hilfsmittel dient. Die sinnliche Wahrnehmung und das Erleben des Besuchers stehen im Mittelpunkt. Die Exponate laden ein, die Faszination Gehen und Greifen mit den eigenen Händen und Füßen zu erkunden. Die Inszenierung der Ausstellung basiert auf dem Leitmotiv der Bewegung und folgt einem ganzheitlichen dynamischen Gestaltungsansatz. Die Medienstationen wirken in ihrer Form, als wären sie aus der Bewegung heraus entstanden. Ihre organischen Rundungen orientieren sich an den Prinzipien der Natur und reflektieren das bionische Grundmotiv.

Interactive media stations on 450 square meters provide information on such themes as how the complex human motor functions work, and how nature serves as a model for highly developed technical aids. Sensory perception and the visitor's experience are at the center of the exhibition. The exhibits invite the visitor to explore the fascination of walking and grasping with their own feet and hands. The staging of the exhibition is based on the theme of the movement and follows a holistic approach to design. The media stations function as if they arise out of the movement. Its organic curves are based on the principles of nature and reflect the basic bionic motif.

Science Center
Science Center

Otto Bock Science Center
Medizintechnik Berlin The Otto Bock
Science Center Medical Technology

Konzeption und Entwicklung von Exponat-Sonderbauten Concept and development of the exhibit's special constructions: ART+COM, Mitarbeiter Otto Bock Holding GmbH & Co.KG

Medienfassade Media facade: ART+COM in Kooperation mit Leurocom und wissenschaftlicher Begleitung vom Biomotionlab ART+COM in cooperation with Leurocom and scientific support from Biomotionlab, Prof. Dr. Nikolaus Troje

männlich
male

schwer
heavy

nervös
nervous

fröhlich
happy

traurig
sad

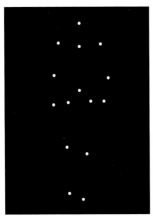

Science Center
Science Center

Otto Bock Science Center
Medizintechnik Berlin The Otto Bock
Science Center Medical Technology

Projektverantwortliche bei Otto Bock
HealthCare Deutschland GmbH
Project Managers at Otto Bock,
HealthCare Germany, LLC.:
Prof. Hans Georg Näder,
Bernhard Kleinhenz

Zu den medialen Höhepunkten gehört die Medienfassade: Eine Bewegungssimulation aus 15 Lichtpunkten, der sogenannte Walker, trägt das Thema weithin sichtbar in den Stadtraum. Eine acht Meter hohe kinetische Installation hinter der gläsernen Frontfassade zieht die Aufmerksamkeit von Passanten auf das Science Center. Auf Pendelarme montierte Bildschirme zeigen virtuelle Hände, die bildschirmübergreifend interagieren.

Among the highlights is the media facade: a motion simulation made of 15 points of light, the so-called Walker, visibly carries the theme well into the urban space. An eight-meter high kinetic installation behind the glassed front facade attracts the attention of passers-by to the Science Center. Monitors mounted on swing arms display virtual hands that interact throughout the screen.

Projektverantwortliche Project Manager ART+COM:
Creative Director Creative Director: Prof. Joachim Sauter
Art Director Art Director: Hermann Klöckner
Leitung Medientechnik Media Technology Management: Satria Isa

Leitung Entwicklung Research and Development Management: Valentin Schunack
Verantwortlich Content Content Manager: Nina Apelt
Projektleiter Project Manager: Michael Jungnickel

Fotos Seiten 349–351, 353–354 und 356 f. Photos pages 349–351, 353–354 and 356 f.: Frank Nürnberger

BESUCHERZENTREN VISITOR CENTERS

Ausstellungen und Museen unterscheiden sich wesentlich von Besucherzentren durch ihre Aufgabenstellung. Originale Objekte und museale Attraktionen sind in Besucherzentren meist nicht zu finden. Vielmehr haben sie die Aufgabe, auf die Attraktionen, meist lokale Sehenswürdigkeiten, Nationalparks, historische Stätten, Wahrzeichen oder Ähnliches, hinzuweisen, den Zugang zum Gegenstand des Interesses zu erleichtern. Besucherzentren begrüßen die Besucher und bieten Informationen. Sie sind oft mit Ausstellungen verbunden und können durchaus attraktiv gestaltet sein, spielen jedoch nicht selbst die Hauptrolle, sondern weisen auf die eigentliche Attraktion oder Sehenswürdigkeit hin. Es gibt jedoch auch Beispiele, wie das Besucherzentrum „Arche Nebra", die selbst als Attraktion gelten. Die nahebei gelegene Fundstelle der Himmelsscheibe von Nebra ist dagegen vollkommen unspektakulär.

Bedarf und Anzahl der Besucherzentren nehmen zu. Als Arbeitsfeld für Planer sind Besucherzentren in Fragen und Überlegungen zu den Bereichen Marketing, Beschilderungen, Leit- und Orientierungssysteme eingebunden. Bei der Gestaltung von Besucherzentren ist eine strenge, konzentrierte Darstellung von großem Interesse, da von einer sehr kurzen Verweildauer ausgegangen werden muss. Die Informationen müssen trotzdem umfassend und vollständig sein und sich einem Publikum mit unterschiedlichsten Ansprüchen mitteilen.

The task of visitor centers is very different from that of exhibitions and museums. As a rule, original objects and museum attractions are not found in visitor centers. Their task is rather one of highlighting attractions such as local points of interest, national parks, historical locations, and landmarks and of making access to the object of interest easier. Visitor centers greet visitors and offer them information. They are often linked to exhibitions and can certainly be attractively designed. However, their role is ultimately a subsidiary one and is generally confined to drawing attention to the real attraction or point of interest. Nevertheless, examples of visitor centers can be found that are regarded as attractions. A good example is the Nebra Arc, a visitor center compared with which the nearby find site of Nebra Sky Disc seems completely unspectacular.

The need for and number of visitor centers is increasing. As a field of work for planners, visitor centers are connected with the areas of marketing, signage, guidance, and orientation systems. The design of visitor centers requires a strict, concentrated presentation that may well only have a short life. Nevertheless, the presented information needs to be comprehensive and complete, and speak to a public with a range of different expectations.

Besucherzentrum Welterbe Regensburg
Visitor Center World Heritage Regensburg

Im Jahr 2006 wurde die Altstadt von Regensburg mit dem angrenzenden Stadtteil Stadtamhof in die Welterbeliste der UNESCO aufgenommen. Im Zweiten Weltkrieg war die Altstadt weitgehend von Zerstörungen verschont geblieben. Regensburg ist damit heute die einzige erhaltene mittelalterliche Großstadt Deutschlands. Die UNESCO würdigte mit dem Welterbetitel zum einen diesen außergewöhnlichen Erhaltungszustand und zum anderen die große Bedeutung, die die Stadt Regensburg im Mittelalter einnahm. Drei Kriterien waren für die Ernennung ausschlaggebend: die besondere, bis heute erhaltene mittelalterliche Architektur, die Rolle, die die Stadt als Ort für Reichsversammlungen spielte, und ihre Bedeutung als Handelszentrum im Mittelalter. Die Stadt Regensburg begreift ihr Welterbeprädikat auch als Aufruf, den Wert ihres kulturellen Erbes aktiv zu vermitteln. Ein zentraler Baustein dafür ist das neu geschaffene Besucherzentrum „Welterbe im Salzstadel". Mit dem Besucherzentrum wurde – direkt an der Steinernen Brücke, dem städtischen Wahrzeichen – eine öffentliche Einrichtung rund um das Thema Welterbe geschaffen. Ziel war, Bürgern und Besuchern eine Anlaufstelle mit Informationen zur Stadt und zum breit gefächerten kulturellen Angebot zu bieten.

Ausgehend vom Thema UNESCO-Welterbe, welches den Einstieg in die Ausstellung darstellt, spiegeln sich in jedem der Themenbereiche die Kriterien der Welterbe-Ernennung und vermitteln diese anschaulich. Der Bereich „Entwicklung der Stadt" bietet so einen Überblick über die über 2000-jährige Siedlungsgeschichte Regensburgs. Die Abteilung „Stadt am Fluss" dreht sich um die Rolle des Handels in Regensburg, und „Leben in der Stadt" befasst sich mit den vielfältigen Aspekten des Alltagslebens, einschließlich Kunst, Kultur und Religion. Ein Regensburger Spezialthema greift der Bereich „Stadt der Reichstage" auf, in dem der Immerwährende Reichstag, der von 1663 bis 1806 in der Stadt tagte, erläutert wird.

In 2006 the old town of Regensburg and the adjoining district of Stadtamhof were included in the UNESCO World Heritage List. Most of the old town came through the Second World War intact and today Regensburg is Germany's only surviving medieval city. In listing Regensburg as a World Heritage site, UNESCO not only recognized the extraordinary degree to which the old town has been preserved but also the significance acquired by Regensburg during the Middle Ages. The central criteria for listing the city were its preserved medieval architecture, the role of the city as a location for meetings of the Imperial Diet, and its significance as a medieval trading center.

The city of Regensburg has responded to its World Heritage listing by launching a program to highlight the value of its cultural heritage. A central building block of these efforts is the new visitor center located in the historic *Salzstadel* (salt storehouse). The center is located directly adjacent to the *Steinerne Brücke*, the stone bridge that is the emblem of Regensburg, and that functioned as an important conduit for medieval trade. The aim behind the establishment of this public facility was to provide the city's residents and visitors with a source of information about the city and its diverse range of cultural offerings.

Based around the theme of the city's role as a World Heritage site, each of the center's thematic sections reflects the criteria for the World Heritage listing. The section "Development of the City" offers an overview of the Regensburg's 2000 years of settlement. The section "City on the River" addresses the city's role as a trading center, and "Life in the City" deals with diverse aspects of everyday life, including art, culture, and religion. The section "City of the Imperial Diet" takes up a very specific Regensburg theme, providing information on the Permanent Imperial Diet that convened in the city from 1663 until 1806.

Besucherzentrum Welterbe Regensburg
Visitor Center World Heritage Regensburg
Salzstadel
Weiße-Lamm-Gasse 1
93047 Regensburg

Gesamtleitung Project Coordination:
Matthias Ripp, Richard Mühlmann
(Welterbekoordination Stadt Regensburg)
(World Heritage Coordination City of Regensburg)

Autoren/Kuratoren/Wissenschaftliches Team Authors/Curators/Research Team:
Dr. Karl Stocker, Erika Thümmel, Dr. Heidi Fell, Judith Huber, Dr. Gerhard Baumgartner, (alle all FH Joanneum Graz), Dr. Ulrike Ziegler, Kunsthistorikerin Art Historian

Die Informationen innerhalb der Themenbereiche sind in zwei Ebenen gegliedert: Neben allgemein Wissenswertem zum Thema werden in „Zooms" Details und besondere Aspekte herausgegriffen und beleuchtet. Die Inhalte der Dauerausstellung bieten den Einstieg in das Thema und laden dazu ein, sich in Museen und Kultureinrichtungen weiter zu vertiefen. Die Ausstellung übernimmt damit eine Lotsenfunktion und zeigt, an welchen Orten sich Informationen zum jeweiligen Thema finden. Zahlreiche Verweise auf diese Orte, die sogenannten Links, sind integriert.

Eine herausgehobene Funktion nehmen sogenannte Leitinstallationen wahr, die stellvertretend für einen gesamten Themenbereich stehen.

Im Themenbereich „UNESCO-Welterbe" befindet sich ein überdimensionaler Globus. Er ist ikonografisches Element der Abteilung und gleichzeitig auch das Markenzeichen des gesamten Besucherzentrums. Auf der Weltkugel sind interaktive Displays angebracht, über die Informationen zu allen Welterbestätten abrufbar sind.

Ein städtebauliches Modell des Welterbe-Ensembles erläutert das Thema „Entwicklung der Stadt". Durch Lichtprojektion auf die Modelloberfläche lässt sich hier die Stadtentwicklung Regensburgs verfolgen. Mit Tastern sind verschiedene Zeitschnitte anwählbar. Über die Projektion, Audioeinspielungen und einen Bildschirm werden zusätzliche Informationen zu dem ausgewählten Zeitschnitt angeboten.

Das Leitobjekt des Themenbereichs „Leben in der Stadt" ist eine Straßenabwicklung aus dem 19. Jahrhundert mit kleinen Dioramen, die Szenen des historischen Alltagslebens darstellen. Als Vorlagen für die Szenen wurden reale Situationen und Räumlichkeiten aus Regensburg mit historischen Abbildungen kombiniert und grafisch neu umgesetzt.

Eine Herausforderung für die Ausstellungsgestaltung stellten die Räumlichkeiten selbst dar: etwa 650 Quadratmeter auf zwei Geschossen. Neben diesem sehr begrenzten Flächenangebot und der denkmalgeschützten Bausubstanz des Gebäudes waren auch

The information provided in each section is structured on two levels. General information on the respective theme is accompanied by "zooms," which highlight and explain particular details and aspects. The contents of the permanent exhibition offer an introduction to themes that can be further explored in other museums and cultural centers. The exhibition therefore also functions as a guide and shows where further information on its respective themes can be found by means of numerous integrated "links."

A particularly notable feature of the exhibition is its so-called signal installations, each of which represents an entire thematic section. For instance, the "UNESCO World Heritage" section features a large world globe, an iconic element that also functions as a trademark of the visitor center as a whole. The globe is equipped with interactive displays that allow visitors to access information on all World Heritage sites. Information on the "Development of the City" is provided in the form of a model of the urban ensemble making up the Regensburg World Heritage site. Light projections onto the model's surface allow visitors to trace the city's historical development, and different periods can be selected via buttons. The projection, audio recordings, and a monitor provide additional information on the selected period.

The signal installation featured in the section on "Life in the City" offers a view of the city's street network in the nineteenth century and includes small dioramas presenting scenes from everyday life constructed using real spaces within Regensburg combined with historical depictions that have been graphically inserted.

One of the major challenges facing the exhibition's designers was the space itself, which measures 650 square meters over two levels. The design had to take into account not only this restricted space and the fact that the *Salzstadel* is under a historical preservation order, but also the building's other uses (restaurant, shops, event auditoriums).

Besucherzentren
Visitor Centers

Besucherzentrum Welterbe Regensburg
Visitor Center World Heritage Regensburg

Wissenschaftlicher Beirat
Scientific Advisory Committee:
Prof. Dr. Michael Fehr, UdK Berlin,
Dr. Peter Germann-Bauer, Museen
der Stadt Regensburg City Museums
of Regensburg, Dr. Peter Morsbach,
Kunsthistoriker, Publizist und Verleger Art
Historian, Publicist and Publisher,

Dr. Wolfgang Muchitsch, Universalmuseum Joanneum Universalmuseum
Joanneum, Sabine Thiele, Regensburg
Tourismus GmbH Regensberg Office of
Tourism, Dr. Eugen Trapp, Stadt Regensburg, Amt für Archiv und Denkmalpflege
City of Regensburg, Department for the
Preservation of Monuments

die Anforderungen der angrenzenden Nutzungen im Gebäude (Restaurant, Geschäfte, Veranstaltungssäle) bei der Planung zu berücksichtigen.

Um angemessen auf diese Rahmenbedingungen reagieren zu können, wurde auf Basis des anvisierten Funktionsprogramms ein Gestaltungswettbewerb durchgeführt, dessen Ziel es war, nachzuweisen, dass die Funktionen Dauerausstellung, Sonderpräsentationsfläche, multifunktionaler Bereich und Servicetheke auf den vorhandenen Flächen untergebracht werden können. Erst im Anschluss daran wurde das inhaltliche Konzept unter Berücksichtigung der Gestaltungsplanung ausgearbeitet.

Das besondere Augenmerk bei der Bewertung der eingereichten Wettbewerbsarbeiten lag daher auf einer überzeugenden räumlich-gestalterischen Lösung, die den unterschiedlichen Belangen der Nutzer und der Charakteristik des Gebäudes Rechnung trägt. Ein sensibler Umgang mit der unter Denkmalschutz stehenden Bausubstanz war ebenso grundlegende Voraussetzung wie die zeitgemäße grafische Präsentation für die Ausstellung.

Die Stadt Regensburg hat mit dem Besucherzentrum eine weitere Attraktion für ihre Bürger und Touristen erhalten. Die umfassende Aufbereitung des Themas UNESCO-Welterbe ist weltweit einzigartig. Im Salzstadel konnte die innovative Verbindung zwischen Besuchererlebnis, Wegweisungsfunktion und Wissensvermittlung geschaffen werden, die alle Altersgruppen anspricht. Mit dem Besucherzentrum hat Regensburg eine Vorbildrolle für die multimediale und interaktive Vermittlung des Themas UNESCO-Welterbe eingenommen.
Richard Mühlmann

Gestaltung

Eine wesentliche Qualität der Räume des Salzstadels entsteht durch die für den Speicher typische Raumstruktur, die auf eine Unterteilung verzichtet. Der Entwurf des Besucherzentrums respektiert diese historische Erscheinungsform und erlaubt lediglich eine sensible Intervention durch von der Decke abgehängte, nach unten offene Körper, die es

The limitations of the space and the functions envisaged for the building were key aspects of the design competition organized to show that a permanent exhibition, special presentation space, multifunctional area, and a service counter could all be accommodated in the available space. It was only afterwards that a thematic concept was elaborated that took into account the possibilities and limitations of the spatial design.

When evaluating competition entries, judges placed particular emphasis on a spatial solution that responded to the needs of the building's users and its specific characteristics. In this context, a sensitive approach to the heritage-listed structure was just as fundamental as a contemporary presentation for the exhibition.

The visitor center has provided the city of Regensburg with yet another attraction for its residents and visitors, and the center's comprehensive approach to the theme of UNESCO World Heritage is unique. In the *Salzstadel*, an innovative link has been forged between the visitor experience, signage and guide functions, and the transmission of knowledge, one that speaks to all age groups. With its visitor center, Regensburg has established a new paradigm for multimedia-based and interactive approaches to the UNESCO World Heritage theme.
Richard Mühlmann

Design Concept

An essential quality of the interior of the Regensburg *Salzstadel* is generated by the spatial structure typical of this type of storage facility, which does not feature any subdivisions. The design of the visitor center respects this historical form and includes only a single sensitive intervention in the form of boxlike structures that hang from the ceiling, and are open at the bottom. They allow visitors to take in the entire area of the floor. The installations divide the space into thematic zones, and can be distinguished from the historical structure by their clear colors, forms and surfaces.

Ausstellungsarchitektur, grafische Gestaltung und Medienkonzeption; Exhibition design, graphic design and media concepts;
Generalplaner allover plan
BERTRON SCHWARZ FREY
Prof. Claudia Frey, Aurelia Bertron, Prof. Ulrich Schwarz

in Kooperation mit in cooperation with:
a-u-r-a architekten: Christian Schmutz, Marisol Rivas Velázquez
Medienrealisation Media Design:
Katrin Jedon und Jens Döring, 2av
Lichtplanung Lighting: Ringo T. Fischer
Illustrationen Illustrations: Monika Richter, Christian Meyer zu Ermgassen

Dauerausstellung Permanent Exhibition
Eröffnung: Mai 2011
Opened on May 2011

ermöglichen, den Boden als durchgehende Gesamtfläche wahrzunehmen. Der Einbau strukturiert den Raum in thematische Zonen und differenziert sich durch seine klaren Farben, Formen und Oberflächen von der historischen Bausubstanz.

„Regensburg – Stadt am Fluss" ist eines der inhaltlichen Leitthemen. Das Blau und die Transparenz ihres Wassers dienten als Ideengeber für die Stimmung des Raumes im Kontrast zur monumentalen Schwere des Gebäudes. Das Besucherzentrum Welterbe Regensburg geht mit seinem musealen Präsentationsansatz über den Anspruch der herkömmlichen Visitor Centers hinaus. Es versteht sich als Entree und Mittler zur Stadt – dem eigentlichen Exponat.

Die Dramaturgie der Ausstellung lebt sowohl formal als auch inhaltlich von dem Spannungsfeld von innen und außen. Die Kabinette bilden mit ihren historischen Abbildungen auf den Innenseiten das Tableau für die Präsentation von thematischen Leitobjekten und haben die Funktion von „Schatzkammern". Großflächige Panoramadarstellungen auf den Außenseiten fungieren als visuelle Verbindung zur Stadt. „Mediale" Ausblicke nach draußen verbinden das Besucherzentrum wirkungsvoll mit der Altstadt und ihrer Geschichte. So entstand ein Ausstellungskonzept, das in ständiger Wechselwirkung zwischen Besucherzentrum und Stadt steht.

One of the central themes of the center is "Regensburg – City on the River." The blue shades and transparent quality of water have inspired the atmosphere evoked by the space, which contrasts with the structure's ponderous monumentality. With its museum-like presentational approach, Regensburg's World Heritage visitor center has greater ambitions than your average tourist office. It is designed to serve as an entrance to and "intermediary" for the city – which is actually the real exhibit.

In formal and thematic terms, the dramaturgy of the exhibition builds on the tension between interior and exterior space. The hanging structures, which feature historical images in their interiors, provide a tableau for the presentation of central thematic objects. They also function as treasure chambers. The large panoramic images on their exteriors create visual ties to the city. "Media" views of the outside world effectively link the visitors' center to the old town and its history. The exhibition concept that has emerged is rooted in the ongoing interaction between the visitor center and the city.

Besucherzentren
Visitor Centers

Besucherzentrum Welterbe Regensburg
Visitor Center World Heritage Regensburg

Träger Supporting Institutions:
Stadt Regensburg, Planungs- und Baureferat City of Regensburg, Planning and Building Division

Ausstellungsfläche Exhibition Area:
650 m²

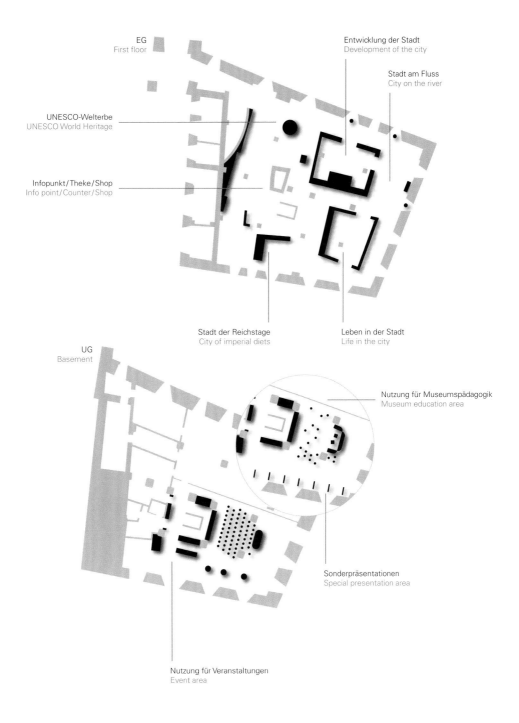

EG
First floor

Entwicklung der Stadt
Development of the city

Stadt am Fluss
City on the river

UNESCO-Welterbe
UNESCO World Heritage

Infopunkt/Theke/Shop
Info point/Counter/Shop

Stadt der Reichstage
City of imperial diets

Leben in der Stadt
Life in the city

UG
Basement

Nutzung für Museumspädagogik
Museum education area

Sonderpräsentationen
Special presentation area

Nutzung für Veranstaltungen
Event area

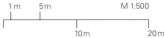

1 m   5 m   M 1:500

                    10 m   20 m

Besucherzentren
Visitor Centers

Besucherzentrum Welterbe Regensburg
Visitor Center World Heritage Regensburg

Entwurfsdarstellungen zur Idee einer „Promenade" mit Ausblicken auf die Altstadt. „Urbanoskope" bieten eine mediale Zeitreise in die historische Stadt.

Design illustrations representing the idea of a "promenade" with views of the Old Town. An "Urbanoskope" provided a historical multimedia journey through time.

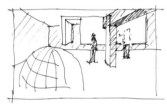

Das Gestaltungskonzept respektiert den Salzstadel als historisches Baudenkmal und Bestandteil des UNESCO-Welterbes Regensburg mit Stadtamhof. Der typische Eindruck der Innenräume mit ungeteilter Lagerfläche sollte in seiner Qualität weitgehend erhalten bzw. wiederhergestellt werden. Dies bedingte einen Rückbau aller Einbauten im EG, Abriss der eingezogenen Wände und Serviceräume des früheren Cafés.

Von der Decke abgehängte, nach unten offene Körper bilden eine thematische Zonierung und machen den Boden als Gesamtfläche wahrnehmbar.

Die Räume erhalten so einen anregenden, freundlich-heiteren Gesamteindruck.

The design concept is one in which the *Salzstadel* is respected as an historic building and as a part of the UNESCO World Heritage Regensburg with Stadtamhof. The typical impression of the interior spaces with one-piece storage area should be largely preserved and restored. This required a dismantling of all fixtures on the ground floor, walls, and demolition of the service rooms of the former cafe. Suspended from the ceiling solids open to the bottom form thematic zonings, which allow the ground to be perceived as a total area. The rooms will have a stimulating, friendly, and cheerful overall impression.

Der selbstleuchtende Globus trägt Displays mit abrufbaren Informationen zu allen Welterbestätten.

The self-illuminating globe displays information about all the World Heritage sites.

Material- und Farbkonzept

Regensburg – Stadt am Fluss.
Das Blau und die Transparenz des
Wassers der Donau dienten als
Ideengeber für die Stimmung des
Raumes im Kontrast zum historischen Bauwerk.
Die in der Ausstellung zu präsentierenden Objekte weisen sehr
nuancierte Farbgebungen auf.
Erd- und Naturtöne überwiegen
und ähneln den Farben, die in der
Bestandsarchitektur Anwendung
finden. Die Ausstellungsgestaltung stellt die Exponate vor das
Gebäude, sie räumt ihnen Vorrang
ein und präsentiert sie vor
leuchtend blauem Hintergrund.

Material and Color Concept

Regensburg – City on the river.
The blue color and the transpar-
ency of the water of the Danube
served as inspiration for the
atmosphere of the room in contrast to the historic building. The
objects presented in the exhibition are of a very nuanced color.
Earth tones and natural shades
predominate and resemble the
colors found in the building's
architecture. The exhibition design
presents the exhibits in front of
the building, so that they have pri-
ority and are represented in front
of the bright blue background.

Das Materialkonzept sieht vor, dass
hauptsächlich Materialien zum Einsatz
kommen, die in ihrer Materialität einen
erkennbaren Kontrast zum historischen
Baudenkmal erkennen lassen und sich
gleichzeitig harmonisch anfügen:

– Glas, mattiert
– Beschichtete Leichtbauplatten, weiß
– Edelstahl, lackiert
– Beschläge, anthrazit
– Einbauelemente, Akzentfarbe Blau
– Diasec, hinterleuchtete Flächen

Grundgedanke bei der Auswahl der Farben für die dienenden Ausstellungselemente, wie Podeste, Sockel, Vitrinen, Halterungen, Untergrund der Informationsflächen u. Ä., ist die Verwendung von unbunten, vornehmlich kalten Farbtönen. Durch die Farbwerte sollen Kontraste lediglich durch den Warm-Kalt-Kontrast, durch Helligkeitskontrast und einen Bunt-Unbunt-Kontrast hergestellt werden. Die Farbigkeit ist mit sehr dunklen Blautönen, vergrauten Weißtönen, verweißlichten und verschwärzlichten Farbtönen und nur spartanisch eingesetzten, in ihrer Menge äußerst begrenzten Akzentfarben sehr zurückhaltend gewählt.

The basic idea in selecting the colors for the exhibition for the foundational elements, such as platforms, pedestals, cabinets, fixtures, etc., is the use of achromatic, mainly cold color shades. Through the color value, the contrasts should be achieved primarily through a warm-cold contrast and through a bright-achromatic contrast. The color is very dark shades of blue, grays, whites, and softened blackened hues which are only sparsely used, and in which very limited accent colors are used lightly.

| The material concept is one in which the materials are used in their "materiality" to bring a discernible contrast to the historical monument and can be seen simultaneously and harmoniously: | – Frosted glass
– Lightweight coated plates, white
– Stainless steel, painted
– Fittings, anthracite
– Built-in elements, with blue accent color
– Diasec backlit areas | |

Farbe und Information

Der Gesamteindruck, die ästhetische Anmutungsqualität, wird durch die am häufigsten auftretenden Farben bestimmt. Dies sind Weiß, z. B. für Untergründe wie mattiertes Glas, und Anthrazit als konturgebende Farbe sowie die Blaupalette auf den Innenseiten der Kabinette als weitere Basisfarben.

Kabinette Außenseite

Monochrom, hell, großflächig reduzierte Farbakzente Aufteilung in Informations- und Bildbereiche/Panoramen

Kabinette Innenseite

Monochrom, gesättigte Farben Farbakzente, detailreich Aufteilung in Informations- und Präsentationsbereiche

Color and information

The overall impression, the aesthetic impression quality, is determined by the most common colors. These are white, for surfaces such as frosted glass, with charcoal as outlining color, as well as the blue line on the inside of the cabinets as an additional basic color.

Cabinets exterior

Monochrome, bright, large area with reduced color accents Used for providing information and in image areas/panoramas

Cabinets inside

Monochrome, color saturated-color accents, detailed and Used in information and presentation areas

Panoramazone
panorama area
Bilder/Illustrativ
images/illustration

Information Kernzone
information area
Höhe 60 cm height 60 cm
Zone Sprachenwechsel
language change area

Überschriften titles
Thema/Orientierung Inhalte
subject/orientation content

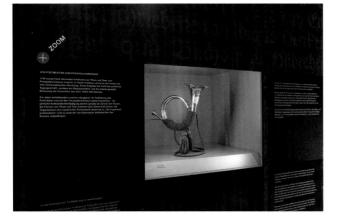

Panoramazone panorama area
Bilder/Illustrativ
images/illustration
Zitat-Zone
quote area

Kernzone Präsentation, Information
Vertiefung presentation area, inform
and additional information
Zone Sprachenwechsel
language change area

Überschriften titles
Thema/Orientierung Inhalte
subject/orientation content

Besucherzentren
Visitor Centers

Besucherzentrum Welterbe Regensburg
Visitor Center World Heritage Regensburg

Oben: Kabinette Außenseite
Narrative Texte/Zitate
Historische Stadtabildungen
im Panoramaformat
Above: Display cabinets outside
Narrative texts/Quotes
Historical city photographs
in panoramic format

t der Stadt
ensburg

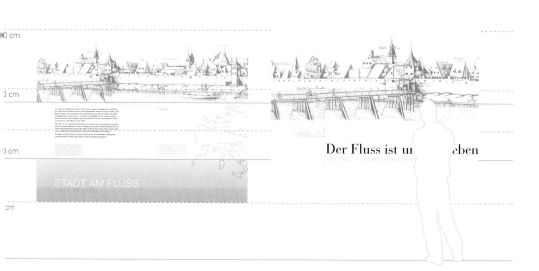

STADT AM FLUSS

Der Fluss ist u...eben

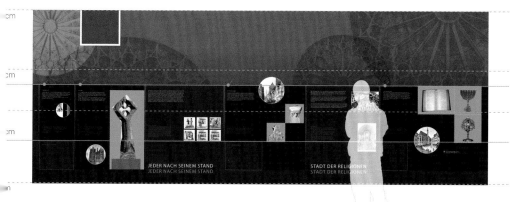

JEDER NACH SEINEM STAND

STADT DER RELIGIONEN

Unten: Kabinette Innenseite
Informationsebene ZOOM
Grafische Markierung
mit runden Bildausschnitten
Below: Display cabinet interior
Information level ZOOM
Graphic lettering with round image
detailing

Informationsebene LINK
Grafische Markierung
Querverweis zu Orten in der Stadt
Information level LINK
Cross references to locations throughout
the city

Objektpräsentation, Inszenierung von
Einzelexponaten
Vitrinenausschnitte in starken Farben
lassen die Exponate „leuchten".
Object presentation, Production of
individual exhibits
Showcases excerpts in bold colors
show that exhibits can "shine".

Seit dem Mittelalter versammelte sich der Kaiser mit
den Reichsständen, den einflussreichsten Vertretern
des Adels, des Klerus und der Freien Reichsstädte, zu
politischen Beratungen. Diese Reichstage fanden ursprünglich
in unregelmäßigen Abständen und an verschiedenen Orten statt.

788 erstmals in Regensburg abgehalten, wurde die Stadt in den folgenden
Jahrhunderten zum häufigen Austragungsort der Reichstage. Als kaiserliche
Pfalz verfügte die Stadt über die nötige Voraussetzung zur Beherbergung und
Versorgung Hunderter Teilnehmer.

Im späten 16. Jahrhundert zog der Reichstag dauerhaft in Regensburg ein.
Die Stadt lag einerseits nicht allzu weit vom Kaiserhof in Wien entfernt und
wurde andererseits sowohl von den protestantischen als auch katholischen
Reichsständen als Tagungsort akzeptiert. 1663 wurde das Alte Rathaus zum Sitz
des Immerwährenden Reichstages, einem ständigen Gesandtenkongress, der
bis zum Ende des Heiligen Römischen Reiches Deutscher Nation 1806 bestand.

Reichstagsmuseum
im Alten Rathaus

STADT DER REICHSTAGE
CITY OF IMPERIAL DIETS

ZWISCHEN KOMPROMISS UND ZEREMONIELL
BETWEEN COMPROMISE AND CEREMONIAL

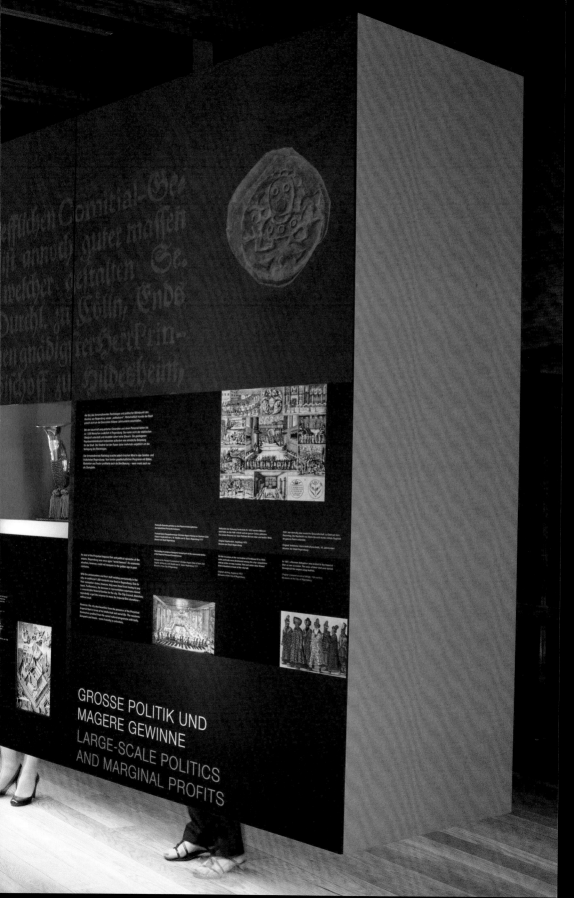

GROSSE POLITIK UND
MAGERE GEWINNE
LARGE-SCALE POLITICS
AND MARGINAL PROFITS

Das durch die kleinen Fensteröffnungen einfallende Tageslicht trägt allenfalls zur Grundbeleuchtung bei. Unter Verwendung der im Bestand befindlichen Installation bietet das neue Beleuchtungssystem eine gleichmäßige, helle Ausleuchtung der Kabinette. Ein in den Volumen der Ausstellungswände integriertes, den Boden erhellendes Effektlicht unterstützt den schwebenden Eindruck der abgehängten Ausstellungswände und betont so die durchgehende Fläche des historischen Salzstadels.

Due to the light passing through the small windows daylight contributes to the lighting scheme. The existing lighting system is completed by new elements which provide a uniform and bright light illuminating the cabinets. An integrated light effect within the exhibition walls illuminate the ground in which the exhibition walls have the appearance of "floating," thus emphasizing the continuous surface of the historic *Salzstadel.*

Besucherzentren
Visitor Centers

Besucherzentrum Welterbe Regensburg
Visitor Center World Heritage Regensburg

Vermittlungskonzept

Das wichtigste Exponat ist die Altstadt selbst. Das Besucherzentrum hat die Aufgabe, seine Besucher zu empfangen und mit Informationen ausgestattet wieder in die Stadt hinauszubewegen. Die Ausstellung bietet für Kinder spezielle Informations- und Interaktionsstationen. Eine typische Regensburger Straße zeigt modellhaft das Leben ihrer Bürger in Form von beleuchteten Mini-Dioramen in Fenstereinblicken.

Communication Concept

The most important exhibit is the Old Town itself; the visitor center's has the mission, to receive visitors and to be equipped with information so that the visitors are able to move back out into the city. The exhibition provides specific information for children and interactive stations. A typical Regensburg street shows the exemplary lives of their citizens in the form of lit miniature dioramas like looking through windows.

Besucherzentren
Visitor Centers

Besucherzentrum Welterbe Regensburg
Visitor Center World Heritage Regensburg

Historischer Straßenzug mit
Mini-Dioramen

Historical streets with mini-slides

Die Geburt der Stadt Regensburg
Birth of the City of Regensburg

Der Medieneinsatz konzentriert sich auf interaktive bzw. autoaktive Installationen und verzichtet auf typische Computerterminals. Das mediale Erlebnis bietet mehr, als das Fernsehen oder der heimische Computerbildschirm. Das dreidimensionale, interaktive Architekturmodell der Stadt Regensburg stellt zusammen mit den „Urbanoskopen" die thematische Verbindung zur Stadt her.

The media program is focused on interactive media and installations and does without the typical computer terminals. The media experience offers more than television or a home computer screen. The three-dimensional, interactive architectural model of the city of Regensburg, together with the "urbanoscopes" connects the city thematic.

Entwurf und Ausführung eines Stadtmodells zur Stadtentwicklung Regensburgs (Material: Kunststein)

Design and implementation of a city model for the the development of Regensburg (Material: artificial stone)

WANDERAUSSTELLUNGEN
TRAVELING EXHIBITIONS

Je nachdem wie lange eine Ausstellung gezeigt wird, sind drei Kategorien zu unterscheiden: Dauerausstellungen sind permanente Ausstellungen, die für einen unbestimmten Zeitraum eingerichtet werden. Zeiträume von zehn und mehr Jahren sind nicht ungewöhnlich. Wechselausstellungen sind temporäre Ausstellungen, die über einen begrenzten und genau definierten Zeitraum von wenigen Wochen, einer Saison oder an einem Ort stattfinden. Wanderausstellungen sind dagegen Ausstellungen, die an verschiedenen Orten gezeigt werden. Wanderausstellungen widmen sich in der Regel speziellen Themen, die sich mit Natur, Archäologie, Geschichte, Kunst oder Wissenschaft befassen. Einer der bekanntesten und gleichzeitig umstrittensten Vertreter dieser Kategorie ist wohl die Ausstellung *Körperwelten*, die seit 1996 plastinierte, überwiegend menschliche Körper zeigt.

Ein wichtiger Aspekt, der bei Wanderausstellungen beachtet werden muss, ist der Transport, da der Standort der Ausstellung in zeitlichen Abständen wechselt. Deshalb werden Wanderausstellungen meist als kompakte Einheit konzipiert, die leicht zu transportieren und möglichst schnell auf- und abzubauen ist. Oft wird der Ausstellungsraum selbst mitgestaltet, zum Beispiel als Box oder Container, der im öffentlichen Raum steht. Diese visuelle Einheit entsteht auch dann, wenn gleichförmige prägnante Grundformen entsprechend im Raum gestaffelt werden. Im folgenden Projektbeispiel, der Ausstellung *Menschen in der einen Welt*, ist die Kreisform der Tafeln die gestalterische Referenz für die Facetten und die differenzierte Betrachtung der „Einen" Welt.

Exhibitions are generally divided into three categories based on where and for how long they are shown. Permanent exhibitions are those mounted for an indeterminate length of time, and periods of ten years or more are not unusual. Temporary exhibitions are those shown at a single location for only a limited and precisely defined period of time, which can amount to a few weeks or a season. By contrast, traveling exhibitions are those that are shown at different locations.

As a rule, touring exhibitions are devoted to special themes dealing with the natural environment, archeology, history, art or science. Probably one of the most well known and also most controversial examples of this category is *Body Worlds*, which has been presenting plastinated, predominantly human bodies since 1996.

Transport is an important aspect of traveling exhibitions, since the location of the exhibition changes at regular intervals. For this reason, traveling exhibitions are usually conceived as compact units that are easy to transport, mount, and dismantle. The exhibition space is itself often part of the design, as in the case of a box or container that is positioned in public space. A visual unit is also created when the same, succinct basic forms are used in a spatial constellation. In the following project example, the exhibition *People In One World*, the rounded form of the display panels provides the design reference for the various facets and differentiated consideration of the concept of "one" world.

Wanderausstellungen
Traveling Exhibitions

Menschen in der einen Welt
People In One World

Menschen in der einen Welt –
Eine Wanderausstellung zum Thema Entwicklungszusammenarbeit
People In One World –
A Traveling Exhibition on the Theme of Development Cooperation

Die Welt wird von fast sieben Milliarden Menschen bevölkert – die digitale Anzeige zu Beginn der Ausstellung gibt die Bevölkerungszunahme im Sekundentakt wieder. Der Begriff „Eine Welt" ist mit Bedacht gewählt, denn unser eigenes Handeln hat immer auch dort Auswirkungen, wo wir es gar nicht vermuten. Die Wanderausstellung zeigt die vielfältigen Zusammenhänge und Abhängigkeiten unserer globalisierten Welt auf. Wer sich die Welt als ein Dorf mit nur 100 Einwohnern vorstellen mag, bekommt einen Eindruck, wie unterschiedlich vieles verteilt ist. Dieser konzeptionelle Ansatz schafft es, die globale Größenordnung dieser Zusammenhänge auf eine für den Betrachter vorstellbare Relation zu bringen. Beispielsweise hätten in dieser Vergleichsgröße 40 Menschen keinen Zugang zu sanitären Anlagen.

Die Grundbedürfnisse bilden den thematischen Einstieg. Alle Menschen benötigen Trinkwasser, Nahrung, Kleidung und eine menschenwürdige Unterkunft. Diese für das Überleben elementaren Bedürfnisse sind nicht für alle Menschen auf der Welt gesichert. In der Ausstellung wird dies durch konkrete Beispiele und authentische Fotos aus anderen Kulturen fassbar.

Die Entwicklung der einen geht oft zu Lasten der anderen. Dies zu ändern ist Ziel der internationalen Entwicklungszusammenarbeit. Sie ist aus der Neuorientierung der internationalen Gemeinschaft und der Gründung der Vereinten Nationen (United Nations, UN) nach dem Zweiten Weltkrieg entstanden. Länder mit einem hohen Lebensstandard, wie beispielsweise Deutschland, engagieren sich für die Entwicklung anderer. Sie haben sich die Sicherung des Weltfriedens, die Einhaltung des Völkerrechts, den Schutz der Menschenrechte, die Förderung der internationalen Zusammenarbeit und die Unterstützung zivilgesellschaftlicher Bereiche zur Aufgabe gemacht. Für derzeit 192 Nationen sind die

The world is populated by almost seven billion people – the digital display at the beginning of the exhibition shows the increase in the world population every second. The term "one world" was chosen as a title in part to emphasize the fact that our own actions have effects in places we do not expect them to. This traveling exhibition focuses on the diverse interconnections and dependencies that characterize our globalized world. Imagining the world as a village populated by one hundred inhabitants provides us with a stark indication of just how unevenly many resources are distributed. This conceptual approach allows the global dimension of these interrelationships to be presented in terms that are easily understandable for the observer. For example, forty people out of one hundred have no access to sanitary facilities.

Basic needs are the thematic starting point of the presentation. All people require drinking water, nourishment, clothing, and decent housing. These elementary needs, which are fundamental to survival, are not available to all the people in the world. In the exhibition, this fact is made comprehensible through the presentation of concrete examples and authentic photos from other cultures.

The development of some is often at the expense of others. Changing this situation is the goal of the international development cooperation launched as a result of the new orientation of the international community, and the establishment of the United Nations following the Second World War. Countries with a high standard of living such as Germany are contributing to the development of other countries. They have made it their task to establish world peace, to ensure the observance of human rights, to promote international cooperation and to support the development of civil society. Currently, 192 nations have adopted the guidelines developed to achieve these goals.

Stiftung Entwicklungs-Zusammenarbeit Baden-Württemberg (SEZ)
Baden-Wuerttemberg Foundation for Development Cooperation
Werastraße 24
70182 Stuttgart

Autoren / Redaktionelles Team
Authors / Editorial Team:
Nicole Kimmel, SEZ
Irene Horn, Stuttgart
Sabine Lehmkühler, Textwerkstatt
Tübingen

Ausstellungseröffnung
Exhibition Opening:
Mai 2009 May 2009

dabei entwickelten Richtlinien bindend. Als Wanderausstellung werden diese wichtigen Themen direkt zu den Menschen getragen und in Schulen, Volkshochschulen, Weltläden, Kirchengemeinden, Stadtverwaltungen oder Vereinen gezeigt. Die Ausstellung eignet sich als Ergänzung zu Unterricht und Seminaren, kann aber auch im Rahmen größerer Veranstaltungen zu Themen der Globalisierung, der Entwicklungspolitik und der *Einen Welt* eingesetzt werden. Neben den Menschenrechten werden auch Bereiche wie Politik und Gesellschaft, kulturelle Globalisierung, Frieden, nachhaltige Entwicklung und Umwelt, Gesundheit, Bildung, Welthandel und internationaler Finanzhandel vertieft.

Verschiedene Vermittlungsebenen sprechen Schüler und interessierte Personen an. Kurze Einführungstexte erläutern die Problematik des Themas. Fragen und Schlagworte springen bereits beim ersten Blick ins Auge. Die konkreten Beispiele werden in interaktiven Spielen, einer Hörstation sowie Schaubildern und Grafiken verständlich und begreifbar.

Ein Turnus von rund vier Wochen je Ausstellungsort erfordert wie erwähnt eine konstruktive Lösung für Transport und Aufbau. Die flexiblen Tafelelemente können über Verbindungspodeste parallel oder im rechten Winkel miteinander kombiniert werden. Somit lassen sich Ausstellungsflächen unterschiedlicher Dimension bespielen. Gleichzeitig tragen die Podeste interaktive Stationen wie einen Globus oder ein Stempelspiel.

Nicole Kimmel, Sabine Lehmkühler

The traveling exhibition brings these themes directly to people and is being presented in schools, adult education centers, fair trade outlets, church community centers, municipal buildings, and the headquarters of civil associations. The exhibition can be used as an adjunct to lessons and seminars as well as in the context of larger events devoted to themes of globalization, development policy, and *One World*. Apart from human rights, it also provides visitors with information in other thematic areas such as politics and society, cultural globalization, peace, sustainable development and the environment, health, education, international trade, and international finance.

The exhibition uses different communicative levels to address school pupils and other interested individuals. Short introductory texts explain the problems associated with a particular theme, quickly drawing attention to questions and key words. Concrete examples are presented in a comprehensible way with the help of interactive games, an audio station, diagrams, and photographs. The exhibition is shown at each location for around four weeks, which necessitates effective strategies for transport and construction. Pedestals have been constructed for the flexible panel elements that allow them to be displayed parallel or at right angles to one another. This means that the exhibition can be adapted to exhibition spaces of various dimensions. The pedestals are also used to support interactive stations involving, for example, a world globe or a stamp game.

Nicole Kimmel, Sabine Lehmkühler

Wanderausstellungen
Traveling Exhibitions

Menschen in der einen Welt
People In One World

Ausstellungsfläche Exhibition Area:
Standfläche ca. 100 m²
Stand area: c. 100 m²

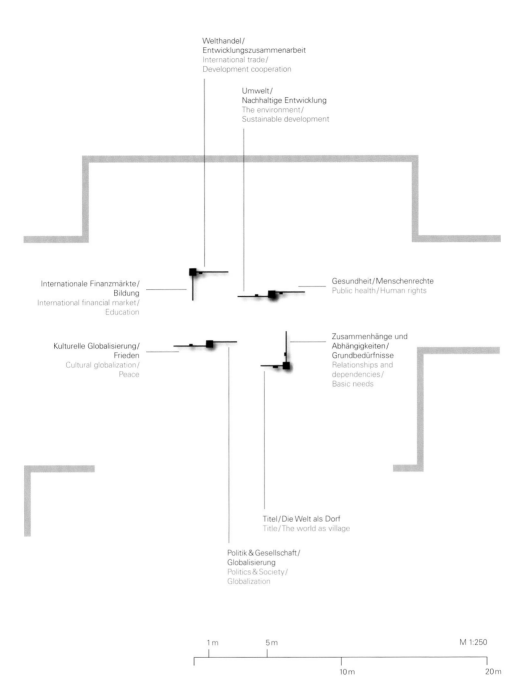

Welthandel/
Entwicklungszusammenarbeit
International trade/
Development cooperation

Umwelt/
Nachhaltige Entwicklung
The environment/
Sustainable development

Internationale Finanzmärkte/
Bildung
International financial market/
Education

Gesundheit/Menschenrechte
Public health/Human rights

Kulturelle Globalisierung/
Frieden
Cultural globalization/
Peace

Zusammenhänge und
Abhängigkeiten/
Grundbedürfnisse
Relationships and
dependencies/
Basic needs

Titel/Die Welt als Dorf
Title/The world as village

Politik & Gesellschaft/
Globalisierung
Politics & Society/
Globalization

1 m   5 m   M 1:250

                         10 m   20 m

Die rund geformten Ausstellungstafeln symbolisieren die Erde und
stellen Beziehungen zu Menschen
und Menschengruppen her. Abbildungen von Menschen in per-
spektivisch natürlicher Proportion
zur Originalgröße beziehen die
Besucher ein und vermitteln das
Gefühl, selbst Teil der Gemeinschaft zu sein.
Die Ausstellungstechnik schafft
durch Verbindungsmodule variable
Möglichkeiten, die Tafeln anzu-
ordnen, und gewährleistet einen
unkomplizierten Auf- und Abbau
der Wanderausstellung.

The round-shaped display panels
symbolize the earth and their relationships with people and socie-
ties. Figures of people in natural
proportions to their original size
draw in the visitors and give
the feeling of being part of the
community itself. The exhibition
technology provides variable ways
to arrange the tables, through
connecting modules which further ensures easy assembly and
disassembly of the exhibition.

Wanderausstellungen
Traveling Exhibitions

Menschen in der einen Welt
People In One World

Farbkonzept
– Blau: „Hausfarbe" der SEZ und
 Assoziation „blauer Planet",
 unteilbare eine Welt
– Grundflächen in warmen Braun- und
 Erdtönen
– Fotos farbig oder monochrom

Color scheme:
– Blue: is the SEZ corporate color and also
 an association of the "blue planet" as one
 world indivisible
– Base areas in warm browns and
 earth tones
– Photos in color or monochrome

Vier Themen-Stationen mit je zwei
Doppeltafeln, die variabel aufgestellt
werden können
Four theme stations, each with two
double panels, which are set up variable.

Foto auf Seite 382 Photo on page 382:
SEZ

ENTWICKLUNGSZUSAMMENARBEIT – GEMEINSAM VERANTWORTUNG TRAGEN

Alle Menschen haben den Wunsch mit Kindern und Enkelkindern in einer friedlichen und gerechten Welt sowie einer intakten Umwelt leben zu können. Doch in vielen Regionen der Erde ist das nicht möglich: Sicherheit, Frieden, Bildung, Wohlstand und Gesundheit sind ungerecht verteilt.

→ **Entwicklungszusammenarbeit** hat zum Ziel, durch technische, finanzielle und personelle Zusammenarbeit die weltweiten wirtschaftlichen, sozialen, ökologischen und politischen Verhältnisse zu verbessern und die Globalisierung gerecht und nachhaltig zu gestalten. Faktoren, die die Entwicklungschancen der armen und ärmsten Länder behindern, soll entgegengewirkt werden. In einer globalisierten Welt kann dies nur durch gemeinsame Anstrengungen aller Länder erreicht werden. Im Jahr 2000 verabschiedeten die damals 189 Mitglieder der Vereinten Nationen, United Nations, UN, die Millenniumserklärung, aus welcher die acht Millenniumsentwicklungsziele, Millennium Development Goals, MDGs, abgeleitet wurden. Ein Hauptaspekt ist die Bekämpfung extremer Armut. Gemeinsam wollen die Mitgliedstaaten die acht Ziele bis zum Jahr 2015 erreichen.

Bis zum Jahr 2015 sollen die acht Millenniumsentwicklungsziele der UN erreicht werden. Um die Erfolge messbar zu machen, wurde das Jahr 1990 als Basisjahr gesetzt. Jedes Ziel besteht aus diversen Teilzielen, deren Verwirklichung mit Hilfe entsprechender Indikatoren gemessen wird.

1981 hatten rund 1,9 Milliarden oder knapp die Hälfte aller Menschen weltweit weniger als einen US-Dollar pro Tag zum Leben. 2008 war es noch fast ein Viertel der Weltbevölkerung.

Die Einschulungsquote im Grundschulbereich stieg in Entwicklungsländern zwischen 1991 und 2006 von 80 auf 88 Prozent. Zwei Drittel des Anstiegs gelang allein nach 1999.

1990 waren weltweit 13 Prozent der Parlamentssitze von Frauen besetzt. 2007 belegten Frauen 17 Prozent der Sitze in den nationalen Parlamenten.

Die Sterblichkeitsrate von Kindern unter fünf Jahren in Entwicklungsländern ging zwischen 1990 und 2005 von 10,6 auf 8,3 Prozent zurück. 1990 starben in der Mongolei 109 von 1 000 Kindern, 2006 waren es nur noch 43.

Die Ausstellung bezieht ihre Besucher ein, lässt sie selbst etwas tun. Datengrafiken sind als einfache, mechanische, robuste Konstruktionen auf drehbaren Scheiben aufgebracht und vermitteln so auf spielerische Weise ihre Informationen.

The exhibition involves visitors in a way that they can do partake in the exhibition themselves. Data graphics are applied as a simple, mechanical, robust designs on rotating discs and thus convey the respective information in a playful manner.

Wanderausstellungen
Traveling Exhibitions

Menschen in der einen Welt
People In One World

Ausstellungsgestaltung
Exhibition Design:
BERTRON SCHWARZ FREY

Entwurfsleitung Head of Design:
Prof. Claudia Frey
Grafische Konzeption und Layout
Graphic concept and Layout:
Monika Richter

2008 wurden 66 Prozent der Geburten weltweit von Hebammen oder Ärzten begleitet, 1990 waren es nur 43 Prozent.

Insgesamt sinkt die Rate weltweiter Erkrankungen an Tuberkulose seit 2003 und stagniert seit 2007. Bleibt dieser Trend konstant, kann das Ziel einer Stagnation oder weiteren Abnahme von Neuerkrankungen noch vor 2015 erreicht werden.

2008 wurden 66 Prozent der Geburten weltweit von Hebammen oder Ärzten begleitet, 1990 waren es nur 43 Prozent.

Weltweit ist die Zahl der arbeitslosen Jugendlichenzwischen 1996 und 2006 von 74 auf 86 Millionen gestiegen. Das ist fast die Hälfte der 195 Millionen Arbeitslosen auf der Welt.

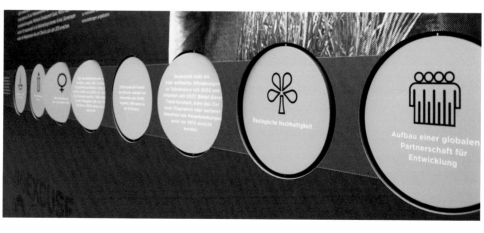

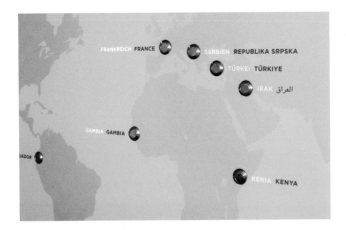

Sprechende Audiostationen mit Berichten und Interviews aus aller Welt machen die Präsentation lebendig.

„Kultur ist vielfältig, beweglich und wandelt sich ständig. Kultureller Austausch und Kulturwandel spiegeln sich in den unterschiedlichsten Aspekten wie Worte, Lieder, Gesten, Kleidungsstile, Musikstücke oder Kunst wider und wandern von einer Gruppe zur nächsten. Dort werden sie aufgenommen, können neu interpretiert werden oder Bestehendes ersetzen. Was früher Jahrhunderte dauerte, kann heute über Nacht den Globus umrunden.
Globale Ideen werden zum Teil ganz unterschiedlich wahrgenommen und in das jeweilige Weltbild eingefügt. Was als zu fremd empfunden wird, wird abgewehrt, vieles aber auch umgewandelt, der eigenen Kultur angepasst und somit vertraut. Die nationale Herkunft spielt dabei eine immer geringere Rolle."

"Talking" audio stations with reports and interviews from around the world make the presentation come alive.
"Culture is diverse, flexible and constantly changing. Cultural exchange and cultural change are reflected in the various aspects such as words, songs, gestures, clothing styles, music or art and move from one group to another. There they are taken, can be reinterpreted or replaced.
What once took centuries can now circumnavigate the globe overnight.
Global ideas are sometimes perceived quite differently, and inserted into each particular world view. What is perceived as too foreign, is refused, but also adapted to their own culture and thus familiar and trusted. National origin, plays an increasingly minor role."

Wanderausstellungen
Traveling Exhibitions

Menschen in der einen Welt
People In One World

Keine Original-Exponate
Not an original exhibit

KULTURELLE GLOBALISIERUNG:
FREMDES UND VERTRAUTES

Kultur ist vielfältig, beweglich und wandelt sich ständig. Kultureller Austausch und Kulturwandel spiegeln sich in den unterschiedlichsten Aspekten wie Worte, Lieder, Gesten, Kleidungsstile, Musikstücke oder Kunst wider und wandern von einer Gruppe zur nächsten. Dort werden sie aufgenommen, können neu interpretiert werden oder Bestehendes ersetzen. Was früher Jahrhunderte dauerte, kann heute über Nacht den Globus umrunden.

Globale Ideen werden zum Teil ganz unterschiedlich wahrgenommen und in das jeweilige Weltbild eingefügt. Was als zu fremd empfunden wird, wird abgewehrt, vieles aber auch umgewandelt, der eigenen Kultur angepasst und somit vertraut. Die nationale Herkunft spielt dabei eine immer geringere Rolle.

Die als „Bollywood" bezeichnete Filmindustrie Mumbais (früher Bombay) ist nach der Hollywoods die bekannteste der Welt. Während zunächst eher traditionelle indische Schönheitsideale und Themen vorherrschten, haben sich die Filme zunehmend dem Weltmarkt angepasst und zeigen eine Mischung aus westlichen und östlichen Elementen. Auch außerhalb Asiens gibt es eine wachsende Begeisterung für Bollywood-Filme.

Wäre die ganze Welt ein Dorf mit nur 100 Einwohnern, gäbe es ...

15 Barbiepuppen

17 Dorfbewohner sprächen Chinesisch und Mandarin
9 Englisch
8 Hindi und Urdu

3 Einwohner könnten in ihrem Leben eine Auslandsreise unternehmen

...ch nicht ... was uns in den Industrie-
...en erscheint, ist anderswo mit viel Mühe
nicht vorhanden.
...Welt als ein Dorf mit nur 100 Einwohnern vor,
...n Eindruck, wie unterschiedlich vieles verteilt ist.

10

6...

Wäre die
mit nur 1

80 Menschen im Dorf hätten keine

15 wären Analphabeten

13 wären unterernährt

2 wären Flüchtlinge

Asiate

100

42 Dorfbewohner hätten ein eigenes Radio
24 einen Fernseher
15 einen Computer
7 ein Auto

...fbewohner wären Kinder unter 15 Jahren

älter als 65 Jahre

100

52 Frauen
48 Männer

ein Dorf
...ern, dann wären ...

Nicht-Weiße
...eiße

...enden Wohnverhältnisse

100

33 Christen
18 Muslime
17 Atheisten

Bevölkerungswachstum

Die Weltbevölkerung wächst schnell. Die Abstände...
...zur nächsten werden kürzer. 1961 lebten rund eine...
der Erde, 1960 waren es bereits drei, 1975 vier und...
Menschen.

Leben zu viele Menschen in einer Region, werden...
Nahrungsmittel knapp. So war es auch in Europa...
überstarken Bevölkerungswachstum führte zu Hu...
hoher Sterblichkeit. Viele Menschen wanderten a...
Aufbau einer wirtschaftlichen Infrastruktur, ange...
nisse und hygienische Bedingungen sowie der a...
Nahrungsgrundlage verbesserten allmählich auch...
Menschen.

Schließlich führten zivilisatorische Fortschritte...
Einführung der allgemeinen Schulpflicht oder b...
Hygienebedingungen auch dazu, dass die Geb...
Die
Bevölkerungsexplosion war gebremst. In der Pl...
vielen europäischen Ländern ein hoher Lebens...
Zunahme der Lebenserwartung messbar ist.

In einer vergleichbaren Situation sind am Anf...
immer viele Länder auf der Erde. Gerade die a...
sen am schnellsten; dadurch verschärft sich de...
Das Risiko einer Frau, bei der Geburt zu sterbe...
ländern 600 Mal höher als bei uns.
Wenn durch Geburtenkontrolle 0,4 Prozent v...
ration geboren werden, bedeutet das für das...
2,4 Prozent weniger Armut.

In der → **Demografie** errechnet man mit Hil...
wie viele Menschen auf der Erde leben. Die...
der Menschen in Entwicklungsländern zu, we...
großen Teil davon ab, wie sich das Bevölke...

Zurzeit bekommt jede Frau im Durchschnitt...
lere Wachstumsvorhersage der Grafik zeigt...
Erde leben, wenn die Geburtenziffer im Do...
Jahr 2050 sinkt.

Ist die Geburtenziffer um 0,5 Kinder je Frau...
das 1,5 Milliarden Menschen mehr oder we...

Quelle: United Nations – Department of E...
(UN/DESA): World Population Prospects...
Urbanization Prospects: The 2003 Revisio...

Bevölkerungswachstum weltweit

hohe, mittlere, ...
Wachstumsprognose

1950   2000

→ **Demografie** beschreibt wie sich Bevölke...
Strukturen wie Alter, Geschlecht, Familie...
Kinderzahl durch demografische Ereignis...
umziehen oder sterben verändern.

→ Die **Geburtenziffer** gibt an, wie viele Kin...
in ihrem Leben zur Welt bringt. Vom Stan...
weltweit noch bei fünf Kindern je Frau...

EINFACHE AUSSTELLUNGEN
SIMPLE EXHIBITIONS

Der Begriff „einfache Ausstellungen" kann auf verschiedene Art und Weise verstanden werden. Zunächst bedeutet „einfach" bescheiden, schlicht und unkompliziert, aber auch leicht verständlich und leicht auszuführen. Der Gesichtspunkt der Einfachheit könnte als Forderung an alle Ausstellungen gerichtet werden. Einfachen Dingen wird nachgesagt, sie seien oft die Schönsten. Einfach kann aber auch bedeuten: nur „ein Objekt" oder nur „ein Gedanke". Komplizierte Dinge einfach auszudrücken hilft, die Kommunikation schneller und verständlicher zu machen. Dieser Gestaltungsansatz fordert von der technischen Umsetzung einfache Materialien im Sinne von billigem oder leicht zu verarbeitendem Material oder auch schlicht „ein Material". Die auf den Seiten 379–389 beschriebene Ausstellung *Eine Welt* kann in Bezug auf ihren Inhalt als einfache Ausstellung verstanden werden. In jedem Fall fördern „einfache Ausstellungen" das Nachdenken über die Möglichkeiten, Ausstellungen einfach zu konzipieren, und können zu neuen Gestaltungsideen anregen. Auf den finanziellen Rahmen eines Projektes bezogen, stellen sie jedoch größte Anforderungen an ihre Macher. Die auf den folgenden Seiten dargestellte Ausstellung über die Berliner Charité verdeutlicht, dass auch mit einfachem Budget ambitionierte Ausstellungen entstehen können. Möglich gemacht hat dies die Kooperation mit Studenten der Universität der Künste Berlin, die aufgrund der mangelnden Ausstattung Berliner Kunsthochschulen geradezu Spezialisten für das Entwerfen außergewöhnlicher Lösungen mit mageren Budgets sind.

The term "simple exhibitions" can be understood in different ways. On the one hand, "simple" can mean modest, plain and uncomplicated, as well as easily understandable and easy to implement. In this sense, simplicity can be seen as a requirement of all exhibitions. It is often said that the simplest is the most beautiful. On the other hand, "simple" can also imply a single object or a single idea. Expressing complicated things simply helps to speed up the process of communication and make it more comprehensible. In technical terms, approaching design with an emphasis on simplicity means using simple components in the sense of cheap or easily workable material or a single material. In terms of its content, the exhibition *One World* described on pages 379–389 can be understood as a simple exhibition. In any case, "simple exhibitions" promote reflection on the possibilities of conceiving exhibitions in simple terms and can generate new design ideas. This becomes particularly important when exhibition designers have only limited financial resources at their disposal. The exhibition on Berlin's Charité hospital presented in this book is a good example of an ambitious exhibition realized using a restricted budget. This was due not least to the contribution made by students from Berlin's University of the Arts, who, due to the lack of resources available to Berlin's art academies, are specialists when it comes to finding remarkable solutions with meager budgets.

Einfache Ausstellungen
Simple Exhibitions

Die Charité zwischen Ost und West.
Zeitzeugen erinnern sich
The Charité between East and West.
Historical Witnesses Remember

Die Charité zwischen Ost und West (1945–1992). Zeitzeugen erinnern sich
The Charité between East and West (1945–1992). Historical Witnesses Remember

Das älteste Berliner Krankenhaus, die Charité, blickt auf eine 300-jährige traditionsreiche Geschichte zurück. Dem jüngsten Abschnitt, der DDR-Geschichte, widmete sich die Ausstellung *Die Charité zwischen Ost und West (1945–1992). Zeitzeugen erinnern sich.* Sie war vom 2. September bis zum 31. Oktober 2010 zu sehen und entstand in Kooperation des Instituts für Geschichte der Medizin und des Berliner Medizinhistorischen Museums der Charité mit der Universität der Künste Berlin und dem Abgeordnetenhaus von Berlin. Das Projekt wurde aus Mitteln der Bundesstiftung zur Aufarbeitung der SED-Diktatur gefördert.

In der Ausstellung galt es, am Beispiel des prestigereichen Berliner Universitätsklinikums vielfältige DDR-spezifische Wirkungsfelder in ihren Dimensionen und Verflechtungen aufzuzeigen – schließlich bestimmten sie den Alltag der Charité-Mitarbeiter. In den acht Ausstellungsstationen standen die Bereiche Versorgung, Forschung und Lehre im Vordergrund. Weitere Themen waren die geografische Lage der Charité an der Berliner Mauer und das Überwachungsinteresse des Ministeriums für Staatssicherheit. In Toncollagen berichten Zeitzeugen der Charité aus den Jahren 1945 bis 1992 über politisch brisante Aspekte ihrer Tätigkeiten. Archivalien, persönliche Fotos und Dokumente bereichern die mündlichen Überlieferungen.

Die DDR-Zeit der Charité ist in großer Vielgestaltigkeit individuellen Erinnerns und zahllosen Dokumenten in diversen Archivbeständen präsent. Sie äußert sich in sehr unterschiedlichen, oft widersprüchlichen Wahrnehmungen und Darstellungen ihrer Protagonisten, die in einem historischen Rahmen kontextualisiert werden.

Die besondere gestalterische Herausforderung der Ausstellung bestand in der Präsentation von Zeitzeugeninterviews, die mit zahlreichen in diesen Jahren dort tätigen Mitarbeitern unterschiedlichster Professionen geführt wurden.

As the oldest hospital in Berlin, the Charité has a history rich in tradition dating back three hundred years. The exhibition *The Charité between East and West (1945–1992). Historical Witnesses Remember* was devoted to its most recent chapter. It ran from September 2 to October 31, 2010, and was the result of a collaboration between the Berlin Parliament, the Berlin University of the Arts, and two institutions affiliated with the Charité: the Institute for the History of Medicine, and the Berlin Museum of Medical History. The project received funds from the Federal Foundation for the Reappraisal of the Dictatorship of the Socialist Unity Party.

The exhibition's goal was to use the prestigious university clinic in Berlin as an example to illustrate the dimensions, and interdependencies of diverse spheres of action that were specific to the German Democratic Republic (GDR), and that ultimately determined everyday life for the Charité staff. The exhibition's eight thematic areas focused on medical care, research, and teaching. Additional subjects included the geographic location of the Charité at the Berlin Wall, and the Ministry of State Security's interest in monitoring the hospital. In audio collages, historical witnesses associated with the Charité between 1945 and 1992 described politically explosive aspects of their work. Archival materials, personal photos, and documents were used to enrich these oral records.

The Charité's East German phase retains a presence in the form of diverse individual recollections, and innumerable documents in various archival holdings. The perceptions and accounts of its protagonists are very different and often contradictory, and the exhibition provided a means by which they could be seen in an historical context.

A special design challenge confronting the exhibition organizers was to present interviews that were conducted with many staff members from different professions who worked at the hospital during these years.

Abgeordnetenhaus Berlin
Berlin House of Representatives
Niederkirchnerstr. 3–5
10117 Berlin

Schirmherr Patron:
Walter Momper, Präsident des Abgeordnetenhauses von Berlin President of the Berlin House of Representatives

Wechselausstellung Temporary Exhibition

Vom Subjekt zum Objekt

Jede thematisch gebundene Ausstellung ist eine Veröffentlichung eigenen Formats. Wie ein schlüssig komponierter Text verfügt sie über eine zentrale These, eine Kernaussage, die sie mit spezifischen Objekten auf einem diskursiven Weg entlang eines Erzählstranges deutlich machen und im besten Falle zur Diskussion stellen will. Wie der lückenhafte Wald der Buchstaben, Silben und Sätze eines geschriebenen Textes ist eine Ausstellung ein gebrochenes Medium. Nie wird ein Themenfeld homogen und damit komplett vorgestellt. Naturgemäß bleibt es bei Informationssplittern, Andeutungen, Mutmaßungen, Fehlstellen, Brüchen und Perspektivwechseln. Vielleicht können sie, ins Positive gewendet und vom Konzept oftmals gar nicht beabsichtigt, Freiräume zwischen den Dingen schaffen, in welchen das Fragen und weitere Nachdenken der Betrachter inspiriert und mit persönlichem Gewinn fortgesetzt werden kann. Konstitutiv für diesen unvermuteten intellektuellen Funkenschlag ist die spezifische Anlage des inhaltlich besetzten, konzeptionell strukturierten und gestalterisch verdichteten Ausstellungsraums.

Thomas Schnalke

Das inhaltliche Ausstellungskonzept

20 Jahre nach dem Ende der DDR schlugen die emotionalen Wellen bei der Frage nach der Ausrichtung und ihrer zeithistorischen Bewertung immer noch hoch. Unter den Zeitzeugen kristallisierten sich zwei Positionen heraus: Die unter schwierigen Bedingungen in der DDR erbrachten Leistungen sollten endlich angemessen gewürdigt werden und in der Tradition des berühmten Krankenhauses ihren Platz finden. Den zahlreichen Negativschlagzeilen, in die der einstige „Leuchtturm des DDR-Gesundheitswesens" seit dem Mauerfall immer wieder geriet, sollte endlich auch ein positives Bild von der beträchtlichen Aufbauleistung und vom Kollektivgeist der Mitarbeiterschaft an die Seite gestellt werden.
Andere Zeitzeugen erwarteten vielmehr, dass der politische Druck und die Gängelung durch Partei und Regierung in den Blick

From Subject to Object

Every theme-based exhibition is a publication in its own format. Similar to a coherently composed text, it has a central thesis or core message that it hopes to discursively illustrate through specific objects along a narrative line. Ideally, it presents this thesis for discussion. Similar to the fragmentary system of letters, syllables, and sentences in a written text, an exhibition is a fractured medium. A subject area is never homogeneous and can therefore never be presented in its entirety. By their very nature, exhibitions can only offer snippets of information, intimations, assumptions, discontinuities, ruptures, and shifts in perspective. When these elements exert a positive effect, one that is often not foreseen in the original exhibition concept, they can create a space between the objects in which viewers are inspired to question, and reflect on the material they are confronted with – a process that can be ongoing and personally fulfilling.
The specific layout of a thematically focused, conceptually structured, and creatively enhanced exhibition space is constitutive of this unexpected intellectual inspiration.

Thomas Schnalke

The Exhibition Concept

Twenty years after the collapse of the GDR, questions about the focus and historical assessment of the Charité caused emotions to run high. Among the historical witnesses, two positions crystallized. Some believed that the work performed under difficult conditions in the GDR should finally be given due recognition and a place in the tradition of the famous hospital. The many negative headlines that the one-time "beacon of the GDR healthcare system" has attracted since the fall of the Wall needed to be contrasted with a positive image of the staff's significant reconstruction efforts, and collective spirit.
Other historical witnesses expected the exhibition to focus on the political pressure exerted by the Communist Party and the GDR government, and their meddling in the way the hospital was run. Opinions differed

Einfache Ausstellungen
Simple Exhibitions

Die Charité zwischen Ost und West.
Zeitzeugen erinnern sich
The Charité between East and West.
Historical Witnesses Remember

Projektleitung Charité 300
Project Management Charité 300:
Reiner Felsberg, Charité

Ausstellungskuratoren Exhibition Curators:
Dr. Rainer Herrn und Laura Hottenrott,
Institut für Geschichte der Medizin der
Charité Institute for the Medical History
of the Charité

genommen werden. Vor allem schieden sich die Geister beim Thema „Stasi", dem Einfluss des Ministeriums für Staatssicherheit auf den Alltag in der Charité. Die Ausstellung verfolgte weder das Ziel, die Positionen polarisierend zuzuspitzen, noch zwischen ihnen befriedend zu vermitteln. Vielmehr schenkte sie individuellen Stimmen Gehör. Uns ging es darum, die Positionen und Erfahrungswelten der Zeitzeugen darzustellen und ihre Biografien im zeithistorischen Kontext verstehbar zu machen. Thematisch war die Ausstellung in sieben separate räumliche Stationen unterteilt, in denen Interviewpassagen als O-Töne zu hören sowie Dokumente und Fotos mit einleitenden Texten auf Ausstellungstafeln zu sehen waren. Eine vertiefende Hörstation bildete den Abschluss des Ausstellungsrundgangs.

1. Die Charité als Sozialgefüge
2. Die Charité als Versorgungsobjekt
3. Die Charité als Grenzobjekt
4. Die Charité als Observationsobjekt
5. Die Charité als politische Arena
6. Die Charité als Prestigeobjekt
7. Die Charité als Medienobjekt

Laura Hottenrott & Rainer Herrn

Gestalterisches Konzept

Der Begriff Oral History meint Erinnerungsinterviews mit Zeitzeugen. Es handelt sich dabei um eine Forschungsmethode, aber auch um eine Methode, in einer Ausstellung ungewöhnliche Vermittlungsmöglichkeiten anzubieten, die einen neuen Blick auf die Vergangenheit provozieren.

Die Oral-History-Methode kommt in der Regel dort zum Einsatz, wo die Geschichte nicht niedergeschrieben ist. Dies ist vor allem im Bereich Alltagsleben der Fall. Die Betrachtung von Erlebnissen Einzelner bietet einen individuellen, emotionalen Zugang zu dem behandelten Thema, lässt aber auch Rückschlüsse auf das Ganze zu. Die Qualität der direkten, persönlich bezogenen Berichterstattung bietet ein hohes Maß an Authentizität und Glaubwürdigkeit.

Die Idee, Oral History als Ausstellungsprojekt umzusetzen, bedeutet eine besondere gestalterische Herausforderung. Zeitzeugen

most when it came to the Stasi (the Ministry of State Security), and its influence on everyday life at the Charité. The exhibition did not pursue the goal of presenting either of these positions in an extreme, polarizing way. Nor did it attempt to mediate between the two. Rather, it gave individuals the opportunity to be heard. It was important for us to present the historical witnesses' positions and worlds, and render their biographies comprehensible in their historical context.

In terms of subject matter, the exhibition was divided into seven separate spatial units where visitors could listen to interview passages in the form of original soundtracks, and view documents and photos with introductory texts presented on exhibition panels. The tour of the exhibition ended at an audio station that provided more in-depth information. The seven areas were:

1. The Charité as a social structure.
2. The Charité as a provider of medical care.
3. The Charité as an object on the border.
4. The Charité as a surveillance object.
5. The Charité as a political arena.
6. The Charité as a prestigious institution.
7. The Charité as a focus of media attention.

Laura Hottenrott & Rainer Herrn

Design Concept

The term "oral history" refers to interviews in which historical witnesses recall the past. It is both a research method, and a strategy for offering unusual presentational possibilities to prompt a new look at the past.

The methods of oral history are usually employed when history does not exist in written form. This is above all the case with everyday life. Examining the experiences of individuals provides an emotive approach to the subject matter under examination, but it does not allow conclusions to be drawn about the whole. The direct personal report ensures a high degree of authenticity, and credibility.

Basing an exhibition project on oral history entails a special challenge for exhibition design. While there is nothing unusual about using interviews with eyewitnesses as

Projektleitung Zeitzeugen Project Management Historical Witnesses: Prof. Dr. Volker Hess, Institut für Geschichte der Medizin der Charité Institute for the Medical History of the Charité, Prof. Dr. Thomas Schnalke, Berliner Medizinhistorisches Museum der Charité Berlin Medical Historical Museum of the Charité

Wissenschaftliche Beratung Scientific Consultant: Dr. Thomas Beddies, Institut für Geschichte der Medizin der Charité Institute for the Medical History of the Charité

Ausstellungszeitraum Exhibition Duration: 1. September 2010 bis 31. Oktober 2010 September 1, 2010 until October 31, 2010

in einer Ausstellung zu Wort kommen zu lassen ist nichts Ungewöhnliches, wenn dies als Ergänzung oder zusätzliche Option eingesetzt wird. Oral History zum tragenden Gestaltungselement zu erheben, ist jedoch ein ungewöhnliches Experiment, das mit medialen Methoden die Aufmerksamkeit des Publikums auf sich zieht.

Wichtigstes „Exponat" sind die Interviews von Zeitzeugen, die sich im Ausstellungsrundgang[1] dramaturgisch zu thematischen Dialogen reduzieren und auf die wesentlichen und eindrucksvollsten Sätze konzentrieren. Die Ausstellungsgestalter setzen diese Hörinstallationen entsprechend den thematischen Spannungsbögen in Szene: das Thema Sozialgefüge als Hörinsel, an der die Besucher um einen Tisch herum sitzen, das Thema Grenzobjekt als Lautsprecher, der von einer Mauer herabschallt, das Thema Observationsobjekt durch in die Wand eingelassene, nicht sichtbare Lautsprecher, die man nur wahrnimmt, wenn man mit dem Ohr direkt an der Wand die Gespräche abhört. Die Ausstellung *Zeitzeugen Charité* zeigt zwar auch Gegenstände, überwiegend Faksimile von Dokumenten, aber die wesentlichen Aussagen fallen in den Interviews mit Zeitzeugen. So steht das gesprochene Wort im Zentrum des Interesses und der Gestaltungsüberlegungen.

Ein besonders reizvoller Aspekt dieses Konzepts ist, dass die Vermittlung von Geschichte durch gesprochene Sprache die wohl ursprünglichste und direkteste Form der Erzählung ist, heute in einem Ausstellungsraum jedoch die wohl ungewöhnlichste. Audioinstallationen als zentrale Vermittlungseinheit entsprechen nicht den gängigen Erwartungen. Genau da liegt die Chance, Wahrnehmungsgewohnheiten zu durchbrechen, um durch eine unerwartete Kommunikationsform gesteigerte Aufmerksamkeit zu erreichen. Der gestalterische Schwerpunkt der Ausstellung liegt auf der Vermittlung von Geschichte durch das gesprochene Wort und der Faszination, die durch die Authentizität von Zeitzeugenberichten entsteht.

supplementary information or an additional option at an exhibition, any attempt to make oral history the main pillar of an exhibition must be seen as an unusual experiment in capturing the audience's attention by media-based methods.

The most important exhibit was the interviews with the historical witnesses. These were dramaturgically reduced to thematic dialogues presented throughout the exhibition tour, and concentrated on the essential and most impressive statements by these witnesses. The exhibition designers orchestrated the audio installations in keeping with the thematic arcs of the show: the topic of "social structure" was realized in the form of an audio island inviting visitors to sit around a table; the theme of "border object" was expressed in the form of a loudspeaker blaring from a wall; the idea of "surveillance object" was presented using invisible loudspeakers set into a wall broadcasting conversations that visitors could only hear by pressing their ears to the wall and "eavesdropping." Although the exhibition at the Charité also presented a number of objects (predominantly facsimiles of documents), it was the interviews that contained the most important statements. Hence the spoken word was the focus of interest, and played a central role in design considerations.

An especially interesting aspect of the concept is that while the presentation of history through the spoken word is probably the oldest, and most direct form of narrative, it is probably the most unusual in exhibition spaces today. The use of audio installations as a central means of presentation runs contrary to common expectations, but it is precisely this method that provides the opportunity to break through perceptual habits, and capture greater attention through an unexpected form of communication. In terms of design, the primary focus of the exhibition was on the presentation of history through the spoken word, and the fascination that emanated from the authenticity of the reports by historical witnesses.

Einfache Ausstellungen
Simple Exhibitions

Die Charité zwischen Ost und West.
Zeitzeugen erinnern sich
The Charité between East and West.
Historical Witnesses Remember

[1] Sebastian Simmert, Dirk Weidlich
[1] Sebastian Simmert, Dirk Weidlich

Träger Supporting Institutions:
Bundesstiftung zur Aufarbeitung der SED-Diktatur, Charité-Universitätsmedizin Berlin State foundation devoted to the examination and reappraisal of the SED dictatorship in East Germany, The Charité School of Medicine, Berlin

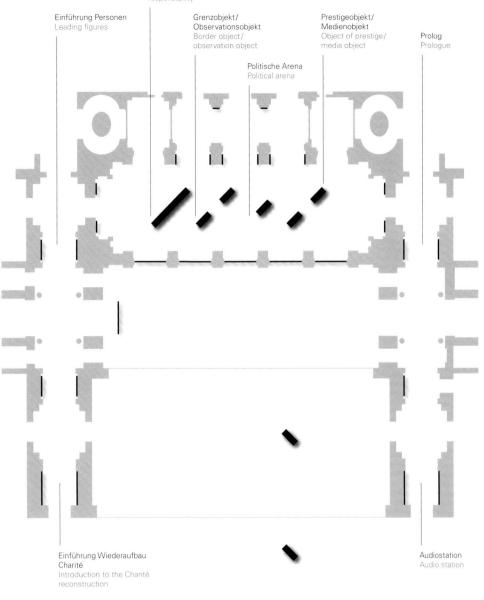

Versorgungsobjekt/
Sozialgefüge
Care facility/social
responsibility

Einführung Personen
Leading figures

Grenzobjekt/
Observationsobjekt
Border object/
observation object

Prestigeobjekt/
Medienobjekt
Object of prestige/
media object

Prolog
Prologue

Politische Arena
Political arena

Einführung Wiederaufbau
Charité
Introduction to the Charité
reconstruction

Audiostation
Audio station

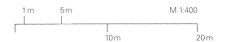

1 m   5 m   M 1:400

                                    10 m   20 m

Themenstationen gliedern sich in ein Hauptthema und davon abzweigend mehrere Unterthemen. Lineare Bezugslinien machen die Struktur aus Texten, Bildern, Dokumenten und Grafiken lesbar.

Theme-based stations are divided into a main theme and several sub-themes. Linear reference lines allow the visitor to read the structure which is made from texts, images, documents, and graphics.

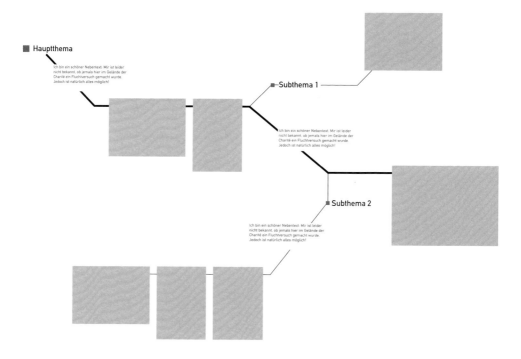

■ Hauptthema

Ich bin ein schöner Nebentext. Mir ist leider nicht bekannt, ob jemals hier im Gelände der Charité ein Fluchtversuch gemacht wurde. Jedoch ist natürlich alles möglich!

■ Subthema 1

Ich bin ein schöner Nebentext. Mir ist leider nicht bekannt, ob jemals hier im Gelände der Charité ein Fluchtversuch gemacht wurde. Jedoch ist natürlich alles möglich!

■ Subthema 2

Ich bin ein schöner Nebentext. Mir ist leider nicht bekannt, ob jemals hier im Gelände der Charité ein Fluchtversuch gemacht wurde. Jedoch ist natürlich alles möglich!

Einfache Ausstellungen
Simple Exhibitions

Die Charité zwischen Ost und West.
Zeitzeugen erinnern sich
The Charité between East and West.
Historical Witnesses Remember

Kooperationspartner Ausstellung
Exhibition Cooperation Partner:
Universität der Künste Berlin

Künstlerische Leitung Artistic Directors:
Prof. Gerhard Diel, Prof. Ulrich Schwarz,
Prof. Jussi Ängeslevä

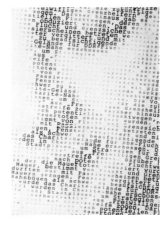

Die Hintergrundbilder der 1,5×3 Meter großen Grafiktafeln generieren sich aus den Texten der Interviews zu großformatigen typografischen Superzeichen.

The background images standing at 1,5×3 meters panels are made from the texts of interviews to large-sized typographic super characters.

Ausstellungsgestaltung und Grafik
Exhibition Design and Graphic Design:
Philipp Hoffmann, Julia Volkmar

Gestaltung digitale Medien
Digital Media Design:
Martin Kim Luge, Clemens Winkler,
Torsten Posselt
Bildbearbeitung Image Editing:
Denis Yilmas

Audio- / Videobearbeitung
Sound and Video Editing:
Sebastian Simmert, Dirk Weidlich

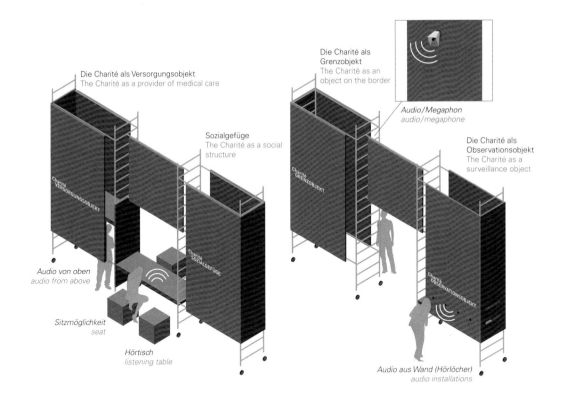

Die Charité als Versorgungsobjekt
The Charité as a provider of medical care

Sozialgefüge
The Charité as a social structure

Die Charité als Grenzobjekt
The Charité as an object on the border

Audio/Megaphon
audio/megaphone

Die Charité als Observationsobjekt
The Charité as a surveillance object

Charité
VERSORGUNGSOBJEKT

Charité
GRENZOBJEKT

Charité
SOZIALGEFÜGE

Charité
OBSERVATIONSOBJEKT

Audio von oben
audio from above

Sitzmöglichkeit
seat

Hörtisch
listening table

Audio aus Wand (Hörlöcher)
audio installations

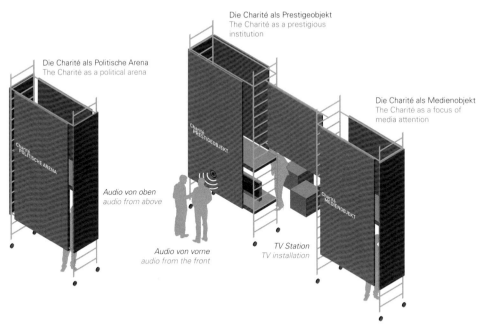

Die Charité als Prestigeobjekt
The Charité as a prestigious institution

Die Charité als Politische Arena
The Charité as a political arena

Die Charité als Medienobjekt
The Charité as a focus of media attention

Charité
PRESTIGEOBJEKT

Charité
POLITISCHE ARENA

Charité
MEDIENOBJEKT

Audio von oben
audio from above

Audio von vorne
audio from the front

TV Station
TV installation

Einfache Ausstellungen
Simple Exhibitions

Die Charité zwischen Ost und West.
Zeitzeugen erinnern sich
The Charité between East and West.
Historical Witnesses Remember

Kooperationspartner Veranstaltungen:
Abgeordnetenhaus von Berlin,
Bundesbeauftragte für die Unterlagen
des Staatssicherheitsdienstes der
ehemaligen Deutschen Demokratischen
Republik

Event cooperation partners:
Abgeordnetenhaus von Berlin (Berlin
House of Representatives), Federal
Commissioner for the Records of the
State Intelligence Agency of the former
German Democratic Republic

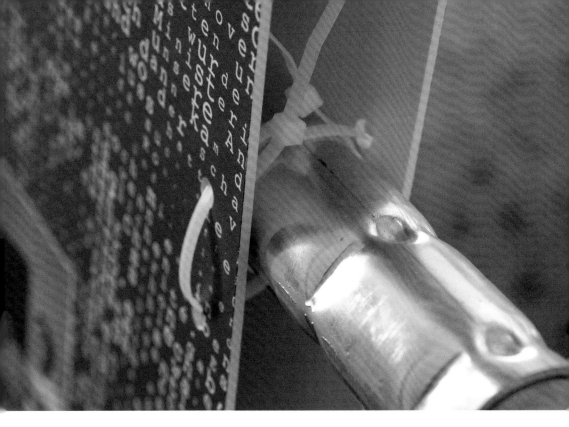

Der Hauptteil der Ausstellung gliedert sich in sieben Themenstationen, die jeweils passende Interviews über unterschiedliche akustische Installationen vermitteln.
So (be-)lauschen die Besucher beim „Observationsobjekt" die Stimmen aus der Wand oder sitzen beim Thema „Sozialgefüge" um einen gesprächigen Hörtisch.

The main part of the exhibition is divided into seven stations in which suitable interviews are distributed across different acoustic installations. In this way the visitors are listening to the voices coming from the wall at the "object observation" or sitting at a chatty table talking about the "social fabric."

Ausstellungssystem, Materialien:
Baugerüststangen, Aluminium,
PVC-Plane, Kabelbinder

Exhibition System, Material:
Scaffolding piles, aluminum, PVC tarp,
cable tie

Hörtisch zum Thema
„Sozialgefüge".
Hörinstallation in der Wand zum
Thema „Observationsobjekt".
Lautsprecher von oben zum
Thema »Grenzobjekt«.

Listening table on the theme
of "social fabric."
Listening installation installed
in the wall on the subject of
"observation object."
Loudspeaker from above on
the subject of "border object."

Einfache Ausstellungen
Simple Exhibitions

Die Charité zwischen Ost und West.
Zeitzeugen erinnern sich
The Charité between East and West.
Historical Witnesses Remember

Querverweis:
Siehe Text „Gestalterisches Konzept",
Seiten 393 ff.
Hyperlink:
See "Design Concept" on pages 393 ff.

DIE CHARITÉ ZWISCHEN
OST UND WEST (1945–1992)
Zeitzeugen erinnern sich.

2. September – 31. Oktober 2010
im Abgeordnetenhaus von Berlin

Aurelia Bertron

Nach ihrem Studium der Visuellen Kommunikation an der Hochschule für Gestaltung in Schwäbisch Gmünd folgten ab 1980 Tätigkeiten in verschiedenen Designbüros in Deutschland und der Schweiz in den Bereichen Grafik Design, Corporate Design, Mode und Ausstellungsgestaltung.

1988 gründete sie zusammen mit Ulrich Schwarz das Büro für Visuelle Kommunikation, Museografie und Ausstellungsgestaltung Bertron & Schwarz. Mit dem Umzug des Büros im Jahr 2000 übernahm Aurelia Bertron die Atelierleitung in Berlin. Ihr Arbeitsschwerpunkt ist die konzeptionelle Aufarbeitung von Inhalten für die visuelle Umsetzung sowie Ausstellungsgrafik und Farbgestaltung.

Als Mentorin unterstützt sie Berufsanfängerinnen bei ihrem Schritt in die Selbständigkeit. Darüber hinaus ist sie passionierte Gärtnerin und arbeitet daran, ihren Berliner Dachgarten in eine großstädtische Prärie zu verwandeln.

After studying visual communications at the Hochschule für Gestaltung in Schwäbisch Gmünd, in 1980 she began working in various design offices in Germany and Switzerland in the fields of graphic design, corporate design, and fashion and exhibition design.

In 1988 together with Ulrich Schwarz she founded Bertron & Schwarz, a firm for visual communications, exhibition design, and museography. With the relocation of the office in 2000 Aurelia Bertron took over the studio management in Berlin. Her work focuses on the conceptual processing of content for the visual implementation as well as exhibition graphics and color.

As a mentor she supports vocational beginners as they step into independence. In addition, she is a passionate gardener and is working to transform her Berlin rooftop garden into an urban prairie.

Prof. Ulrich Schwarz

Ulrich Albert Schwarz, 1956 in Triberg im Schwarzwald geboren, studierte Visuelle Kommunikation, arbeitete danach als selbständiger Designer und gründete 1988 Bertron & Schwarz, Gruppe für Gestaltung GmbH.

Seit 2000 ist Ulrich Schwarz Professor für Grundlagen des Entwerfens an der Universität der Künste Berlin, Institut für Transmediale Gestaltung.

Er ist als Autor und Herausgeber u. a. durch Publikationen wie *Designing Exhibitions, Raum Zeit Zeichen, Museografie und Ausstellungsgestaltung* sowie in *Information Graphics* und dem *Information Design Source Book* vertreten.

Neben der Entwurfstätigkeit als Ausstellungsgestalter verfasst er Studien und Gutachten im Bereich der Besucherleitsysteme, Museografie und Ausstellungsgestaltung.

Ulrich Albert Schwarz was born in 1956 in Triberg in the Black Forest. He studied visual communications, then worked as a freelance designer, and in 1988 founded Bertron & Schwarz Design Inc.

Since 2000, Ulrich Schwarz is a professor of design fundamentals at the Universität der Künste Berlin, Institute of Design. He is the author and editor several publications such as *Designing Exhibitions, Raum Zeit Zeichen, Museografie und Ausstellungsgestaltung, Information Design Sourcebook,* and *Information Graphics.*

In addition to his activities as an exhibition designer, he has authored studies and reports in the field of visitor management systems, museography, and exhibition design.

Prof. Claudia Frey

Claudia Frey studierte von 1993 bis 1997 Visuelle Kommunikation an der Hochschule für Gestaltung in Schwäbisch Gmünd. Während dieser Zeit arbeitete sie bereits bei Catherine Baur im Atelier Perluette in Lyon. Nach ihrem Studium war sie als Projektleiterin für Bertron & Schwarz tätig. 1999 erhielt sie ein DAAD-Stipendium und studierte an der Hochschule für Gestaltung und Kunst in Zürich.

Im Jahr 2000 schloss sie dort den Nachdiplomstudiengang Szenisches Gestalten in Scenic Design/Scenography ab. Im gleichen Jahr wurde Claudia Frey geschäftsführende Gesellschafterin der Bertron Schwarz Frey GmbH mit Geschäftssitz in Ulm.

Seit Herbst 2011 ist Sie Professorin für „Visuelle Gestaltung im Raum" an der Fakultät Gestaltung der Hochschule für Angewandte Wissenschaften Würzburg-Schweinfurt.

Entsprechend ihrer Ausbildung und Erfahrung liegt ihr Arbeitsschwerpunkt auf der szenischen Gestaltung musealer Räume.

From 1993 to 1997 Claudia Frey studied visual communications at the Hochschule für Gestaltung in Schwäbisch Gmünd. During this time she worked with Catherine Baur at Perluette in Lyon. After completing her studies, she worked as project manager for Bertron & Schwarz. In 1999 she received a DAAD grant and studied at the School of Art and Design in Zurich.

In 2000 she completed her postgraduate studies in scenic design. That same year Claudia Frey served as the managing partner of Bertron Schwarz Frey headquartered in Ulm. Since autumn of 2011 she is a professor for "visual design in space," in the Design Faculty of the Hochschule für Angewandte Wissenschaften Würzburg-Schweinfurt.

In line with her education and experience her main focus is on the scenic design of museum spaces.

BERTRON SCHWARZ FREY sind die Herausgeber des Buches und Autoren aller nicht namentlich gekennzeichneten Artikel.
Weitere Autoren in der Reihenfolge ihres Erscheinens im Buch:
BERTRON SCHWARZ FREY are the publishers of the book and the authors of all texts not specified by name. More authors in the order in which they appear in this book:

Dr. Ferdinand Damaschun

Jahrgang 1950, 1970 bis 1974 Studium der Kristallografie an der Humboldt-Universität zu Berlin. 1980 Promotion im Fach Mineralogie.
Seit 1974 zuerst als wissenschaftlicher Assistent und danach als Kustos für die Gesteins- und Lagerstättensammlung im Museum für Naturkunde Berlin. In den Jahren 1992 und 1993 Amtierender Direktor des Museums für Naturkunde. Von 1993 bis 2005 Leiter der Abteilung Öffentliche Ausstellungen, 2006 Übernahme der Leitung der neu eingerichteten Abteilung Ausstellungen und öffentliche Bildung und Ernennung zum Stellvertreter des Generaldirektors. Seit 1. Januar 2011 Amtierender Generaldirektor des Museums.
Das besondere wissenschaftliche Interesse gilt der Wissenschaftsgeschichte und materialwissenschaftlichen Untersuchungen zur Denkmalpflege.
Born in 1950 Ferdinand Damaschun studied crystallography from 1970 to 1974 at Humboldt-Universität zu Berlin. In 1980 he earned his Ph.D. in mineralogy. Beginning in 1974 he first worked as a research assistant, and later as curator of the rock and deposit collection at the Museum für Naturkunde Berlin. Between 1992 and 1993 he was Acting Director of the Museum für Naturkunde. From 1993 to 2005 he was director of the Department of Public Exhibitions; in 2006 he resumed the responsibility of the newly created Department of Exhibitions and Public Education, and was subsequently appointed as the deputy director general. Since January of 2011 he is the Acting Director General.
He is particularly interested in the history of science, and material science and research concerning the preservation of historical monuments.

Prof. Dr. Albert-Dieter Stevens

Albert-Dieter Stevens, 1957 in Ostfriesland geboren, studierte Biologie in Gießen und Brasilia und promovierte über die Blütenbiologie von Trompetenblumengewächsen in den Savannen Zentral-Brasiliens. Nach langjährigen Projekten im Amazonasgebiet und in Südamerika kam er 2001 an den Botanischen Garten und das Botanische Museum Berlin-Dahlem der Freien Universität Berlin. Dort ist er als Professor und Direktor wissenschaftlich zuständig für die Pflanzensammlungen im Botanischen Garten und Herbarium und leitet die entsprechende Abteilung. Neben den vielfältigen Aufgaben der Weiterentwicklung, Erschließung und Nutzung der wissenschaftlichen Sammlungen für Forschung und Bildung ist er verantwortlich für eine Reihe von Projekten insbesondere zum Ausbau der Saatgut- und Erhaltungssammlungen gefährdeter Pflanzenarten.
Albert Dieter Stevens, born 1957 in Ostfriesland, studied biology in Gießen and Brasilia, and earned his doctorate in the flowering biology of trumpet flowers in the savannas of central Brazil. After many years of participating in projects in the Amazon and in South America, in 2001 he joined the Botanical Garden and Botanische Museum Berlin-Dahlem of the Freie Universität Berlin. There, he is a professor and scientific director responsible for the plant collections at the botanical garden and herbarium, and director of the respective departments. In addition to the various tasks of development, exploration, and utilization of scientific collections for research and education, he is responsible for a number of projects, particularly in the conservation of seed collections of endangered plant species.

Dr. Susanne Jaschko

Susanne Jaschko promovierte in Kunstgeschichte an der RWTH Aachen. Von 1997 bis 2000 war sie Kuratorin der transmediale, Festival für Kunst und digitale Kultur in Berlin. Von 2001 bis 2004 war sie dort auch stellvertretende Leiterin. Von 2008 bis 2009 leitete sie das Ausstellungs- und Veranstaltungsprogramm sowie das Artist-in-Residence-Programm des Netherlands Media Art Institute in Amsterdam, Niederlande. Seit 2004 ist sie auch als freie Kuratorin und Dozentin international tätig. Regelmäßig spricht sie auf Fachkonferenzen und publiziert zu Themen, die im Zentrum ihrer kuratorischen Praxis stehen. 2011 gründete sie die prozessagenten, eine Agentur für räumliche und soziale Prozesse mittels Kunst und Design.
Susanne Jaschko earned her doctorate in art history at the RWTH Aachen. From 1997 to 2000 she was curator of the Transmediale Festival for Art and Digital Culture in Berlin; from 2001 to 2004 she was also deputy director. From 2008 to 2009 she managed the exhibition and events program as well as the artist-in-residence program of the Netherlands Art Media Institute in Amsterdam. Since 2004 she has worked internationally as a freelance curator and lecturer. She regularly speaks at conferences and has published essays on curatorial topics. In 2011 she founded the prozessagenten, an agency for spatial and social processes by means of art and design.

Dr. Birte Frenssen

Birte Frenssen (geb. 1967) studierte Kunstgeschichte in Göttingen und Köln. Nach der wissenschaftlichen Assistenz an der Hamburger Kunsthalle baute sie das Pommersche Landesmuseum mit auf, wo sie heute als Kuratorin und stellvertretende Direktorin arbeitet.
Birte Frenssen (born in 1967) studied art history in Göttingen and Cologne. After working as a research assistant at the Hamburg Kunsthalle she helped establish the Pomeranian Landesmuseum where she is currently curator and deputy director.

Prof. Dr. h.c. Walter Smerling

Walter Smerling, geboren 1958, studierte Betriebswirtschaft und Kunstgeschichte. Nach einer TV-Hospitanz beim SWF arbeitete er ab den 1980er-Jahren als Autor, Regisseur und Moderator für das Fernsehen und produzierte zahlreiche Beiträge, Schwerpunkt: kulturelle Features, Reportagen, Künstlerportraits. Von 1980 bis 1984 war er Vorstand im Bonner Kunstverein, seitdem organisiert er Ausstellungen und anderweitige Kulturprojekte im In- und Ausland. Walter Smerling ist Geschäftsführender Vorstand der Stiftung für Kunst und Kultur e.V., Direktor des MKM Museum Küppersmühle in Duisburg sowie künstlerischer Leiter des Kunstprojekts Salzburg. 2010 wurde er zum Honorarprofessor für Kunst- und Kulturvermittlung an der Universität Witten/Herdecke ernannt.

Walter Smerling, born in 1958, studied business administration and art history. After an internship at SWF TV, in the 1980th year he worked as a television writer, director, and moderator; and wrote numerous articles with a focus on cultural features, documentaries, and artists portraits. From 1980 to 1984 he was director at the Bonner Kunstverein, and has since organized numerous exhibitions and other cultural projects at home and abroad. Walter Smerling is Managing Director of the nonprofit organization Foundation for Art and Culture, in addition to the director of the Museum Küppersmühle in Duisburg and artistic director of the Salzburg Art Project. In 2010 he was appointed Honorary Professor of Art and Cultural Education at the University of Witten Herdecke.

Steffi Cornelius M.A.

Steffi Cornelius, 1960 in der Pfalz geboren und dort aufgewachsen, studierte an der Universität Tübingen Empirische Kulturwissenschaft, Politikwissenschaft und Neuere Deutsche Literatur. Im Jahr 1988 schloss sie ihr Studium mit dem Magister Artium ab. Es folgte ein wissenschaftliches Volontariat im Westfälischen Freilichtmuseum Hagen. Im Jahr 1991 wurde sie wissenschaftliche Mitarbeiterin des damals im Aufbau befindlichen Freilichtmuseums im Kreis Esslingen. Seit 1993 ist die Kulturwissenschaftlerin Museumsleiterin und seit 1995 zugleich Amtsleiterin des Freilichtmuseums in Beuren. Das in Trägerschaft des Landkreises Esslingen befindliche Museum ist das jüngste von insgesamt sieben regionalen ländlichen Freilichtmuseen in Baden-Württemberg.

Steffi Cornelius (1960) born and raised in Palatinate, studied empirical cultural studies, political science, and contemporary German literature at the University of Tübingen. In 1988 she completed her studies with a master of arts; and a subsequent academic internship in the Westphalian Open-air Museum Hagen. In 1991 she was a research associate at the open-air museum in Esslingen, which at the time was still under construction. Since 1993 she has served as museum director (cultural science) and in addition as the director of the museum in Beuren since 1995. The museum located in the district of Esslingen is the newest of seven regional rural Open Air Museums in Baden Württemberg.

Dr. Alfons Schmidt

Alfons Schmidt, Leitender Baudirektor, Jahrgang 1962, studierte von 1983 bis 1989 Architektur an der Universität Hannover und Università di Firenze. 1989 bis 1993 Dissertation und Arbeit als freiberuflicher Architekt. 1995 erlangte er den Grad eines Doktors der Ingenieurwissenschaften an der Universität Hannover. 1996 Postgradualstudium Denkmalpflege an der Universität Dresden. Von 1991 bis 1992 Leiter des Stadtplanungsamtes der Stadt Kronach/Bayern. 1993 bis 1995 Referendariat für den höheren technischen Verwaltungsdienst mit dem Abschluss als Bauassessor, bis 2001 in der brandenburgischen Landesbauverwaltung als Baubeamter eingesetzt. Seit 2000 Nebenamt als Prüfer für die Fachrichtung Hochbau im Oberprüfungsamt im Bundesbauministerium. Seit 2001 Leiter der Abteilung Baudenkmalpflege der Stiftung Preußische Schlösser und Gärten Berlin Brandenburg.

Alfons Schmidt, Executive Planning Director, born 1962, studied architecture at the University of Hannover and Università di Firenze from 1983 to 1989. From 1989 to 1993 he wrote his dissertation and worked as a freelance architect. In 1995 he obtained his doctorate in engineering from the University of Hanover. In 1996 he completed postgraduate studies on the conservation of historical monuments at the University of Dresden. From 1991 to 1992 he served as the Director of the Urban Planning Office in Kronach, Bavaria. From 1993 to 1995 he completed a traineeship in technical management services, graduating with a degree in construction assessment, and worked in the Brandenburg state construction administration as a building official until 2001. Since 2000, he has served an auditor for the Department of Building Construction in the Federal Ministry of Transport, Building and Urban Development. Since 2001 he has served as the director of the Department of Architectural Conservation of the Foundation for Prussian Palaces and Gardens Berlin Brandenburg.

Prof. Dr. Hartmut Troll

Hartmut Troll studierte Landschaftsökologie und Landschaftsgestaltung in Wien an der Universität für Bodenkultur, arbeitete als freiberuflicher Planer in Bremen und Berlin, lehrte als wissenschaftlicher Mitarbeiter an der Hochschule Neubrandenburg, promovierte an der Universität Kassel und ist nun Referent für historische Gärten bei der Staatlichen Schlösser- und Gärtenverwaltung in Baden-Württemberg. Außerdem ist er Lehrbeauftragter und seit Kurzem Honorarprofessor für Gartenkunst und Gartendenkmalpflege am Institut für Europäische Kunstgeschichte der Universität Heidelberg.

Hartmut Troll studied landscape ecology and landscape design in Vienna at the University of Agricultural Sciences, worked as a freelance planner in Bremen and Berlin, taught while a research assistant at the University of Neubrandenburg, received his Ph.D. from the University of Kassel and is currently an advisor for historical gardens at the Department State Palaces and Gardens in Baden-Württemberg. He is also a lecturer and recently an honorary professor of horticulture and historical garden conservation at the Institute for European Art History at the University of Heidelberg.

Bernolph Freiherr von Gemmingen-Guttenberg

Bernolph von Gemmingen studierte nach dem Wehrdienst und einer Banklehre in Freiburg, St. Gallen und Fontainebleau Volks- und Betriebswirtschaft. Er arbeitete fünf Jahre für die amerikanische Unternehmensberatung Arthur Andersen & Co. in Frankfurt am Main, bevor er 1996 ins Neckartal auf die Burg Guttenberg ging. Dort leitet der Burgherr in der 16. Generation seiner Familie alle kleineren und größeren Aktivitäten, die sich um die alte Stauferburg ranken (Forstwirtschaft, Holzhandel HolzLand, Tourismus Deutsche Greifenwarte und Burgmuseum Burg Guttenberg). Neben seiner Tätigkeit im Neckartal ist er seit 1999 geschäftsführender Administrator der gemeinnützigen v. Schad'schen Stiftung sowie der Cronstett- und Hynspergischen evangelischen Stiftung in Frankfurt am Main, die sich in vielfältigen sozialen und kulturellen Projekten engagieren. Bernolph von Gemmingen ist verheiratet und hat drei Kinder.

After completing his military service Bernolph von Gemmingen studied business administration and economics, and worked as a bank clerk in Freiburg, St. Gallen, and Fontainebleau. For five years he worked for the American management consultancy firm Arthur Andersen & Co. in Frankfurt am Main, before moving in 1996 to the Neckar Valley and Guttenberg Castle. It was there that he took on the responsibilities of overseeing all the minor and major activities related to the old castle such as forestry, timber trade, "Holzland" tourism, the German Raptor Research Center, as well as the Guttenberg Castle Museum. Besides his activities in the Neckar Valley, he is the managing director of the nonprofit foundation Schad'schen Stiftung since 1999, as well as the Cronstett and Hynspergischen Protestant Foundation in Frankfurt am Main, which is engaged in diverse social and cultural projects. Bernolph von Gemmingen is married and has three children.

Prof. Dr. Matthias Wemhoff

Geboren 1964 in Münster, Studium der Vor- und Frühgeschichte, Mittlere Geschichte und Kirchengeschichte in Bamberg und Freiburg, 1992 Leiter des Museums in der Kaiserpfalz in Paderborn und seit 2002 des Westfälischen Landesmuseums für Klosterkultur in Kloster Dalheim. Seit 2008 Direktor des Museums für Vor- und Frühgeschichte der Staatlichen Museen zu Berlin und Landesarchäologe von Berlin. Honorarprofessor an der Freien Universität Berlin.

Born in 1964 in Münster, studied pre- and early history, medieval history, and church history in Bamberg and Freiburg. Since 1992 he has served as the director of the Imperial Palace Museum in Paderborn, and since 2002 the Westphalian State Museum of Monastery Culture in the Dalheim monastery. Since 2008 he is the director of the Museum of Prehistory and Early History of the Berlin State Museums, and archaeologist for the state of Berlin. He holds a honorary professorship at the Freie Universität Berlin.

Karin Birk M.A.

Karin Birk studierte an der Johannes-Gutenberg-Universität Mainz Vor- und Frühgeschichte, Anthropologie und Historische Geografie und schloss das Studium 1998 mit dem Magister Artium ab. Während dieser Zeit nahm sie an zahlreichen archäologischen Ausgrabungen teil. Nach ihrem Studium war sie als Kuratorin und Projektleiterin großer Ausstellungen am Historischen Museum der Pfalz Speyer tätig. Dort leitete sie unter anderem ab 1999 das Kindermuseum Junges Museum.

Seit 2005 betreut Karin Birk im Landesmuseum Württemberg in Stuttgart die archäologischen Ausstellungen als Projektmanagerin. So übernahm sie unter anderem die Projektsteuerung der Ausstellung *Ägyptische Mumien – Unsterblichkeit im Land der Pharaonen* 2008 und *Schätze des Alten Syrien – Die Entdeckung des Königreichs Qatna* 2010.

Karin Birk earned her masters degree in pre- and early history, anthropology, and historical geography from the Johannes Gutenberg University Mainz in 1998. During this time she participated in numerous archaeological excavations.

After graduation, she worked as the curator and project manager of major exhibitions at the Palatinate Speyer Historical Museum. There she was responsible for the children's museum program (1999).

Since 2005 Karin Birk is the archaeological exhibitions project manager at the Württemberg State Museum in Stuttgart. It was there that she oversaw the exhibition project *Egyptian Mummies – Immortality in the Land of the Pharaohs* in 2008, and in 2010 *The Treasures of Ancient Syria – Discovery of the Kingdom of Qatna*.

Rolf Schaubode M.A.

Rolf Schaubode studierte Ethnologie, Ur- und Frühgeschichte und Spanisch an der Universität Köln, 1989 Abschluss mit dem Magisterexamen.

Von 1991 bis 1995 Beschäftigung an der Pädagogischen Hochschule Weingarten als wissenschaftlicher Mitarbeiter bei der Vorbereitung, Durchführung und Abwicklung der Ausstellung *900 Jahre Heilig-Blut-Verehrung in Weingarten*, außerdem Leitung eines Seminars zu den Grundlagen der Ur- und Frühgeschichtsforschung.

Ab 1996 wissenschaftliche Konzeption der Dauerausstellung des Stadtmuseums im Schlössle. Nach Eröffnung des Museums 2001 Gestaltung von ca. 50 Wechselausstellungen. Ab 2007 Mitarbeit bei der Neugestaltung des Weingartener Alamannenmuseums und der Konzeption des Museums für Klosterkultur.

Rolf Schaubode studied anthropology, pre- and early history, and Spanish at the University of Cologne; in 1989 graduated with a master's degree.

From 1991 to 1995 he was employed at the Weingarten College of Education as a research assistant for the preparation, implementation, and development of the exhibition commemorating 900 years of devotion to the Holy Blood in Weingarten, in which he also held a seminar on the fundamentals of pre- and early historical research.

From 1996 he was responsible for the scientific conception of the permanent exhibition at the Schlössle City Museum. After the opening of the Museum of Design in 2001 he was responsible for the design of approximately 50 temporary exhibitions. From 2007 he has been involved in the redesign of the Weingarten Alamanni Museum, and the design and conception of the Museum of Monastery Culture.

Prof. Dr. Bernd Lindner

Bernd Lindner, 1952 in der Lutherstadt Wittenberg geboren, studierte 1974 bis 1978 Kultur- und Literaturwissenschaften sowie Soziologie an der Humboldt-Universität zu Berlin, an der er 1985 auch promovierte. Von 1978 bis 1992 arbeitete er als Kultursoziologe in der Jugendforschung, zuerst am Zentralinstitut für Jugendforschung Leipzig, nach 1990 am Deutschen Jugendinstitut München. 1995 habilitierte er sich in Soziologie an der Universität Karlsruhe, an der er seit 2001 eine apl. Professur innehat. Seit 1994 ist er als wissenschaftlicher Mitarbeiter am Zeitgeschichtlichen Forum Leipzig bei der Stiftung Haus der Geschichte der Bundesrepublik Deutschland tätig und dort als Kurator vieler zeitgeschichtlicher und kulturhistorischer Ausstellungen hervorgetreten.

Er ist Autor zahlreicher wissenschaftlicher Publikationen und Sachbücher zur Jugendkultur, Generationsproblematik, Zeitgeschichte sowie zur Kultur- und Kunstsoziologie.

Bernd Lindner was born in Wittenberg in 1952, and from 1974 to 1978 he studied cultural and literary history, and sociology at Humboldt-Universität zu Berlin, where he graduated in 1985. From 1978 to 1992 he worked as a cultural sociologist in youth research, first at the Central Institute for Youth Research in Leipzig, and after 1990 at the German Youth Institute in Munich.

In 1995 he pursued his doctorate in sociology at the University of Karlsruhe, where since 2001 he has held an adjunct professorship. Since 1994 he has been a research associate at the Contemporary History Forum Leipzig, and at the "House of History" of the Federal Republic of Germany where he has served as a curator of many exhibitions of contemporary and cultural history.

He is the author of numerous publications and nonfiction books for youth culture, generational issues, contemporary history as well as culture and art sociology.

Dr. Stefan Fassbinder

Stefan Fassbinder, aufgewachsen in Algerien und Schwaben, studierte in Freiburg im Breisgau und in Aix-en-Provence Ur- und Frühgeschichte, Geschichte, Kunstgeschichte und Biblisch-historische Theologie. Er schloss das Studium 1996 mit der Promotion zu einem Thema aus der frühneuzeitlichen Frömmigkeitsgeschichte ab. 1996 bis 1999 arbeitete er als Ausstellungssekretär in Paderborn für die Ausstellung *799 – Kunst und Kultur der Karolingerzeit. Karl der Große und Papst Leo III. in Paderborn*. Anschließend trat er die Stelle des Historikers am neu gegründeten Pommerschen Landesmuseum in Greifswald an. Seine Hauptaufgabe ist der Aufbau der Dauerausstellung zur Geschichte und Kultur der Region Pommern.

Stefan Fassbinder, grew up in Algeria and Swabia, and studied pre- and early history, history, art history, and biblical and historical theology in Freiburg and in Aix-en-Provence. He graduated in 1996 with a doctorate writing his thesis on the history of early modern religious piety. From 1996 to 1999 he worked as an exhibition assistant for the *799 – Arts and Culture of the Carolingian Period, Carl the Great, and Pope Leo III in Paderborn*. He then joined the newly established Pomeranian Museum in Greifswald as a historian. His main task is to build a permanent exhibition on the history and culture of the region of Pomerania.

Dr. Rainer Y

Rainer Y studierte Kunstgeschichte, Klassische Archäologie und Theatergeschichte an den Universitäten München und Regensburg. Sein Studium schloss er 1983 mit einer Dissertation über die utopischen Architekturentwürfe von Fidus (1868-1948) ab.

Von 1983 bis 1988 war er – zunächst als Volontär, dann als wissenschaftlicher Mitarbeiter – am Württembergischen Landesmuseum Stuttgart und bei der Bayerischen Verwaltung der staatlichen Schlösser, Gärten und Seen in München beschäftigt.

Seit 1988 betreut Rainer Y die Kostüm- und Textilsammlung der Landesmuseums Württemberg. Als Oberkonservator in der Abteilung Kunst- und Kulturgeschichte war er für die Konzeption des im Schloss Ludwigsburg gegründeten und 2004 eröffneten Modemuseums verantwortlich.

Rainer Y studied art history, classical archeology, and theater history at the University of Munich and Regensburg. He graduated in 1983 writing his dissertation on the utopian architectural designs of Fidus (1868–1948).

From 1983 to 1988 he worked first as a volunteer, and then as a researcher at the Württemberg State Museum Stuttgart and at the Bavarian Administration of State Palaces, Gardens, and Lakes in Munich. Since 1988, Rainer Y serves as director of the costume and textile collection of the Württemberg State Museum. As chief curator in the department of art and cultural history, he was responsible for the design concept of the Museum of Fashion in Ludwigsburg Castle, which subsequently opened in 2004.

Dr. Gabriele Kleiber

Studierte Kunstgeschichte, Geschichte, Baugeschichte und Germanistik an den Universitäten Karlsruhe und Stuttgart. Ihre Magisterarbeit beschäftigte sich mit dem Thema „Die Wiederentdeckung El Grecos in Deutschland" ihre Doktorarbeit mit „Schilde im 19. Jahrhundert unter besonderer Berücksichtigung der Ehrenschilde". Sie war beim Badischen Landesmuseum in Karlsruhe tätig, wo sie auch ihr Volontariat verbrachte und betreute 1983 in St. Blasien die Ausstellung *Das tausendjährige St. Blasien*. Im Landesmuseum Württemberg in Stuttgart bearbeitete sie einen klassizistischen Keramikfund. Seit 1989 ist sie bei den Staatlichen Schlössern und Gärten Baden-Württemberg angestellt. Viele Jahre war sie für Klöster in Württemberg zuständig. Seit 2009 betreut sie die kurpfälzischen Schlösser Heidelberg, Mannheim und Schwetzingen.

Gabriele Kleiber studied art history, history, architectural history, and Germanic studies at the Universities of Karlsruhe and Stuttgart. Her thesis dealt with the theme of "The Rediscovery of El Greco's in Germany," her thesis was entitled "Shields in the 19th Century: Honor shields." She was at the Baden State Museum in Karlsruhe, where she completed her internship and in 1983 supervised the exhibition in St. Blaise celebrating a thousand years of St. Blaise. In the Württemberg State Museum in Stuttgart, she updated a classical ceramic Fund. Since 1989 she has been employed at the State Palaces and Gardens of Baden Württemberg. For many years she was responsible for monasteries in Württemberg. Since 2009 she manages the Palatine palaces of Heidelberg, Mannheim, and Schwetzingen.

Dr. Kirsten Fast
Kirsten Fast, 1943 in Ankara/Türkei geboren, studierte nach einigen Jahren Tätigkeit im Tourismus Kunstgeschichte, Archäologie und Nordistik an der Ludwig-Maximilians-Universität München und schloss 1980 mit der Promotion ab. Mehrjährige Arbeit in einem Projekt des Württembergischen Landesmuseums Stuttgart, bis 1985 Betreuung des Funk-kollegs Kunst beim DIFF in Tübingen. Ab 1987 Aufbau der Esslinger Histo-rischen Museen: Stadtmuseum, J.F. Schreiber-Museum und Archäologisches Museum St. Dionys. Bis zum Ruhestand im Jahr 2009 Erarbeitung zahlreicher Ausstellungen – besonders zu Esslinger und Baden-Württemberg-Themen. Bis 2008 war Kirsten Fast neun Jahre lang Präsidentin des Museumsverbandes Baden-Württemberg und Mitglied in verschiedenen Vorständen und Beiräten anderer deutscher Museen und Museumsorganisationen.

Kirsten Fast was born in 1943 in Ankara, Turkey. After several years in the tourism industry she studied art history, archeology, and Nordic studies at the Ludwig-Maximilians-Universität München and graduated in 1980 with her doctorate degree. She was involved in a project for several years the Württemberg State Museum Stuttgart, and until 1985 at the DIFF (Deutsches Institut für Fernstudien) in Tübingen.
From 1987 she was involving in the establishment of the Esslinger Historical Museum: City Museum, J.F. Schreiber Museum, and the Archaeological Museum of St. Dionysius. In the years up to her re-tirement in 2009, she was involved in the development of numerous exhibitions – especially concerning themes related to Essling and Baden-Württemberg.
By 2008, Kirsten had severed almost nine years as president of the Museum Association of Baden-Württemberg, and as a member of various boards and advi-sory boards of other German museums and museum organizations.

Maren Krüger
Maren Krüger studierte Judaistik in Berlin und Jerusalem. Nach einem Museums-volontariat arbeitete sie freiberuflich für Museen und Ausstellungsprojekte, wissenschaftliche Einrichtungen und Verlage. Thematisch beschäftigte sie sich mit der Geschichte und Kultur der Juden in Deutschland. Sie war unter anderem an der Vorbereitung der Dauerausstellung der Stiftung Neue Synagoge Berlin – Centrum Judaicum beteiligt. Seit 1999 arbeitet Maren Krüger für das Jüdische Museum Berlin. Sie gehörte zunächst einem Team von Kuratoren an, das die Eröffnung der Dauerausstellung *Zwei Jahrtausende deutsch-jüdische Geschichte* vorbereitete. Seit der Eröffnung des Jüdischen Mu-seums im September 2001 ist die Pflege und Weiterentwicklung der Dauerauss-tellung ihr Arbeitsgebiet.

Maren Krüger studied Jewish studies in Berlin and Jerusalem. After serving as a museum volunteer she subse-quently worked on a freelance basis for museums and exhibition projects, and academic institutions and publishers. She has primarily focused on themes that concern the history and culture of Jews in Germany. She was involved in the preparation of the permanent exhibition of the the New Synagogue Berlin – Centrum Judaicum Foundation. Since 1999, Maren Krüger works for the Jewish Museum Berlin. She was part of a team of curators that were responsible for the permanent exhibition *Two Millennia of German Jewish History*. Since the opening of the Jewish Museum in September 2001, her work involves the maintenance and continual development of the permanent exhibition.

Dr. Jörg Skriebeleit
Jörg Skriebeleit studierte Empirische Kulturwissenschaft/Europäische Ethnologie an der Universität Tübingen und der Humboldt-Universität zu Berlin. Schwerpunkte waren dabei neben zeit-geschichtlichen Themen Museumstheorie und -praxis. Promotion am Zentrum für Antisemitismusforschung der TU Berlin. Seit 1999 Leiter der KZ-Gedenkstätte Flossenbürg. Zahlreiche Publikationen zu erinnerungskulturellen und museolo-gischen Themen. Lehraufträge an Universitäten in Berlin, Marburg, München und Wien. Verantwortlich für die Neukon-zeption der KZ-Gedenkstätte Flossenbürg. Wissenschaftlicher Berater bei diversen Memorial-Projekten wie dem Mahnmal für die ermordeten Juden Europas in Berlin, der KZ-Gedenkstätte Mauthausen und dem Denkort U-Boot Bunker Valentin Bremen.

Jörg Skriebeleit studied empirical cultural studies and European ethnology at the University of Tübingen and Humboldt-Universität zu Berlin. He focused on con-temporary issues in addition to museum theory and practice. He earned his Ph.D at the Center for Research on Antisemitism at the TU Berlin.
Since 1999 he has served as director of Flossenbürg Memorial. he has published numerous publications on cultural remembrance and museological issues. He has held lectureships at universities in Berlin, Marburg, Munich, and Vienna. He was responsible for the redesign of the Flossenbürg Memorial. He served as a scientific consultant at various memorial projects such as the Memorial to the Murdered Jews of Europe in Berlin, the Mauthausen Concentration Camp Memorial, and the U-Boat Bunker Valentin Memorial in Bremen.

Ulrich Fritz
Ulrich Fritz, Jahrgang 1969, studierte in Freiburg, Boston und Konstanz Literatur-wissenschaften und Geschichte. Von 1999 bis 2001 arbeitete er als wissenschaft-licher Mitarbeiter beim Humanitären Hilfsfonds für ehemalige Zwangsarbeiter der Siemens AG. Von 2001 bis 2010 war er an der KZ-Gedenkstätte Flossenbürg am Aufbau des Archivs sowie an den beiden Dauerausstellungen *Konzentrationslager Flossenbürg 1938–1945* und *Was bleibt – Nachwirkungen des Konzentrationslagers Flossenbürg* maßgeblich beteiligt.
Seit 2011 arbeitet er bei der Stiftung Bayerische Gedenkstätten im Projekt „KZ-Außenlager in Bayern". Sein Doktorvater Wolfgang Benz (TU Berlin) wartet sehn-süchtig auf die Fertigstellung einer Arbeit zu den Außenlagern des KZ Flossenbürg.

Fritz Ulrich was born in 1969 and studied literature and history in Freiburg, Boston, and Constance. From 1999 to 2001 he worked as a researcher at the Siemens Humanitarian Relief Fund for Former Forced Laborers. From 2001 to 2010 he worked on archive development at the Flossenbürg Concentration Camp Memo-rial as well as on the two permanent exhibitions *Concentration Camp Flossen-bürg 1938–1945* and *What Remains – The aftermath of the Flossenbürg Concentra-tion Camp* in which he was significantly involved. Since 2011 he is employed at the Bavarian Memorial Foundation in the Concentration Camps in Bavaria project. His supervisor Wolfgang Benz (TU Berlin) eagerly awaits the completion of his work on the peripheral Flossenbürg concentra-tion camps.

Dr. Tobias Wolff
Tobias Wolff, 1967 in Hannover geboren, studierte Geologie in Freiburg und Amherst, Massachusetts und promovierte an der Universität Bremen. Nach einer halbjährigen Tätigkeit am Exploratorium in San Francisco ergänzte er 1999 das Entwicklungsteam für das Universum Science Center Bremen an der Universität Bremen. Seit Sommer 2000 ist er als Ausstellungsleiter der Universum Manage-mentgesellschaft für die wissenschaftlich-gestalterische Leitung des Universum verantwortlich. Sein Tätigkeitsschwerpunkt liegt in der Entwicklung von temporären und permanenten Ausstellungen im Universum, von Wanderausstellungen sowie von Ausstellungen für externe Auftraggeber.

Tobias Wolff was born in 1967 in Hanover, he studied geology in Freiburg and Amherst, Massachusetts and graduated from the University of Bremen. After working for six months at the Exploratorium in San Francisco in 1999 he contributed to the development team for the Universum Science Center Bremen at Bremen University. Since the summer of 2000 he is an exhibition director at Universum in which he is responsible for scientific design management. His focus lies in the development of temporary and permanent exhibitions in the Universum Science Center and traveling exhibitions, as well as exhibitions for external clients.

Alexandra Grossmann

Alexandra Grossmann studierte Humanmedizin an der Humboldt-Universität zu Berlin. Während dieser Zeit war sie in der klinischen Forschung mit dem Schwerpunkt Revisionsendoprothetik von 2004 bis 2009 in der Orthopädischen Klinik Markgröningen tätig. Seit der Eröffnung des Science Centers, der Hauptstadtrepräsentanz des niedersächsischen Unternehmens Otto Bock HealthCare GmbH, im Juni 2009 ist sie als wissenschaftliche Koordinatorin am Standort eingesetzt. Ihr Tätigkeitsschwerpunkt bezieht sich auf die Vermittlung und Erstellung der wissenschaftlichen Inhalte des Science Centers sowie den Ausbau der Kooperationen mit Verbänden und branchenaffinen Multiplikatoren.

Alexandra Grossmann studied medicine at Humboldt-Universität zu Berlin. During this time she was in clinical research with a focus in revision arthroplasty and from 2004 to 2009 active in the Markgröningen Orthopaedic Clinic. Since the opening of the Science Center, the representative office of the lower Saxtony company Otto Bock HealthCare, she has served as a research coordinator since June 2009. The main activities are concerned with the placement and preparation of the scientific content of the Science Center, and the expansion of cooperation with industry associations and established multipliers.

Richard Mühlmann

Richard Mühlmann studierte Stadtplanung an der Fachhochschule Nürtingen von 2000 bis 2005. Während und nach seinem Studium war er in verschiedenen Planungsbüros in Budapest, München und Stuttgart tätig. 2006 wechselte er in die Stadtverwaltung Regensburg.
Dort arbeitete er zunächst an städtebaulichen Planungen und Konzepten für den Altstadtbereich. Nach der Ernennung Regensburgs zum UNESCO-Welterbe war er 2007 am Aufbau der Welterbekoordination beteiligt und arbeitet seitdem als Projektleiter in diesem Bereich. Seine Arbeitsschwerpunkte liegen im Bereich des Welterbe-Managements und bei den Themen Bewusstseinsbildung und Vermittlung des Welterbetitels.
Neben seiner beruflichen Tätigkeit studiert Richard Mühlmann seit 2010 International Building Project Management an der Hochschule für Technik in Stuttgart.

Richard Mühlmann studied urban planning at the University of Applied Sciences Nürtingen from 2000 to 2005. During and after his studies he worked in various planning offices in Budapest, Munich, and Stuttgart. In 2006 he was employed at the Regensburg City Administration. There he worked on urban planning and concepts for the Old Town area. Following the appointment of Regensburg as a UNESCO World Heritage Site in 2007 he was involved in establishing the World Heritage Committee and has since worked as a project coordinator in this area. His research interests include World Heritage management and in the issues of consciousness-building and mediation of the World Heritage title. In addition to his professional activities, since 2010 Richard Mühlmann has studied international building project management at the University of Applied Sciences in Stuttgart.

Nicole Kimmel M.A.

Nicole Kimmel studierte Politikwissenschaft, Neuere und Neueste Geschichte sowie Kommunikationswissenschaft an der Universität Augsburg. Seit 1998 ist sie Referentin bei der Stiftung Entwicklungs-Zusammenarbeit Baden-Württemberg (SEZ) mit Sitz in Stuttgart. Aktuell ist sie dort für die Presse- und Öffentlichkeitsarbeit verantwortlich. Ihre fachlichen Schwerpunkte liegen im Bereich der Kommunalen Entwicklungszusammenarbeit, des Nachhaltigen Tourismus, in der Corporate Social Responsibility (CSR) und auf Themen der Nachhaltigkeit.
Als gemeinnützige und unabhängige Stiftung errichtet, zielt das Wirken der SEZ auf die Sensibilisierung breiter Bevölkerungskreise für globale Themen.

Nicole Kimmel studied political science, contemporary history and communication science at the University of Augsburg. Since 1998 she has been a consultant for SEZ Baden-Württemberg based in Stuttgart. She is currently in charge of press and public relations. Her professional interests are in the area of municipal development cooperation, sustainable tourism, corporate social responsibility (CSR) and sustainability issues. Established as a non-profit and independent foundation the work of the SEZ is aimed at raising awareness concerning global issues.

Sabine Lehmkühler M.A.

Sabine Lehmkühler studierte Kunstgeschichte, Archäologie (Vor- und Frühgeschichte) und Anthropologie in Tübingen, Wien und Ulm. Nach der Mitarbeit an verschiedenen wissenschaftlichen und museumsdidaktischen Projekten, unter anderem an der Universität Tübingen und am Württembergischen Landesmuseum Stuttgart, machte sie sich 1996 mit der kulturwerkstatt tübingen selbständig. Seither arbeitet sie als freie Kulturwissenschaftlerin und Autorin, unterstützt unter anderem Unternehmen bei der Suche nach der eigenen Geschichte, bei der Entwicklung von tragfähigen Kommunikationskonzepten oder bei der griffigen und facettenreichen Aufbereitung komplexer Zusammenhänge und Inhalte.

Sabine Lehmkühler studied art history, archaeology (pre- and early history) and anthropology in Tübingen, Vienna and Ulm. After working in various scientific and educational museum projects, including the University of Tübingen and the Württemberg State Museum Stuttgart; in 1996 she started providing a cultural workshop on a freelance basis. Since then she has worked as a freelance writer and cultural theorist in which she has supported companies in search of their own history, through the development of viable communication concepts or in the efficient and multifaceted treatment of complex relationships and content.

Prof. Dr. Thomas Schnalke

Thomas Schnalke, geboren 1958, Studium der Medizin in Würzburg und Marburg, 1985 medizinisches Staatsexamen, 1987 Promotion, ab 1988 wissenschaftlicher Assistent am Institut für Geschichte der Medizin der Universität Erlangen-Nürnberg, 1993 Habilitation für Geschichte der Medizin, 2000 Berufung auf die Professur für Geschichte der Medizin und Medizinische Museologie an der Medizinischen Fakultät Charité der Humboldt-Universität zu Berlin, verbunden mit der Leitung des Berliner Medizinhistorischen Museums der Charité.

Thomas Schnalke was born in 1958 and studied medicine in Würzburg and Marburg, in 1985 he earned his medical degree; in 1987 his doctorate and since 1988 he is research associate at the Institute for the History of Medicine at the University of Erlangen-Nuremberg; in 1993 at the Habilitation for the History of Medicine; in 2000 an appointment as Chair of the History of Medicine and Medical Museology at the Medical Faculty Charité, Humboldt-Universität zu Berlin, in cooperation with the leadership of the Berlin Medical Historical Museum the Charité.

Dr. Rainer Herrn

Rainer Herrn, geboren 1957, ist Mitarbeiter des Instituts für Geschichte der Medizin der Charité. Zahlreiche Ausstellungen, Publikationen, Lehrveranstaltungen und Vorträge zu medizinhistorischen, sexual- und geschlechtswissenschaftlichen Themen.

Born in 1957, Rainer Herrn is an employee of the Institute for History of Medicine at Charité. He has participated in numerous exhibitions, publications, courses and lectures on the history of medicine, as well as sexual and gender research topics.

Laura Hottenrott

Laura Hottenrott schloss ihr Studium der Geschichtswissenschaften, Ibero- und iberoamerikanischer Geschichte und Rechtswissenschaften im Jahr 2002 an der Universität Bielefeld ab. Seitdem arbeitete sie für verschiedene Gedenkstätten und Zeitzeugen-Projekten zur NS- und DDR-Geschichte, unter anderem als Co-Autorin der neuen Dauerausstellung der Gedenkstätte Geschlossener Jugendwerkhof Torgau zur Geschichte repressiver Heimerziehung in der DDR. Zuletzt war sie Co-Kuratorin der Ausstellung *Die Charité zwischen Ost und West (1945–1992). Zeitzeugen erinnern sich* am Institut für Geschichte der Medizin, Charité.

Laura Hottenrott completed her studies at the University of Bielefeld in History and Ibero-American history and law in 2002. Since then she has worked for various memorials and witness projects concerning national socialist and German Democratic Republic history; and is co-author of the new permanent exhibition of the Closed Juvenile Correctional Facility Torgau on the history of repressive home education in the GDR. She was most recently co-curator of *The Charité between East and West (1945–1992). Historical Witnesses Remember* of the Institute for the History of Medicine, Charité.

Impressum
Imprint

Grafik Design, Layout und Typografie
Graphic Design, Layout, Typography
Bertron Schwarz Frey GmbH
Büro für visuelle Kommunikation
Museografie und Ausstellungsgestaltung
www.bertron-schwarz-frey.de

Aurelia Bertron
Ulrich Schwarz
Claudia Frey
Susanne Asenkerschbaumer
Claudius Hog (Bildbearbeitung photoshopping)
Dinah Lohrer (Mitarbeit assistance)

Titelfoto: Volker Kreidler
www.volkerkreidler.de

Übersetzung Deutsch – Englisch
Translation German – English:
Joseph O'Donnell

Lektorat Copyediting:
Thomas Menzel (Deutsch German)
Leina Gonzales Bird (Englisch English)

Verlag Publisher
Robert Steiger
Werner Handschin
Katharina Kulke

Bibliographic information published
by Die Deutsche Bibliothek.
Die Deutsche Bibliothek lists this
publication in the Deutsche National-
bibliografie; detailed bibliographic
data is available on the Internet at
<http://dnb.ddb.de>.

© 2012 Birkhäuser, Basel
Postfach, CH-4002 Basel,
Switzerland,
www.birkhauser.ch
Ein Unternehmen von De Gruyter

Printed on acid-free paper produced
of chlorine-free pulp. TCF ∞
Printed in Germany

ISBN: 978-3-0346-0775-9

9 8 7 6 5 4 3 2 1